X Windows on the World

Developing Internationalized Software with X, Motif,® and CDE

Hewlett-Packard Professional Books

Blinn	Portable Shell Programming: An Extensive Collection of Bourne Shell Examples
Blommers	Practical Planning for Network Growth
Costa	Planning and Designing High Speed Networks Using 100VG-AnyLAN, Second Edition
Crane	A Simplified Approach to Image Processing: Classical and Modern Techniques in C
Fernandez	Configuring CDE—The Desktop Environment
Fristrup	The Essential Web Surfer Survival Guide
Fristrup	USENET: Netnews for Everyone
Grady	Practical Software Metrics for Project Management and Process Improvement
Grosvenor, Ichiro, O'Brien	Mainframe Downsizing to Upsize Your Business: IT-Preneuring
Gunn	A Guide to NetWare® for UNIX®
Helsel	Graphical Programming: A Tutorial for HP VEE
Helsel	Visual Programming with HP VEE
Kane	PA-RISC 2.0 Architecture
Knouse	Practical DCE Programming
Lewis	The Art & Science of Smalltalk
Lund	Integrating UNIX® and PC Network Operating Systems
Madell, Parsons, Abegg	Developing and Localizing International Software
Malan, Letsinger, Coleman	Object-Oriented Development at Work: Fusion in the Real World
McFarland	X Windows on the World: Developing Internationalized Software with X, Motif®, and CDE
McMinds/Whitty	Writing Your Own OSF/Motif Widgets
Phaal	LAN Traffic Management
Poniatowski	The HP-UX System Administrator's "How To" Book
Poniatowski	HP-UX 10.x System Administration "How To" Book
Thomas	Cable Television Proof-of-Performance: A Practical Guide to Cable TV Compliance Measurements Using a Spectrum Analyzer
Witte	Electronic Test Instruments

X Windows on the World

Developing Internationalized Software with X, Motif®, and CDE

Thomas C. McFarland

Hewlett-Packard Company

Prentice Hall PTR
Upper Saddle River, New Jersey 07458

Editorial/production supervision: *Craig Little*
Manufacturing manager: *Alexis R. Heydt*
Acquisitions editor: *Karen Gettman*
Editorial assistant: *Barbara Alfieri*
Cover design: *The Works*
Cover design director: *Jerry Votta*
Patricia Pekary, Manager Hewlett-Packard Press

Published by Prentice Hall PTR
Prentice-Hall, Inc.
A Simon & Schuster Company
Upper Saddle River, New Jersey 07458

The publisher offers discounts on this book when ordered in bulk quantities.
For more information, contact:

Corporate Sales Department
Prentice Hall PTR
1 Lake Street
Upper Saddle River, NJ 07458

Phone: 800-382-3419, Fax: 201-236-7141
E-mail: corpsales@prenhall.com

Printed in the United States of America
10 9 8 7 6 5 4 3 2 1

ISBN 0-13-359787-3

Prentice-Hall International (UK) Limited, *London*
Prentice-Hall of Australia Pty. Limited, *Sydney*
Prentice-Hall Canada Inc., *Toronto*
Prentice-Hall Hispanoamericana, S.A., *Mexico*
Prentice-Hall of India Private Limited, *New Delhi*
Prentice-Hall of Japan, Inc., *Tokyo*
Simon & Schuster Asia Pte. Ltd., *Singapore*
Editora Prentice-Hall do Brasil, Ltda., *Rio de Janeiro*

Contents

Preface   ix

1. Designing for International Markets   1

1.1 What Is Internationalization and Why Should You Care?......................1
1.2 Custom Localized Software...2
    1.2.1 Benefits of Custom Localized Software 3
1.3 Internationalized Software 6
    1.3.1 Customers Benefit from I18N...7
    1.3.2 Developers Benefit from I18N 8
    1.3.3 Costs of Using I18N 11
1.4 Standards Controlling I18N 13

2. Locale-Sensitive Operations: Handling Text Data   15

2.1 Initializing I18N Tools: setlocale().....................................16
    2.1.1 Using setlocale() in Your Application 17
    2.1.2 When Should You Call setlocale()?....................................20
    2.1.3 Summary: Using setlocale()...20
2.2 About Text Data...20
    2.2.1 Characters, Character Sets, Coded Character Sets, and
           Code Sets 21
    2.2.2 Code Set Independence or Universal Character Set? 27
2.3 Locale-Sensitive Operations: Text Manipulation 31
    2.3.1 Storing and Manipulating Character Data in Memory 32
    2.3.2 Parsing and Truncation 40

2.3.3 Character Identification and Classification 45
2.3.4 Case Conversion 47
2.3.5 Sorting 48
2.3.6 Converting Characters from One Code Set to Another 49

3. Locale-Sensitive Operations: Messages and Data Formats   51

3.1 Messaging Mechanisms 51
    3.1.1 Resource Files 52
    3.1.2 Message Catalogs 52
3.2 Message Catalog Example 55
3.3 What Needs to Be Translated? 58
3.4 What about Icons? 59
3.5 Hints and Common Mistakes 60
    3.5.1 Don't Build Messages from Fragments 60
    3.5.2 Don't Reuse Messages 60
    3.5.3 Allow for Text Growth in Translations 61
3.6 Formatting Text according to Local Custom 61
    3.6.1 Time and Date Formats 62
    3.6.2 Floating Point Numbers 64
    3.6.3 Monetary Values 65
3.7 Reading and Writing Text Data 67
3.8 Summary 69

4. Displaying Local Language Characters with X11R5   71

4.1 The Problem with Using Fonts 71
    4.1.1 One Font Isn't Enough for Some Code Sets 72
    4.1.2 Character Value Isn't Always Identical to the Glyph Index 72
    4.1.3 Getting the Right Font for the Locale 73
4.2 Font Sets: the X11R5 Solution 73
    4.2.1 X Logical Font Description 73
    4.2.2 Creating a Font Set with XCreateFontSet() 74
    4.2.3 Manipulating and Freeing Font Sets 76
4.3 Drawing with Font Sets 76
4.4 Calculating Metrics with Font Sets 78
    4.4.1 Ink metrics vs. logical metrics 79
    4.4.2 Example: Calculating Metrics with Font Sets 80

4.5 Example Program: Using Font Sets to Draw Characters......................81
4.6 Summary 87

5. Displaying Local Language Characters with X11R6   89

5.1 Overview..89
5.2 Connecting to an X Output Method..92
5.3 Obtaining Information from the Output Method 92
     5.3.1 Example: Connecting to and Querying an Output Method 95
5.4 Creating an Output Context 97
     5.4.1 Calling XCreateOC() 98
5.5 Querying and Changing an Output Context 98
     5.5.1 XOC Values..98
5.6 Using an Output Context 102
5.7 Summary 103

6. Keyboard Input: Background and Overview   105

6.1 When a Key Is Pressed ... .105
6.2 Input Methods 106
     6.2.1 Background..106
     6.2.2 Keyboard Interaction Models 107
     6.2.3 Input Method Styles..111

7. Keyboard Input with X Windows   115

7.1 Open a Connection to an Input Method..116
     7.1.1 Determine Which Input Method to Use....................................116
     7.1.2 Connecting to the Input Method 117
7.2 Determine Which Styles the Input Method Supports 117
7.3 Choose the Preedit Style and Status Style 119
     7.3.1 Example: Choosing an XIM Style..119
7.4 Create an Input Context 121
     7.4.1 XIC Data Values 122
     7.4.2 Creating Variable Length Lists..122
     7.4.3 Example: Creating an XIC..123
7.5 Identify Which Events the Input Method Needs................................124
7.6 Allow the Input Method to Examine Events before Processing
     Them 125
7.7 Process KeyPress Events 125

7.8 Setting and Querying XIC Data Values.. 127
   7.8.1 Which Attributes Should You Set?.. 128
7.9 Tell the Input Method When Keyboard Focus Is Gained or Lost........ 128
7.10 Example: Putting It All Together... 129
7.11 Summary: Internationalized Keyboard Input with X11R5................ 140
7.12 Frequently Asked Questions 140

8. Keyboard Input: Supporting Over-the-Spot and Off-the-Spot
   Preedit and Status Styles   **145**

8.1 Supporting Over-the-Spot Style... 145
8.2 Adding Support for Off-the-Spot Preedit and Status Styles............... 147
   8.2.1 Provide Required Data When Creating the XIC...................... 148
   8.2.2 Select for Window Size Change Events 149
   8.2.3 Negotiate with the Input Method for the Geometry Needed 149
   8.2.4 Notify the Input Method When the Window is Resized.......... 154
8.3 Example 155

9. Keyboard Input with On-the-Spot Preedit and Status Styles   **165**

9.1 Adding support for On-the-Spot Preedit and Status Styles 165
   9.1.1 PreeditStartCallback 166
   9.1.2 PreeditDoneCallback 167
   9.1.3 PreeditDrawCallback 167
   9.1.4 PreeditCaretCallback 171
   9.1.5 StatusStartCallback 173
   9.1.6 StatusDoneCallback.. 174
   9.1.7 StatusDrawCallback.. 174
9.2 Example: Using On-the-Spot Style... 175
   9.2.1 Initial Design Decisions... 175
   9.2.2 Example: Accessing Application Data in the Callbacks 178
   9.2.3 Example: PreeditStartCallback 179
   9.2.4 Example: PreeditDoneCallback 182
   9.2.5 Example: PreeditDrawCallback.................................. 185
   9.2.6 Example: PreeditCaretCallback 190
   9.2.7 Example: Using the Callbacks in an Application 191

10. Keyboard Input with X11R6   **195**

10.1 Setting Input Method Values 196

10.2 Managing Memory with XGetIMValues() 197
10.3 When Input Methods Start Up 197
    10.3.1 Example Usage 199
10.4 When Input Methods Stop Working 202
10.5 Finding and Controlling the Input Method's Preedit State 203
    10.5.1 Does the Input Method Support Setting/Querying Preedit
        Mode? 204
    10.5.2 Querying the Input Method's Preedit State 205
    10.5.3 Setting the Input Method's Preedit State 205
    10.5.4 Controlling the Input Method's Default Preedit State 206
    10.5.5 Finding Out When the Input Method's Preedit State
        Changes... 206
10.6 Forcing the Input Method to Ignore Keys 207
10.7 Asking the Input Method to Perform String Conversions 209
10.8 Allowing the Input Method to Request String Conversions 210
10.9 Standard Protocol for Input Method Implementers 212
10.10 Summary: New Input Method Values 213
    10.10.1 XNResourceName and XNResourceClass 215
    10.10.2 XNDestroyCallback.. 215
    10.10.3 XNQueryIMValuesList and XNQueryICValuesList........... 215
    10.10.4 XNVisiblePosition 216
    10.10.5 XNR6PreeditCallback 218
10.11 Summary: New XIC Values 219
    10.11.1 XNDestroyCallback.. 221
    10.11.2 XNResetState... 221
    10.11.3 XNHotKey 221
    10.11.4 XNHotKeyState 221
    10.11.5 XNStringConversion 222
    10.11.6 XNStateConversionCallback 222
    10.11.7 XNPreeditState 222
    10.11.8 XNPreeditStateNotifyCallback.. 223

11. Data Interchange and Internationalization   **225**

11.1 A Typical Data Exchange 226
11.2 Exchanging Text Data with Internationalized Software.................... 226
11.3 Performance Hints for Text Data Interchange 230
11.4 Example 231

11.4.1 Selection Owner...231
11.4.2 Selection Requestor 235
11.5 Summary: Data Interchange for Internationalized Software 239

12. Using Resources and the Xt Toolkit with Your Internationalized Software **241**

12.1 Localized Resources 242
12.2 Initializing the Locale of Xt-Based Software 242
12.2.1 Locale Command Line Option and Locale Resource............243
12.2.2 Default Language Procedure 244
12.3 Finding Locale-Specific Files...244
12.3.1 Finding Locale-Specific Resource Files 246
12.4 Font Set Resource Converter 247
12.5 Event Loops, I18N, and Xt 248

13. Developing Internationalized Software with Motif **249**

13.1 Displaying Local Language Characters with Motif...........................249
13.1.1 Motif Font Lists and fontList Resources 250
13.1.2 Compound Strings 251
13.2 Obtaining Local Language Characters from the Keyboard 252
13.2.1 Controlling Input with Motif 253
13.3 Data Interchange Using Motif 254
13.4 Setting Localized Titles and Icon Names 254
13.5 Locale Sensitive Motif Resources 255
13.5.1 Which to Use: Resources or Message Catalogs?....................255
13.6 Locale Sensitive Pixmaps 255
13.7 Limits of Motif I18N Support...257
13.8 Example Internationalized Motif Program 258
13.9 Summary 270

14. Advanced Topics: I18N for the Motif Widget Writer **271**

14.1 Creating Font Lists...271
14.2 Extracting Font Sets from Font Lists 273
14.3 Obtaining Local Language Characters from the Keyboard 274
14.3.1 Overview: XmIm* Routines 274
14.3.2 Connecting to the Input Method: XmImRegister()................275

14.3.3 Sending Values to the Input Method:
XmIm[Va]SetValues() 276
14.3.4 Gaining Focus: XmIm[Va]SetFocusValues() 277
14.3.5 Losing Focus: XmImUnsetFocus() 278
14.3.6 Handling Key Events: XmImMbLookupString() 278
14.3.7 Breaking Connection with the Input Method:
XmImUnregister() 279

15. I18N and the Common Desktop Environment (CDE 1.0)   281

15.1 Setting Font Resources with CDE 282
15.2 Controlling Locale and Input Method Selection with CDE 284
15.2.1 Controlling the choice of input method 285
15.3 Integrating Your Software with the CDE Workspace Menu 285
15.4 Integrating Your Software with the Application Manager 286

**Appendix A. Quick Reference: C Library Internationalization
Routines   287**

A.1 Tools for Converting between Multibyte and Wide Character 287
A.2 Tools for Parsing and Scanning 289
A.3 Tools for Character Classification 289
A.4 Tools for Case Conversion... 290
A.5 Tools for Sorting 290
A.6 Tools for Converting between Code Sets 291

**Appendix B. X11R5: XIC Values, Preedit Attributes, and Status
Attributes   293**

B.1 XIC Data Values 293
B.1.1 Preedit and Status Attributes 295

Appendix C. Example Program: Keyboard Input with X11R5   301

Appendix D. Example: Keyboard Input Using XmIm*   323

Appendix E. Quick Reference: Localizable Motif Resources   341

Glossary   347

Index   355

Preface

X Windows on the World: Developing International-ized Software with X, Motif®, and CDE describes how to develop graphical user interface software that can easily be made to operate according to the rules and customs of the user's native language.

Localized software is software in which all modifications necessary to make the product work correctly in the user's local language have been performed. For example, all messages, help text, and manuals have been translated. All fonts and local language methods necessary are available at application start-up. *Internationalization* is a design approach that makes it easier to localize software.

It seems every time you walk into the book store, someone has a new book out telling you how to create internationalized or localized software. What makes this book different? Just this — this book focuses on the graphical user interface portion of your application. With Release 5 of the X Window System™ (X11R5), the X Consortium provided a new set of Application Programmatic Interfaces (APIs) allowing graphical user interface applications to interact with users in their native language; this functionality was extended in Release 6 (X11R6). Release 1.2 of the Motif Toolkit is built on top of X11R5; one of the key focuses of Motif 1.2 was to enable the development of internationalized software.

At the time of this writing, no other book describes in detail how to use the internationalization functionality of X11R5, X11R6, and Motif 1.2. This book shows you how to use these features of X11R5, X11R6, and Motif 1.2; through the liberal use of examples, you can see exactly how to use these new functions in your own applications.

The Common Desktop Environment (CDE) is also based on X11R5 and Motif 1.2 but provides some additional widgets as well. This book describes how to create internationalized software with the facilities CDE offers. In addition, there are aspects of the environment that affect internationalized software you develop for CDE. This book describes how you develop and integrate an internationalized application into CDE.

Audience

If you create software that has a graphical user interface and you would like to be able to sell that software in multiple countries, this book is written for you. Even if you are not selling your graphical user interface software (for example, your software is shareware or freeware) and simply want to make it usable by as many people as possible, this book is for you. It describes

- Different design approaches you can take to create software that meets the special needs of customers who speak a language different than yours.
- The problem areas that your software must address to be marketable in other countries.
- How to use the various internationalization tools available to overcome these problems.

If you manage a software project and intend to sell the software in other countries, you will benefit from this book as well. It provides solutions to the problems that must be dealt with by your project team. Additionally, you will gain an overview of the total process of providing localized solutions to your customer. From initial design through final product release, this book explains the process of developing and delivering internationalized graphical user interface software.

Topics and Objectives

This book answers the following questions:

- What is internationalization and why should I care?
- What are the advantages of internationalization over other design methodologies?
- What software operations are sensitive to the application user's language, local customs, and data encoding methods?
- What tools are available that perform the software operations that are dependent on the user's language, local customs, and data encoding methods?
- How standard are these tools? Alternately phrased: How portable is an application that uses these tools?
- How do I obtain local language characters from the keyboard of a graphical user interface application written with X11R5, X11R6, Motif 1.2, or CDE?
- How do I display local language characters in my graphical user interface application?
- How do I interchange local language characters with other graphical user interface applications?
- How do I handle local language characters in resource files?
- How do I test my graphical user interface application once I've used the tools explained in this book?
- Besides using the tools as explained in this book, what else do I need to do to create the local language version of my product?

The objectives in writing this book will be met if, after reading the book, you know the answers to these questions, or at least know where to look for the answers.

Topics Not Covered

This book is not a general book on internationalization. There are several excellent books already on the market on that topic, such as Sandra Martin O'Donnell's *Programming for the World*.[1]

Also, this is not a linguistics book. I make no attempt to describe the software challenges presented by every language of the world. Such an analysis might be interesting from an academic standpoint, but from a practical standpoint, it would probably be a waste of your time to read and my time to write. The computer industry in many countries is not developed to a state where it is profitable to develop software for them. In addition, the software tools that are needed to write internationalized software for many of these countries don't exist or are not yet standard. For example, the international capabilities of X11R5 and Motif 1.2 allow development of internationalized software for Western Europe, Central Europe, Eastern Europe, the Americas, and some languages of the Pacific Rim. They do not provide support for many languages of Africa, the Middle East, India, Thailand, and others.

Finally, I do not attempt to cover the languages discussed in this book to the same depth. This should not be construed as a bias against any language. Rather, the intent is to illustrate the problems of writing software for a particular language or group of related languages and then describe the tools that are available to deal with those problems. Different languages have different problems, requiring a different depth of discussion.

Assumptions

In writing this book, I found it necessary to make some basic assumptions. For example, I have written the book assuming the reader is an English-speaking American software developer or project manager. This isn't to say that the book is not useful for other readers. Rather, I made this assumption in an attempt to keep the book more readable. I started out trying to write the book to be culturally neutral. This led to what might kindly be termed "interesting paragraphs." For example:

> *Once the product is completed in the "home" country, it is announced and shipments begin there. At that time, investigation is usually just beginning on the local language version. (Local to where?)*

Maybe this just exposes my limits as a writer, but I prefer to think that a book written in this fashion would be boring at best and unreadable at worst.

---

1. *Programming for the World, A Guide to Internationalization*, by Sandra Martin O'Donnell. Published by Prentice Hall. ISBN 0-13-722190-8.

This book describes how to create software for use in multiple countries. In particular, it describes how to create the graphical user interface of such applications using X11R5, X11R6, Motif 1.2, and/or CDE. I chose to use the C Programming Language in the text and in example programs. While bindings to other programming languages for these tools do exist, their primary use is with C.

I assume that you are familiar with C; I do not attempt to teach it in this book. In creating the examples for the book I went out of the way *not* to optimize the code. When you look at the example sources, I believe you will understand the concept being illustrated. I also expect that many of you will say to yourselves, "That could sure be coded a lot more efficiently!"

Typographical Conventions

The following conventions are used in this book:

Typographic Conventions

italic	Used for general emphasis. Also used when a new term or concept is first introduced.
`Computer Font`	Used to represent data types, function names, and example programs, such as `char*` and `setlocale()`.
`Italic Computer Font`	Used to identify parameters when listing a function specification — a value that should be replaced by a program variable or data when the function is actually used. For example, `setlocale(category, locale)`.

Road Map

Technical books such as this are typically not the book of choice to curl up with for a little pleasure reading. You are reading this book because you want to make your graphical user interface application work in other languages. You want to do this as quickly and as painlessly as possible. The following sections summarize the content of each chapter, allowing you to decide with which chapters to spend your time.

Chapter 1 — "Designing for International Markets"

Chapter 1 describes the motivations behind making your software work in languages other than English and for geographic regions other than the United States. It describes two models for making your software work in other languages and explains the costs and benefits of each. The chapter concludes with a discussion of standards that aid in making your software work for other languages. This helps you make design decisions — balancing between portability and functionality.

Chapter 2 — "Locale-Sensitive Operations: Handling Text Data"

Chapter 2 describes the software operations whose expected results vary depending on the language and location of the software user. Although some graphical user interface concepts are introduced here, the main focus is on non-graphical portions of applications including

- the variety of ways text characters are encoded.
- the choices available for storing textual data in memory and the performance and convenience trade-offs for each choice.
- the nature of the language and cultural sensitive software operations.
- the tools available to perform language and cultural sensitive operations and the standard that defines each tool.

Chapter 3 — "Locale-Sensitive Operations: Messages and Data Formats"

Chapter 3 describes how to provide local language messages and data formatted according to local customs in internationalized software.

Chapter 4 — "Displaying Local Language Characters with X11R5"

Chapter 4 describes how to code your application so that it can render the characters of the user's language. It describes the X11R5 concept of font sets and their use.

Chapter 5 — "Displaying Local Language Characters with X11R6"

Chapter 5 describes the changes made to the way text is rendered using X11R6 in internationalized software. It introduces the concepts of output methods and output contexts, showing you how to apply them in your application.

Chapter 6 — "Keyboard Input: Background and Overview"

Chapter 6 describes the general concepts of how you obtain characters from the keyboard in an X Windows application. It provides an overview of the different ways coded characters for different languages are generated from the keyboard.

Chapter 7 — "Keyboard Input with X Windows"

Chapter 7 describes the concepts of input methods and input contexts, first introduced in X11R5. It shows how the same application code allows a Japanese user to enter Kanji characters from the keyboard, a Russian user to enter Cyrillic characters from the keyboard, and a German user to enter accented and special characters needed for German from the keyboard. The chapter provides many examples showing you how to code your application to generate characters from the keyboard.

Chapter 8 — "Keyboard Input: Supporting Over-the-Spot and Off-the-Spot Preedit and Status Styles"

Chapter 8 expands on the techniques introduced in Chapter 7, describing how to support over-the-spot preedit style and off-the-spot preedit and status styles. Examples in the chapter build on the example introduced in Chapter 7.

Chapter 9 — "Keyboard Input with On-the-Spot Preedit and Status Styles"

Chapter 9 describes how to use a special style of input method that provides "on-the-spot" feedback.

Chapter 10 — "Keyboard Input with X11R6"

Chapter 10 describes how to obtain coded characters from the keyboard using the internationalization features added to X11R6. X11R6 extends the keyboard capabilities introduced in Chapter 9, providing features such as notification when input methods quit functioning and notification when input methods are ready for connection.

Chapter 11 — "Data Interchange and Internationalization"

Chapter 11 describes how to exchange textual data with another graphical user interface application. While text data interchange isn't strictly a problem of internationalized applications, the fact that there are internationalized applications increases the likelihood that two different applications displayed to the same screen may want to exchange data encoded in different ways. This chapter describes how you use the concepts of the X Window System's Inter-Client Communications Conventions Manual (ICCCM) to exchange text data between applications that may run in different languages with different character encodings.

Chapter 12 — "Using Resources and the Xt Toolkit with Your Internationalized Software"

Chapter 12 describes how to create and use local language resources in your application. It also describes the internationalization features added to the Xt toolkit.

Chapter 13 — "Developing Internationalized Software with Motif"

Chapter 13 describes how to write an internationalized application using Motif 1.2 widgets. Because Motif is built on top of the internationalization capabilities of X11R5, it shields you from the complexities of the underlying internationalization architecture in X11R5. While relatively brief, this chapter describes everything you need to do to internationalize your Motif application.

Chapter 14 — "Advanced Topics: I18N for the Motif Widget Writer"

Chapter 14 describes advanced Motif internationalization concepts. Most application developers use the existing Motif widgets as provided. However, sometime you may find that you need to write your own widget, or that you need to use a widget in a way for which some capabilities are lacking (such as performing keyboard input in a `DrawingArea` widget). This chapter helps you ensure that the software developed in this manner is internationalized.

Chapter 15 — "I18N and the Common Desktop Environment (CDE 1.0)"

Chapter 15 describes how you create an internationalized application with CDE and integrate it into the common desktop.

Appendix A — "Quick Reference: C Library Internationalization Routines"

Appendix A provides several tables, grouping logically related internationalization routines together. For example, Table A.1 lists all I18N routines used to convert between multibyte and wide character representations of character data. The tables also identify in which standards the routines are defined.

Appendix B — "X11R5: XIC Values, Preedit Attributes, and Status Attributes"

Appendix B lists and describes the data values your software uses to communicate when generating local language characters from the keyboard.

Appendix C — "Example Program: Keyboard Input with X11R5"

Appendix C is a program listing that illustrates all the support input styles supported by X11R5. It is built from the initial example introduced in Chapter 7 and later expanded in Chapters 8 and 9.

Appendix D — "Example: Keyboard Input Using XmIm*"

Appendix D illustrates the use of Motif's XmIm* routines for obtaining local language characters from the keyboard.

Appendix E — "Quick Reference: Localizable Motif Resources"

Appendix E contains tables which list Motif resources that may need to be modified when your software is localized.

Glossary

The glossary defines the internationalization related terms introduced in this book. Since the book assumes that you already understand the X Window System and Motif, it does not define terms commonly used with those systems.

Acknowledgments

I have been fortunate in having the help and support of many wonderful people throughout this project. Don McMinds not only initially suggested the project to me, but also worked with me through its entire length. Don tirelessly reviewed several drafts of the book, catching many of my errors and lending his writing expertise. Thanks, Don!

I've had the privilege to work with Frank Rojas for the last seven years as we struggled to internationalize the X Window System, the OSF/Motif toolkit, and the Common Desktop Environment. Through his many reviews, Frank has been instrumental in helping keep the book technically accurate. He has given his time repeatedly to help me wade my way through the murkier parts of the X11R6 specification. In addition, Frank has given me a non-HP® perspective on the topics and has made sure the example programs compile and run on IBM®'s AIX® systems.

Sandra Martin O'Donnell has not only been a good friend throughout the project — she has also lent her expertise in internationalization of the operating system to several draft reviews.

Several friends and colleagues have reviewed portions of the book, providing technical feedback and adding different perspectives on how the material should be presented. My thanks go to Ehood Baratz, Thaddeus Konar, and Bill McMahon.

Many others have given their time to answer questions and provide information needed for the book: Charlie Amacher, Claudia DeBlau, Ken Fujisawa, Tim Greenwood, Hideyuki Hayashi, Toshikazu Hirasawa, Hideki Hiura, Vania Joloboff, Nelson Ng, Bob Scheifler, Yuichi Takashima, and Joe Whitty.

I would also like to thank Karen Gettman and Camille Trentacoste of Prentice Hall — Karen for her patience with my optimistic schedules and Camille for her continual good humor despite my many questions. Craig Little and Martha Williams have both worked hard to catch my errors in grammar, punctuation and style. Thanks!

Finally, I want to thank Jan and Stephanie McFarland. Their love and support made it possible to complete the book. Thank you for tolerating my frequent absences from family life and for boosting my spirits when I felt as if the book would never be completed.

Though all of these folks have generously given of their time and support, any errors this book contains are mine and mine alone.

Obtaining Copies of the Examples

The program examples in this book are available on-line via anonymous `ftp` from `ftp.prenhall.com`. When you `ftp` to this location, change directories to:

`pub/ptr/hewlett_packard_professional_books.w-064/mcfarland/xwindows.wld`

When you `ftp` to `ftp.prenhall.com`, supply the user name: `anonymous`. You will be asked to supply your e-mail address as a password.

There you will find a compressed tar file, `xwow.tar.Z` and the text file, README. README describes how to extract the sources for the example programs from `xwow.tar.Z`. The programs have been built and tested successfully on HP-UX 9.*, HP-UX 10.*, and AIX 4.1 systems.

If you have comments on the book, or suggestions for improvement, please send me e-mail at either of the following addresses:

```
xwow@hpcvlx.cv.hp.com
xwow@cv.hp.com
```

Your comments and suggestions are welcome and appreciated.

Designing for International Markets

T his chapter describes the motivation for making software usable in countries other than those for which the software was designed. It describes two commonly used approaches for creating software for other countries, listing the benefits and costs of each approach. This chapter provides a high-level architectural look at the design approach known as internationalization (I18N).

The acronym "I18N" (pronounced "eye eighteen en") is an aid for lazy typists; it literally means a word that starts with the letter "I," followed by 18 more letters, and ends with the letter "N." The computer industry is often derided in the press for continually creating new acronyms and buzz words. And the acronym I18N may seem like another valid example of this practice. After working in I18N for eight years, I feel that the term is not a buzz word; it is a necessity. Try typing a detailed message to your manager describing internationalization and the reasons you want to use it. Then go back and count how many times you typed "internationalization" before reverting to the acronym "I18N."

This chapter concludes with a look at the various standards that support the I18N model and the types of tools specified by each. The latter information should help you, the developer of internationalized software, make an informed decision regarding the trade-offs between functionality and portability.

1.1 What Is Internationalization and Why Should You Care?

One prime objective of a software developer's job is to provide the most customer-required functionality for the lowest possible cost. This allows you to sell as many copies of an application at as little cost as possible. That may sound mercenary and academics may deride the approach, but nearly all software development is done with an eye toward profit.

One of the fastest ways to leverage software development cost is to sell the same products in additional markets, including other countries. The problem from a software design standpoint is that users in other countries expect the software to correctly process their written language and interact with them in that language. They expect the following features:

- The product must allow input, processing, and display of characters of the user's language. For example, a word processing application should allow the user to type in the characters of his language. Additionally, the user expects that once the characters are entered, they should be displayed and printed correctly.
- The product must interact with the user in his or her language. For example, prompts, error messages, and help screens must be displayed in the user's language. (Would you buy a VCR if the manual were written in a language you didn't understand or if all its buttons were labeled in a language you didn't understand?)
- Data must be formatted according to the user's local customs.
- Data must be processed according to the rules of the user's language.

For an application to sell well in a country or region, the product must at least meet these user expectations. The same is true of software developed for non-commercial purposes.

There are two primary ways to meet these user expectations: custom localized software and internationalized software.

1.2 Custom Localized Software

One approach to meeting the needs of international customs is to create special, custom *localized* versions of the original product targeted specifically at that region. (You will sometimes see this referred to as *local language software*, *language-specific software*, or *local version* of the software.) In this book, the term localized means that all modifications necessary to make the product work correctly in the user's local language have been performed. For example, all messages, help text, and manuals have been translated. All fonts and local language methods necessary are available at application start-up. Internationalization is a design approach that makes it easier to localize a software product.

A typical scenario in companies that utilize this approach is listed below.

1. The marketing team identifies features and requirements for the U.S. market and the U.S. design team creates the product.
2. Once the U.S. product is completed, all project materials (such as design documents, source code, documentation, and illustrations) are bundled up and sent to a remote design team in the new target region.
3. The remote design team begins evaluating and investigating the U.S. product to determine what changes must be made to make it acceptable to the local customers. The team then makes those changes.

4. The U.S. design team begins work on the next release of the product or perhaps even the replacement product. This work proceeds at the same time the remote design team is beginning its work on the current release of the product.

This process is repeated for each remote market. While there are some specific benefits to this type of approach, the costs for developing custom localized versions of the software are extensive.

1.2.1 Benefits of Custom Localized Software

Customers benefit from this approach in that they *eventually* receive a product carefully tailored for their needs in the remote location.

The original software development team benefits in that once the original product is released, they don't have to worry about making it work correctly in other countries. It becomes somebody else's problem. The original development team can immediately proceed to work on the next project.

1.2.1.1 Costs of custom localized software

The costs of custom localized software solutions are borne by the customer and by the software developers. Costs to the customer include

- late delivery of the localized product to the customer,
- inconsistent operation between different localized versions of what is supposed to be the same product, and
- limited selection of localized versions of the product.

Costs to the developer include

- extra staffing expense,
- difficulty in maintaining the product,
- difficulties in updating and enhancing the product, and
- reduced window of opportunity to sell localized versions.

1.2.1.2 Late availability of product

The customer may have to wait a long time to get a version of the product that works in his or her language. Once the product has been completed by the original design team, it is usually announced and shipments begin there. At that time, investigation is usually just beginning in the remote country for creating the localized version of the product. Depending on the size and complexity of the software, the size of the local development team, and the completeness and accuracy of the design documentation, customers in the remote country may not see a version of the product that speaks their language for six to nine months — or even longer.

1.2.1.3   Different language versions, different results

Each local engineering team has control of the source code, with the opportunity to change functionality, introduce new features, and remove others. This means that the Spanish version of the product and the German version of the product may have very different features. In some cases, the only things different localized versions of a product share in common are the product title and the source code from which they were developed. Consistent operation across localized versions of the product is a high priority for big, multinational companies — the kind of customer you want to purchase your software. Creating custom localized versions of your software makes it difficult to meet the needs of these customers.

1.2.1.4   Cost prohibitive

Customers may not be able to obtain localized versions for some languages of interest simply because the cost is too great for the software developer. The number of sales anticipated in a country may not justify the cost of hiring a local development team to redesign the product. The result: Customers have fewer choices and you sell your software into fewer markets.

1.2.1.5   Staffing expense

This cost is the most obvious. You must hire a staff of software developers in the target country to redesign your original product and to test the localized version. It is extremely expensive to staff a remote software development team. And you still need to hire local language experts to translate text messages and documents. Technical writers or professional translators are better suited than software engineers to craft the prompt, message, or help text that is most appropriate for the products' intended audience. This is just as true in English as it is for the localized version of the product.

1.2.1.6   Increased software maintenance costs

Since the remote software team uses the product source code, that source code is heavily modified as the localized version of the product is created. Unless great care is taken, the localized version can diverge from the original version, leading to support nightmares as shown in Figure 1.1. When a bug is found and fixed in the original version, someone has to determine if the fix is applicable to the different localized versions. When a bug shows up in a localized version, each localized version has to be examined to see if it suffers the same problem. This may not be a simple task, because the source code for the localized versions may be wildly divergent.

1.2.1.7   Expensive to enhance

Enhancements to the original version are difficult to apply to the localized version. When the remote development team receives version two of the product, team members must first determine how version two differs from the original version. Then they must determine how the localized version differs from the original version. They must decide how to apply

Figure 1.1
Creating custom localized versions can be costly. Designing, implementing, supporting, and updating
multiple custom, localized versions of a product can be overwhelming.

the changes in the new version to the localized version before finally modifying the changes
to be correct for the local language. All of this adds significantly to the time (and cost) of creating the localized version.

1.2.1.8   Reduced window of opportunity

The window of opportunity for selling the localized software product is usually much
smaller than that of the original version of the product. This is because the localized version
of the product is usually not available until some time after the product announcement and
release in the original version. Suppose that the localized version is completed six months
after release of the original product. Software sales should presumably follow the same pat-
tern as they did in the United States. However, the original software development team has
been busy developing the next, new and improved, release of the product. Suppose that they
announce and ship the updated product one year after releasing the original version in the
United States; this is just six months after release of the localized product. Experience has
shown that sales of the localized product will rapidly taper off as the new updated product is
announced in the United States. It doesn't matter that the localized version of the updated
product will not occur for another six months. Customers see the new features announced in
the updated U.S. product and are unwilling to pay for the original version.

The high cost of producing custom localized versions of the software means that typically only large software companies use this approach — and then only in markets where
they can be assured of large enough volume of sales for the margins to cover the high cost of
creating the localized version and still return some profit.

Until about ten years ago, most software and hardware companies used this approach to
reach remote markets. However, for all the reasons cited above, these same companies now
are pursuing a different approach, called internationalization.

1.3 Internationalized Software

Internationalization is a software design methodology that allows software to interact with a user in his or her written language. Internationalized software operates on data according to the language rules and customs of its user. And best of all, I18N does not require source code changes, recompilation, or relinking to provide these capabilities.

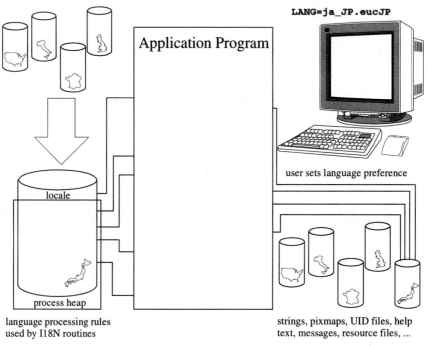

LANG=ja_JP.eucJP

Application Program

user sets language preference

locale

process heap

language processing rules
used by I18N routines

strings, pixmaps, UID files, help
text, messages, resource files, ...

Figure 1.2
I18N: Conceptual Model.

With the I18N model, the application is designed and implemented once. As Figure 1.2 shows, any data that might need be to changed for correct local language operation (for example, messages, data format strings, and font specifications) is made external to the application. When starting an application, the user indicates in which *locale* he or she desires the application to operate. The locale is a collective term for the language of the user, the location or territory of the user (which determines locale customs, such as currency formats), and the code set in which the user's data is represented. The locale is also a physical data file and/or collection of routines that are used to initialize an application's language sensitive environment. The definitions are often used interchangeably since the physical file is an implementation or instantiation of the language, territory, and code set.

I18N routines called by the application load the data and methods for that locale before beginning execution of the application. A single application executable — created from a single set of application source code — provides correct operation in any supported locale.

1.3.1   Customers Benefit from I18N

Customers benefit from the I18N approach in may ways. They get the same main benefit obtained with the custom localized version approach: correct operation in the user's local language. They receive consistent behavior of the application across all languages they use (especially important for large, multinational companies). Localized software created with the internationalization approach is generally much more quickly available to customers than localized software created with the custom localized version approach. At the same time, I18N provides for more user customization of the product.

1.3.1.1   Correct behavior in the user's local language

I18N provides the same correct local language behavior as is provided by custom localized versions. Algorithms are written generically with specific behavior controlled by table information loaded at application start-up. Alternatively, dynamic loading is used to bring in a custom language version of a language sensitive function or procedure at application start-up.

1.3.1.2   Consistent operation across local languages

With an I18N approach, a single source, single executable is produced, and that single executable is used for all supported languages. Since only your development team has access to that source, it isn't possible for the *localizers* to change the behavior of the application; only your development team can do that. (The term localizer refers to the person who readies the application for use in another language. With an I18N design approach, the localizer typically translates only text files and manuals.)

1.3.1.3   Localized version available more quickly

If an application has been internationalized correctly, the only real tasks remaining to create the localized version are to translate text files and to translate documentation. Both of these processes can be started well before the final version of the product is finished in the United States. In fact, many companies today make it a point to ensure that localized versions are ready for shipment at the same time as the original version. They accomplish this by picking a freeze date after which no changes can be made to product behavior, thus allowing product documentation to be completed; similarly, after the freeze date no changes can be made to application text (for example, help files, messages, and resource files). Translation can begin on the freeze date for the external text files and documentation. If the amount of translation isn't overwhelming, the localized version can usually be released on the same date as the U.S. version.

1.3.1.4   Customization by the user

I18N is based on the concept that language-sensitive data can be stored external to the application source and executable. For example, messages are stored externally in message catalogs; widget labels and initial text values may be stored either in message catalogs or in resource files. It is possible to protect these message catalogs and resource files from modification by the customer. But it is more common to make these files modifiable by the user. This allows customization of the software by the user. For example, users might want to control the font used by the application or might want to customize an error message or prompt.

1.3.2   Developers Benefit from I18N

While there are many benefits of the I18N approach for the customer, there are even more benefits for the software developer. Foremost among these is that no application source code changes are required to localize the software as long as the I18N design approach is used. No source code changes means no remote software development team is needed. It also means that localized versions share exactly the same source code and executable, making support, maintenance, and enhancements much easier than with custom localized versions. The I18N approach makes it easy to add support for new languages, usually without software source code changes. These all result in lower costs to enter a particular local language market. This means that for a given amount of money, your software can be made available in more local language markets than was possible with custom localized versions. And because the cost is low, the I18N approach is available to small- and medium-sized software companies. Finally, applications developed with the I18N approach are still highly portable across platforms.

1.3.2.1   Less expensive

With I18N, the application is designed and implemented once. There is no need to hire local language programmers to redesign and reimplement the application for correct operation in a local language. *Localization* of an internationalized application consists chiefly of translating text files. Localization (sometimes referred to as *L10N*) is a term that refers collectively to all work needed to make a product acceptable and work correctly for use in a different locale. This includes translating all text to be displayed to the user, translating documentation, modifying the behavior of language sensitive operations, and providing fonts and other special functionality when needed.

With I18N, localization can be done much more cheaply than reimplementing or redesigning the product. All that is required is local language expertise, not language and software design expertise.

Because localized versions can be produced so inexpensively, the I18N approach makes it less risky to enter new local language markets. It requires a smaller investment to enter the market, which means fewer sales need be made to reach the break-even point for the local language product.

The lower cost of reaching local language markets also means that medium- and small-sized software companies can have access to local language markets. For example, a software company in the United States consisting of a dozen software engineers is unlikely to hire engineering teams in Japan, Germany, France, and Spain in order to reach those markets. To create custom localized versions for those markets would require them to triple or quadruple their staff. Assuming the capital is available to do this, it is still a risk that few small companies are willing to take. However, with I18N it may be necessary to hire only a single translator in each country. Or it may even be possible to find native speakers of those languages in the United States (for example, international students at a local university) who can perform the necessary translations inexpensively.

1.3.2.2 Easier to maintain, easier to enhance

Because there is only one version of the source code, bugs are easier to isolate and correct. There is no question about whether a bug was in the original product or was caused by changes made by one of the remote development teams; there is only one source. When a bug is patched for one language version, it is automatically patched for all supported language versions. That's the advantage of one of the key tenets of I18N: a single source, a single executable.

For the same reason, it is much easier to enhance internationalized software products. With one development team modifying the source, only the external language sensitive bits need to be localized, and then only those portions that have changed since the previous release.

1.3.2.3 Easy to support new languages

When creating internationalized applications, all potentially language-sensitive operations are performed by standard I18N function calls. An I18N function performs its operations according to the locale of the user, obtaining the data needed to return the correct results from a location external to the application — a single function performs correctly for all supported locales. Though specific to the implementation of the I18N function, this is typically done by loading tables from the file system, or by dynamically loading a locale-specific method to perform the operation. From a software design standpoint, you don't really need to care how the I18N functions work, as long as they provide the correct result and don't affect your software.

The bulk of this book focuses on how to create applications in this manner. But for now, accepting this generalization, you can see that if all language-sensitive operations are external to the application source, you need only modify the external data and methods to make the application work correctly for a new language.

Actually, the preceding is a bit of an oversimplification. The effort required to internationalize software is a function of the language or languages for which you target your application. The languages of the world can be grouped by characteristics of the language:

- languages that are written in a single direction and for which the shape of a character does not depend on which characters are adjacent,[1] such as English, French, and German.
- *bidirectional* languages, such as Hebrew, in which some portions are written from right to left while other portions are written left to right — within a single sentence. Such languages are referred to as bidirectional languages. These languages present special challenges to the developer of graphical user interface software. For example, just figuring out which portions of text are drawn in one direction and which are drawn in the other, and then calculating a starting x,y position to pass to the drawing routines can present a significant challenge.
- *context-sensitive* languages. In the written form of some languages the shape of an individual character (e.g., the glyph used to render it) depends on the shape of the character(s) that precede it and follow it. For example, in cursive English the shape of an "r" depends on the shape of the character that precedes it. If the "r" follows a low-ending shape, such as "a," the beginning of "r" is also low — near the baseline. If the "r" follows a high-ending shape, such as "o," the beginning of "r" is also high. You can prove this to your self by writing the words "dare" and "door" in cursive script. Languages where the shape of a character depends on the shapes of the characters that surround it are called context-sensitive languages. And while English has a non-cursive (and non-context-sensitive) form, some context-sensitive languages such as Arabic have no alternate writing form. Context-sensitive languages prove a challenge for the graphical user interface programmer in many ways. For example, the application must determine how much of a string must be redrawn when a single character changes — the shape of the new character may require that the characters surrounding it be redrawn since their shapes are affected by the shape of the new character.

In general, if you internationalize software for one language in a group, you pick up support for other languages in that group with no additional effort. For example, suppose you design your application to be internationalized, targeting France for localization. French is a Latin-based language, written left to right with block letters; French needs only a few additional letters beyond those used in the English alphabet. If you internationalize your application correctly with French in mind as a target market, the resulting application can also support German, Italian, or any other major Western European language without application modification. Additional localization is required, but no application source code changes.

1.3.2.4   Application portability

The ability to port their product from one platform to another with minimum of effort is of key importance to most software developers. Portability is not sacrificed when you internationalize your software.

---

1. Some I18N engineers break this single group into two subgroups: languages for which each character can be encoded with one data byte and languages that require more than one data byte for a character.

The tools that enable internationalized software design are standard tools. Graphical user interface tools for I18N are standardized in the X Window System, releases 5 and 6 (also known as X11R5 and X11R6), and in Motif release 1.2 and later. Other tools are standardized in the C programming language by various standards bodies. The advantage of standards is that any application written to comply with them is (or should be) easily portable to any platform that conforms with those standards. Since I18N is supported by standards such as X11R5, Motif 1.2, ANSI C, ISO/IEC C, and POSIX, internationalized applications should not have their portability restricted by the fact that they are internationalized.

1.3.3   Costs of Using I18N

While there are many benefits of internationalization, they don't come completely free of charge. Creating internationalized applications requires some additional planning at the start of the project, as well as some additional coding during software development. And, there are some performance implications for internationalized software, though these generally are small (or at least can be minimized through careful software design).

1.3.3.1   Planning

To properly internationalize software, some additional planning is required. First, you must know the countries in which the software will be sold. But unless you want to redesign your software after version 1 is released, you must have an idea of where versions 2, 3, or 4 may be sold as well. No product marketing team can answer this with a complete guarantee of accuracy,. so a best guess must be made. The reason for knowing the potential markets is so that the product design team can know which classes of languages they must support. For example, suppose product marketing tells you: "We'll initially sell in Germany and France. And if things go well, we'll expand into Italy, Spain, Switzerland, Belgium, and Holland. But no matter what, we won't expand into Asia." This tells you that you only need to design your software to support languages written from left to right and that have a small number of characters (representable in eight bits of data per character). There is no need to worry about the problems associated with characters requiring more than one byte of storage. The task is relatively easy.

Suppose however that product marketing said: "We'll initially release the software in Germany, France, the United Kingdom, Italy, and Japan. If things go well in Japan, we'll look at Korea and China. And the Middle East is a possibility as well." As mentioned previously, the languages of Europe are all very similar and require the same capabilities of an internationalized application. However, the languages of the Pacific Rim (such as Japanese, Korean, Traditional Chinese, and Simplified Chinese) put additional requirements on your software. For example, the number of bytes required to represent a single character in the language can vary from character to character, between one and four bytes per character. Some applications for the Pacific Rim may require vertical writing (that is, text is written in columnar form as opposed to linear form that you are now reading) — though neither X11 nor Motif currently support this capability.

As you can see, there is a new class of problems to be planned for if Asian languages are to be supported by the software. Similarly, the bidirectional and context-sensitive languages of the Middle East put yet another set of design problems on the application developer.

Standard tools exist to deal with nearly all of the requirements of the different language groups. Yet each requires additional work on the part of the application designer and implementor.

What does all this additional planning and additional coding do to the project schedule? Experience shows that I18N adds about 10 percent – 15 percent to the project schedule. However, that increase is more than offset by the decrease in the project schedule for all the localized versions of the product to be produced.

1.3.3.2   Some tools don't exist

Though standard C language tools exist that address many language and cultural problems, there are still gaps. Tools for handling bidirectional and context-sensitive languages are not yet standard. A collection of tools known as the Layout Services are working their way through X/Open's internationalization working group. But at the time of this writing the Layout Services specification had not yet been adopted. Because no standard C tools exist to process bidirectional or context-sensitive languages, the X Window System does not provide direct support for these language groups.

For these reasons, software targeted for users of these languages must either take advantage of vendor proprietary tools for these languages (and limit portability of the software) or plan on creating custom localized software for users of these languages.

1.3.3.3   Performance

Any discussion about the costs and benefits of internationalization would be incomplete without a discussion of performance. As described earlier, internationalization is achieved through the use of generalized algorithms that use local language specific data loaded at application start-up in order to perform language-sensitive operations correctly. Generalized algorithms are always slower than those custom designed for processing a particular language. Fortunately, language-sensitive operations (such as collation, display of messages, and formatting of text data) tend to be a very small percentage of the total computing done by an application. So, the overall impact of these slower algorithms is usually negligible. The next chapter explains about implementation trade-offs you can make between coding simplicity and maximum performance.

In addition to slower algorithms, there is a performance cost to load the language sensitive data at application start-up. For graphical user interface applications that load significant amounts of resources and do a great amount of widget initialization at application start-up, the performance impact of loading internationalized data is usually small in comparison. Again, there are design trade-offs to be considered that can minimize even this small performance hit. For example, deciding when to use a message catalog and when to use a toolkit or Motif resource can impact performance. Trade-offs such as these are explored in coming chapters.

1.4 Standards Controlling I18N

The tools that enable development of internationalized software are controlled by a number of consortiums or standards bodies. The I18N capabilities of the X Window System are controlled by the X Consortium; the I18N capabilities of the Motif Toolkit are controlled by the Open Software Foundation. The bulk of this book is devoted to exploring these capabilities as well as discussing the potential future directions of these tools.

However, an internationalized graphical user interface application cannot be written solely with the tools provided by X and Motif. What about tools for the non-graphical, language-sensitive operations performed by the application? These tools are specified by programming language standards and by operating system standards. Since most X and Motif applications are written in the C programming language and run on UNIX[®2], it's worth understanding which standards bodies and consortia define I18N support for C and UNIX. In the next chapter, as language-sensitive operations and the tools the handle them are described, the standards governing each tool are listed. And, as different platforms support different standards, the list of I18N tools and the standards that define them will allow you to make an informed decision about which tools you will use when developing your application.

---

2. UNIX is a registered trademark in the United States and other countries, licensed exclusively through X/Open Company Limited.

Locale-Sensitive Operations: Handling Text Data

The correct result of some software operations depends on the user's language, location, and *data encoding*. The encoding of text data is the code set used to represent written text in a computer. A unique numeric value, or code, is assigned to each character. (Code sets are discussed in detail in section 2.2.1 on page 21.)

For example, suppose your software lists a large catalog of car parts; each car part has a description and a price. If the users of that software are in Germany, they expect the description of each part to be in German. Further, they may expect the price to be listed in deutsche marks, and formatted as German monetary values are normally formatted. Japanese users of the same software expect the description of each part to be in Japanese, with the price listed in Japanese yen.

Fortunately, relatively few software operations need to be sensitive to the user's locale. The next two chapters explain which operations are locale-sensitive, providing background information when necessary. They also explain which tools allow your internationalized software to provide the behavior the user expects.

The purpose of these two chapters is not to define how each locale-sensitive operation should behave with every language of the world. Rather, for each locale-sensitive operation, each chapter gives one or two examples to demonstrate the nature of that sensitivity. It then introduces one or more software tools that allow you to meet the locale-specific requirement.

Which operations are locale sensitive? They can be broadly classed as

- text data manipulation (parsing, sorting, case shifting)
- text messages to the user
- formats of data displayed to the user and entered by the user
- text input from the keyboard
- text rendering or displaying text data
- text data interchange with other applications
- graphical symbols displayed to the user

Locale-sensitive text data manipulation is discussed in this chapter. Locale-sensitive messages and data formats are dealt with in the next chapter. These operations are not specific to graphical user interface software — they are operations that must be performed by every internationalized application (with or without a graphical user interface). The last four operations in the list are specific to graphical user interfaces. The remaining chapters of this book are devoted to those topics. All operations are governed by the application's locale.

2.1 Initializing I18N Tools: setlocale()

The I18N tools described in the remainder of this book require the application to initialize the *locale*. The locale is a collection of data and/or methods that cause internationalized C library and X library functions to behave correctly for the user's language, local customs, and data encoding. The locale is global in the application process — that is, locale data is subject to the same rules that govern any process global data.

The locale is initialized by calling the `setlocale()` function, as is shown in Figure 2.1 on page 17. (As you will see in a later chapter, the routine `XtSetLanguageProc()` should be used in some situations instead of `setlocale()` to initialize the locale.)

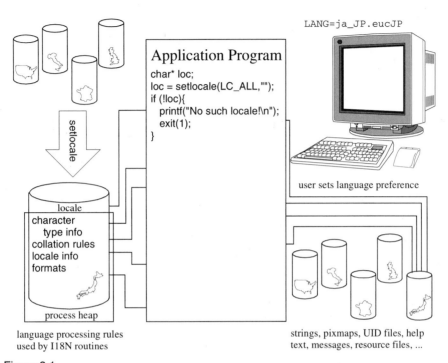

LANG=ja_JP.eucJP

Application Program
```
char* loc;
loc = setlocale(LC_ALL,"");
if (!loc){
    printf("No such locale!\n");
    exit(1);
}
```

setlocale

user sets language preference

locale

character
    type info
collation rules
locale info
formats

process heap

language processing rules
used by I18N routines

strings, pixmaps, UID files, help
text, messages, resource files, ...

Figure 2.1

setlocale() copies local specific data onto the global data space stored on the process heap. In some implementations, it also initializes locale-specific methods that perform locale-sensitive operations. In both cases, setlocale() causes the I18N routines to perform in a locale-specific manner. The locale is usually specified by setting one of several standard environment variables.

2.1.1   Using setlocale() in Your Application

setlocale() takes two parameters: a category and a locale:

```
char * setlocale(int category, char* locale);
```

The *category* parameter allows you to control which portions of the locale are initialized to locale *locale*. As the architecture of I18N was forged through various working groups and standards bodies, some of the architects felt it would be useful in some cases to be able to set portions of the locale to one language and other portions to a different language. It is not uncommon for several languages to be used within a single country. German, French, and Italian are all commonly used languages in Switzerland. A user in Switzerland might want to process data in German, have prompts presented in French, and yet want monetary values printed with Swiss formats and currency symbol.

To allow for needs such as this, setlocale() can control functionally separable pieces of the locale independently. This is done by breaking the locale into functional subcomponents, called categories. `setlocale()` can initialize one or more categories to a specified locale, and other categories can be initialized to a different locale. These categories are described in Table 2.1.

Table 2.1 Locale Categories and Their Functions

Category	Function
LC_ALL	affects the behavior of all internationalized functions; controls the behavior of all the categories listed below. Except for special cases, most calls to `setlocale()` use the LC_ALL category, initializing all categories to the same locale.
LC_COLLATE	affects the behavior of regular expressions and the internationalized functions used to collate strings.
LC_CTYPE	affects the behavior of regular expressions, character classification functions, character conversion functions, and any function that processes multibyte data (discussed in the next section).
LC_MESSAGES[†]	affects the language of messages displayed to the user; affects the processing of affirmative and negative responses.
LC_MONETARY	affects the internationalized functions used to format monetary values.
LC_NUMERIC	affects the handling of the radix character in internationalized functions that convert between string and floating point representations, and between string and integer representations. Also affects the formatting of numeric quantities.
LC_TIME	affects the behavior of internationalized time and date conversion functions.

†. The LC_MESSAGES category is not an ISO, ANSI, o POSIX standard category. It was added to the X/Open Portability Guide for Issue 4 (XPG4). This category is only guaranteed to be present on XPG4 conforming systems.

For example, the following call in your application causes messages to be displayed in the fictional locale FooSpeak:

```
(void)setlocale(LC_MESSAGES, "FooSpeak");
```

This example uses a fictional locale to make a point. The values for locale names are defined by all the standards bodies as vendor and implementation dependent. This means that to select European Spanish, the value to be passed to the second parameter of `setlocale()` depends on which system the application runs. For example, on HP-UX 9.0 the correct value is "spanish," on HP-UX 10.0 the correct value is either "spanish" or "es_ES.roman8," while on Solaris® 2.3 the correct value is "es_ES." This could be a problem except for one thing — any application that includes the locale name in the application source code is not internationalized anyway. In such a case, the source code would have to be changed and the application recompiled to make it work in a different locale. Instead of coding a locale name in your application, the typical way of calling `setlocale()` is with an empty string as the second parameter. When the empty string is passed, `setlocale()` queries the environment for one or more environment variables that tell it the locale value to use. For example, the following directs `setlocale()` to initialize its monetary information according to the user's preferences, as specified by environment variables:

```
(void)setlocale(LC_MONETARY, "");
```

Which environment variables control which categories? Each category has an associated environment variable with the identical name that controls the locale of that category. In the preceding example, the user would set the `LC_MONETARY` environment variable to a string value for the language desired.

In addition to the environment variables that control individual categories, there are two environment variables that control multiple categories: `LANG` and `LC_ALL`. When `LANG` is set, it directs `setlocale()` to use its value whenever the environment variable for an individual category is not set. For example, suppose the user sets `LC_MESSAGES` to "fr_FR.iso88591," `LANG` to "de_DE.iso88591," and the locale is initialized with `setlocale(LC_ALL, "")`. In this case, the `LC_MESSAGES` category is initialized to "fr_FR.iso88591" with the result that messages are displayed in French. All other categories are initialized to "de_DE.iso88591." For example, since the `LC_TIME` environment variable isn't specified, the `LC_TIME` category is controlled by the `LANG` environment variable. Time and date strings are therefore formatted according to German customs.

When the environment variable `LC_ALL` is set, it directs `setlocale()` to ignore the `LANG` environment variable and any other `LC_*` environment variable; `LC_ALL` overrides all other locale controlling environment variables for `setlocale()`. Like the value of the second argument to `setlocale()`, the values assigned to these environment variables is vendor dependent.

In nearly all cases, your application should call `setlocale()` with the category `LC_ALL`. The main reason to call `setlocale()` with one of the other category specifiers is if you are trying to fine-tune application performance and you know that your application uses only a specific portion of the locale. In this instance you might specify one of the categories in an effort to limit the amount of I18N data that `setlocale()` loads at application initialization.

Though rarely done, another reason to call `setlocale()` is to query the current locale to determine the setting of a particular category. Calling `setlocale(category, NULL)` causes `setlocale()` to return a string for *category* identifying the locale of that category. This is known as a locale query operation. The value returned is implementation dependent and may be different from the value assigned to the associated environment variable. However, it can be passed to a future call to `setlocale()` to restore the locale to the same locale as when queried.

2.1.2   When Should You Call setlocale()?

setlocale() must be called before any I18N function is called. The safest thing to do is to call setlocale() immediately after the opening main brace of your application. It doesn't hurt to call it then, and it ensures that you don't inadvertently call an I18N function before initializing the locale.

If you are developing code for a library instead of an application, you should not call setlocale(). Instead, assume the application using your library calls setlocale() for you. If your library code calls setlocale(), it potentially changes the global locale and in the process, destroys some state information that cannot be recovered.

2.1.3   Summary: Using setlocale()

- Call setlocale() as the first executable after your application's opening main brace.
- Use LC_ALL for the setlocale() category parameter, unless you have a compelling reason not to do so.
- Never code the locale name into the call to setlocale(). Instead, use the empty string for the locale parameter, allowing the user to specify environment variables that control which locale setlocale() loads. Alternatively, initialize the environment variables in an application start-up shell script; the localizers for your application can then set the variables when they localize the shell script.
- If the code you are writing is part of a library (instead of being an application executable), do not call setlocale() from the library. Doing so changes the locale global state without the application's knowledge. As a library developer, you should use the rest of the I18N routines described in this book and assume that the user of your library calls setlocale(). Documentation for your library should point this out clearly. If an application fails to call setlocale(), your library still functions; it just doesn't have internationalized behavior. There is no way to tell if the application has called setlocale().

2.2 About Text Data

If the only operation your software performs on text data is to read/write complete strings or to read/write byte streams, then you don't have to worry about locale-sensitive text data manipulation issues. On the other hand, if your software searches, parses, or modifies text data in any fashion, then your software needs to take into account locale-sensitive text data manipulation operations. For example, if your software searches for a substring within text data, if it parses text data, or if it normalizes text data, then it is performing operations where the results need to vary depending on the user's language, location, and data encoding.

As a software designer, you have the ability to affect the types and complexity of locale-sensitive operations your software must deal with. Each design decision involves an engineering trade-off — for example, memory usage verses performance. To make these design decisions, you need to have a basic understanding of the issues that constrain the possible choices:

- How is text data represented in memory and on disc — what are characters, character sets, coded character sets, and code sets?
- Which data type should be used to store text in memory — `char*` or `wchar_t*`?
- Which text manipulation operations are sensitive to the user's locale?

2.2.1   Characters, Character Sets, Coded Character Sets, and Code Sets

If your software deals with text data, then you must have at least a passing familiarity with the concept of characters, character sets, coded character sets, and code sets. At a minimum, you must be able to decide which code set(s) your software will support and understand the impact of this decision on your design. Your decision about which code sets to support is usually dictated by market requirements for the countries in which you plan to sell your software.

It is best to start with some basic definitions. Though most people will tell you that they *know* what a character is, few topics in the various I18N mail lists generate the volume of e-mail discussions as do discussions of what a character is, what a character set is, what a coded character set is, and what a code set is. Within this book, the following definitions are used:

character — any of the symbols (letters, numbers, punctuation, controls) used in the writing of a language. For example, the letter "A" is a character. A Japanese kanji or ideograph is a character.

character set — a collection of characters used to write one or more languages. For example, the letters a – z and A – Z, coupled with a set of punctuation marks and numbers are a character set used to write the English language. The term *repertoire* is commonly used to mean character set.

coded character set — a character set for which a unique numeric identifier or code has been assigned to each character. Computers can't easily deal with abstract graphical symbols the way you and I can. Instead, they assign a numeric value or code point to each character. This code point allows the character to be stored and manipulated in software. For example, in ASCII (American Standard for Character Information Interchange), the character "A" has a value of hexadecimal 41 (0x41). In American EBCDIC (a coded character set sometimes used on IBM systems), the character "A" has a coded value 0xC1.

encoding method — a method, scheme, or set of rules for combining several coded character sets in a data stream. Examples of encoding methods include ISO 2022, Compound Text, and EUC — Extended Unix Code. When an encoding method is applied to a specific collection of coded character sets, the result is an implementation of an encoding method. For example, EUC is an encoding method that combines up to four coded character sets in a data stream. When the rules of EUC are used to combine JISX0201, JISX0208, and JISX0212 (these Japanese Industrial Standard code sets are described in the following table), the result is Japanese EUC — an encoding method implementation.

code set — either a coded character set or an encoding method implementation. Each locale requires that data be represented in either a coded character set or an encoding method implementation. For example, the code set of the U.S. English locale en_US.iso88591 is ISO 8859.1; the code set of Japanese Korean locale ko_KR.eucKR is the encoding method implementation eucKR — Korean EUC.

There are a large variety of code sets in existence today, each supporting a different language or collection of languages. Some examples are listed in Table 2.2. There are a number of national standard code sets as well as international code sets. In addition, many vendors support proprietary code sets that they created while the national and international standard code sets were being formed. Typically, vendors developed their proprietary code sets because they wanted to sell systems into regions where national or international standard code sets did not yet exist.

Table 2.2 Example Code Sets

Code Set	Languages Encoded
U.S. ASCII	U.S. English
ISO 8859.1	The major languages of Western Europe, plus English
ISO 8859.2	The Latin-based languages of Central and East Europe, plus English
ISO 8859.5	The Cyrillic based languages of East Europe and Russia, plus English
ISO/IEC 10646	Most of common commercially used languages of the world, plus many less frequently used languages
HP Roman8	A Hewlett-Packard proprietary code set encoding the major languages of Western Europe, plus English
German EBCDIC	German, plus English
JISX0201	Japanese Katakana, plus English
JISX0208	Approximately 6350 Japanese kanji characters, plus symbols used in Cyrillic, Greek, English, and mathematics
JISX0212	Approximately 6000 Japanese kanji characters
Shift-JIS	A code set that combines the characters of U.S. ASCII, JISX0201 and JISX0208
Japanese EUC	A code set that combines the characters of U.S. ASCII, JISX0201, JISX0208, and in some implementations JISX0212
CNS 11643	A large collection of ideographic characters used in Taiwan

Table 2.2 Example Code Sets (Continued)

Code Set	Languages Encoded
Big5	Another large collection of ideographic characters used in Taiwan
GB 2312	Simplified Chinese, used in the Peoples Republic of China

One of the code sets most commonly used today is also one of the oldest — U.S. ASCII. U.S. ASCII, shown in Table 2.3, is a coded character set that uses seven bits of data to represent its repertoire of characters. The repertoire includes graphical characters, as well as some control characters. Control characters are special characters used to control a device as opposed to characters that represent a graphical symbol. For example, Form Feed is a control character that instructs a device to advance to the next logical page of data. Control characters are represented in this book's code set tables as a shaded area.

Table 2.3 U.S. ASCII Coded Character Set Table

US ASCII Coded Character Set															
0	**1**	**2**	**3**	**4**	**5**	**6**	**7**	**8**	**9**	**A**	**B**	**C**	**D**	**E**	**F**
			0	@	P	`	p									(0)
		!	1	A	Q	a	q									(1)
		"	2	B	R	b	r					U				(2)
		#	3	C	S	c	s					N				(3)
		$	4	D	T	d	t					U				(4)
		%	5	E	U	e	u					S				(5)
		&	6	F	V	f	v					E				(6)
		`	7	G	W	g	w					D				(7)
		(	8	H	X	h	x									(8)
		)	9	I	Y	i	y									(9)
		*	:	J	Z	j	z									(A)
		+	;	K	[	k	{									(B)
		,	<	L	\	l	|									(C)
		-	=	M	]	m	}									(D)
		.	>	N	^	n	~									(E)
		/	?	O	_	o										(F)

Most programmers are familiar with U.S. ASCII; nearly all code sets used on UNIX systems include U.S. ASCII as a base. ASCII uses seven data bits to represent its 95 graphic characters and 33 control characters. An individual coded character is identified by the byte

value of that character; the eighth data bit of the byte is not used in U.S. ASCII. By convention, characters in a code set table are ordered according to their byte value; the most significant *nibble*[1] of the byte is the horizontal index while the least significant nibble of the byte is
the vertical index. This is a convenient format for a code set table because it lets you quickly
obtain the hexadecimal value of a character from the table. The horizontal index is the most
significant digit, while the vertical is the least significant digit. For example, the coded value
for the character "a" in the U.S. ASCII code set is 0x61 — column 6, row 1.

From Table 2.3, you can see code values in ASCII range from 0x00 through 0x7F, or in
binary 0000 0000 through 0111 1111 — as you can see from the binary values, the eighth
data bit of the byte is not used. ASCII contains most of the characters needed for text communication in the English language in the United States.

To develop internationalized software, it isn't necessary to understand every code set in
popular use. However, it is useful to know that all commonly used code sets in the UNIX
world are superset U.S. ASCII — they all include seven-bit U.S. ASCII within them. In some
cases, countries need only a few additional coded characters for their languages. They created
their code sets by using the eighth data bit to encode the additional characters needed for their
language. The eighth data bit added 128 code values for encoding the additional characters
(represented by the plain white areas in the U.S. ASCII table, code values 0x80 through

---

1. A nibble is one-half of a byte, or four data bits.

0xFF). For example, ISO 8859.1 (see Table 2.4) is an eight-bit code set that includes the characters needed to write most Western European languages and the languages used in the Americas.

Table 2.4 ISO 8859.1 Coded Character Set Table

ISO 8859.1 Coded Character Set															
	0	**1**	**2**	**3**	**4**	**5**	**6**	**7**	**8**	**9**	**A**	**B**	**C**	**D**	**E**	**F**
0				0	@	P	`	p				°	À	Ð	à	ð
1			!	1	A	Q	a	q			¡	±	Á	Ñ	á	ñ
2			"	2	B	R	b	r			¢	²	Â	Ò	â	ò
3			#	3	C	S	c	s			£	³	Ã	Ó	ã	ó
4			$	4	D	T	d	t			¤	´	Ä	Ô	ä	ô
5			%	5	E	U	e	u			¥	µ	Å	Õ	å	õ
6			&	6	F	V	f	v			¦	¶	Æ	Ö	æ	ö
7			'	7	G	W	g	w			§	·	Ç	×	ç	÷
8			(	8	H	X	h	x			¨	¸	È	Ø	è	ø
9			)	9	I	Y	i	y			©	¹	É	Ù	é	ù
A			*	:	J	Z	j	z			ª	º	Ê	Ú	ê	ú
B			+	;	K	[	k	{			«	»	Ë	Û	ë	û
C			,	<	L	\	l	|			¬	¼	Ì	Ü	ì	ü
D			-	=	M	]	m	}				½	Í	Ý	í	ý
E			.	>	N	^	n	~			®	¾	Î	Þ	î	þ
F			/	?	O	_	o				¯	¿	Ï	ß	ï	ÿ

Similar eight-bit coded character sets were codified in the ISO 8859 standard for other alphabetic languages of Europe and Africa.

Table 2.4 and Table 2.5 are useful for introducing some terms that will be needed during the discussion of rendering international text characters with X11R5 in the next chapter. An eight-bit coded character set table such as the ISO 8859.1 table is often broken up into four general areas:

- *C0* — control characters whose eighth bit is zero. A set of 33 control characters assigned to code values 0x00 through 0x1F, plus 0x7F.
- *G0* or *GL (graphics left)* — graphical characters whose eighth data bit is zero. A set of 95 graphical characters assigned to code values 0x20 through 0x7E.
- *C1* — control characters whose eighth bit is one. A set of 32 control characters assigned code values 0x80 through 0x9F.

• *G1* or *GR (graphics right)* —graphical characters whose eighth data bit is one. A set of 96 graphical characters assigned to code values 0xA0 through 0xFF. (Some eight-bit coded character sets use code value 0xFF as a C1 character instead of a G1 character.)

Table 2.5 General Structure for an Eight-Bit Coded Character Set

	Eight-Bit Coded Character Set			
	0 1	2 3 4 5 6 7	8 9	A B C D E F
0 1 2 3 4 5 6 7 8 9 A B C D E F	CO	G0 Graphics Left	C1	G1 Graphics Right

For other languages, even eight data bits aren't enough to encode all the characters needed to represent the language. For example, current popular Japanese code sets encode between 6500 and 13,000 characters. Code sets for these languages typically are created to mix one-byte characters with characters requiring more than one byte for their coded character value. For example, Japanese EUC (Extended UNIX Code) mixes the coded characters from several Japanese Industrial Standard (JIS) coded character sets in a data stream, yielding a mixture of one-byte, two-byte, and three-byte characters together in a data stream.

Japanese EUC, an extremely popular code set in Japan, is described in Table 2.6.

Japanese EUC is just an example. There are many code sets used in the world in which the number of bytes per character varies within the code set; Japanese EUC is just one such set. Other examples include Japanese Shift-JIS, Taiwan Big5, Taiwan EUC, Taiwan CCDC, and Korean EUC.

Table 2.6 Japanese EUC Code Set

Subset Name	# Bytes	Character Code Value (Binary)	Coded Character Set
Code set 0	1	0xxxxxxx	U.S. ASCII[†]
Code set 1	2	1xxxxxxx 1xxxxxxx	JISX0208—1990
Code set 2	2	10001110 1xxxxxxx	JISX0201—1976
Code set 3	3	10001111 1xxxxxxx 1xxxxxxx	JISX0212—1990

JIS X 0208-1990, *Code of the Japanese Graphic Character Set for Information Interchange*, is a JIS coded character set encoding 6879 characters, including 6355 kanji characters.

JIS X 0201-1976, *Code for Information Interchange,* is JIS coded character set encoding the 94 characters of ASCII plus 63 katakana characters.

JIS X 0212-1990, *Code of the Supplementary Japanese Graphic Character Set for Information Interchange*, is a JIS coded character set encoding 6067 characters, including 5801 kanji characters.

†. The graphic for \ is usually replaced with the Japanese yen symbol, ¥.

The intent of this section is not to make you an expert on code sets. Rather, the intent is to help you understand that your customers throughout the world need some way to encode the characters of their language — and the way that character data is encoded can vary drastically.

2.2.2   Code Set Independence or Universal Character Set?

There are two potential ways to deal with the multitude of code sets when writing internationalized software:

- Write your software to assume all data is in one code set, choosing a *universal coded character set* that encompasses all the characters that could be needed by users in all of your target markets. When data external to the application is represented with some different code set (for example, when reading data from a file created by a different application), convert that data to your chosen universal character set.
- Write your software to be *code set independent*. That is, write your software such that it makes no assumptions about the number of bytes required to represent a character. And write your software such that it makes no assumptions about the value of any coded character.

2.2.2.1   Universal coded character set

Code set dependent software assumes all character data is encoded in a single, coded character set. Internationalized code set dependent applications typically utilize a large, universal coded character set, such as Unicode or ISO/IEC 10646.[2]

A universal coded character set attempts to encode all possible characters needed to represent all languages and data of interest. By definition, such character sets are very large.

For example, ISO 10646 BMP (also known as *UCS2*) requires two bytes[3] for each coded character. ISO 10646 encodes approximately 33,000 characters and reserves an additional 6000 code positions for private use. ISO 10646 provides a single coded character set for languages as diverse as Arabic, Armenian, Bengali, Chinese, Devanagari (an alphabet in which Sanskrit and many modern Indian languages are written), German, Greek, Japanese, Thai, and Tibetan.

There are distinct advantages and disadvantages to making your internationalized software dependent on a universal coded character set.

Advantages

The main advantage of making your software dependent on a universal coded character set is that it allows many disparate languages to be displayed and processed at the same time. Although this capability is theoretically possible with a code set independent design, in practice few UNIX implementations today support a universal code set in a form that is usable with a code set independent design approach.

Another benefit of making your software dependent on a universal coded character set is that your software is more compatible and interoperable with Microsoft®'s NT. NT is built on top of Unicode, the most common universal coded character set in use today. NT not only processes textual data internally as Unicode, but also allows software to read and write Unicode directly.

Code values for universal coded character sets typically use the same number of bytes for each character. Such fixed-size code sets make it possible to perform quick offsets into memory to reach a given character position. It also makes it possible to parse backward through a string of characters. Fixed-size code sets are possible with a code set independent design approach. However, data typically has to be transformed on input to the application and transformed again on output. (This is discussed in more detail in section 2.3.1 on page 32.)

Disadvantages

There are a number of drawbacks to designing internationalized software to depend on a single, universal code set. Foremost among these is that universal code sets are relatively new. Most UNIX system vendors do not directly support universal code sets. And, when writing internationalized graphical user interface software, both operating system support and support within the X library are required for any code set to be used.

---

2. At the time of this writing, Unicode and the Basic Multi-Lingual Plain (BMP) of ISO 10646, the part of ISO 10646 for which characters are defined, are identical. This book uses the term ISO 10646 to refer both to Unicode and to ISO 10646 BMP.

3. The ISO 10646 standard uses the term octet instead of byte. The standard is trying to specify that two eight-bit values are used to represent a single character. While technically accurate, few C compilers or library routines are written to process octets. Since this book focuses on practical programming problems, byte is used instead of octet.

Further, no standard APIs exist to perform internationalized operations on universal code set data. If you want to write your software to depend on a universal code set, you will need to create your own routines to perform locale-sensitive operations.

When you make your software dependent on a universal coded character set, every character requires a fixed number of bytes to store in memory — two bytes per character for Unicode and ISO/IEC 10646 UCS2 (BMP), four bytes per character for ISO/IEC 10646 UCS4. This may be an acceptable cost to users who want the capability to mix Arabic, Japanese, and Danish together in a document. However, most software users work in a single language or a pair of languages. Software users in Western Europe, Central Europe, Eastern Europe, the Americas, and North Africa have standard coded character sets that meet their monolingual or bilingual needs — and each character requires only one byte of memory.

While a fixed number of bytes per character is an advantage for many operations (such as parsing), it is debatable whether or not ISO 10646 actually provides a fixed number of bytes per character. ISO 10646 defines every code point as a character. And since each code point is a fixed size, by definition, each character is the same size. You need to take this with a large grain of salt. ISO 10646 includes some control characters and many non-spacing characters that only make sense when combined with other characters. For example, ISO 10646 includes a single code point for the A-diaeresis (Ä): 0x00C4. It also includes a code point for A (0x0041)and a code point for non-spacing diaeresis "character" (0x0308). So, A-diaeresis (Ä) can be represented by two bytes (0x00C4) or by four bytes (0x0041 0x0308).

Before deciding to make your software depend on a universal coded character set, check on the availability of fonts for that code set — few fonts exist for universal code sets today.

At the time of this writing, the typical practice among those supporting universal coded character sets is to ship a composite font made up of commonly used characters; such fonts typically include *glyphs*[4] for less than 20 percent of the characters encoded in a universal code set. From an X Window System standpoint, this is a very reasonable approach. The X server is required to load and calculate font metrics across all glyphs in the font, whether they will be used or not. However, shipping limited fonts reduces the key advantage that universal code sets offer — namely, the ability to mix many diverse languages together on the display.

Another disadvantage of making your software depend on a universal coded character set is that, despite inclusion of "universal" in the name, universal coded character sets are not universal. They do not include every known character of all writing systems from all ages. No matter how universal the designers of a universal code set intend to be, someone *always* finds that they need additional characters that are not present in the universal code set. For example, ISO 10646 includes a section that encompasses all the commonly used Japanese, Chinese, and Korean characters — at least all the commonly used characters at the time ISO 10646 was drafted. Currently, users in Taiwan are using the full repertoire of characters

---

4. A *glyph* is a graphical representation of a character, independent of coded character value. For example, each of the following is a glyph for the first character of the English alphabet: a, *a*, a, and a.

encoded in the CNS 11643 Taiwan standard. Only portions of these characters are present in ISO 10646. Until these characters are incorporated into ISO 10646, users in Taiwan might find a universal code set based solution lacking.

Perhaps the biggest drawback to universal coded character sets is that they cannot be directly used by an application in C string functions or in internationalization routines. ISO 10646 BMP uses a fixed width, two bytes per character; values for each byte can range from 0x00 through 0xFF. This means that a byte value of 0x00 can exist in an ISO 10646 character value. The ISO/IEC C standard, as well as the ANSI-C standard, require that the basic execution character set use a NULL byte (e.g., 0x00) to terminate character strings. So, an ISO 10646 character cannot be directly copied into a `char*` data storage if C library string routines (such as `strcpy()` and `strcat()`) are exercised on the data. Of course, ISO 10646 data could be placed into `short*` or `int*` data types, but no string processing routines exist for character data stored as `short` or `int`.

2.2.2.2   Code set independence

The remainder of this book talks about the specifics of how to develop internationalized code set independent software. It is relatively easy to write your software such that it doesn't matter which code set is used; a few guiding principles provide the foundation for writing code set independent software:

- The number of bytes required to store a character is not fixed. The size of a character can vary from one code set to another. In fact, the size of a character can vary from one coded character to another within the code set of a given locale.
- All code sets supported on a system are supersets of the *basic execution character set*. The ISO and ANSI C Programming Language standards define the basic execution character set as the 26 uppercase and 26 lowercase letters of the English alphabet, 29 graphic characters (including punctuation marks, brackets, and parentheses), plus several control characters (space, horizontal tab, vertical tab, and form feed). The characters of the basic execution character set must be included in every code set supported by the system; the value of any character in the basic execution character set must be the same in every code set supported by the system.

The repertoire of the basic execution character set is fully contained in ASCII. As a practical matter, all code sets in common use on UNIX systems today are superset ASCII. This includes the ISO 8859.* collection of coded character sets, all the EUC code sets used throughout the Pacific Rim, as well as country de facto standard code sets, such as Taiwanese Big5 and Japanese Shift-JIS.

Further, the ANSI-C standard and the ISO C standard say that the basic execution character set must have the character repertoire identical to that of ASCII, including many of the control characters. So while not explicitly requiring ASCII, ISO pretty well limits the choices of basic execution character set to superset ASCII.

Armed with these two key principals and the software tools described throughout the rest of this book, you can write code set independent, internationalized software.

There are advantages and disadvantages to using a code set independent software design approach. Every major UNIX system vendor has examined the advantages and disadvantages, and each has chosen a code set independent approach. Further, the C Programming Language standards bodies of ISO and ANSI, as well as X/Open® and the X Consortium, have also elected to follow a code set independent design approach. For these reasons, the remainder of this book assumes a code set independent design approach.

Advantages

If you design internationalized software to be code set independent, no source code changes are required to support new locales or code sets — assuming the new code set is superset ASCII.

ISO C Programming Language Standard and the X/Open Portability Guide include many standard C library APIs to aid in the development of code set independent internationalized software. Since all major UNIX system vendors implement these standards, you can develop internationalized, code set independent software that is also portable.

As you will see in later sections, code set independent software can be more memory efficient than software developed to depend on a universal code set. If the user chooses an eight-bit code set, then only one byte of memory per character will be used to store a character. In a universal code set design approach, every character requires at least two bytes of memory.

Another advantage of code set independent software is that it can more easily accommodate changes to code set standards. If code values change or additional code points are defined, code set independent software typically does not have to be modified.

Disadvantages

Since you can't assume anything about the user's character data (such as the size in bytes of an individual character), it can be less efficient to process. Your software must use C library routines just to identify where each character starts and to determine how many bytes it contains. Standard C library routines exist that perform transformations of character data to a fixed size data storage. But even these transformations are operations that need not be performed with a universal code set design approach.

2.3 Locale-Sensitive Operations: Text Manipulation

Most operations performed on text data are affected by the locale of the software user — from decisions as seemingly simple as deciding how to store character data in memory to deciding how to collate strings. This section describes the most common locale-sensitive operations that are performed on text data, and identifies the tools that allow your software to perform those operations in a locale-sensitive way. In Appendix A, you will find a summary of these tools, along with tables that help you know which standards support which tools.

2.3.1   Storing and Manipulating Character Data in Memory

One of the first decisions you must make when designing internationalized, code set independent software is how you will store and process character data within the software.

Character data can be stored in memory and processed as either *multibyte* or *wide character* data.

Multibyte is a term that means the data is stored as a sequence of bytes — one or more bytes per character; the data type for multibyte data is `char*`. The size of a single multibyte character can vary from character to character; this is a function of the locale. For example, multibyte Japanese EUC data may contain one-byte, two-byte, and three-byte characters, all mixed together in the same `char` array. On the other hand, German ISO 8859.1 data contains only one-byte characters.

Wide character is a term meaning that data is stored in fixed width elements, one character per element. The data type for wide character data is `wchar_t` (one wide character) or `wchar_t*` (a wide character string). Type `wchar_t` is an integral data type whose content is opaque. This means that the value of a wide character may or may not be the same as its multibyte representation. Except for characters of the basic execution character set,[5] a wide character can only be generated by calling a C library API that converts a multibyte character into a wide character. The size of `wchar_t` is implementation defined. Further, the result of converting a given multibyte character to a wide character is not only implementation defined, but also locale dependent. For example, the result of converting a multibyte A-diaeresis to wide character in the German locale may be different than converting a multibyte A-diaeresis to wide character in the Swiss locale. Given these constraints, wide characters are not written directly to disc, nor are they suitable for passing directly to another application.

2.3.1.1   Multibyte or wide character?

Which data type should you choose in your software? As with any engineering decision, there are trade-offs associated with each. The choice you make depends on the type of processing to be performed, your software's sensitivity to performance or memory usage, and the availability of supporting APIs on the platforms on which your software runs.

The following sections highlight the chief advantages and disadvantages of multibyte and wide character storage. Then, as different locale-sensitive operations are examined, examples of processing with multibyte and with wide character are provided. These should help you make your decision about which to use in your software.

Advantages of multibyte

The biggest advantage of using multibyte is that it is almost always more efficient in terms of memory usage than using wide characters. There are no wasted bytes with multibyte. If a coded character is only one byte long, then only one byte of memory is used to store that

---

5. Both the ANSI and ISO C Programming Language Specifications say that the wide character value of any member of the basic execution set must be identical to its multibyte value cast to an integer.

character. With wide characters, `sizeof(wchar_t)` bytes are used to store every character, regardless of the number of bytes required to represent the character in its code set.

An additional advantage of multibyte is that the data encoding in memory is identical to that on disc. No conversions are necessary when reading from or writing to disc. When reading or writing wide characters, conversions are always necessary. Software that internally stores characters as multibyte avoids the conversion from multibyte to wide character when the data comes into the software.

Disadvantages of multibyte

The chief disadvantage of using multibyte is that it is very inefficient for parsing or performing random offsets into character data. The reason for this inefficiency is that individual multibyte characters can be different sizes (occupy different numbers of bytes) within a string. In Asian locales, it is common to find one-byte, two-byte, three-byte and four-byte characters mixed together in a string. When parsing or performing offsets into multibyte text data, it is imperative that operations be performed on character boundaries. But determining where character boundaries are located in a string is inefficient. If your application is simply reading, copying, and writing null terminated strings, without manipulating their content, there is no inefficiency in using multibyte character data — the disadvantage disappears.

How inefficient is multibyte for parsing and performing random offsets into character data? Performance varies from platform to platform, but experience has shown that the impact is reasonably small, even in cases where large quantities of data are being manipulated or where large quantities of text data are being modified. For example, the Motif Text Widget internally processes most of its data as multibyte data.

Besides being less efficient than wide character for certain operations, multibyte can lead to more complex software. You can judge this for yourself by comparing the multibyte parsing example and the wide character parsing example in the section 2.3.2 on page 40.

An additional disadvantage of multibyte is that few standard APIs currently exist for performing locale-sensitive operations on multibyte character data. If portability restricts you to using only ANSI C or ISO-C library routines, the only multibyte locale-sensitive routines available are those that convert between multibyte and wide character, and those that identify the number of bytes in an individual character. X/Open Portability Guide Version 4 (XPG4) has additional locale-sensitive routines for processing multibyte characters, but not quite as extensive functionality as is provided for processing wide characters.

Advantages of wide character

There are several good reasons to use wide character storage for your character data. First, there are many standard locale-sensitive APIs defined in XPG4 and in ISO-C for processing wide characters. This means that applications developed with these APIs have access to more I18N functionality than applications that use multibyte and remain very portable.

The other key advantage of wide characters is that the size of every character is the same. This makes it easy to write software that performs random offsets into a given text position within a block of text data. It is easy to parse backward through a wide character string — something that is not even possible with multibyte. Because wide characters are all the same size, parsing code is much easier to write and even easier to understand when examining the source.

Disadvantages of wide character

There are some disadvantages to using wide characters. First, the data type `wchar_t` is a `typedef`; its size differs from system to system. This means that your software can never depend on the size of a wide character.

Another disadvantage is that wide characters are not directly readable from the file system or directly writable to the file system. Only multibyte characters can be stored in files. This means that for every character read into the application and for every character written by the application, a conversion is necessary. There are many standard C library routines that perform these conversions, but the conversion must still be done.

Though ISO-C and XPG4 define many standard I18N wide character APIs, vendors are sometimes slow in making the wide character I18N APIs available on their platforms. For example, XPG4 I18N APIs are first available on HP-UX 9.05, Solaris 2.4, OSF/1 R1.1, and AIX 3.2. Customers are often even slower in moving to a vendor's new operating system (OS) release; this can limit availability of the APIs on the target platforms for your software.

The biggest disadvantage of using wide characters is that each character requires `sizeof(wchar_t)` bytes to store — regardless of the locale and regardless of the number of bytes required to store the character in multibyte. Many systems define `wchar_t` to be of type `int`. This means that on most hardware, storing a single character uses four bytes of memory. For Japanese and Chinese users, this represents a non-trivial growth in memory requirements; most characters in these languages require two or three bytes per character in multibyte. However, the biggest cost by far is to users in Europe and the Americas. The code sets used in these countries typically require only one byte per character to store a multibyte character. With wide characters, these users are seeing a fourfold increase in memory required to internally store string data.

If the amount of data your software is storing is relatively small, then the growth probably won't be noticed. Similarly, if your software is performing lots of offsets into large amounts of text data or is making many random modifications to large amounts of text data (operations common to text editor applications), then the performance gained by using wide characters may make the increased memory usage acceptable — though the performance gain is tempered by the performance cost of the conversion to and from multibyte.

2.3.1.2   Summary: multibyte verses wide character

When should you use wide characters and when should you use multibyte? For graphical user interface applications, a good general rule is to use multibyte character representation unless

• the amount of text data being processed is small,

- your software needs to perform locale-sensitive operations for which only wide character APIs exist, or
- your software needs to perform random offsets into large amounts of text data or perform backward searches on large amounts of text data.

As a software developer, you must examine the benefits and cost of each before determining when to use wide characters and when to use multibyte. For example, I had to make this same evaluation when coding Motif 1.2, the internationalized version of Motif. In that case, I chose multibyte in almost every situation because I found multibyte to be the least expensive in terms of memory and performance overhead. The one exception was the implementation of Motif's TextField Widget. Wide characters were deemed acceptable for Text-Field since it was designed to allow entry and manipulation of only a small number of characters. And even then, wide character storage was used only for locales in which a multibyte character might require more than one byte. (This is determined at run time using the MB_CUR_MAX macro, described in Table 2.11 on page 40.)

2.3.1.3   Converting between multibyte and wide characters

There are a number of standard routines for converting between multibyte character representation and wide character representation. All of these functions require that the setlocale() routine be successfully called in order for the conversion routines to work properly. Their behavior is governed by the LC_CTYPE category of the current locale.

The ISO/IEC 9899:1990 C standard (hereafter referred to as ISO C) and the ANSI C standard define tools for converting between multibyte and wide character representations. These tools are shown in Table 2.7.

Table 2.7 ANSI C and ISO C Routines for Converting between char* and wchar_t*

Name	Description
mbtowc(w,s,n)	Examines at most n bytes of the multibyte array s and converts the first valid multibyte character found into a wide character, storing it in the wchar_t pointed to by w. The number of bytes converted (e.g., the size of the multibyte character) is returned. If an invalid multibyte character is found, −1 is returned.
mbstowcs(w,s,n)	Converts an entire string of multibyte characters from the string s into an array of wide characters, storing no more than n wide characters in the array pointed to by w. If no error occurs, the number of wide characters stored is returned; otherwise, −1 is returned.
wctomb(s,w)	Converts the wide character w into a multibyte representation, storing the result in the char* array pointed to by s; at most MB_CUR_MAX[†] bytes are stored. If no error occurs, the number of bytes comprising the multibyte character is returned; otherwise, −1 is returned.
wcstombs(s,w,n)	Converts a sequence of wide characters pointed to by w into multibyte, storing them in the array pointed to by s. The conversion stops if a multibyte character would exceed the limit of n total bytes or if a null character is converted. If no error occurs, the number of bytes written to s (not including the null character) is returned; otherwise, −1 is returned.

†. MB_CUR_MAX is a macro initialized by setlocale(). MB_CUR_MAX evaluates to a positive integer expression whose value is the maximum number of bytes in a multibyte character for the current locale (category LC_CTYPE).

In 1994, Amendment 1 to the ISO/IEC 9899:1990 C Programming Language Standard was published. This amendment, often referred to as the *MSE* (Multibyte Support Extensions), adds many I18N routines to the ISO C standard. The I18N routines in this extension are described separately in this book because the amendment was so recently published and because it takes time for vendors to implement standards. Before using the routines provided by the MSE, you should verify that each vendor's system on which your software will ship supports the MSE routines.

Table 2.8 identifies the routines added in the MSE that support conversion between multibyte and wide character.

Table 2.8 MSE Routines for Converting between char* and wchar_t*

Name	Description
fprintf() printf() sprintf() vfprintf() vprintf() vsprintf()	The MSE adds the l qualifier to the %c and %s format specifiers. When the specifier is preceded by the l qualifier, the character (%c) or string (%s) is converted from wide character to multibyte before writing the value.
fwprintf() wprintf() swprintf() vfwprintf() vwprintf() vswprintf()	The MSE defines these wide character equivalent of the fprintf() and vfprintf() routines. Functionally equivalent to their multibyte counter parts, these functions accept wide character and wide character string arguments. Wide characters are converted to multibyte before output.
fscanf() scanf() sscanf()	The MSE adds the l qualifier for the %c and %s format specifiers. When the specifier is preceded by the l qualifier, multibyte characters read in are converted to wide characters and then stored in the wide character variables identified by the arguments.
fwscanf() wscanf() swscanf()	The MSE defines these wide character equivalent of the fscanf(). Functionally equivalent to their multibyte counter parts, these functions accept wide character and wide character string from the input stream, storing them in wide character variables or converting them to multibyte characters according to directives of the format specifiers.
getwc() fgetwc()	Reads a multibyte character from a file and converts it to a wide character.
getwchar()	Equivalent to getwc() called on stdin.
fgetws()	Reads multibyte characters from a file, converting them to wide characters. Reading ends when the specified number of multibyte characters have been read, when a newline character has been read, or when an end of file is encountered.
fputwc() putwc()	Converts a wide character to multibyte and writes the byte(s) to a file.
fputws()	Converts a sequence of wide characters to multibyte and writes the bytes to a file.
putwchar()	Equivalent to fputwc() performed on stdout.
ungetwc()	An "undo" function for a previous call to getwc(), fgetwc(), or getwchar(). Converts a wide character back to multibyte and pushes the resulting bytes back onto an input stream.
btowc()	Identifies if the argument is a one-byte multibyte character. If it is, btowc() converts it to a wide character.

Table 2.8 MSE Routines for Converting between char* and wchar_t* (Continued)

Name	Description
wctob()	Determines if the wide character argument corresponds to a one-byte multibyte character. If so, wctob() converts the wide character to multibyte.
mbrtowc() wcrtomb() mbsrtowcs() wcsrtombs()	The functions are identical to the similarly named functions described in Table 2.7. However, these functions include an extra parameter — a pointer to a state object. This state object allows you to convert between multibyte and wide character in one data stream without impacting the state of conversion in a different stream.

In addition to the ISO C and ANSI C routines, XPG4 defines a number of routines that convert between multibyte and wide character. In general, these functions allow for conversion from multibyte to wide character when reading characters from a stream or file, and allow for conversion from wide character to multibyte when writing characters to a stream or file. These functions are described in Table 2.9. Their behavior is governed by the LC_CTYPE category of the current locale. Note that many of the XPG4 routines are similar to those provided by the MSE. X/Open is currently working on aligning XPG I18N routines with those in the MSE.

Table 2.9 XPG4 Routines for Converting between char* and wchar_t*

Name	Description
fprintf() printf() sprintf() vfprintf() vprintf() vsprintf()	XGP4 adds the %C and %S format specifiers which allow a wide character and a wide character string (respectively) to be specified as arguments. Wide characters are converted to multibyte before printing.
fscanf() scanf() sscanf()	XGP4 adds the %C and %S formats which allow a wide character and a wide character string (respectively) variables to be specified as arguments. Multibyte characters read in are converted to wide characters and then stored in the wide character variables identified by the arguments.
getwc() fgetwc()	Reads a multibyte character from a file and converts it to a wide character.
getwchar()	Equivalent to getwc() called on stdin.
fgetws()	Reads multibyte characters from a file, converting them to wide characters. Reading ends when the specified number of multibyte characters have been read, when a newline character has been read, or when an end of file is encountered.
fputwc() putwc()	Converts a wide character to multibyte and writes the byte(s) to a file.
fputws()	Converts a sequence of wide characters to multibyte and writes the bytes to a file.

Table 2.9 XPG4 Routines for Converting between char* and wchar_t* (Continued)

Name	Description
putwchar()	Equivalent to fputwc() performed on stdout.
ungetwc()	An "undo" function for a previous call to getwc(), fgetwc(), or getwchar(). Converts a wide character back to multibyte and pushes the resulting bytes back onto an input stream.

2.3.1.4   Identifying character boundaries with multibyte

If you choose to store and process data as multibyte, it is important to remember that to be internationalized, all operations must be done on complete characters. To do this, you need some way to identify the size (the number of bytes) of a character as it occurs in a char* buffer. You must also be able to determine where one multibyte character ends and the next one starts. Fortunately, several ISO C, ANSI C, and XPG standard tools exist for this purpose. These tools are listed and described in Table 2.11. Each of these functions requires that the software's locale has first been initialized with a call to setlocale(). Their behavior is controlled by the LC_CTYPE category of the current locale.

Table 2.10 ANSI C, ISO C, and XPG Multibyte Character Size and Boundary Identification Routines

Name	Description
MB_CUR_MAX	Identifies the maximum number of bytes per multibyte character for the current locale. A multibyte character requires between one and MB_CUR_MAX bytes of memory for the current locale.
MB_MAX_LEN	Identifies the maximum number of bytes per multibyte character across all locales supported by the system.
mblen(s,n)	Examines at most n bytes and returns the size of the multibyte character beginning at s; if the character is invalid, it returns a –1.
mbtowc(w,s,n)	Examines at most n bytes of the multibyte array s and converts the first valid multibyte character found into a wide character, storing it in the wchar_t pointed to by w. The number of bytes converted (e.g., the size of the multibyte character) is returned. If an invalid multibyte character is found, –1 is returned.
mbstowcs(w,s,n)	Converts an entire string of multibyte characters from the string s into an array of wide characters, storing no more than n wide characters in the array pointed to by w. If no error occurs, the number of wide characters stored is returned; otherwise, –1 is returned.

Each of these routines aids in identifying the size of a multibyte character or in identifying the boundary between multibyte characters. The MSE defines additional routines to aid in these tasks. The MSE routines are described in Table 2.11.

Table 2.11 MSE Multibyte Character Size and Boundary Identification Routines

Name	Description
`mbrlen(s,n,ps)`	Examines at most n bytes and returns the size of the multibyte character beginning at s; if the character is invalid, it returns a -1. The state pointer ps keeps track of the conversion state for this particular call.
`mbrtowc(w,s,n,ps)`	Examines at most n bytes of the multibyte array s and converts the first valid multibyte character found into a wide character, storing it in the `wchar_t` pointed to by w. The number of bytes converted (e.g., the size of the multibyte character) is returned. If an invalid multibyte character is found, -1 is returned. The state pointer ps keeps track of the conversion state for this particular call.
`mbsrtowcs(w,s,n,ps)`	Converts an entire string of multibyte characters from the string s into an array of wide characters, storing no more than n wide characters in the array pointed to by w. If no error occurs, the number of wide characters stored is returned; otherwise, -1 is returned. The state pointer ps keeps track of the conversion state for this particular call.

2.3.2   Parsing and Truncation

Remember one basic concept when searching a string in internationalized software: Perform all comparisons on complete coded characters, making sure that pointers always point to boundaries between coded characters. If you are using wide character storage, this is transparent. Once data is in wide character, you are guaranteed that each wide character contains a complete coded character.

However, if you are using multibyte character storage, it is imperative that you compare only complete coded characters. This means making sure that the pointers to the search string and the match string are aligned on a character boundary. It also means making sure that the size of the characters being compared in the search string and the match string are identical.

For example, suppose that you want to search a string for the second occurrence of the "/" character. In all multibyte code sets on a given system, "/" has the same value and is one byte in size. However, there are some code sets in which the second byte of an Asian multibyte character has the same value as the single one-byte "/" character. For this reason, you must take care when searching a multibyte character string for a match. If you simply search the string looking for any byte that matches the byte value of "/", you might match a portion of an Asian character instead of matching the "/" character as desired. This is illustrated in Figure 2.2.

The following example programs demonstrate how a search for the "/" might be done with multibyte and with wide character. The program takes advantage of the ANSI and ISO C

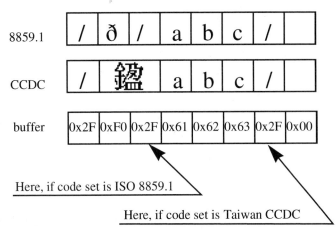

Figure 2.2
Parsing for "/" (code value 0x2F) in a multibyte buffer.

Programming Language Specification specification that says the basic execution character set must contain the one-byte "/" character, and it must be present and have the same value in every code set processed by a C program.

In the multibyte example, you know the character you are searching for is one byte in size across all locales. So, you design your search to use `mblen()` to first identify one-byte characters, since they are the only ones that can possibly match "/". Once you have identified a one-byte character, you can legitimately compare it to "/" for equality.

`mblen()` requires a parameter specifying the maximum number of bytes to be examined to identify the size of a character. The macro `MB_CUR_MAX` is initialized by `setlocale()` to identify the largest number of bytes per multibyte character in the current locale. So `MB_CUR_MAX` is a good macro to pass in as the maximum number of bytes parameter in `mblen()`.

```
/* Example of searching buffer for a "/" with
 * multibyte storage. */
#include <locale.h>
#include <stdio.h>
#define MAX_BUF 256
main(){
  char buffer[MAX_BUF + 1];
  int index, char_size;

  /* Initialize the locale by calling setlocale. It
   * reads environment variable to identify which locale
   * the program user wants. */
  (void)setlocale(LC_ALL, "");
```

```
/* A fully internationalized program would use message catalog
 * calls for strings displayed to the user. They are not
 * included here since the calls have not yet been introduced
 * in the book. */

/* Buffer is initialized from stdin by scanf(). */
printf("Please enter the path name.\n");
(void)scanf("%s", &buffer[0])
for (index=0,char_size=mblen(&buffer[0],MB_CUR_MAX);
     buffer[index] != NULL, char_size >= 0;
     index+=char_size,
     char_size=mblen(&buffer[index], MB_CUR_MAX)){
     if (char_size == 1 && buffer[index]=="/"){
       printf("Found it!\n");
       break;
     }
}
if (char_size < 0){
   printf("Invalid multibyte character was found.\n");
   exit(1);
}
if (index == strlen(buffer))
   printf("No '/' was found.\n");

}
```

Now consider the same search operation performed with wide character storage. In this example, the scanf() format specifier %S is used to convert multibyte characters read from stdin into wide characters and store them in the wide character buffer. The %S format specifier is specified in XPG4; in the MSE this same functionality is achieved using the l qualifier to the %s format specifier. If your system does not support the XPG4 or MSE format specifier, use %s and read the data into a char* buffer as in the multibyte example above. Then use mbstowcs() to convert the multibyte data into wide character. (This is shown in the example program with #ifdef NO_XPG4.)

```
/* Example of searching buffer for a "/" with
 * wide character storage. */
#include <locale.h>
#include <stdio.h>
#include <stdlib.h>
#define MAX_NUM_CHARS 256
main(){
  wchar_t wbuf[MAX_NUM_CHARS + 1];
```

```c
    int index;
#ifdef NO_XPG4
    char buf[(MAX_NUM_CHARS * sizeof(wchar_t)) + 1];
    size_t ret;
#endif /* NO_XPG4 */

    /* Initialize the locale by calling setlocale it will
     * read environment variable to identify which locale
     * the program user wants. */
    (void) setlocale(LC_ALL, "");

    /* A fully internationalized program would use message catalog
     * calls for strings displayed to the user. They are not
     * included here since the calls have not yet been introduced
     * in the book. */

    printf("Please enter the path name.\n");

#ifdef NO_XPG4
    /* Buffer gets initialized from stdin; %s directs
     * scanf to read multibyte from stdin; the program
     * then converts it to wide character with mbstowcs. */
    (void)scanf("%s", &buf[0]);
    ret=mbstowcs(wbuf, buf, MAX_NUM_CHARS);
    if(ret == -1){
      printf("An invalid multibyte character found!\n");
      exit(1);
    }

#else /* We have XPG4 capability */
    /* Buffer gets initialized from stdin; %S directs
     * scanf to read multibyte from stdin and convert it
     * to wide character. */
    (void)scanf("%S", &wbuf[0]);
#endif /* NO_XPG4 */

    for (index=0; wbuf[index]!=L'\0' && wbuf[index]!=L'/';
         index++){}
    if (wbuf[index]==L'\0')
      printf("No '/' was found.\n");
    else
      printf("'/' was found at index %d.\n", index);
}
```

Note that in the wide character example, the for loop in which the actual searching is done is extremely simple;[6] the body of the loop is actually empty.

The two preceding programs are good examples of how to write internationalized programs that parse a string. However, the multibyte program is also an excellent example of a common mistake made when using multibyte storage — the problem of truncation in the middle of a multibyte character. Although the program does check for valid multibyte characters (the call to `mblen()` returns -1 if an invalid or incomplete multibyte character is encountered), it does nothing about the possibility that `scanf()` read an incomplete multibyte character from `stdin`. Ideally, if `mblen()` returned -1, the program should have checked if the end of the buffer had been reached. If it had, then the last bytes in the buffer probably represent the start of an incomplete multibyte character, the rest of which is waiting to be read from `stdin`. So, the program should have retained those last bytes, copying them into the beginning of the buffer and read the rest of the buffer from `stdin`, concatenating them with the remaining bytes from the previous `scanf()` call.

In addition to these techniques, there are I18N wide character routines that can aid in parsing operations, if your systems supports the MSE. These routines are described in Table 2.12.

Table 2.12 MSE Wide Character Scanning and Parsing Routines

Name	Description
wcschr(*wcs*, *wc*)	Locates the first occurrence of the wide character *wc* in the wide character string *wcs*.
wcscspn(*wcs1*, *wcs2*)	Calculates the number of wide characters in the initial segment of *wcs1* that consists entirely of wide characters not present in *wcs2*.
wcspbrk(*wcs1*, *wcs2*)	Locates the first occurrence in the wide character string *wcs1* of any wide character present in *wcs2*.
wcsrchr(*wcs*, *wc*)	Locates the last occurrence of the wide character *wc* in the wide character string *wcs*.
wcsspn(*wcs1*, *wcs2*)	Calculates the number of wide characters in the initial segment of *wcs1* that consists entirely of wide characters present in *wcs2*.
wcsstr(*wcs1*, *wcs2*)	Locates the first occurrence in the wide character string *wcs1* of the wide character string *wcs2*.

---

6. The for loop uses two wide character constants: L'\0' (the wide character NULL) and L'/' (the character "/" converted to a wide character). ANSI and ISO C specify the prefix L as a way to specify a wide character constant. NULL and "/" are part of the C Language basic execution character set. The C Language specification says that these characters must have the same value (as char and as wchar_t) in all locales and code sets supported on a system. Therefore, it is safe to code these wide characters as constants using the L prefix.

Table 2.12 MSE Wide Character Scanning and Parsing Routines (Continued)

Name	Description
wcstok(*wcs1*, *wcs2*, *ptr*)	Breaks the wide character string *wcs1* into a sequence of tokens, each of which is delimited by a wide character from *wcs2*.
wmemchr(*wcs*, *wc*, *n*)	Locates the first occurrence of the wide character *wc* in the first *n* wide character of the wide character string *wcs*.

2.3.3 Character Identification and Classification

Ideally, an internationalized application shouldn't be concerned with individual character attributes. However, some software has a need to know certain characteristics of an individual character. For example, is the character a graphic character? Is it a control character? The answers to these questions depend on the locale of the user and on the code set of the data. As the developer of internationalized code set independent software, you want to perform these operations in a locale-sensitive manner.

XPG4 and the MSE define a number of routines that allow your software to perform such character classifications in a locale-sensitive way; these routines are listed and described in Table 2.13. These routines operate only on wide character data. Their behavior is governed by the LC_CTYPE category of the current locale. So, you must first call setlocale() before calling these functions.

Table 2.13 XPG4 and MSE I18N Character Classification Routines

Name	Description
iswalnum(*wc*)	Returns true if the wide character is an alphabetic character or a digit.
iswalpha(*wc*)	Returns true if the wide character is an alphabetic character.
iswcntrl(*wc*)	Returns true if the wide character is a control character.
iswctype(*wc*, *cl*)	Returns true if the wide character is of the character class *cl*, where the character class is defined by a call to wctype().
iswdigit(*wc*)	Returns true if the wide character is a digit character (for example, 1, 2, 3).
iswgraph(*wc*)	Returns true if the wide character is a character with graphical representation. Internationalized graphical user interface software should call an X library function to examine a character's font metrics when determining if a character is graphical or not. For details on obtaining a character's font metrics, see section 4.4 on page 78.
iswlower(*wc*)	Returns true if the wide character is a lowercase alphabetic character. Many languages do not have the concept of upper- and lowercase. You need to carefully examine your use of this function in an internationalized application.

Table 2.13 XPG4 and MSE I18N Character Classification Routines (Continued)

Name	Description
iswprint(*wc*)	Returns true if the wide character is a printable character. iswprint() is identical to iswgraph() except that it also returns true if the wide character is the space character — iswgraph() returns false for a wide character space. Internationalized graphical user interface software should call an X library function to examine a character's font metrics when determining if a character is graphical or not. For details on obtaining a character's font metrics, see section 4.4 on page 78.
iswpunct(*wc*)	Returns true if the wide character is a punctuation character (for example, colon, period, question mark).
iswspace(*wc*)	Returns true if the wide character causes white space in displayed text. Examples include space, tab, carriage return, newline, vertical tab, and form feed.
iswupper(*wc*)	Returns true if the wide character is an uppercase alphabetic character. Many languages do not have the concept of upper- and lowercase. You need to carefully examine your use of this function in an internationalized application.
iswxdigit(*wc*)	Returns true if the wide character is a character used to represent a hexa-decimal digit.
wctype(*ch_class*)	Returns a value that can be passed to iswctype(). The classification must be either one of the reserved classes or a new class defined in the locale's LC_CTYPE category. This allows vendors and developers to create new character classes to be used with iswctype().

Currently, there are no I18N routines that perform character classification operations on multibyte character data when more than one byte is required to represent the character. XPG3 does specify locale-sensitive character classification routines for char data, but these are specified such that they cannot operate on characters that require more than one byte to represent.

A note of caution: Just because your software uses the internationalized character classification routines doesn't mean that the software is internationalized. For example, an application might use the iswspace() function to determine if a character is a white space character or not. This can be done in a locale neutral way. However, you have to ask the question, "Why do I want to know if the character is a white space character?" If the answer is "Because I want to break my string on a word boundary," then your software still isn't internationalized. Not all languages use white space as a valid line-break criterion. Unfortunately, there are no internationalized routines yet that can tell you where a line can be broken.

2.3.4   Case Conversion

Occasionally, it may be necessary for software to convert the case of characters. Since the concept of case does not apply to all languages of the world, this generally isn't a great idea for internationalized software. However, there are instances (such as normalizing data before doing comparisons) where it cannot be avoided.

The rules for the result of converting a lowercase character into an uppercase character vary from language to language. For example, converting a lowercase accented character to an uppercase character in Canadian French results in an uppercase accented character. Converting the same lowercase accented character to uppercase in European French may cause the accent to be dropped.

Ideally, the developer of internationalized software wants to call a routine that just does "the right thing." If the concept of case conversion is relevant for the user's locale, the correct conversion is performed; otherwise, the character is unmodified.

XPG4 and the MSE define wide character functions that perform case conversion in a locale-sensitive manner. These functions are listed and described in Table 2.14. You must first call `setlocale()` for these functions to operate correctly. Their behavior is governed by the `LC_CTYPE` category of the current locale.

Table 2.14 XPG4 and MSE I18N Case Conversion Routines

Name	Description
`towlower(wc)`	Returns the corresponding lowercase wide character to the wide character argument. If there is no corresponding lowercase wide character argument, the argument is returned unmodified.
`towupper(wc)`	Returns the corresponding uppercase wide character to the wide character argument. If there is no corresponding uppercase wide character argument, the argument is returned unmodified.

Note that round trip conversion with the case conversion routines is not guaranteed. For example, suppose that you have a lowercase e-grave (è) encoded as a wide character. Calling `towupper()` on that character, and then passing the result to `towlower()` may not result in a wide character e-grave.

The MSE defines two additional functions for extending the kinds of conversions that you can perform on wide characters: `wctrans()` and `towctrans()`. Use of these functions for anything other than conversion between uppercase and lowercase characters is vendor dependent and requires modification to the locale data base. Locale modifications such as these are almost always done by the operating system provider. Since you cannot depend on these modifications being made on all possible platforms, these functions shouldn't be used if the software is to be portable.

2.3.5   Sorting

The software you develop may need to display a sorted list of strings (such as customer names or city names) to the software user. The way a user expects strings to be sorted depends on the user's locale. For example, a list of names sorted according to the rules and customs of a German user would have to be reordered to be acceptable for a Spanish user. Similarly, an American user might have trouble finding a name in a list of names sorted according to the rules and customs of a Spanish user.

As the developer of internationalized software, you want the ability to call a routine that orders strings according to the language and customs of the software user. XPG4 and ISO-C provide several routines that tell you if, according to the user's locale, string A should sort prior to or after string B. These routines are listed and described in Table 2.15. You must first call `setlocale()` for these routines to operate correctly. Their behavior is governed by the `LC_COLLATE` category of the current locale.

Table 2.15 XPG4 and ISO C I18N Sorting Routines

Name	Descriptions
`strcoll(s1,s2)`[†]	Returns –1, 0, or 1 if $s1$ should collate before, equal to, or after $s2$ according to the rules of the current locale.
`strxfrm(s1,s2,n)`[†]	Transforms the multibyte string $s2$, placing no more than n bytes of the transformed string in $s1$. Two transformed multibyte strings can be compared with the non-internationalized routine `strcmp()` and still obtain internationalized results. This is useful when repeated comparisons are to be done on the same strings. A reverse transform operation is not available, so applications must maintain a link between the transformed string and the non-transformed string.

†. This function was originally defined in XPG3. It is also part of the ANSI C standard.

The MSE and XPG4 also define several routines that tell you if, according to the user's locale, wide character string A should be sorted prior to or after wide character string B.

These routines are listed and described in Table 2.16. The behavior of these routines is governed by the LC_COLLATE category of the current locale.

Table 2.16 XPG4 and MSE I18N Sorting Routines

Name	Descriptions
wcscoll(ws1,ws2)	Returns −1, 0, or 1 if ws1 should collate before, equal to, or after ws2 according to the rules of the current locale.
wcsxfrm(ws1,ws2,n)	Transforms the wide character string ws2, placing no more than n transformed wide characters in ws1. You can compare two transformed wide character strings with the non-internationalized routine wcscmp() and still obtain internationalized results. This is useful when repeated comparisons are to be done on the same strings. A reverse transform operation is not available, so applications must maintain a link between the transformed string and the non-transformed string.

2.3.5.1   Comparing strings for equality

Not all string comparisons are sensitive to the user's locale. The result of a comparison for string equality generally does not depend on the user's locale. To compare two strings for equality, use the non-internationalized multibyte functions strcmp() and strncmp(), or the internationalized wide character functions wcscmp() and wcsncmp().

When using the multibyte string comparison functions to compare for string equality, make sure that the pointers passed in point to the beginning of a multibyte character. Additionally, take care when using strncmp() to perform comparisons on complete characters. Since n specifies the number of bytes to be compared, it is possible to specify a value for n that causes a comparison to be performed on a partial coded character. This can have unexpected and undesired results.

2.3.6   Converting Characters from One Code Set to Another

Occasionally, your software may receive data that is not encoded in the code set of the current locale. Similarly, your software may need to write text data encoded in a code set that is not the same as that used by the current locale. In such cases, you need the ability to convert between the external encoding and the code set of the current locale. XPG4 defines a set of routines as well as a command that performs these conversions. These functions and the command are listed and described in the table titled Table 2.17 on page 50. Note that the functions are not sensitive to the current locale and, as such, are not internationalization routines — setlocale() does not affect their behavior. However, the existence of internationalized software does increase the possibility that your software can encounter data encoded in different code sets.

Table 2.17 XPG4 Code Set Conversion Tools

Name	Description
`iconv_open(`*`to, from`*`)`	Returns a conversion descriptor for a converter that converts coded characters from the code set *from* to the code set *to*.[†]
`iconv_close(`*`cd`*`)`	Deallocates the conversion descriptor *cd* and all other associated resources allocated by `iconv_open()`.
`iconv(`*`cd, in, m, out, n`*`)`	Converts coded characters from the buffer *in* into a sequence of corresponding characters in another code set, storing them in *out*. The conversion performed is controlled by the conversion descriptor *cd*.
`iconv -f` *`from`* `-t` *`to`* `[`*`file...`*`]`	Converts the coded characters in the input files from the code set identified by *from* to characters encoded in the code set identified by *to* and writes the results to standard output.[†]

†. Tags used to identify code sets as well as the permitted combinations are implementation dependent.

Note that in the case of data interchange for graphical user interface applications (such as cut and paste or drag and drop), X11R5 defines a set of ICCCM compliant routines to perform the necessary conversions. These routines and their use are covered in depth in Chapter 11.

Locale-Sensitive Operations: Messages and Data Formats

Perhaps the most obvious aspect of internationalizing software is that strings displayed to the users (for example, error messages, prompts, and help text) must be translated and presented in the user's language. But even something as obvious as translating messages presented to the user requires additional thought and planning in creating internationalized software. To make your software internationalized, you must separate the text to be translated from your application source code. This is essential if you are to use the internationalization model — single source, single executable software, working correctly for local language users without source code modification. You can choose from several mechanisms, such as message catalogs and resource files, to accomplish this.

Once you decide which mechanism to use, you have to decide which text needs to be translated. This isn't as easy as it might seem. And, you must make sure that the translated text is presented in a format acceptable to the user.

Finally, there is always the temptation for developers of graphical user interface software to say: "Forget about text. We'll use icons for everything. Pictures are about as international as you can get." While there is a certain amount of truth to this view, it is as easy to design non-internationalized icons as it is to design non-internationalized software. (See section 3.4 on page 59 for more details.)

3.1 Messaging Mechanisms

There are two mechanisms you can use to separate translated text from the source code for your graphical user interface software: resource files and message catalogs.

3.1.1   Resource Files

Resource files[1] are loaded by X11 and Motif in a language-sensitive fashion. If you have initialized the application's locale, the current locale is used to determine which resource files are loaded. The current locale is also used to parse the localized resources as they are loaded — the X11R5 specification says that resource values are to be interpreted as being encoded in the code set of the current locale.

So, a graphical user interface software designer *might* decide to place all translatable strings in a resource file. At application start-up, the resource manager loads the resource files based on the current locale. The application then retrieves the translated strings from the resource data base as it needs them.

It is feasible to use the resource manager as a general mechanism for handling localized text messages for the user. However, it has a few distinct disadvantages. X11's resource manager loads, parses, and stores in memory all resources defined in the resource databases at application start-up — whether or not the resources are ever actually referenced by the software. Loading, parsing, and merging resources are not cheap operations. If your application defines many resources in its resource databases, application start-up can be slow.

So, should you avoid using localized resources? No. Just use them judiciously. Use localized resources for strings that must always be loaded by the application. For example, use localized resources for most localized widget values, such as push button widget label strings, small initial text widget values, label widget label strings, and list widget initial values. These are values that are usually specified at widget create time anyway.

3.1.2   Message Catalogs

Message catalogs are files containing text strings needed by the software. A message catalog is usually something more than a plain text file and less than a binary file. For example, a message catalog is often implemented to be a large text file of messages prefaced with an index table identifying the byte length of each message along with its byte offset in the file. This allows quick access and retrieval of an individual message from the file. Such message catalogs are created by passing structured message catalog source files through a compiler or generator (such as X/Open's `gencat` command).

Typically, the message catalog is opened during software initialization. Individual strings are read from the catalog as they are needed. The most commonly implemented message catalogs allow similar messages to be grouped together in sets. For example, you might group all prompts in one set, all error messages in another set, and all initial values in yet another set. Individual messages within a set are referenced by either a numeric tag or a string identifier.

Unfortunately, neither ANSI C nor ISO C specify message catalog routines in their standards. X/Open specifies message catalog routines in XPG3 andXPG4. Although there are

---

1. The resource file mechanism is discussed in detail in Chapter 12.

a number of message catalog systems on different platforms, the XPG message catalog system is probably the most common.

Table 3.1 lists and describes the XPG message catalog routines and commands.

Table 3.1 X/Open Message Catalog Tools

Name	Description
catopen(*name*,*flag*)	Opens the message catalog identified by *name*, returning a message catalog file descriptor. If no catalog is found, catopen returns −1.
catclose(*fd*)	Closes the specified message catalog.
catgets(*fd*,*set*,*num*,*def*)	Returns a pointer to an internal buffer containing the message identified by *num* in set *set* from the specified catalog. The maximum size of the buffer is defined by NL_TEXTMAX in <limits.h>; the maximum value for *set* and *num* are determined by NL_SETMAX and NL_MSGMAX respectively, also defined in <limits.h>. If an error occurs for any reason, it returns a pointer to the default string, *def*.
gencat *outfile infile* ...	Creates a message catalog from one or more message catalog source files.[†] If *outfile* does not exist, gencat creates it. If *outfile* exists, gencat merges the new messages with the existing messages in *outfile*.

†. The syntax and structure of message catalog source files are specified by XPG3 and XPG4. See your system's man page for gencat for a complete description.

In XPG3, the message catalog routines were not affected by the current locale. However, XPG4 made the behavior of catopen() depend on the LC_MESSAGES category of the current locale (*not* the environment variable of the same name), if the *flag* parameter was set to NL_CAT_LOCALE. This is emphasized here because, if flag is set to NL_CAT_LOCALE, your software must call setlocale() before calling catopen(). This is a common mistake even among experienced I18N software developers.

catopen() searches for a message catalog by searching a series of colon separated paths specified in the NLSPATH environment variable. If it can't find the specified message catalog, catopen() searches a series of system defined default paths for the catalog. Each path can contain wild card characters. These wild cards and their meanings are listed in Table 3.2.

Table 3.2 Wild Cards Used in NLSPATH and in System Default Message Catalog Search Path

Wild card	Meaning
%N	Value of the *name* argument passed to `catopen()`.
%L	If *flag* is zero, the value of the LANG environment variable. If *flag* is NL_CAT_LOCALE, this is replaced with the value of the LC_MESSAGES category.
%l	If *flag* is zero, the language component of the LANG environment variable. If *flag* is NL_CAT_LOCALE, this is replaced with the language component of the LC_MESSAGES category.
%t	If *flag* is zero, the territory component of the LANG environment variable. If *flag* is NL_CAT_LOCALE, this is replaced with the territory component of the LC_MESSAGES category.
%c	If *flag* is zero, the code set component of the LANG environment variable. If *flag* is NL_CAT_LOCALE, this is replaced with the code set component of the LC_MESSAGES category.
%%	A single % character.

It is up to the implementation of the C library to determine how to replace the %l, %t, and %c wild cards. The intent was to support systems where the locale was defined to identify a language, a territory where that language is spoken, and the code set used to encode characters of that language. For example, French as spoken in Canada, with data encoded in ISO 8859.1, might have %l replaced with "fr", %t replaced with "CA", and %c replaced with "iso88591". This maps well to operating systems that define the locale name as language_territory.codeset (such as LANG=fr_CA.iso88591). However, since locale names are not standardized, the implementation of the C library decides how to map these wild cards. This should not affect your ability to write internationalized software. However, it will impact where the message catalogs for your software are installed on different platforms.

Many XPG compliant vendors offer an extension to the XPG message catalog tools that allow you to obtain the source for a message catalog file directly from the message catalog — you can think of it as un-`gencat`. For example, HP-UX provides the `dumpmsg` command. `dumpmsg` generates a message catalog source file from a message catalog. The `dspcat` command shipped with AIX 3.2 (and later) provides similar capabilities.

In addition to the XPG message catalog tools, some specialized subsystems have invented their own mechanisms for separating software source and translated text. For example, the Common Desktop Environment (CDE) help subsystem uses its own mechanism for making help text separate from the application. Motif's UIL (User Interface Language) is a static initialization language for specifying the initial appearance of a Motif application. It enables you to create a locale-specific UID (User Interface Description) file — the result of compiling a UIL file.

3.2 Message Catalog Example

This section introduces a simple C program that is modified to use message catalogs. Later, as you read about locale-sensitive data formats, the example is expanded to show how message catalogs and data formats are often used together.

So, to start, consider the notorious C language program "Hello World!"

```c
#include <stdio.h>
main(){
    printf("Hello World!\n");
    exit(0);
}
```

Now, to internationalize this, a few things must be done:

1. Add a call to `setlocale()` to initialize the application locale.
2. Add a call to `catopen()` to open the message catalog.
3. Add a call to `catgets()` to retrieve the localized message from the catalog, passing the result to `printf()`.
4. Add a call to `catclose()` to close the message catalog before exiting.
5. Create a message catalog source file, using your favorite text editor.
6. Use the `gencat` command to create a message catalog from the message catalog source file.
7. Decide where to place the localized message catalog.
8. Set the `NLSPATH` environment variable to ensure that `catopen()` can find the message catalog you just created.

Applying steps 1 through 4 yields the following variation of the program:

```c
#include <stdio.h>
#include <locale.h>
#include <nl_types.h>
main(){
    nl_catd  my_cat;
    char *ret_val;
    ret_val=setlocale(LC_ALL,"");
    if(!ret_val){
        printf("Locale not supported!\n");
        exit(1);
    }
    my_cat=catopen("hello",NL_CAT_LOCALE);
    if (my_catd < 0)
        printf("No message catalog!\n");
    printf(catgets(my_cat,1,1,"Hello World!\n"));
```

```
    catclose(my_cat);
    exit(0);
}
```

The first thing you notice from this example is that adding I18N and message catalogs doesn't exactly qualify as software-lite — a 3line program grows to 16 lines. However, you can take solace in that adding message catalogs to a 20,000-line application has no more overhead than that required for this simple program.

Now that you've recovered from the shock of the increased size, take a closer look at what was added. Two additional `#include` statements provide the definitions needed for `setlocale()` and for `catopen()`.

The call to `setlocale()` initializes the I18N environment for the application. In this example, all categories of the locale are initialized (LC_ALL is used). Since message catalogs are the only I18N functions used in this program, LC_MESSAGES could have been substituted for LC_ALL. This would have resulted in a lighter weight `setlocale()` call — the data for the LC_CTYPE category, the LC_COLLATE category, and the other categories would not have been loaded from disc. However, the example will be expanded in later sections and other locale categories will be needed.

Notice that the application checks the return from `setlocale()` to let the user know if the user's requested locale (indicated by the user's LANG environment variable) is not supported or has failed. The error message is displayed without benefit of a message catalog since the localized message catalog can't be opened if `setlocale()` fails.

Next, the application opens its message catalog with

```
    . . .
      catopen("hello",NL_CAT_LOCALE);
```

The string "hello" is not necessarily the name of the catalog to be opened. XPG does not specify the name to be used for message catalogs. A common convention is to use the application executable name with a ".cat" suffix attached. The actual file name of the message catalog is usually some variation of the string passed to catopen, for example `hello.cat`.

The file name for which `catopen()` looks is determined by the NLSPATH environment variable and the vendor defined default path. For example, the default message catalog search path on HP-UX is `/usr/lib/nls/%L/%N.cat`, where $%L$ is a wild card replaced with the value of the LC_MESSAGES category and $%N$ is a wild card replaced with the value of the first argument to `catopen()`. For example, suppose the internationalized "Hello World!" program is run with LANG=ja_JP.eucJP. With `catopen()` coded as in the example, HP-UX would look for the message catalog by default in

```
    /usr/lib/nls/ja_JP.eucJP/hello.cat.
```

Next, the program verifies that the `catopen()` call succeeded, warning the user if it does not.

Finally, the message is retrieved and is passed to `printf()`:

```
...
    printf(catgets(my_catd,1,1,"Hello World!\n"));
```

The first parameter to `catgets()` is the message catalog file descriptor returned by `catopen()`. Following that are two arbitrary numbers, the set number and the message number. The application can use any numbers it wants,[2] as long as they are the same as the set number and message number that are used for the message in the message catalog source file. The final parameter is the default string — the string to be returned if `catgets()` fails for any reason. Using the original string as the default string helps in source code documentation, as well as ensuring that at least some reasonable message is returned in case something happens to the message catalog.

Now that you understand the internationalized "Hello World!," it's time to create the message catalog the program uses. XPG specifies the format of the message catalog source file. It can be simplified to the following rules:

- All messages must be grouped into message set(s). The `$set`*n* directive in the message catalog source file identifies the set number.
- `\n` in a message is replaced with a newline character by `gencat`. `\t` in a message is replaced by tab.
- Any line beginning with $ that is not followed by one of the few reserved key words (such as `set`) is considered to be a comment. You can use comments to document your message catalog source files for the person who will translate them.
- Any line beginning with a number is considered to be a line identifying a message associated with that message number. A single space character separates the message number from the message text. All text after the initial space and up to the first non-escaped newline is considered to be part of that message. The backslash (`\`) can be used to escape a newline in a message, so that a single line message can span multiple lines in the message source. For example,

```
$ This is an example comment followed by an example message.
1 Hello!\nThis is a two line greeting \
that spans three lines in the \
message catalog source file!\n
```

---

2. Any value within limits — specifically those limits specified in the system header file `limits.h`.

Using these simple rules, the message catalog source file (named `hello.msg`) might look like the following:

```
$
$ Message catalog source file for hello.c.
$
$set1
$
$ This is the initial greeting message.
1 Hello World!\n
$ This is a good place for notes to the translator to help them
$ understand how this particular message will be used and what
$ response is desired of the reader. This helps ensures the best
$ translation of the message.
```

With the message catalog source file complete, you create the actual message catalog with the following command:

```
gencat hello.cat hello.msg
```

Make sure LANG is set to the locale of the messages in the catalog when actually executing `gencat` on a translated message catalog source. `gencat` is an internationalized application that calls `setlocale()` to make sure it correctly parses the localized text in the message catalog source file.

To test the application with the newly generated message catalog, set NLSPATH to identify the location of the message catalog. For example, suppose you put the catalog in `~/my_test_catalogs/hello.cat`. You could test your internationalized "Hello World!" by setting

```
NLSPATH=~/my_test_catalogs/%N.cat
```

Notice that since %L is not used in NLSPATH, it is not necessary to even set LANG to test your application's ability to access the message catalog.

3.3 What Needs to Be Translated?

You should plan to translate all text displayed to the user. This includes prompts, help text, error messages, push button widget labels, application title bars, icon titles, initial values of text displayed in text widgets, and strings values of label widgets.

In addition, you may need to translate strings used to format data, such as `printf()` and `scanf()` format strings. These strings can contain positional indicators for the format specifiers, allowing the translator to change the order in which parameters are displayed to the user or are read from the user.

You must decide if you will translate command line options and flags. (Command line options and flags are usually *not* translated.) Suppose the fictional command `foobar` supports a command line option `-file`. Do you want to allow the flag `-file` to be translated? Allowing translation might cause problems if the command is run on systems for which the shell(s) have not been internationalized. If the system shells support localized characters on the command line, then you need to consider what mechanisms exist to support localized flags. If your software uses `yacc` and `lex` to parse command line options, you must first determine if these system commands are internationalized on your development systems. If they are not, then you must either perform command line parsing yourself or disallow localized flags. If you implement command line parsing yourself and you decide to allow for localized flags, then the flags you search for must be translated as well.[3]

3.4 What about Icons?

When developing graphical user interfaces, there is a temptation to believe that icons and other graphic symbols are immune to internationalization and localization. Icons are pictorial representations of ideas. What's more internationalized than an actual picture, right? The trouble is that what is plainly conveyed by a graphic symbol in your culture might be meaningless in another culture. Or even worse, the symbol might have an unintended or offensive meaning in another culture.

For example, I had the opportunity to consult for internationalization on one early graphical user interface based e-mail project. The design team chose to place on the desktop a mailbox icon for the mailer and a cylindrical icon for the trash can. The graphic symbol chosen for the mailbox was a typical U.S. rural mailbox, complete with a flag to indicate when new mail had arrived. The trash can was a simple cylinder. The application was well received in the United States and Canada. However, numerous complaints of lost mail flowed in from customers in the UK. It turned out that the U.S. rural mailbox was a complete mystery to some UK users. However, the cylinder strongly resembled the mailbox used by the Royal Post. The result? Users in the UK were dropping their outgoing mail in the trash can and wondering why it wasn't being delivered. The moral of the story is that pictures are not necessarily universally understood across all cultures.

If you plan to use icons or pictures in your software product, do not hard code the graphic into your software. Instead, load it at run time the same way you do a message catalog. (Motif and X11 provide routines that allow you to locate icons and other bitmap files in a language-sensitive fashion.) In this way, you can provide a different graphic for some locales or cultures without modifying your software.

---

3. This sounds obvious, but at least one software project made the effort to parse the command line with I18N character handling tools — and forgot to make the flags translatable.

3.5 Hints and Common Mistakes

When making text external to your software source, there are a few guiding principles that may make life easier when translating that text later.

3.5.1   Don't Build Messages from Fragments

One of the more common mistakes an engineer makes when introduced to message catalogs is to try and make all messages as "efficient" as possible. For example, when looking at the messages displayed by your program, suppose you find a number of similar messages that start with the phrase "Accessing ..." — "Accessing the printer," "Accessing user Bob," "Accessing help volume." In an effort to minimize the amount of text in the message catalog, you might decide to create a single message for the phrase "Accessing" and a collection of messages that are combined with it to form complete messages.

Efficiency is usually a *good* thing, but this is an example of a good thing taken too far. Attempting to translate such message catalogs nearly always fails. The reason is that English is an ambiguous language with loose rules for sentence structure. This isn't true for other languages. For example, the translation of "Accessing" in German depends on what is being accessed; the verb form changes depending on the object. Additionally, the translation of a phrase may require that the phrase be split into pieces. All of this usually means that a reasonable translation is not possible.

As a general rule, make messages complete sentences. It is usually safe to allow parameter substitution in a message, such as a file name or a value. When in doubt, ask the person performing the translation for guidance.

3.5.2   Don't Reuse Messages

Unless the message occurs due to identical circumstances or the user is expected to respond in exactly the same way, do not reuse a message. English is a wonderfully ambiguous language. A single sentence can have a completely different meaning depending on context — which can be both a blessing and a curse. It's wonderful as long as everyone knows the context. When they don't, the results can be disastrous at worst and humorous at best. (If you doubt it, go to your local video store and check out a copy of Abbot and Costello's *Who's on First?* comedy routine.)

Other languages are not blessed/cursed with the ambiguity of English. So, when tempted to use a single message in multiple places in your software, ask yourself the following questions: "When the message is displayed by the different parts of the software, are the circumstances identical that would cause the message to be displayed?" "Should the user do exactly the same thing in each situation when that shared message is displayed?" If the answer to either of these questions is no (or even *maybe*), play it safe by creating separate messages in your software and in the catalog.

3.5.3   Allow for Text Growth in Translations

The amount of space required to convey an idea in English is not necessarily the same as that required to convey the same idea in another language. Some languages require less room to express the same idea; some languages require more room.

Human factors engineers say that applications should leave a certain amount of white space when displaying text data. The amount of white space recommended varies, but all agree that a dialog box packed border to border with solid text is not user friendly. Suppose that you carefully design your dialog box to ensure that you have the amount of white space that your human factors team tells you is needed. Further assume that, as a good designer of internationalized software, you place the text for that dialog in a resource file or a message catalog. Now you have a problem. You can be sure that in at least one of the language translations the text will fill or overflow your dialog.

To avoid this problem, a couple of precautionary steps should be taken. First, assume that at least for one translation, the size of the text will grow. By how much? It's hard to say. However, a commonly used guideline is that the most verbose translation uses about 60 percent more space than that used by English language text. So, one solution might be to pad your original English language message by an additional 60 percent and then lay out the geometry for your dialog box. (Remember to strip out the padding before sending the text for translation.)

This solution can have the negative effect of making your English language messages look too sparse in their windows. A different solution is to ensure that the size (geometry) of the dialog is not hard coded and is placed in a resource file. In this way, you can customize the size of the dialog to fit the size of the translated text. Of course, you still must take care not to create an English language text so large that the translated text cannot be displayed with reasonable human factors considerations.

3.6 Formatting Text according to Local Custom

It is not enough that text is displayed in the user's local language. It must also be formatted according to their regional customs and expectations.

For example, suppose you are creating a file manager application. When displaying a detailed list of files to a user, you probably will include the time and date showing the last modification of that file. Or, the user might want to see only files modified after a certain date and time. When prompted to enter the date and time for the files to be displayed, the user expects to enter that date and time in the formats he or she uses every day.

Local data formats are not limited to time and date representation. You expect the currency symbol to change with the user's locale, but you probably hadn't anticipated that the *location* of the currency symbol depends on local custom — it does, and sometimes in unusual ways. Internationalized software that displays or allows entry of monetary values must deal with these variations.

The next few sections discuss the most common variations in locally formatted data. How common? Common enough that X/Open and ISO C adopted interfaces allowing applications to deal with them.

3.6.1   Time and Date Formats

The way in which time and date are formatted vary from country to country. In the United States, the date is always written with the month listed before the day of the month. For example, 11/12/94 is obviously November 12, 1994, right? In the United States, this is the correct interpretation. However, in the United Kingdom, 11/12/94 would be interpreted as 11 December 1994.

It isn't just the order of day, month, and year that varies. The character used to separate the day, month and year varies as well. For example, in the United States, November 12, 1994 is written 11/12/94; in Germany, it is written 12.11.94. Similarly, in the United States you write 12:05 pm to represent the time 5 minutes past noon. In France, this same time is represented as 12h05.

Even the way the year is calculated depends on your country and culture. In the United States and in Western Europe, the Gregorian calendar is used. The year is the number of years since the birth of Christ — or at least it was based on the year of Christ's birth based on the best calculations at the time the calendar was established. However, there are many other calendar systems in common use in the world today. For example, in Japan the year is based on the date that the current emperor ascended the throne. With each new emperor, a new Era begins and the year count starts over. For example, the late Emperor Hirohito presided over the Era of Showa. With his passing, Emperor Akihito ascended the throne and proclaimed this to be the Era of Heisei. At the time of this writing, it is currently the seventh year of Heisei.

Figure 3.1 shows just some of the variations in which time and date are represented in the world.

A complete description of time and date variations would fill many, many pages. And while it might be interesting, it would not help you write internationalized software capable of dealing with the variations. It's enough to realize that there are variations. The big question is, "How do I write my software to be independent of these variations?"

Locale	Time/Date Format
France	Mardi 29 novembre 1994 20:20:23
Germany	Di., 29. Nov. 1994, 20:20:23
Japan	平成6年11月29日 （火），午後 8時20分23秒
Korea	1994년11월29일 （화），오후 8시20분23초
Portugal	29/11/1994 20.20.23
Spain	Mar, 29 Nov 1994 20:20:23
Taiwan	中華民國83年11月29日 星期二，20時20分23秒
United Kingdom	Tue. 29 Nov, 1994 08:20:23 PM
United States	Tue, Nov 29, 1994 08:20:23 PM

Figure 3.1

Sample time and date formats from around the world.

ISO C defines only one routine to help your software display correctly formatted time and date quantities. It is described in Table 3.3.

Table 3.3 ISO C I18N Time/Date Formatting Tools

Name	Description
strftime()	Takes a `struct tm` and returns a formatted time/date string. The routine uses a supplied format string, substituting locale-specific values from the current locale. If no format string is supplied, a locale-specific default format is used. The structure `tm` is defined in `time.h` and populated by any of several standard C library routines, such as `localtime()`.

The MSE defines one additional routine that helps your software to display correctly formatted time and date quantities. This routine is described in Table 3.4.

Table 3.4 MSE I18N Time/Date Formatting Tools

Name	Description
wcsftime()	Takes a `struct tm` and returns a formatted time/date wide character string. The routine uses a supplied format string, substituting locale-specific values from the current locale. If no format string is supplied, a locale-specific default format is used.

XPG4 defines a variety of routines that allow your software to display correctly formatted time and date quantities. In addition, XPG4 defines a routine that parses a locally formatted time/date string into something your software can process. These routines are described in Table 3.5.

Table 3.5 XPG4 I18N Time/Date Formatting Tools

Name	Description
`nl_langinfo()`	Allows the application to query for many time/date format related values (such as the local name for month 11) for the current locale, including default format strings.
`strftime()`	Takes a `struct tm` and returns a formatted time/date string. The routine uses a supplied format string, substituting locale-specific values from the current locale. If no format string is supplied, a locale-specific default format is used. The structure `tm` is defined in `time.h` and populated by any of several standard C library routines, such as `localtime()`.
`strptime()`	Takes a locally formatted time/date string and using a supplied format string, fills in a `struct tm`. If no format string is supplied, a locale-specific default format is used.
`wcsftime()`	Takes a `struct tm` and returns a formatted time/date wide character string. The routine uses a supplied format string, substituting locale-specific values from the current locale. If no format string is supplied, a locale-specific default format is used.

The format string used by many of the time and date formatting routines is an excellent candidate for a message catalog (if you decide not to use the locale default format string). Placing the format string in a message catalog allows the localizer to customize the format for each locale.

3.6.2   Floating Point Numbers

The way in which floating point values are written varies from region to region. In the United States, the decimal point (.) is used as the *radix*. The radix is the symbol in floating point values used to separate whole numbers from their fractional portions. For example, in the United States the approximate value of pi would be written 3.141. In Germany, this same quantity would be expressed as 3,141. Similarly, the character used to group characters (such as the thousands separator) varies from region to region. For example, in the United States the number three thousand one hundred forty one would be written 3,141 while in Germany the same quantity would be written 3.141. Confusing? Perhaps, but not if you use the XPG4 routines to handle these differences in formatting for you. These routines are listed and described in Table 3.6.

Table 3.6 XPG4 Numeric Formatting Tools

Name	Description
localeconv()	Queries the numeric formatting conventions of the current locale, returning the radix character and grouping character, as well as other locale-specific information.
nl_langinfo()	Allows queries for individual locale-specific attributes, such as radix character and grouping character.
fprintf() printf() sprintf() vfprintf() vprintf() vsprintf()	Inserts the correct radix character when converting a floating point value to a string.
fscanf() scanf() sscanf()	Uses the locale's radix character when identifying and converting string representations of floating point values.
strtod()	Converts a formatted string representation of a numeric value to a double precision floating point value. The current locale's radix character is used when evaluating the string to be converted.
wcstod()	Converts a formatted wide character string representation of a numeric value to a double precision floating point value. The current locale's radix character is used when evaluating the wide character string to be converted.

ANSI C and ISO C provide little in the way of tools to help you process locally formatted string numeric data. Table 3.7 describes the sole function provided by ANSI C and ISO C.

Table 3.7 ANSI C and ISO C Numeric Formatting Tools

Name	Description
localeconv()	Queries the numeric formatting conventions of the current locale, returning the radix character and grouping character, as well as other locale-specific information.

The MSE provides no additional tools to help you process locally formatted string numeric data.

3.6.3 Monetary Values

While most people know that the currency symbol used to represent monetary values depends on the country of the user, it is less intuitive that the position of that currency symbol also depends on the country of the user. For example, the United States and Portugal both use $ as their currency symbol. In the United States, the currency symbol occurs before the amount. In Portugal, the currency symbol replaces the radix. Figure 3.2 shows just some of the variation in the ways monetary values are represented around the world.

Locale	Monetary Format
France	10,25 FF
Germany	DM 10,25
Japan	¥10.25
Korea	₩10.25
Portugal	10$25
Spain	+Pts10,25
Taiwan	NT$10.25
United Kingdom	£10.25
United States	$10.25

Figure 3.2
Position of currency symbol varies from country to country.

Another variation in the way monetary values are presented is that the number of characters used to form a currency symbol varies from country to country. XPG4 (and to a lesser extent, ISO C) provide tools to aid in formatting monetary strings. These tools are listed and described in Table 3.8.

Table 3.8 XPG4 Monetary Formatting Tools

Name	Description
localeconv()	Queries the monetary formatting conventions of the current locale, returning the local currency symbol, the international currency symbol, monetary radix character, the monetary grouping character, the number of characters in each set of grouped digits in a monetary string, and the positive and negative signs used in representing monetary values.
nl_langinfo()	Returns the currency symbol used for the current locale, along with an indication of whether the currency symbol is displayed before the value, after the value, or replaces the radix.
strfmon()	Generates a formatted string representation of a monetary value using a program supplied format string.

Table 3.9 describes the monetary formatting tools supported by the ISO C standard. The MSE provides no additional tools for handling monetary values.

Table 3.9 ISO C Monetary Formatting Tools

Name	Description
`localeconv()`	Queries the monetary formatting conventions of the current locale, returning the local currency symbol, the international currency symbol, monetary radix character, the monetary grouping character, the number of characters in each set of grouped digits in a monetary string, and the positive and negative signs used in representing monetary values.

3.7 Reading and Writing Text Data

All of the functions for reading and writing internationalized text data have already been listed in the section comparing wide characters and multibyte character storage. However, the `printf()` and `scanf()` family of functions have an additional capability that is worth special attention. Sometimes it is highly desirable when reading or writing strings to be able to swap the order of parameters to meet local data formats and customs. For example, suppose your software generates a parts list for a CAD/CAM drawing. The part list consists of columns of data, with the first column containing the part number, the second column containing the drawing reference number, the third column containing the supplier number, and the fourth column contains the price for the part. A typical code fragment for printing the parts list might be

```
...
printf("Part#:\tRef#:\tSupplier:\tPrice:\n");
for (i=0; i<num_parts; i++)
    printf("%d\t%d\t%d\t%f",part,ref,supplier,
           price);
```

Further suppose that, as a good international code designer, you add your call to `setlocale()` and put the format header and format strings in a message catalog:

```
...
printf(catgets(my_fd,1,27,
           "Part#:\tRef#:\tSupplier:\tPrice:\n"));
for (i=0; i<num_parts; i++)
    printf(catgets(my_fd,1,28,"%d\t%d\t%d\t%f\n"),
           part,ref,supplier,price);
```

Now suppose that when localizing the product, one of your marketing persons approaches you and says: "Great! When localizing the product for the FooBar locale, we found out that local practice there is to list the price immediately after the part number." What do you do now? To reorder the report requires source code changes at a minimum.

Fortunately, the XPG4 printf() and scanf() family of routines support positional parameters in their format strings. A positional parameter is an addition to the format specifier that allows you to tell the routine which of the parameters is to be associated with the given format specifier. The form of the positional parameter is a modified format specifier. If the original format specifier is %s, the positional format specifier is %$n$$s, where n is the number of parameter to be substituted.

Here's how the previous code fragment would look using positional parameters:

```
...
printf(catgets(my_fd,1,27,
             "Part#:\tRef#:\tSupplier:\tPrice:\n"));
for (i=0; i<num_parts; i++)
   printf(catgets(my_fd,1,28,
                   "%1$d\t%2$d\t%3$d\t%4$f\n"),
            part,ref,supplier,price);
```

Now, when the request comes in to change the order of the items in the report, you simply modify the message catalog as follows:

```
$set1
$ Originally was:
$   Part#:\tRef#:\tSupplier:\tPrice:\n
$   %1$d\t%2$d\t%3$d\t%4$f\n
$
$ Translated for locale FooBar:
27 Part#\tPrice\tRef#\Supplier\n
28 %1$d\t%4$f\t%2$d\t%3$d\n
```

Message 28 in the catalog tells printf() to convert the first parameter (part), an integer quantity, to string and print it followed by a tab. Next, it tells printf() to convert the fourth parameter (price), a floating point value, to string and print it followed by a tab. It then tells printf() to convert the second parameter (ref), an integer quantity, to string and print it followed by a tab. Finally, it tells printf() to convert the third parameter (supplier), an integer quantity, to string and print it followed by a newline. Suppose the original (non-localized) output looks like the following:

```
    part#:    Ref#:    Supplier:          Price:
    1234-56   A-1111   T-MacAir, Inc.   $325.00
    6789-00   A-7351   T-MacAir, Inc.   $1.25
```

CHAPTER 3 69

Using the FooBar message catalog with positional parameters changes the parts list to look like this:

```
part#:      Price:    Ref#:     Supplier:
1234-56     $325.00   A-1111    T-MacAir, Inc.
6789-00     $1.25     A-7351    T-MacAir, Inc.
```

As you can see, by placing format strings in message catalogs and by taking advantage of positional parameters, you can tell `printf()` (and `scanf()`) to alter the order in which they deal with parameters — without modifying the application source code.

3.8 Summary

As a developer of internationalized software, there are certain design decisions you must make:

1. Identify the regions where your software is likely to be sold during the lifetime of the product.
2. Determine the hardware and software platforms to which your software will be ported. Then identify which set of standards are supported on each. For example, do they all support XPG4? Do they all support ISO C (ISO/IEC 9899-1990)? Do they all support the 1994 Amendment to ISO C? What code sets are supported on each?
3. Decide if your code will be based on a principal of code set independence or whether you will build a dependence on a single, universal code set. The answer to item 2 may limit your options.
4. Decide whether you will store and process text data as multibyte (`char *`) and where you will store and process text as wide character (`wchar_t *`); it is not unusual to use both multibyte and wide character in the same software. Your decision may be constrained by the standards supported on the platforms to which your software will be ported.
5. Identify which tasks performed by your software may be affected by the locale of the users and the encoding of their data.
6. Make sure your application initializes the locale by calling `setlocale()` before calling any other I18N routine.
7. Add I18N calls for all situations identified in item 5.
8. Make sure that any text that could potentially need to be translated is not coded into the software. Decide if you will use message catalogs, resource files, or a combination of the two to make the text external to your software's source code. Don't forget that icons may need to be localized as well.

Displaying Local Language Characters with X11R5

$\mathbf{T}$he graphical user interface portion of an application is affected by internationalization in just a few key areas: generating characters from the keyboard that are appropriate for the user's locale, displaying those characters correctly, and interchanging character data with other X-based software (e.g., cut and paste, drag and drop).

This chapter explains how to display characters encoded in the code set of the user's locale. In the process, you will learn about the X11R5 concept of *font sets* and the drawing routines that use them. You will also find new routines to calculate text metrics (such as ascent, descent, and spacing between lines) when displaying text data. Finally, and most importantly, you will see how to use these routines in your software so that a single version of your software displays any character of any locale supported by the X Window System on your platform.

4.1 The Problem with Using Fonts

A font is a collection of glyphs. Individual glyphs within the font are addressed by a numeric value called the *glyph index*. For bitmap fonts, the glyph index is defined by the glyph's ENCODING keyword in the font.

Prior to Release 5 of X11, the implementation and specification of the X Window System assumed that

- Only a single font need be open in order to render text data.
- The coded value of a character was identical to that character's glyph index in the font used.
- The font opened was appropriate for the coded character data of the user's locale.

These assumptions placed an incredible burden on the software you developed. It meant that you had to keep track of the user's locale and open one or more fonts whose encoding matched the encoding of the user's data. If the coded value of a character was not identical to a font's glyph index, you had to map the code value to the glyph index. If multiple fonts were required to render all of the characters of the user's language, you were required to know when to use which font for which characters. An internationalized application had to do all these things for every locale supported on the system.

4.1.1   One Font Isn't Enough for Some Code Sets

Releases of the X Window System prior to X11R5 assumed that a single font contained all the glyphs needed to render text characters. If more than one font was needed, it was the application's responsibility to open any additional fonts and switch the font in the graphics context (GC) when it was time to render with the new font. This was a workable (if limited) solution, as long as you were only concerned with supporting the languages of the Americas or of Europe. However, this solution fails miserably for the languages of Asia.

For example, Extended UNIX Codes (EUC) as used in Japan is actually a combination of four separate coded character sets (see Table 2.6 on page 27). A typical Japanese EUC data string contains characters from each of component coded character sets: ASCII, JISX0201, JISX0208, and JISX0212. Each of these component coded character sets requires its own font. Using the X11R4 model, the application was responsible for opening a font for each of the constituent coded character sets of EUC, breaking the Japanese EUC string into coded character set consistent segments, and changing fonts in the GC before rendering each segment. An added problem occurred because the coded character value in Asian code sets was usually not identical to the glyph index in the font. So, the coded character value had to be mapped to the glyph index before the render call was made.

Fortunately, X11R5 provides a mechanism that allows software to be oblivious to whether 1 font or 40 fonts are required to render the user's data.

4.1.2   Character Value Isn't Always Identical to the Glyph Index

Prior to X11R5, X11 rendering routines assumed that the coded character value of each character was identical to the font's glyph index for that character. For example, if an application was operating in a locale based on the ISO 8859.1 coded character set, then the glyph index of the character Å (code value 0xc5) must also be 0xc5. If not, the application was responsible for mapping each code point to the appropriate glyph index.

For many languages in Asia, the coded character value is often *not* identical to the font glyph index. For example, the coded character value of the Japanese Katakana character *ka* in EUC is 0x8ec6; its glyph index is 0xc6. Similarly, the Japanese Shift-JIS coded character value for the Kanji character for month is 0x8c8e; the glyph index for that character is 0x376e.

Prior to X11R5, internationalized software had to code into the software source this mapping knowledge for every code set it wanted to support. As a practical matter, this mapping was either handled by the vendor's implementation of the X library, or software was not internationalized for Asian languages. Fortunately, the X11R5 internationalized rendering routines perform these mappings for you.

4.1.3 Getting the Right Font for the Locale

Prior to X11R5, the user or the application was responsible for ensuring that the font opened was appropriate for the user's data. For example, if your application was operating in the German locale using the ISO 8859.1 code set, the user or the application was responsible for ensuring that an ISO 8859.1 font was opened and used to render text data.

X11R5 provides a mechanism to automatically open and use all the right fonts needed to render characters encoded in the code set of the locale.

4.2 Font Sets: the X11R5 Solution

The designers of X11R5 believed that applications should not have to know anything about the relationship between the character encoding of text data and the font(s) used to render them. For example, they believed an application designer should be able to say, "I have some text data encoded in the code set of the user's locale. Open the font(s) needed and render the text at position *x,y*." They felt obtaining font metrics for a string should be the X library's responsibility, not the application's; if multiple fonts are required to render text in the user's locale, the application shouldn't have to worry about calculating font metrics across the different fonts.

As a solution, the designers of X11R5 introduced a new concept and a new data type: the *font set* (data type XFontSet). They also created new rendering and font metric routines that utilized font sets.

A font set is a list of one or more fonts, providing glyphs for every printing character in the code set of the locale. It is created by calling XCreateFontSet(). To understand how XCreateFontSet() works and how to use it, you need to be familiar with the X Logical Font Description (XLFD).

4.2.1 X Logical Font Description

When creating a font set, you must pass a list of font names — a comma separated list of XLFDs.

X uses an XLFD to uniquely identify a font. Font files contain a font name property that is represented as an XLFD; users and applications use an XLFD[1] to identify what font they want to use. The XLFD is a series of hyphen (–) separated fields, with each field provid-

---

1. Actually, users often supply an *alias* to an XLFD. There is a file named fonts.alias in the directory where the font file resides. This file is used to map simple names to the font's actual font name, which is almost always an XLFD. In addition, this file can contain the entry "FILE_NAMES_ALIASES". This says that the file name of the font is an alias to its actual font name. The font's actual name is stored in properties within the font. Though not required to use XLFD for its name, as a practical matter almost all fonts for use with X created since X11R3 use an XLFD name.

ing some information about the font. The last two fields of an XLFD specify the coded character set used to encode the glyphs. These are the character set registry
(CHARSET_REGISTRY) and the character set encoding (CHARSET_ENCODING) fields of
the XLFD. For example, consider the following XLFD:

```
-adobe-times-bold-o-normal--8-80-75-75-p-110-iso8859-1
```

Without going into a complete description of the XLFD, this basically identifies a font
created by Adobe Corporation. The typeface of the font is named Times. Its glyphs are bold,
oblique (slanted), and 8 points high on a 75 x 75 DPI resolution monitor. The last two fields
(iso8859-1) say that the font contains the glyphs for the ISO 8859.1 coded character set
and that the glyphs in the font are indexed according to that coded character set. These last
two fields of the XLFD are the CHARSET_REGISTRY and CHARSET_ENCODING fields.
For example, the ISO 8859.1 coded character value for Å is 0xc5. Similarly, 0xc5 is the glyph
index for the glyph Å in a font whose CHARSET_REGISTRY-CHARSET_ENCODING is
iso8859-1.

So, if your user were working in an ISO 8859.1 based locale, you would want an XLFD
font name with the last two fields "iso8859-1".

4.2.2   Creating a Font Set with XCreateFontSet()

From a software developer's standpoint, the key thing to remember about
XCreateFontSet() is that it opens fonts that allow you to display text data encoded in
the code set of the user's locale. If the user runs the software in a German ISO 8859.1 locale,
ISO 8859.1 fonts are opened. If the user runs the software in a Japanese EUC locale,
JISX0201, JISX0208, and JISX0212 fonts are opened; the font for JISX0201 usually con-
tains glyphs for ASCII as well as the JISX0201 characters.

If the operating system adds support for a new locale, no software changes are required
on your part. The implementation of the X library may change and the X locale database may
be modified, but you won't need to modify your software.

To get these benefits from XCreateFontSet(), you need to call it properly. It has
this syntax:

```
XFontSet XCreateFontSet(display,
                        base_font_name_list,
                        missing_charset_list_return,
                        missing_charset_count_return,
                        def_string_return)
Display *display;
char *base_font_name_list;
char ***missing_charset_list_return;
int *missing_charset_count_return;
char **def_string_return;
```

When you call `XCreateFontSet()`, it does several things for you. First, it queries for the current locale of the application. This establishes the *locale of the font set* that is being created. It then checks a vendor specific database to get a list of which `CHARSET_REGISTRY-CHARSET_ENCODING` pairs must be found in the fonts of the font set if all characters in the user's locale are to be rendered. Armed with this list of `CHARSET_REGISTRY-CHARSET_ENCODING` fields, it then looks at what attributes (such as typeface and point size) you have requested for the fonts in the font set. These attributes are specified in the *base_font_name_list* argument to `XCreateFontSet()`.

The *base_font_name_list* is a comma separated list of one or more *base names*. The base name specifies a collection or family of fonts with similar characteristics. The value of a base name is an XLFD; one or more of the fields in the XLFD can be replaced with a wild card. For example, `*-medium-r-normal--18-*` is a base name that specifies all fonts that have a medium weight, a roman slant, an empty `ADD_STYLE_NAME` field, and are 18 pixels high.

If a base name supplied to `XCreateFontSet()` includes `CHARSET_REGISTRY-CHARSET_ENCODING` fields, `XCreateFontSet()` checks to make sure that the specified fields match those from the vendor database. If they match, `XCreateFontSet()` uses the specified XLFD to open the matching font in the font set. This allows the application or the user to control more closely which fonts are used to build the font set.

`XCreateFontSet()` opens all the fonts needed to display any character in the code set of the user's locale. The exact mechanism that `XCreateFontSet()` uses is implementation dependent, though all implementations perform similar tasks. The following describes the algorithm used in Hewlett-Packard®'s implementation of X11R5.

`XCreateFontSet()` queries the X server for a list of all fonts that match the base name supplied — that is, all fonts that have the attributes you requested. In the list returned by the server, `XCreateFontSet()` searches for the first font it can find that matches the first `CHARSET_REGISTRY-CHARSET_ENCODING` pair retrieved from the X library vendor's database. It repeats this search until it has found one font for each `CHARSET_REGISTRY-CHARSET_ENCODING` pair in the database.

If `XCreateFontSet()` is completely successful, it returns an `XFontSet`; it sets *missing_charset_list_return* and *missing_charset_count_return* to NULL and zero, respectively.

If `XCreateFontSet()` is unable to find a font for one or more `CHARSET_REGISTRY-CHARSET_ENCODING` entries in the X locale database, it sets the number of missing fonts in *missing_charset_count_return*. It also places into *missing_charset_list_return* a list of the `CHARSET_REGISTRY-CHARSET_ENCODING` pairs for which no fonts could be found. The memory for this list is allocated by the X library and should be freed by a call to `XFreeStringList()`. In addition, if *def_string_return* is not NULL, it is set to a string that represents the glyphs that are drawn when X is requested to render characters with a font set and the character maps to one of the fonts in the font set for which no font could be opened. If `XCreateFontSet()` returns the empty string in this parameter, characters for which there is no font in the font set will not be rendered. If the string is not empty, then the X library calls that use font sets will use some glyph (such as space) to render characters belonging to the missing character sets in the font set.

4.2.3   Manipulating and Freeing Font Sets

X11R5 provides several routines that allow you to obtain information about the fonts in a font set and to free a font set. Except for freeing a font set, most software will rarely, if ever, need to call these routines. They are listed and briefly described here in case your software is one of the rare cases that does need the functionality provided by these calls.

If you find that your software no longer has a need for a font set, the font set should be destroyed and its memory freed by calling `XFreeFontSet()`. This call causes the individual font structures that comprise the font set to be freed, along with function internal memory used for storing the base name list, font name list, and font metrics.

X11R5 provides three routines that allow you to obtain information about a font set. These are described in Table 4.1.

Table 4.1 Miscellaneous Font Set Routines

Name	Description
`XLocaleOfFontSet()`	Returns the name of the locale that was current at the time the font set was created.
`XBaseFontnameListOfFontSet()`	Returns the original list of base names supplied when `XCreateFontSet()` was called.
`XFontsOfFontSet()`	Returns the list of `XFontStruct`s that comprise the font set.

4.3 Drawing with Font Sets

To render data encoded in the code set of the user's locale, you need a font set and any of the internationalized rendering functions added for X11R5. Most of these functions closely parallel the non-internationalized rendering functions provided prior to X11R5. For example, `XDrawString()` and `XmbDrawString()` perform the same function — they both render the specified text with the foreground pixel at the specified location (the background is not modified). One key difference is that `XmbDrawString()` takes an additional argument, an `XFontSet`. `XmbDrawString()` uses the font set to render the characters while `XDrawString()` uses the font in the GC to render the characters. The other key difference is that `XmbDrawString()` renders characters encoded in the code set of the font set's locale, while `XDrawString()` assumes its argument is a string of single byte (eight-bit) characters whose coded value is identical to the glyph index of the font in the GC. (The font set's locale is the locale that was the current locale when the font set was created.)

The internationalized X11R5 rendering routines come in two varieties: a multibyte version (prefixed with Xmb) and a wide character version (prefixed with Xwc). Data passed to the Xmb routines is assumed to be encoded in the same code set as the code set of the font set's locale. Data passed to the Xwc routines is assumed to have been generated in the same locale as the font set's locale. This is not an issue for you if your software does not change the locale (i.e., it calls `setlocale()` only once).

The Xmb and Xwc rendering routines are listed and described in Table 4.2.

Table 4.2 X11R5 Internationalized Rendering Functions

Name	Description
XmbDrawString()	Draws a multibyte string, encoded in the code set of the font set's locale, with the foreground pixel. The background is not modified.
XwcDrawString()	Draws a wide character string with the foreground pixel. The background is not modified.
XmbDrawImageString()	Calculates the size of the rectangle defined by the logical extents of the multibyte string, using the metrics of the font set.[†] It fills the rectangle with the background pixel, then draws the multibyte string, encoded in the code set of the font set's locale, with the foreground pixel.
XwcDrawImageString()	Calculates the size of the rectangle defined by the logical extents of the wide character string, using the metrics of the font set.[††] It fills the rectangle with the background pixel and then draws the wide character string with the foreground pixel.
XmbDrawText()	Draws a multibyte string, encoded in the code set of the font set's locale, with the foreground pixel. The background is not modified. It allows switching among multiple font sets for the multibyte string rendered, for example, allows switching among a normal and a bold or italic font set.
XwcDrawText()	Draws a wide character string with the foreground pixel. The background is not modified. It allows switching among multiple font sets for the wide character string rendered. For example, allows switching among a normal and a bold or italic font set.

[†]. Metrics are the overall logical metrics returned by XmbTextExtents(). Font metrics are discussed in section 4.4 on page 78.

[††]. Metrics are the overall logical metrics returned by XwcTextExtents(). Font metrics are discussed in section 4.4 on page 78.

4.4 Calculating Metrics with Font Sets

Applications and libraries frequently need to know how big a string will be when rendered. For example, they need to know how high above the base line the tallest character rises, how far below the base line the lowest descender hangs, how many pixels separate the origins of adjacent characters, and how many pixels separate baselines when displaying multiple lines of text (see Figure 4.2 on page 81). Prior to the introduction of font sets, these metrics could be obtained by directly examining the font structure or by using any of several X library routines, such as `XTextWidth()`.

With the introduction of font sets, applications could no longer directly examine the font structure to obtain font metrics because the metrics of one font in the font set might be different from the metrics of the other fonts in the font set. The old font metric routines from X11R4 couldn't be used since they were defined to accept a font ID or an `XFontStruct` argument.

To correct this deficiency, X11R5 provides a number of new routines that allow you to calculate the metrics of a particular string. X11R5 also provides routines that return the maximum and minimum combined metrics over all fonts in the font set. Table 4.3 describes the functionality these routines provide.

Table 4.3 X11R5 Font Metric Routines

Name	Description
`XmbTextEscapement()`	Returns the number of pixels in the primary draw direction between the origins of the first character in the multibyte string and the multibyte character that begins at a specified byte offset in the multibyte string. This value (the escapement) is always positive, regardless of character rendering order.
`XwcTextEscapement()`	Returns the number of pixels in the primary draw direction between the origins of the first character in the wide character string and the nth wide character, where n is an argument to the routine. This value (the escapement) is always positive, regardless of character rendering order.
`XmbTextExtents()` `XwcTextExtents()`	Returns two `XRectangles` that describe the overall ink metrics and the overall logical metrics of the supplied multibyte or wide character string.
`XmbTextPerCharExtents()` `XwcTextPerCharExtents()`	Returns two arrays of `XRectangles`. One array contains an `XRectangle` for each character in the multibyte or wide character string — the rectangle describes the ink metrics for that character. The other array contains an `XRectangle` for each character in the string — the rectangle describes the logical metrics for that character. The routine also returns the same pair of `XRectangles` returned by `XmbTextExtents()` or `XwcTextExtents()`.

Table 4.3 X11R5 Font Metric Routines (Continued)

Name	Description
XExtentsOfFontSet()	Returns two XRectangles. One describes the maximum ink extents across all glyphs defined in the font set. The other describes the maximum logical extents across all glyphs defined in the font set.

Notice that many of the font set metric routines use an XRectangle to return the font metrics. Most confusion about font metrics seems to be based on misunderstanding the relationship of the bounding box (an XRectangle) and the character origin contained in the bounding box. Figure 4.1 explains the relationship.

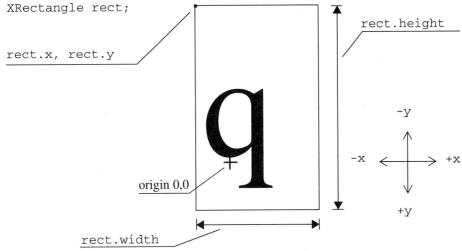

Figure 4.1
Relationship of bounding box to character origin. Notice that rect.y is in the negative *y* direction from the origin. Similarly, rect.x is in the negative *x* direction from the origin. rect.x and rect.y are typically negative numbers for XRectangles used to obtain font set metrics.

4.4.1   Ink metrics vs. logical metrics

Many of the X11R5 internationalized font metric routines provide two types of metrics: *ink metrics* and *logical metrics*.

An ink metric is a measurement that describes the space occupied by the pixels of the characters being measured. A logical metric is a measurement that describes the space occupied by the pixels of the characters being measured *plus* any additional space required to ensure correct separation of characters or lines. Use ink metrics when you want to know the smallest rectangle that encloses the displayed characters. (For example, use ink metrics when determining if an `ExposeEvent` should cause a line of text to be redrawn.) Use logical metrics when determining the amount of space to allow between lines of text data or the amount of space between adjacent characters — the logical metrics include the space designed in by the font designer for interline and intercharacter spacing. For example, if you were designing a text widget, you would use logical metrics to determine how many pixels should separate the baselines of text displayed in the widget.

4.4.2   Example: Calculating Metrics with Font Sets

Suppose that you call `XmbTextExtents()` on the string "y":

```
XmbTextExtents(fontset, "y", 1, &ink, &logical);
```

Both `ink` and `logical` are `XRectangles` that describe a bounding box for the character "y". These bounding boxes and their associated metrics are shown in Figure 4.2. The rectangle height is the height of the bounding box; the rectangle width is the width of the bounding box. The x and y positions of the rectangle identify the upper left corner of the bounding box relative to the origin of the character "y". Therefore, the key font metrics (ascent, descent, left bearing, and right bearing) can be easily calculated.

The ascent is simply the negative y value of the rectangle. For example, the logical ascent is `-logical.y`. This is because the y coordinate of the rectangle is the location of the upper left corner of the bounding box *relative to the character origin*. Since the character origin is below the upper left corner of the bounding box and since X measures positive y moving top to bottom, you must use the negative of the rectangle's y coordinate to get a positive ascent. The descent then must be the rectangle height minus the ascent.

The left bearing is simply the negative x value of the rectangle. For example, the logical left bearing is `-logical.x`. Again, the reason for negating the value is because the rectangle coordinate is relative to the character origin. The origin of the rectangle is in the negative x direction from the character origin as X measures the horizontal direction. The right bearing is then just the rectangle width minus the left bearing.

The metrics for a character (logical or ink) can be calculated quickly from the `XRectangle` returned by an X11R5 font set metric routine:

```
ascent = -rectangle.y
descent = rectangle.height - ascent
left_bearing = -rectangle.x
right_bearing = rectangle.width - left_bearing
```

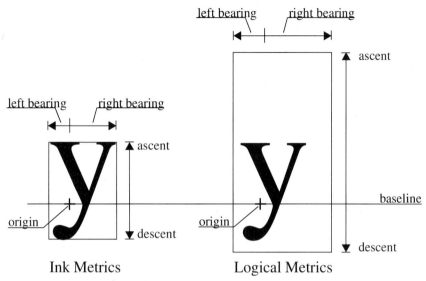

Figure 4.2
Ink metrics compared to logical metrics for the character "y".

4.5 Example Program: Using Font Sets to Draw Characters

Remember the challenging example program introduced in Chapter 3 called "Hello World!"? OK, so it wasn't so challenging. But it is coming back to haunt you now. The following example is a variation of "Hello World!" The program has been modified to output to the X Window System using X11R5 font sets and associated calls. The first thing that should catch your eye is that the simple, three-line, non-internationalized C program has grown as it becomes internationalized and moves to X.

An analysis and explanation of the example program, organized into functional blocks, is provided immediately following the program listing.

```
#include <stdio.h>
#include <X11/Xlib.h>
#include <locale.h>
#include <limits.h>
#include <nl_types.h>

/* Use defines for message catalog sets; this makes
 * your message catalog calls easier to read. */
#define PROMPTS 1
#define ERR_SET 2
#define DEFAULTS 3
```

```
#define MARGIN_X 10
#define MARGIN_Y 10

main(argc, argv)
  int argc;
  char *argv[];
{
  Display *dpy;
  int screen;
  Window win;
  GC gc;
  XGCValues gcv;
  XEvent event;
  XFontSet fs;
  char *program_name=argv[0];
  char greeting[NL_TEXTMAX+1];
  nl_catd my_cat;
  unsigned long gcv_mask;
  char def_basename[]="-*-medium-r-normal-*-24-*";
  char *basename;
  char **missing_charsets;
  int num_missing_charsets=0, i=0;
  char *default_string;
  int x_start, y_start, width, height;
  XRectangle ink_return, logical_return;

  (void)setlocale(LC_ALL, "");
  my_cat=catopen("xhello", NL_CAT_LOCALE);
  if ((dpy=XOpenDisplay(NULL)) == NULL) {
    fprintf(stderr,
            catgets(my_cat, ERR_SET, 1,
                    "%s: cannot open Display.\n"),
            program_name);
    exit(1);
  }

  basename=catgets(my_cat, DEFAULTS, 1, def_basename);
  fs=XCreateFontSet(dpy, basename, &missing_charsets,
                    &num_missing_charsets, &default_string);

  if (!fs){
    fprintf(stderr,
            catgets(my_cat, ERR_SET, 2,
```

```
                             "No font set! Exiting ....\n"));
   exit(1);
}
if(num_missing_charsets > 0){
  fprintf(stderr,
            catgets(my_cat, ERR_SET, 3,
                     "Incomplete font set!\n"));
   for (i=0; i< num_missing_charsets; i++){
     fprintf(stderr,
              catgets(my_cat, ERR_SET, 4,
                       "\tmissing: %s\n"), missing_charsets[i]);
   }
   XFreeStringList(missing_charsets);
}
sprintf(greeting,
          catgets(my_cat, PROMPTS, 1, "Hello World!"));
(void)XmbTextExtents(fs,greeting,strlen(greeting),
                        &ink_return, &logical_return);
width=ink_return.width + (2*MARGIN_X);
height=ink_return.height + (2*MARGIN_Y);
x_start=MARGIN_X;
y_start=MARGIN_Y - ink_return.y;
screen=DefaultScreen(dpy);
win=XCreateSimpleWindow(dpy,RootWindow(dpy,screen),
                          0, 0, width, height, 2,
                          BlackPixel(dpy,screen),
                          WhitePixel(dpy,screen));

gcv.foreground=BlackPixel(dpy,screen);
gcv.background=WhitePixel(dpy,screen);
gcv_mask=GCForeground | GCBackground;
gc=XCreateGC(dpy, win, gcv_mask, &gcv);

XSelectInput(dpy,win, ExposureMask);

XMapWindow(dpy,win);

while(1) {
  XNextEvent(dpy, &event);

  switch (event.type) {
    case Expose:
      if (event.xexpose.count == 0)
        XmbDrawString(dpy, win, fs, gc, x_start, y_start,
```

```
                              greeting, strlen(greeting));
        break;
    }
  }
}
```

As you can see, "Hello World!" has grown in its move to X Windows. However, the I18N portions of the program are relatively small and easy to understand.

In the `#define` block, three symbolic names have been defined: PROMPTS, ERR_SET, and DEFAULTS. The messages in the message catalog are grouped into sets of similar messages. This helps organize a large message catalog. Using well-chosen symbolic names makes the individual message catalog calls easier to understand when debugging your software or when someone else inherits your software.

The program calls `setlocale()` as the first executable statement in the program. This ensures that the locale is loaded and available for any internationalization function that needs it. The program opens the message catalog by calling `catopen()`, immediately following the call to `setlocale()`:

```
  ...
  (void)setlocale(LC_ALL, "");
  my_cat=catopen("xhello", NL_CAT_LOCALE);
```

A robust program would check for errors when loading the locale and when opening the message catalog. In your software, you will have to determine what action should be taken if the user's locale cannot be loaded or if the local language message catalog cannot be opened. You could consider either failure to be a critical error and exit the application. You could issue a warning message to the user and continue operation in the default locale or with the default messages. Or you could create a dialog to inform the user of the error, offering the option to terminate execution or to continue using defaults.

The example program next opens the display, issuing a message from the message catalog if the display cannot be opened. Notice the symbolic name for the message set (ERR_SET) tells you at a glance that the message occurs as the result of an error condition; using symbolic names for set numbers makes your source code more readable:

```
  ...
  if ((dpy=XOpenDisplay(NULL)) == NULL) {
    fprintf(stderr,
            catgets(my_cat, ERR_SET, 1,
                    "%s: cannot open Display.\n"),
            program_name);
    exit(1);
  }
```

The program next calls `catgets()` to retrieve the base name list from the message catalog. Placing the base name list in a message catalog allows it to be customized for different locales. Using the retrieved base name list, the program creates a font set by calling `XCreateFontSet()`. If no font set can be created, the program exits:

```
...
basename=catgets(my_cat, DEFAULTS, 1, def_basename);
fs=XCreateFontSet(dpy, basename, &missing_charsets,
                  &num_missing_charsets, &default_string);

if (!fs){
  fprintf(stderr,
          catgets(my_cat, ERR_SET, 2,
                  "No font set! Exiting ....\n"));
  exit(1);
}
```

Notice also that the program checks to see if any of the fonts needed for the font set are missing; this is indicated by `num_missing_charsets`. If there are missing fonts in the font set, the program warns the user that some characters may not be rendered. If a partial font set is created, `XCreateFontSet()` allocates memory to return a list of `CHARSET_REGISTRY-CHARSET_ENCODING` values identifying which fonts in the font set could not be found. This memory must be freed by calling `XFreeStringList()`, as this part of the example program shows:

```
...
if(num_missing_charsets > 0){
  fprintf(stderr,
          catgets(my_cat, ERR_SET, 3,
                  "Incomplete font set!\n"));
  for (i=0; i< num_missing_charsets; i++){
    fprintf(stderr,
            catgets(my_cat, ERR_SET, 4,
                    "\tmissing: %s\n"), missing_charsets[i]);
  }
  XFreeStringList(missing_charsets);
}
```

Once the font set is created, the application can calculate the size of the window needed to display the message. To do so, the program retrieves the string to be displayed from the message catalog. It then passes the string to `XmbTextExtents()` to obtain the font metrics for the string. This function returns both ink metrics and logical metrics. In this particular case, there is only one line of text to be displayed — there is no need to worry about interline spacing. So the program uses ink metrics to define the size of the string. It also uses predefined margins (X_MARGIN and Y_MARGIN) that provide a little white space around the string. The program calculates the size of the window needed as the size of the ink metrics plus the margins. It then creates the window

```
    . . .
    sprintf(greeting,
            catgets(my_cat, PROMPTS, 1, "Hello World!"));
    (void)XmbTextExtents(fs,greeting,strlen(greeting),
                         &ink_return, &logical_return);
    width=ink_return.width + (2*MARGIN_X);
    height=ink_return.height + (2*MARGIN_Y);
    x_start=MARGIN_X;
    y_start=MARGIN_Y - ink_return.y;
    screen=DefaultScreen(dpy);
    win=XCreateSimpleWindow(dpy,RootWindow(dpy,screen),
                            0, 0, width, height, 2,
                            BlackPixel(dpy,screen),
                            WhitePixel(dpy,screen));
```

The program next creates the GC. Notice that since all rendering is done with the font set created, there is no need to specify a font in the GC. The program specifies only the foreground and background colors when creating the GC.

As in any other X application, the program next selects for the events of interest. Since this program's only purpose is to display a string, the only event of interest is an expose event. The message is rendered by calling XmbDrawString() in the programs expose event loop:

```
    . . .
    switch (event.type) {
      case Expose:
        if (event.xexpose.count == 0)
          XmbDrawString(dpy, win, fs, gc, x_start, y_start,
                        greeting, strlen(greeting));
        break;
    }
```

Figure 4.3 shows a sample output of the program run in different locales with different message catalogs. The only differences among the three sample windows are that the greeting message was changed in the catalog, the base name list was changed in the catalog, and the value of LANG was changed for each execution of the program.

You can obtain similar results. Enter and compile the program. Then, set your environment variables to control access to the message catalog. A useful option is to set NLSPATH to point to a local test directory. For example, you might set NLSPATH as follows:

```
$NLSPATH:./%L/%N.cat:./%N.cat.
```

This allows you to put test message catalogs in the same directory as your test program. It also allows you to use locale-specific subdirectories of your test directory to contain localized test messages.

Depending on what text you put in your message catalog, the results should look something like Figure 4.3.

Figure 4.3
Example output from the internationalized, X Windows version of "Hello World!", using X11R5 font sets, X11R5 internationalized rendering routines, and X11R5 internationalized font metrics routines.

In this example, the frame and title bar decorations are generated automatically by Motif's window manager. The frame, decorations, and shadowing depend on the window manager you use and the resources you set.

4.6 Summary

To internationalize your application, use Table 4.4 to help you choose among the many font handling, font metric and text rendering routines.

Table 4.4 Drawing Internationalized Text

Use these internationalized routines ...	instead of these old X11R4 routines ...
XCreateFontSet()	XLoadQueryFont() XLoadFont()
XmbDrawString()[†] XwcDrawString()	XDrawString() XDrawString16()
XmbDrawImageString()[†] XwcDrawImageString()	XDrawImageString() XDrawImageString16()

Table 4.4 Drawing Internationalized Text (Continued)

Use these internationalized routines ...	instead of these old X11R4 routines ...
XmbDrawText()[†] XwcDrawText()	XDrawText() XDrawText16()
XmbTextEscapement()[†] XwcTextEscapement()	XTextWidth() XTextWidth16()
XmbTextExtents()[†] XwcTextExtents()	XQueryTextExtents() XQueryTextExtents16() XTextExtents() XTextExtents16()
XmbTextPerCharExtents()[†] XwcTextPerCharExtents()	XFontStruct xfs; xfs->per_char[n];
XExtentsOfFontSet()	XFontStruct xfs; xfs->min_bounds; xfs->max_bounds; xfs->ascent; xfs->descent;

†. An Xmb*() routine and its corresponding Xwc*() routine are both internationalized routines. Both will return identical results for a given locale. The only difference is in the data type used for the string argument.

Displaying Local Language Characters with X11R6

T he X11R5 font set mechanism and drawing routines described in the previous chapter are still supported in X11R6. In fact, they still provide the only I18N text rendering and font metric mechanisms for X11R6. Only a few new I18N rendering capabilities are provided with X11R6. And even these new capabilities are of questionable usefulness.

Unless you are writing your software for a platform that has proprietary software for handling bidirectional or context-sensitive languages, skip this chapter and use the X11R5 font set and drawing routines described in Chapter 4.

5.1 Overview

Drawing text with X11R6 differs from drawing text with X11R5 in two fundamental ways:

- X11R6 provides a more object-oriented model for drawing text. In this model your software opens a *method,*[1] called an output method, which is software that actually draws the text. Your software controls the text that is drawn and the attributes of the text drawn by manipulating an object called an output context.
- X11R6 provides new routines that allow your software to ask if the current version of the X library supports rendering of bidirectional languages or context-sensitive languages.

---

1. The term *method* here is used in the same way method is used in object-oriented programming. A method is software that performs a function on behalf of your application. It may be in-line code within the X library, or it may be a separate server process that is shared by many applications. The actual implementation is transparent to the software that accesses the method.

For context-sensitive languages, an individual character may be drawn with any of several shapes. The correct shape for a character depends on the characters that surround it. A single character code may be rendered with one of several different shapes depending on the characters that surround it. With *implicit shaping*, the shape of the character is determined by examining the code values of the characters surrounding a particular character. In *explicit shaping*, the shape of a character is determined by an explicit flag or escape sequence that accompanies the character. Software that performs character shaping usually examines the character in context and converts the coded character to a new value that causes the glyph for the correct shape to be used from the font.

For bidirectional languages, the direction of a segment of text can be determined either *explicitly* (by means of some added data, such as an escape sequence or flag) or *implicitly*. When determined implicitly, the direction of a segment of text is divined by examining character code values of the characters of the segment and the character code values of the characters surrounding the segment. When determined explicitly, directional flags are embedded in the text data; each flag indicates the rendering direction for the associated segment of text.

<u>Note</u>

X11R6 does not require an implementation of the X library to support rendering of bidirectional or context-sensitive languages. The sample implementation of X11R6 supplied by the X Consortium does not support rendering such languages. You should also note that X library support alone is not sufficient to properly render text for these languages. To correctly render bidirectional and context-sensitive languages, your software needs additional software that performs character shaping for context-sensitive languages and reorders text correctly for screen display of bidirectional languages. (In bidirectional languages, the order in which characters are stored in memory is usually not the same as the order in which characters are displayed on the screen.) No standard software exists today that performs these services.

Because the X11R6 specification does not state the behavior of the library for implementations that support bidirectional or context-sensitive languages, this book only describes how you use the new standard X11R6 library interfaces. It does not attempt to show you how to write software for systems where the implementation of the X library supports bidirectional or context-sensitive languages.

The new X11R6 rendering model is based on the concept of an output method (data type XOM), and an output context (data type XOC). An output method is locale-specific software that knows how to draw text according to the locale. An output context contains the data (such as the font set) needed by an output method to draw the text. Your software draws text and calculates metrics using the same routines it used with X11R5, such as `XmbDrawImageString()`. However, your software passes an XOC to the routine instead of an `XFontSet`. This is based on the X11R6 specification, section 13.7:

> *An XOC can be used anywhere an XFontSet can be used, and vice versa; XFontSet is retained for compatibility with previous releases. The concepts of output methods and output contexts include broader, more generalized abstraction than font set, supporting complex and more intelligent text display, and dealing not only with multiple fonts but also with context dependencies.*

Confused? Figure 5.1 should help. It shows two partial sample programs — one using an X11R5 font set, and the other using an X11R6 output method and output context. The programs produce identical results. Why use output methods and output contexts? The only real reason to use them is that they may make it easier for your software to take advantage of future standard X11 internationalized rendering capabilities or vendor proprietary implementations of bidirectional and context-sensitive languages.

Sample X11R5 Program

```
main(argc,argv)
   int argc;
   char* argv[];
{
   (void)setlocale(LC_ALL,"");
   ...

   fs=XCreateFontSet(dpy,basename,
      &missing_charsets,
      &missing_cs_count,
      &default_string);
   ...
   XmbTextExtents(fs,buf,
      strlen(buf),&ink_return,
      &logical_return);
   XmbDrawImageString(dpy,win,fs,
      gc,x,y,buf,strlen(buf));
   ...
   XFreeFontSet(dpy,fs);
```

Sample X11R6 Program

```
main(argc,argv)
   int argc;
   char* argv[];
{
   (void)setlocale(LC_ALL,"");
   ...
   om=XOpenOM(dpy,NULL,NULL,NULL);
   oc=XCreateOC(om,XNBaseFontName,
                 basename,NULL);
   ...

   XmbTextExtents(oc,buf,
      strlen(buf),&ink_return,
      logical_return);
   XmbDrawImageString(dpy,win,oc,
      gc,x,y,buf,strlen(buf));
   ...
   XDestroyOC(oc);
   XCloseOM(om);
```

Figure 5.1
Comparison of X11R5 and X11R6 sample programs for internationalized text rendering.

With X11R6, your software draws text and calculates font metrics in exactly the same way that it did with X11R5. The only real differences with X11R6 are in the way the font set is created, in the way errors in font set creation are detected, and in the additional information available to your software identifying the capabilities of the X library it is using. These differences are discussed in the remainder of this chapter.

5.2 Connecting to an X Output Method

Your application connects to an output method in one of two ways:

- You can explicitly connect to an output method by calling XOpenOM(). If there are multiple output methods supported for a locale on your system, a vendor defined *modifier* can be used to control which XOM is returned by XOpenOM().
- You can establish a connection to the locale's default XOM by calling XCreateFontSet(). The X11R6 implementation of XCreateFontSet() creates a connection to the locale's default output method automatically for you.

A modifier is a string that is used to modify the default behavior of a locale-dependent function. X modifiers are set by passing the modifier as an argument to the XSetLocaleModifiers() function or by setting the XMODIFIERS environment variable. X11R6 does not define standard modifiers that affect the output method. However, individual X library vendors may define modifiers used by their implementation of the X library.

Your software should connect to an output method by calling XOpenOM() since this allows the user to control which output method is used when multiple output methods are supported.

When your software has finished using an output method, you can use XCloseOM() to disconnect from the output method.

5.3 Obtaining Information from the Output Method

Table 5.1 lists and describes the functions you can use to connect to an output method and to obtain information from the output method.

Table 5.1 X11R6 Output Method Functions

Name	Description
XOpenOM()	Establish a connection to an output method, returning an XOM.
XCloseOM()	Closes a specified output method.
XSetOMValues()	Controls the output method by setting properties or features of an output method. There are no standard values defined by X11R6 that can be set.
XGetOMValues()	Allows your software to query the output method for certain information and capabilities. See Table 5.2 for a list and description of the information that can be queried.
XDisplayOfOM()	Returns the display associated with the output method — the display that was passed to XOpenOM().
XLocaleOfOM()	Returns a vendor defined string identifying the locale associated with the output method.

Note that the lack of standard values that can be set for an output method makes the function XSetOMValues() almost useless. Your X library vendor may define values that can be set for its particular implementation of XSetOMValues(). Check the man page for this function for more information. If your X library vendor does define output method values that can be set, coding those values into your software will require software changes when porting the software to other platforms.

Table 5.2 describes the standard X11R6 output method values your software can query from an XOM. Your software can query them by calling XGetOMValues(). Note that the values *cannot* be set with XSetOMValues().

Table 5.2 X11R6 Output Method Values

Name	Description
XNRequiredCharSet	Querying for this value returns a structure of type XOMCharSetList. This structure contains a pointer to a list of CHARSET_REGISTRY-CHARSET_ENCODING fields that *may* be used for creating font sets for the current locale. (Despite the name, not all fonts in the list are necessarily required to render characters in the current locale.) The list should not be modified or freed by the caller. It will be freed automatically by XCloseOM(). Until freed, the X library will not modify the value of the list.
XNQueryOrientation	Querying for this value returns a structure of type XOMOrientation. This identifies the default *global orientation* of text when drawn with the output method. Figure 5.2 shows the possible orientations. You must free the memory for the returned value by calling XFree(); this also frees the contents of the structure.
XNDirectionalDependentDrawing	Querying for this value returns a Boolean. If the return value is True, the implementation of the rendering functions supports *implicit* handling of directional text (such as Hebrew and Arabic). If it does support directional text, the implementation of the internationalized drawing routines in the X library internally reorders the string as necessary before rendering. It is up to the application to decide how much text must be passed into a drawing routine for it to correctly reorder the string for display.
XNContextualDrawing	Querying for this value returns a Boolean. If the return value is True, the implementation of the rendering functions support *implicit character shaping* (explained below) for context-sensitive languages (such as Thai and Arabic). If it does, the drawing routine selects the glyph shape for each coded character passed to it. It is up to the application to decide how much text must be passed into a drawing routine for it to correctly determine the shape of each glyph in the string to be drawn.

XGetOMValues() allows your software to determine the default global orientation for text data in the current locale. For example, it identifies if the text is written from left to right within a line of text or if it is written right to left within a line of text. The orientation of the output method is the default orientation. It can be overridden by the orientation of the output context used to communicate with the output method. Figure 5.2 illustrates four of the five possible values that may be returned when querying the output method for text orientations.

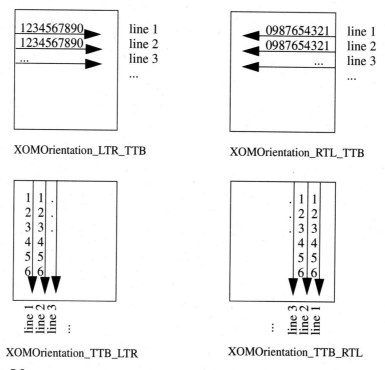

Figure 5.2
This illustration shows the sequence of characters within a line of text, and the sequence of lines of text within a document for each of the possible text orientation values. The arrows indicate the direction of text within a single line of text.

The boxes in Figure 5.2 represent pages of text. The arrows in each box show the direction of text within a single line of text. The line numbers show the sequence of lines within a body of text. Most of the orientations are self-explanatory. XOMOrientation_Context is an orientation that is not easily illustrated, and needs a little explanation. For this orientation, the global direction is determined by the direction of the first character in a string. That is, when XOMOrientation_Context is set, the global orientation is not determined until the first call to an I18N sensitive rendering or metric function. The orientation of the first character in that call determines the global orientation for all future calls — unless the global orientation is change by calling XSetOCValues().

5.3.1   Example: Connecting to and Querying an Output Method

The following example shows how to connect to an output method and how to query for the various information obtainable from the output method.

```c
/* This program allows you to determine which optional X11R6
 * rendering functionality is supported on a platform. Because
 * the program is simply a tool for you, it does not use
 * message catalogs for the many strings of data displayed.
 * If this program was meant to be localized, all text currently
 * hard coded in printf() statements would be retrieved from a
 * message catalog. */
#include <stdio.h>
#include <X11/Xlib.h>
#include <locale.h>
#include <limits.h>
#include <nl_types.h>

/* Use defines for message catalog sets; this makes
 * your message catalog calls easier to read. */
#define PROMPTS 1
#define ERR_SET 2
#define DEFAULTS 3
main(argc, argv)
int argc;
char *argv[];
{
  Display *dpy;
  nl_catd my_cat;
  XOMCharSetList charsets;
  XOMOrientation dirs;
  XOM om;
  Boolean directional, contextual;
  char* loc_of_om;
  char* err;
  int i;

  (void)setlocale(LC_ALL, "");
  my_cat=catopen("xom_test", NL_CAT_LOCALE);
  if ((dpy=XOpenDisplay(NULL)) == NULL) {
```

```
        (void) fprintf(stderr,
                    catgets(my_cat, ERR_SET, 1,
                            "%s: cannot open Display.\n"),
                    program_name);
        exit(1);
    }
/* Cause user defined modifiers to be read, then
 * connect to an output method. */
    if (XSetLocaleModifiers("") == NULL){
        (void)fprintf(stderr, catgets(my_cat,ERR_SET,1,
                        "Warning: cannot set locale modifiers.\n"));
        exit(1);
    }
    om=XOpenOM(dpy,NULL,NULL,NULL);
/* Query for the locale name associated with the output method. */
    loc_of_om=XLocaleOfOM(om);
    printf(catgets(my_cat,PROMPTS,1,
                "Locale of the output method is %s\n."),
            loc_of_om);
    /* Query for rendering info from the output method. */
    err=XGetOMValues(om,XNRequiredCharSet, &charsets,
                        XNDirectionalDependentDrawing,&directional,
                    XNContextualDrawing, &contextual,
                    XNQueryOrientation, &dirs, NULL);
    if(!err){

    /* Report support for bidirectional and context-sensitive
     * text by the X library. */
    if(directional)
        printf(catgets(my_cat,PROMPTS,2,
            "X library supports directional text!\n"));
    if(contextual)
        printf(catgets(my_cat,PROMPTS,3,
                "X library supports context-sensitive text!\n"));

    /* Print the CHARSET_REGISTRY-CHARSET_ENCODING pairs that
     * will be used when creating a font set for the current
     * locale. */
    printf(catgets(my_cat,PROMPTS,4,
                "List of CHARSET_REGISTRY-CHARSET_ENCODING:\n"));
    for(i=0; i < charsets.charset_count; i++)
        printf(catgets(my_cat,PROMPTS,5,"\t%s\n"),
            charset.charset_list[i]);
```

```
/* Print the default orientation of text for the
 * current locale. */
for (i=0; i < dirs.num_orientation; i++){
  if(dirs[i]->orientation==XOMOrientation_LTR_TTB){
    printf("A line of text is written LTR.\n");
    printf("Lines are written horizontally.\n");
    printf("Lines of text proceed top to bottom.\n");
    break;
  }
  if(dirs[i]->orientation==XOMOrientation_RTL_TTB){
    printf("A line of text is written RTL.\n");
    printf("Lines are written horizontally.\n");
    printf("Lines of text proceed top to bottom.\n");
    break;
  }
  if(dirs[i]->orientation==XOMOrientation_TTB_LTR){
    printf("Text is written vertically.\n");
     printf("The first column of text is on the left.\n");
     printf("Subsequent columns proceed to the right.\n");
    break;
  }
  if(dirs[i]->orientation==XOMOrientation_TTB_RTL){
    printf("Text is written vertically.\n");
     printf("The first column of text is on the right.\n");
     printf("Subsequent columns proceed to the left.\n");
    break;
  }
  if(dirs[i]->orientation==XOMOrientation_Context){
     printf("Direction of a line of text is determined by \
the first character of text.\n");
     break;
  }
 }
 }
}
```

5.4 Creating an Output Context

There are two ways to create an output context:

- You can explicitly call XCreateOC() to create the output context. When calling the function, you must identify which output method will be controlled by the output context. In addition, you may pass XCreateOC() a variable length argument list of output context values. These values specify the behavior of the output method when you pass the output context to a I18N drawing or text metric function.

- You can create a font set by calling `XCreateFontSet()`. This opens a connection to the default output method and returns an `XFontSet`. The X11R6 specification states that an `XFontSet` is an opaque type equivalent to the type `XOC`. You can think of an `XFontSet` as an `XOC`, with default output context values, that is associated with the locale's default output method.

When your software no longer needs an output context, it should be destroyed. An output context created with `XCreateOC()` should be destroyed by calling `XDestroyOC()`. An output context created with `XCreateFontSet()` should be destroyed with `XFreeFontSet()`. If for some reason your software isn't sure how the output context was created, it can query for an output context value (`XNOMAutomatic`) which indicates how the output context was created.

5.4.1   Calling XCreateOC()

`XCreateOC()` has the following syntax:

```
XOC XCreateOC(om, ...)
XOM om;
```

The ellipses (`...`) in the syntax definition indicate that a variable length list of arguments can be passed to `XCreateOC()`. The possible output context values that you may pass to `XCreateOC()` are described in Table 5.3. At a minimum, you must pass an `XOM` and a base font name list when calling `XCreateOC()`. `XCreateOC()` uses the base font name to create a font set for the output context. If not even a single font can be found for the font set, `XCreateOC()` returns NULL; an output context is not created.

5.5 Querying and Changing an Output Context

You use an output context to control the behavior of the output method. For example, every output context includes a font set. The output context controls the output method by telling the output method which font set to use when drawing text.

Occasionally, you may want to obtain some information about how the output method will behave with a particular output context. X11R6 provides the `XGetOCValues()` routine, allowing you to query the output context to determine its current values. Similarly, you may want to modify the behavior of the output method. This can be done by setting values for the output context with the routine `XSetOCValues()`.

5.5.1   XOC Values

Table 5.3 lists the `XOC` values defined in X11R6. It also shows you which values must be specified with `XCreateOC()`, which values have a default value if not specified, which values can be changed with XSetOCValues(), and which values can be queried with XGetOCValues(). In each case, it shows you the data type associated with the value. It also shows if you can get the same information or behavior using a different interface. Following Table 5.3 is a description of each of the XOC values.

Table 5.3 X Output Context Values

XOC value	Control	Data type	Alternative interface
XNBaseFontName	C-G	char*	XCreateFontSet()
XNMissingCharSet	G	XOMCharSetList*	XCreateFontSet()
XNDefaultString	G	char*	XCreateFontSet()
XNOrientation	D-S-G	XOrientation*	(none)
XNResourceName	S-G	char*	(none)
XNResourceClass	S-G	char*	(none)
XNFontInfo	G	XOMFontInfo*	XFontsOfFontSet()
XNOMAutomatic	G	Boolean*	(none)

Key	Meaning
C	The value *must* be specified when creating the XOC with XCreateOC().
D	If not specified, the value is set to a default value inherited from the output method.
S	The value can be set by calling XSetOCValues().
G	The value may be queried by calling XGetOCValues().

5.5.1.1   XNBaseFontName

XNBaseFontName is a list of base font names used to create the font set contained in the XOC. The list is a null-terminated string, containing a comma separated list of base font names. The same rules that govern a base name list passed to XCreateFontSet() apply to the XNBaseFontName XOC value.

When querying for XNBaseFontName, the memory containing the base font name list is owned by the X library. You should not free or alter the contents of the memory.

5.5.1.2   XNMissingCharSet

XNMissingCharSet identifies which (if any) CHARSET_REGISTRY-CHARSET_ENCODING pairs needed to create a font set could not be found. If there are no missing values, the charset_list element of the XOMCharSetList structure is set to NULL and the charset_count element is set to zero. Otherwise, charset_list is set to a list of one or more null-terminated strings and charset_count is set to the number of null-terminated strings. Each string contains the CHARSET_REGISTRY-CHARSET_ENCODING of a required font that could not be located when creating the font set for the XOC.

The memory associated with charset_list is owned by the X library. You should not modify or free this memory. The memory is freed when you destroy the output context by calling XDestroyOC(). Until freed, the X library does not modify the contents of charset_list.

5.5.1.3   XNDefaultString

When you use an XOC in which all fonts needed for the font set could not be found, some characters in the locale cannot be drawn. In such cases, the internationalized drawing functions draw a default string in place of the locale characters for which no font is available. You can query for this default string using the XNDefaultString output context value. You might want to do this in order to calculate the font metrics of characters drawn with the default string.

If the result of the query is the empty string (""), then no characters are drawn for characters for which fonts are missing. If you use a text metric function (such as XmbTextExtents()) on these characters, each character's escapement is zero.

The memory associated with the default string is owned by the X library. You should not modify or free this memory. The memory is freed when you destroy the output context by calling XDestroyOC(). Until freed, the X library does not modify the default string.

5.5.1.4   XNOrientation

XNOrientation identifies the orientation of text when drawn with the output context. The orientation is of type XOrientation. The possible values are illustrated in Figure 5.2. If you do not specify the orientation when you create the XOC, the XOC inherits a default orientation from the output method. This default orientation is the orientation returned by a call to XGetOMValues() using the XNQueryOrientation value.

Contrary to what you might expect, changing the orientation of the XOC does not change the prime drawing direction for the X library drawing functions. The X11R6 specification says that the prime drawing direction is left to right. So what does the orientation do? If the implementation supports implicit directionality, the orientation tells the implementation how to reorder the string before rendering it in the prime drawing direction. That's because the convention for most systems is to store text data in memory in the order in which it is typed or spoken — sometimes called *keyboard order*, or *phonetic order*. Figure 5.3 shows a string stored in memory that is drawn on the screen from right to left using the locale's orientation XOMOrientation_RTL_TTB. In the figure, the string contains some characters in the locale that are drawn from right to left; these are the characters represented by alphabetic characters (A-F). These characters are mixed together in a string with other characters that are drawn from left to right; the left to right characters are represented by numeric characters (1-3). This is a common situation with languages such as Arabic and Hebrew.

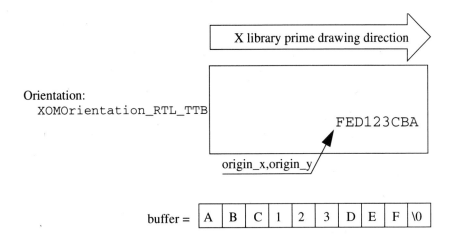

```
XmbDrawString(dpy, gc, fontset, origin_x, origin_y,
              buffer, strlen(buffer));
```

Figure 5.3
When XNOrientation indicates right to left in an implementation that supports implicit directionality, the implementation of the X library routine "reorders" the characters before drawing in the prime drawing direction.

5.5.1.5   XNResourceName and XNResourceClass

XNResourceName and XNResourceClass specify the full name and class used to set and query output context values set via resources. You should use these values as prefixes for name and class when setting or looking up resources that may vary from one output context to another.

Note that the output method values described in Table 5.2 on page 93 cannot be set as resources.

When querying for the resource name and resource class, the memory returned by XGetOCValues() is owned by the X library. You should not modify or free it. The memory is freed when you destroy the output context via a call to XDestroyOC() or when you change the associated value by calling XSetOCValues().

5.5.1.6   XNFontInfo

XNFontInfo is a structure providing you with information about the fonts in the font set of the output context. The structure has the following definition:

```
typedef struct {
    int num_font;
    XFontStruct **font_struct_list;
    char **font_name_list;
} XOMFontInfo;
```

The structure element `num_font` identifies the number of fonts described in the structure. `font_struct_list` is a list of X font structures that comprise the font set. `font_name_list` is a list of null-terminated font names. The order of `font_struct_list` corresponds to the order of `font_name_list`. So the second entry in `font_name_list` is the font name of the second entry in `font_struct_list`.

When you create the XOC, the fonts needed for the font set are not necessarily loaded from the server. An implementation of the X library may choose to delay loading a font in the font set until it is needed for drawing or to compute text metrics. Therefore, you should not count on the existence of `per_char` metrics in an individual `XFontStruct` in `font_struct_list`.

Never free the `XOMFontInfo` struct yourself. The structure is freed when the XOC is destroyed.

5.5.1.7   XNOMAutomatic

`XNOMAutomatic` is a boolean that identifies if the XOC was created by `XCreateOC()` or by `XCreateFontSet()`. You need to know this so that you can destroy the output context correctly. If `OMAutomatic` is `True`, the output context was created by calling `XCreateFontSet()`; it should be destroyed by calling `XFreeFontSet()`. If `OMAutomatic` is `False`, the output context was created by `XCreateOC()`; it should be destroyed by calling `XDestroyOC()`.

5.6 Using an Output Context

You use an X11R6 output context in exactly the same way you use an X11R5 font set. For example, with X11R5 you pass a font set to `XmbDrawImageString()`. With X11R6, you pass an output context to `XmbDrawImageString()` instead of a font set. Wherever a font set can be used in a drawing function or a text metric function, an output context can be used in its place. The X Consortium did not even change the signature or syntax of the internationalized text functions in X11R6 to accommodate output contexts. For example, the specification for `XmbDrawImageString()` still says that it requires an `XFontSet` argument, not an output context. Use the output context exactly as you would a font set. Because there is no difference between the use of font sets and output contexts, the internationalized "Hello World!" example is not reproduced here using output contexts.

5.7 Summary

To internationalize your application, use Table 5.4 to help you choose among the many font handling, font metric and text rendering routines.

Table 5.4 Drawing Internationalized Text

Use these internationalized routines ...	instead of these old X11R4 routines ...
XOpenOM()	XLoadQueryFont()
XCreateOC()	XLoadFont()
XmbDrawString()[†]	XDrawString()
XwcDrawString()	XDrawString16()
XmbDrawImageString()[†]	XDrawImageString()
XwcDrawImageString()	XDrawImageString16()
XmbDrawText()[†]	XDrawText()
XwcDrawText()	XDrawText16()
XmbTextEscapement()[†]	XTextWidth()
XwcTextEscapement()	XTextWidth16()
XmbTextExtents()[†]	XQueryTextExtents()
XwcTextExtents()	XQueryTextExtents16()
	XTextExtents()
	XTextExtents16()
XmbTextPerCharExtents()[†]	XFontStruct xfs;
XwcTextPerCharExtents()	xfs->per_char[n];
XExtentsOfFontSet()	XFontStruct xfs;
	xfs->min_bounds;
	xfs->max_bounds;
	xfs->ascent;
	xfs->descent;

†. An Xmb*() routine and its corresponding Xwc*() routine are both internationalized routines. Both will return identical results for a given locale. The only difference is in the data type used for the string argument.

Keyboard Input: Background and Overview

In the next few chapters you will learn how to generate characters encoded in the code set of the user's locale from the keyboard. This chapter provides some basic background, defining the concepts and terms you need to understand how to generate characters from the keyboard in internationalized X-based software. In this chapter, you will learn what happens when a user presses a key on the keyboard — what the X server does and what your software should do. You will also find out the relationship between your keyboard, the X server's keymap, and the coded character generated. You will read about a variety of ways that users expect to interact with their keyboard to generate the characters of their language.

6.1 When a Key Is Pressed ...

For X Window System based graphical user interface software, the X server plays two key roles. The first is to manage resources, such as fonts, atoms, window IDs, and properties. The second is to funnel each user action (each mouse movement, mouse button press, key press, and key release) to clients connected to that server that have expressed interest in the information. Software interested in knowing about user actions tells the server it is interested in one or more particular types of *events* that occur in a specific window; it does this by calling XSelectInput(). Then, when an action occurs (for example, the user presses a key or moves the mouse), the server generates an XEvent. An XEvent is a structure containing

- a field identifying what kind of event occurred,
- a field identifying the display where the event occurred,

- a field identifying the window[1] where the event occurred, and
- event specific data.

For internationalized keyboard input, you will be primarily concerned with events of type XKeyEvent. The event specific data provided with each XKeyEvent includes a *key code* — a device-specific value that identifies which physical key on the keyboard was pressed. You can think of the key code (data type KeyCode) as a value that identifies the row and column on the keyboard of the key that was pressed. Additionally, the event includes a value that indicates what *modifiers* (such as Shift or Control) were active when the event occurred. While perhaps interesting, the device key code and modifiers associated with the event aren't much help in finding out the character the user wanted to enter. Neither your software nor the X server has any way to know what coded character the user was trying to enter. To convert an XKeyEvent into a coded character, you need an *input method*.

6.2 Input Methods

An input method (IM) is a procedure, a macro, or sometimes a separate process that converts KeyPress events into a character encoded in the code set of the current locale. For each locale supported by X11R5 and X11R6 on your system, at least one input method is provided — though a vendor often provides several input methods for a locale. Each input method has its own paradigm for which combination of key presses result in a given character. Users often get extremely attached to a particular input method — touch typists become used to typing a specific set of key sequences to generate a specific character. This is similar to the attachment some people feel about their chosen editor or word processor. Some people are devout vi users while others believe that emacs is the only editor to use. User attachments to a particular input method are often no less strong.

6.2.1 Background

Prior to the addition of input methods in the X11R5 specifications, applications were pretty much on their own to convert a KeyPress event into a coded character. X11R4 provided some limited help by supplying XLookupString() — a routine that converts a single KeyPress event into an ISO 8859.1 coded character. The routine is not useful for developing internationalized software since it produces only ISO 8859.1 coded characters. But even if that limit were removed, the routine still has one fundamental problem. It assumes that for each key pressed on the keyboard, a single character should be generated. This assumption was fine for languages needing a small number of characters. A typical keyboard has around 100 keys, nearly half of which are dedicated to non-character generating functions (such as the Escape key, the Enter key, and the Backspace key). That leaves about

---

1. Actually, it is set to a window that is convenient to toolkit dispatchers, but for practical purposes you can think of it as the window where the event occurred.

50 keys, plus combinations with the Shift key and the Meta or Alt key, to generate all the characters needed for the user's language. While many European languages can be squeezed onto 50 keys, the tens of thousands of characters needed for Asian languages cannot.

Further, even European language users have come to expect that certain characters needed for their language are generated by typing combinations of key sequences. These expectations may have been set from using physical terminal devices that had their own mechanisms for character generation built in to them. Or they may have come from using personal computers that also have their own mechanisms for generating characters.

6.2.2   Keyboard Interaction Models

The ways that users type on their keyboards can be classified into three general models: simple input, compose or dead-key input, and complex input. The following descriptions of these models will help you understand how users expect to interact with the keyboard in order to enter characters of their language. You need this information to understand how to use the input method routines developed for X11R5 and expanded for X11R6.

6.2.2.1   Simple input model

In the simple input model, the character that the user wants is engraved on the key cap. Pressing the key causes the character to be generated. Pressing the Shift key in combination with the key causes the uppercase version of the character to be generated. For example, if the keyboard has a key engraved with the letter A-diaeresis (Ä), pressing that key generates a-diaeresis (ä). Pressing the Shift key in combination with the A-diaeresis key generates A-diaeresis (Ä). It's a simple model — one key press generates one character.

6.2.2.2   Compose or dead-key input model

In this model, some characters are generated by pressing a sequence of keys. For example, suppose the keyboard has a diaeresis key. Using the compose input model, the user might first press and release the diaeresis key, then press and release the A key. When the diaeresis key is pressed, the cursor doesn't advance. Instead, the next key pressed generates its normal character and is then modified by having a diaeresis added. In other words, when the user presses the diaeresis key, it appears to have no affect. However, if the user then presses the A key, an a-diaeresis (ä) is generated.

The actual mechanism used varies from vendor to vendor. Some vendor models dictate that an accent mark (such as diaeresis, grave, acute, or cedilla) be typed before typing the character that is modified by the accent. Other vendor models require the user to press a multikey while simultaneously pressing the accent key and the key for the character modified by the accent. Still other models have the user press a deadkey in combination with the accent key. This tells the input method to combine the accent with the character that follows. For most of these models, there is no visual feedback to the user that a character is being composed. For example, when the user presses the diaeresis key, typically nothing is displayed at all until the next character is entered.

Most vendors support multiple compose or dead-key models; they do this to ease the transition to their systems for users coming from other vendor platforms.

As a developer of internationalized software, you needn't care which dead-key or compose model is used to generate characters. You only need to be aware that sometimes a user presses multiple keys on the keyboard before a character is finally produced. And you must avoid building assumptions into your software about the order in which keys are pressed to generate a character. The input method APIs described later in this chapter allow you to do this.

6.2.2.3   Complex input models

For languages with large numbers of characters, even dead-key or compose input models are not sufficient for generating all the characters needed for the user's language. These languages typically use very complex input models in which several keys are pressed just to enter one character. It is not uncommon to type ten or more keys just to generate one character. Complex input methods have special requirements that impact the way you write your internationalized software. To understand these requirements, you need to understand how users interact with complex input methods.

In complex input models, the user presses a special key to tell the input method that he is ready to generate a character. Next, the user types a sequence of keys that help the input method determine which character the user wants to enter. This may be a phonetic representation of the way the character is pronounced, it may be a series of keys that identify the brush strokes a user would make when drawing the character by hand, or it may even be the hexadecimal code value for the character. Regardless, the input method displays the intermediate form of the character being generated as the user types. This is displayed in an area or window called the *preedit area*.

A complex input method typically displays some indication of its current status (for example, the input method is active, the input method is in phonetic input mode, or the input method is in stroke mode). The status is displayed in a window or area called the *status area*.

When the user is ready to finally generate the character, a key press tells the input method to convert what has been typed so far into a character, if possible. If the input method cannot generate a unique character, or if it simply wants to confirm the character before passing to the application, it may display the choices in the status area or in the preedit area. Some input methods display the choices in a separate window called the *auxiliary area*.

It is easiest to understand these complex input methods by following an example. Figure 6.1 shows how a user enters Japanese Kanji characters into an application using one vendor's phonetic input method. While the keys pressed and the user interaction will be different for different languages and for different input methods, the general sequence of events applies to nearly all complex input methods. The figure contains a series of screen images during the input process. Each screen sample is numbered. The paragraphs following the figure help you understand what you are seeing in each numbered screen image.

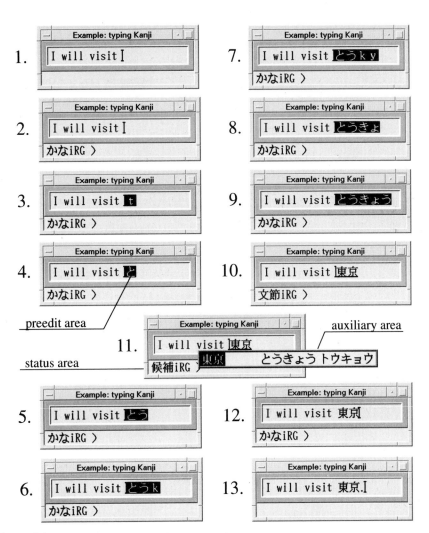

Figure 6.1
Example of using complex input method.

1. The user has typed English characters into a text widget and is preparing to start generating the Kanji characters for name of the city, Tokyo. In this case, the input method utilizes both a simple input model (for typing ASCII characters) and a complex input model (for typing Kanji characters).

2. The user pressed the Kanji start key, indicating that she wants to start preediting (to type in Kanji characters). The label in the diagram for step 11 shows the status area, indicating that the user is preediting characters.

3. The user now types out the name Tokyo phonetically. The phonetic representation of Kanji presented in ASCII characters is called Romaji. The Romaji for Tokyo is "tou-kyou". So the user begins typing Romaji for Tokyo by typing first the letter "t". After typing "t", it is displayed in the preedit area.

4. The user continues typing the phonetic representation by typing "o". With this input method, as soon as a full syllable is typed in (such as "to"), the syllable is immediately converted to Hiragana, a form of phonetic Japanese used to write words of Japanese origin. The Hiragana for the syllable "to" is displayed in the preedit area.

5. The user continues typing the phonetic representation by typing "u". Since "u" is Romaji for a Hiragana character, it too is immediately converted to a Hiragana and displayed next to the Hiragana for "to."

6. The user continues typing the phonetic representation by typing "k". Notice that the letter k is displayed next to the Hiragana for "u" in the preedit area.

7. The user types the letter "y". Again, the preedit area reflects what has been typed in so far.

8. The user types the letter "o," forming Romaji that is immediately converted into two Hiragana by the input method. The preedit area now contains the Hiragana for "to," "u," and "kyo."

9. Now the user completes typing the Romaji for Tokyo by typing "u". As before, the Romaji "u" is immediately converted to a Hiragana character. The preedit area now contains the full Romaji for Tokyo (toukyou), converted into Hiragana.

10. Next, the user presses the Convert key, a key that tells the input method to convert the contents of the preedit area into Kanji. This particular input method searches its databases and displays in the preedit area the last Kanji entered into the input method that were pronounced "toukyou."

11. If the Kanji displayed were not the representation desired, the user would press the Convert key again, causing the input method to display a list of all Japanese characters (Kanji, Hiragana, and Katakana) that are pronounced "toukyou." Though the Kanji displayed in step 10 is correct, the Convert key was pressed here to illustrate the auxiliary area in which multiple choices are sometimes displayed by an input method.

12. The user selects the correct Kanji for the "toukyou" that is the capital of Japan. The input method finally passes the Kanji characters to the application.

13. The user presses the Kanji stop key, to quit generating Kanji. Notice the change in the status area. The user types the ASCII "." to complete the sentence.

6.2.3   Input Method Styles

Each input method has its own set of styles for how the preedit area, status area, and auxiliary area are displayed to the user. It is important for you to understand these different styles. Each style implies a different amount of work for the application using that input method. As the developer of internationalized software that must talk to these complex input methods, you will have to choose which style(s) you are willing to support.

6.2.3.1   Preedit styles

The location of the preedit area can vary greatly. Human factors experts say that the preedit area should be as close as possible to the location where the generated characters are eventually placed. This allows the user to see the context of the characters being generated with the input method.

There are four commonly used locations or *styles* for the preedit area. A complex input method may support more than one preedit style, allowing users to choose which style best fits their needs. The common names for the preedit styles are *root*, *off-the-spot*, *over-the-spot* and *on-the-spot*, where *spot* refers to the location of the text cursor or the point where the composed character is eventually displayed. These are described in Table 6.1 and illustrated in Figure 6.2.

Table 6.1 Preedit Styles

Style	Description
root	The preedit window is displayed somewhere on the root window. It may or may not be anywhere near the window where the generated characters will be placed.
off-the-spot	The preedit window is attached to the application's main window, but not necessarily the child window where the generated characters will be placed.
over-the-spot	The preedit window is laid over the top of the application window. The location for the preedit window is at the cursor location, or the *x,y* location in the application window where the generated character will be placed. The preedit window may obscure some portions of text in the application window.
on-the-spot	The *application draws the preedit data* on behalf of the input method. The application moves any existing characters out of the way to make room for the preedit data, making sure that none of the existing characters in the window are obscured by the preedit data.

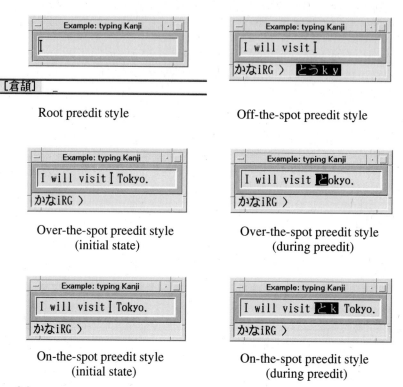

Figure 6.2
Four different preedit styles are supported by X11: root, off-the-spot, over-the-spot, and on-the-spot.

X11R5 uses the data type `XIMStyle` to identify a particular preedit style. Each preedit style has a unique `XIMStyle` value; each places special requirements for data that you must send to the input method when using that style. The following sections describe this data in detail and show you how and when to communicate the data for each preedit and status style.

6.2.3.2   Status styles

As with the preedit area, the location of the status area can vary greatly. There are three locations or styles for the status area: root, off-the-spot, and on-the-spot. A complex input method may support more than one status style, allowing users to choose which style best fits their needs. Table 6.2 describes the various status styles.

Table 6.2 Status Styles

Style	Description
root	The status window is displayed somewhere on the root window. It may or may not be anywhere near the window where the generated characters will be placed.
off-the-spot	The status window is attached to the application's main window, but not necessarily the child window where the generated characters will be placed.
on-the-spot	The *application draws the status information* on behalf of the input method.

Root status style is shown in Figure 6.2; the status area is displayed at the left side of the separate window shown for root preedit style. The same figure shows off-the-spot status style in the remaining examples. The figure does not show on-the-spot status style. Theoretically, the style exists, but I have yet to see a working example of it.

Keyboard Input with X Windows

In this chapter you will learn how to write your software so that a single source, single object version of your software can

- Obtain characters, coded in the code set of the current locale, from the keyboard.
- Interact with the user in the style of his choice without modification to your software.

This chapter describes and demonstrates the use of the routines in the X library that enable keyboard input. The examples in this chapter show you how to write your software so that it supports the root preedit and status style. This is the easiest style to support and it provides a good overview to the set of steps your software must perform to support all preedit and status styles. The next two chapters expand on the concepts introduced here, showing you how to add support for off-the-spot, over-the-spot, and on-the-spot styles.

Writing internationalized software to use input methods for keyboard input is actually pretty simple. The following list outlines the steps your software needs to perform to talk to an input method. These steps are discussed in detail in the remainder of the chapter:

1. Open a connection to the input method.
2. Ask the input method which preedit styles and which status styles it supports.
3. Choose a preedit style and status style that the input method supports and that you are willing to support.
4. Create an *input context*, specifying the chosen styles and any initial data required by those styles. An input context is an object used for all communication between your software and the input method.
5. Identify which events the input method needs to know about. Combine those events with the events your software is interested in when selecting for input.
6. Allow the input method to examine events before your software processes them. You do this by calling `XFilterEvent()` immediately after calling `XNextEvent()`.

7.   Process `KeyPress` events by calling `XmbLookupString()` or
      `XwcLookupString()`, depending on whether your software wants multibyte char-
      acters or wide characters returned. Both routines pass the event to the input method,
      which eventually converts `KeyPress` events into characters coded in the code set of
      the current locale.

8.   Tell the input method any time data required by the chosen styles changes.

9.   Tell the input method when keyboard focus is gained or lost.

That's all there is to it! The following sections examine each of these steps more
closely, using example code to illustrate the concepts.

7.1 Open a Connection to an Input Method

To establish a connection between your software and an input method, your software
must

1.   Let the X library determine which input method the user wants to use by calling
      `XSetLocaleModifiers()` from your software.

2.   Open a connection to the input method by calling `XOpenIM()`.

7.1.1 Determine Which Input Method to Use

It is common, particularly in Asia, for a system to have several different input methods
for one locale. Users control which input method is used with their application by specifying
a *locale modifier*. Typically they do this by setting the `XMODIFIERS` environment variable,
though your software may decide to implement a resource to supplement the ways in which a
user can specify the modifier. For example, Motif's VendorShell widget defines the
`XmNinputMethod` resource as an additional way to specify a locale modifier.

The X11R5 specification says that a modifier must have the form `"@im=value"`,
where *value* is implementation defined. For example, if you want your HP-UX 9.0 or HP-
UX 10.0 based software to talk to HP's `xjim` Japanese input method, you would set
`XMODIFIERS` as follows:

```
XMODIFIERS="@im=_XIMP_japanese.eucJP#xjim.0" /* HP-UX 9.0 */

XMODIFIERS="@im=_XIMP_ja_JP.eucJP#xjim.0"    /* HP-UX 10.0 */
```

On AIX systems, if you want your software to talk to IBM's Japanese input method,
you might set `XMODIFIERS`:

```
XMODIFIERS="@im=DoubleByte"
```

The documentation for the input methods supported on your system should include a
description of the modifier setting needed to connect to the input method.

The value of the modifier is read by the X library when your software calls `XSetLocaleModifiers()`. You should make this call after initializing the locale with `setlocale()` and prior to opening the input method.

7.1.2 Connecting to the Input Method

Once you have initialized the locale and allowed the X library to determine which input method the user wants to use, open a connection to that input method by calling `XOpenIM()`. The syntax of `XOpenIM()` is

```
XIM XOpenIM(display, db, res_name, res_class)
    Display *display;
    XrmDataBase db;
    char *res_name;
    char *res_class;
```

`XOpenIM()` examines the current locale and any locale modifiers set to determine which input method should be used for that locale. The routine returns an `XIM`, which is an opaque data structure identifying the connection to the input method. Some input methods may use their own private resources to affect their appearance or behavior. These values can be passed to the input method via the resource database *db*. If the input method may be connected to many different applications, you may want the ability to control the appearance or behavior specifically for your application's connection to the input method. For this reason, you may want to supply your software's name and class in the *res_name* and *res_class* parameters. This allows the input method to look up resources specific for that name and class when parsing the resource database. In practice, the resource database, the resource name, and resource class are all typically specified as NULL.

7.2 Determine Which Styles the Input Method Supports

Input methods are often implemented to support multiple preedit and status styles. Once your software has a connection to the input method, it needs to determine which preedit and which status styles are supported by the input method. To obtain this information, call the routine `XGetIMValues()`. The syntax for this routine is

```
char * XGetIMValues(im, ...)
    XIM im;
```

The ellipses (. . .) in the syntax indicate that the routine accepts a variable length argument list. The arguments identify the input method value (XIM value) being queried and a location where the returned information should be stored. The variable length argument list must be null-terminated. With X11R5, only one standard argument is defined for `XGetIMValues()` — `XNQueryInputStyle`. A call to query for supported input styles looks like the following:

```
main(){
    XIMStyles *im_supported_styles;
    XIM my_im;
    Display dpy;

    (void)setlocale(LC_ALL,"");
    dpy = XOpenDisplay(NULL);
    XSetLocaleModifiers("");
    my_im = XOpenIM(dpy, NULL, NULL, NULL);
    (void)XGetIMValues(my_im, XNQueryInputStyle,
                       &im_supported_styles, NULL);
```

The variable `im_supported_styles` now identifies all styles supported by the input method `my_im`. How do you interpret the contents of `im_supported_styles`? `XIMStyles` is a structure defined as

```
typedef struct{
    unsigned short count_styles;
    XIMStyle *supported_styles;
}XIMStyles;
typedef unsigned long XIMStyle;
```

The values for `XIMStyle` are listed and described in Table 7.1.

Table 7.1 XIMStyle Values

XIMStyle	Value	Description
XIMPreeditArea	0x0001L	This is off-the-spot preedit style.
XIMPreeditCallbacks	0x0002L	This is on-the-spot preedit style.
XIMPreeditPosition	0x0004L	This is over-the-spot preedit style.
XIMPreeditNothing	0x0008L	This is root preedit style. This is also the preedit style used with compose and dead-key input models.
XIMPreeditNone	0x0010L	The input method does not provide any preedit information.
XIMStatusArea	0x0100L	This is off-the-spot status style.
XIMStatusCallbacks	0x0200L	This is on-the-spot status style.
XIMStatusNothing	0x0400L	This is root status style. This is also the status style used with compose and dead-key input models.
XIMStatusNone	0x0800L	The input method does not provide status information.

XIMStyle values are allocated so that they can be logically OR'd together to represent a combination of preedit and status styles. For example, expanding on the preceding example, the following code fragment shows how you can determine if the input method supports XIMPreeditPosition style:

```
if (im_supported_styles | XIMPreeditPosition){
    /* Supports over-the-spot preedit style!*/
```

7.3 Choose the Preedit Style and Status Style

Once you know which styles the input method supports, how do you choose which preedit style and status style to use for your software? Human factors research indicates that preedit feedback should appear as close to the final location of the generated character as possible. This implies that you should choose XIMPreeditCallbacks whenever it is supported by the input method. But this may be more trouble than it's worth under some circumstances. For example, this style makes little sense when inputting characters into a small window. You must decide for each situation which style(s) are appropriate for your software. Each style requires your software to perform a different amount of work on its behalf. It is not uncommon for software to support only a subset of styles. For example, Motif 1.2 and Motif 2.0 support only root, off-the-spot, and over-the-spot preedit styles; similarly, they support only root and off-the-spot status styles. The chapters that follow, coupled with Appendix B, will help you decide which styles to support.

7.3.1   Example: Choosing an XIM Style

Once you have decided which style(s) you are willing to support, you must try to choose the best match between styles supported by the input method and the styles you are willing to support. The example routines SelectStyle() and BestStyle() illustrate one way you might find the "best match." You may want to make these example routines part of your personal library if you plan to write much code handling internationalized keyboard input.

SelectStyle() is a routine that you might call from your software. It accepts an input method and an XIMStyle. The XIMStyle parameter identifies the collection of preedit and status styles (in any combination) your software is willing to support. SelectStyle() queries the input method to find out which styles it supports. It then checks each preedit and status style combination returned by the input method to see if your software is willing to support them. When SelectStyle() finds multiple matches, it uses the routine BestStyle() to choose which of the styles is best from a human factors standpoint. The user is usually interested most in preedit feedback. So the preedit style is used to decide which style is best. In case there are more than one preedit/status style combinations that support the "best preedit style," the status style is used to decide which style is best.

```
/*
 * This code is developed from an example provided in
 * "Programmer's Supplement for Release 5",
 * copyright 1992 O'Reilly & Associates, Inc.
 *
 * SelectStyle() accepts an XIMStyle from the application
 * which indicates the complete collection of preedit and
 * status styles it is willing to support.
 *
 * SelectStyle() queries the IM for the styles it supports.
 * For each pair of preedit and status styles supported by
 * the IM, it checks to see if both the preedit and status
 * are supported by the application. SelectStyle() uses
 * the routine BestStyle() to choose the "best style" (from
 * a human factors view) when multiple preedit and status
 * styles are supported by both the IM and the application.
 *
 * If SelectStyle() finds that not even one preedit and
 * status style can be found in common, it returns 0,
 * indicating that the caller should either reconsider the
 * set of styles it is willing to support or should forget
 * about obtaining keyboard input for the user.
 */

XIMStyle BestStyle(s1, s2)
XIMStyle s1;
XIMStyle s2;
{
    XIMStyle pe_mask = XIMPreeditCallbacks | XIMPreeditPosition
        | XIMPreeditArea | XIMPreeditNothing | XIMPreeditNone;
    XIMStyle st_mask = XIMStatusCallbacks | XIMStatusArea
        | XIMStatusNothing | XIMStatusNone;
    if (s1 == 0) return s2;
    if (s2 == 0) return s1;
    if (s1 == s2) return s1;

    s1_preedit = s1 & pe_mask;
    s2_preedit = s2 & pe_mask;
   /* Choose based on best preedit style. */
    if ((s1 & pe_mask) != (s2 & pe_mask)){
        if ((s1 | s2) & XIMPreeditCallbacks)
          return((s1 & XIMPreeditCallbacks)?s1:s2);
        if ((s1 | s2) & XIMPreeditPosition)
          return((s1 & XIMPreeditPosition)?s1:s2);
```

```
      if ((s1 | s2) & XIMPreeditArea)
        return((s1 & XIMPreeditArea)?s1:s2);
      if ((s1 | s2) & XIMPreeditNothing)
        return((s1 & XIMPreeditNothing)?s1:s2);
      if ((s1 | s2) & XIMPreeditNone)
        return((s1& XIMPreeditNone)?s1:s2);
    } else {
    /* Same preedit style; choose based on status style. */
      if ((s1 | s2) & XIMStatusCallbacks)
        return((s1 & XIMStatusCallbacks)?s1:s2);
      if ((s1 | s2) & XIMStatusArea)
        return((s1 & XIMStatusArea)?s1:s2);
      if ((s1 | s2) & XIMStatusNothing)
        return((s1 & XIMStatusNothing)?s1:s2);
      if ((s1 | s2) & XIMStatusNone)
        return((s1 & XIMStatusNone)?s1:s2);
    }
}


XIMStyle SelectStyle(im, app_style)
XIM im;
XIMStyle app_style;
{
    XIMStyles *im_styles;
    XIMStyle best = 0;
    XIMStyle tmp_style;
    int i;

    XGetIMValues(im, XNQueryInputStyle, &im_styles, NULL);

    for(i=0; i < im_styles->count_styles; i++){
       tmp_style = im_styles->supported_styles[i];
       if ((tmp_style & app_style) == tmp_style)
          best = BestStyle(best, tmp_style);
    }
    XFree(im_styles);

    return(best);
}
```

7.4 Create an Input Context

When your software has decided which preedit and status style it will use, it must communicate its choice to the input method when creating an *input context* (data type XIC). An input context is an opaque object used for all communications between your software and the input method. You create an input context by calling `XCreateIC()`. The syntax for this routine is

```
XIC XCreateIC(im, ...)
    XIM im;
```

The ellipses (. . .) in the syntax indicate a variable length argument list; the list must be null-terminated. At a minimum, the argument list must contain the preedit style, the status style, and any additional data required by those styles. This information is passed as XIC data values. The optional and required data required for each style is listed and described in Appendix B.

7.4.1   XIC Data Values

XIC data values are used to pass information between your software and the input method. They are listed and described in Table B.1. Table B.2 shows which XIC data values must be set for each preedit and status style. Two XIC data values *must* be specified when creating the XIC, regardless of the chosen style: `XNPreeditAttributes` and `XNStatusAttributes`.

7.4.1.1   Preedit and status attributes

`XNPreeditAttributes` is an XIC data value used to pass preedit *attributes* to the input method. Preedit attributes are collections data needed to display preedit feedback information to the user. Similarly, `XNStatusAttributes` is an XIC data value used to pass status *attributes* to the input method. Status attributes are collections of data needed to display status feedback information. Both preedit attributes and status attributes are passed as null-terminated variable length lists. X11R5 defines 14 preedit attributes and 12 status attributes. Not all attributes are relevant for every preedit style and status style.

You will use `XNPreeditAttributes` and `XNStatusAttributes` to pass attributes needed for your chosen preedit and status style. Table B.3 describes each preedit attribute; Table B.4 describes each status attribute. Table B.5 and Table B.6 show for each style:

- which attributes must be set when creating the XIC,
- which can be queried,
- which can be set after creating the XIC, and
- which attributes are ignored.

7.4.2   Creating Variable Length Lists

When you create the XIC, you must specify the initial XIC data values, including preedit and status attributes. There's one small problem though. XIC data values are passed as a null-terminated variable length argument list to `XCreateIC()`. Two of the XIC data values you must pass in (XNPreeditAttributes and XNStatusAttributes) are also null-terminated variable length arguments. The function XVaCreateNestedList() allows you to create a variable length argument (data type XVaNestedList) that can be passed as part of another variable length argument. Its syntax is

```
XVaNestedList XVaCreateNestedList(dummy, ...)
int dummy;
```

The ellipses (. . .) in the syntax indicate a variable length argument list; the list must be null-terminated. The argument *dummy* specifies an unused argument, as is required by ANSI C when using variable length argument lists. This function allocates memory and copies the variable length list of arguments into that memory. The arguments are copied as supplied, so the data pointed to by pointer arguments must not be modified until the list is no longer needed.

When you no longer need the nested list created with this routine, you should free the memory associated with it by calling XFree().

7.4.3   Example: Creating an XIC

The routine XCreateIC() was introduced on page 121. Now that you know a little bit about XIC data values, you can see how the routine is used. Assume that you have queried the input method for supported styles and have decided to use XIMPreeditPosition and XIMStatusNothing styles. Using the tables in Appendix B, you see that at least the preedit position and the font set must be specified at create time. The tables also show that some additional values (such as the foreground and background color) will receive implementation defined defaults if not supplied. The following code fragment shows how you would prepare for and call XCreateIC(), passing these preedit and status attributes.

```
XVaNestedList preedit_att, status_att;
int dummy = 0;
XIMStyle my_style;
XPoint spot;
XFontSet my_fontset;
Window my_win;
Display dpy;
XIM my_im;
int screen = DefaultScreen(dpy);
...
/* In a real program, the initial cursor x,y location
 * would be based on font set logical metrics. For this example,
 * just use 0,0 as the cursor location. */
spot.x=0; spot.y=0;
/* For preedit style XIMPreeditPosition, we must pass in the
 * font set and the cursor location. In addition, if the
```

```
 * foreground and background are not supplied, implementation
 * defined defaults will be used. The values are easy to get,
 * so pass them in as well. */
preedit_att = XVaCreateNestedList(dummy,
                            XNSpotLocation, &spot,
                            XNForeground, WhitePixel(dpy, screen),
                            XNBackground, BlackPixel(dpy, screen),
                            XNFontSet, my_fontset, NULL);
/* For status style XIMStatusNothing, no values are required.
 * However, the font set, background, and foreground will all
 * get implementation defined defaults if not supplied. And we
 * have the values available already. So we might as well pass
 * them in. */
status_att = XVaCreateNestedList(dummy,
                            XNForeground, WhitePixel(dpy, screen),
                            XNBackground, BlackPixel(dpy, screen),
                            XNFontSet, my_fontset, NULL);
my_style = XIMPreeditPosition | XIMStatusNothing;
my_ic = XCreateIC(my_im, XNInputStyle, my_style,
                       XNClientWindow, my_win,
                       XNFocusWindow, my_win,
                       XNPreeditAttributes, preedit_att,
                       XNStatusAttributes, status_att, NULL);
XFree(preedit_att);
XFree(status_att);
```

The preceding code fragment illustrates how to use nested variable length lists as required when creating the input context. Later in this chapter you will find a complete example that combines opening the input method, negotiating for preedit and status style, creating the input context, and using the input method to process keyboard events.

7.5 Identify Which Events the Input Method Needs

Once you have created the XIC, you need to find out which events are needed by the input method. You can do this by querying for the XIC data value, `XNFilterEvents`. The general syntax used for setting and querying XIC data values is described in section 7.8 on page 127. For now, the following example shows you have to determine which events the input method needs and include those when telling the X server which events your software is interested in.

```
...
  long im_event_mask;
  long event_mask;
```

```
/* Here are the events my software is interested in. */
  event_mask = KeyPressMask | FocusChangeMask | ExposureMask;

/* Find out what events the input method needs. */
  XGetICValues(ic, XNFilterEvents, &im_event_mask, NULL);

/* Combine these masks and make the request to the X server. */
  event_mask |= im_event_mask;
  XSelectInput(dpy, win, event_mask);
```

7.6 Allow the Input Method to Examine Events before Processing Them

Once you have connected to the input method and created the input context, your software is ready to process key events. Because some input methods want the chance to examine and use key events before your software obtains them, your software should call `XFilterEvent()` before processing any event. The syntax is

```
Bool XFilterEvent(event, win)
  XEvent *event;
  Window win;
```

event   identifies the event to filter.

win   specifies the window for which the filter is to be applied. If *win* is NULL, the filter is applied to the window in the event structure.

An input method can register one or more filters with the X library. Calling `XFilterEvent()` allows the input method's filter to process the event. If the input method needs the event, `XFilterEvent()` returns `True`; otherwise it returns `False`. If `XFilterEvent()` returns `True`, your software should discard the event and not process it.

If your software uses Xt to dispatch events, `XtDispatchEvent()` calls `XFilterEvent()` for you. For more information, see section 12.5 on page 248.

7.7 Process KeyPress Events

If the input method does not need the event passed to `XFilterEvent()`, the routine returns `False`. Your software can then process the event as usual. If the event is a `KeyPress` event, your software can convert the event into a coded character by calling either `XmbLookupString()` or `XwcLookupString()`. The two routines function identically except that `XmbLookupString()` returns characters in multibyte form while `XwcLookupString()` returns characters in wide character form. The syntax for these two routines is

```
int XmbLookupString(ic, event, buffer, bytes_buffer,
                    keysym, status);
  XIC ic;
  XKeyPressedEvent *event;
  char *buffer;
  int bytes_buffer;
  KeySym *keysym;
  Status *status;

int XwcLookupString(ic, event, w_buffer, num_wchars,
                    keysym, status);
  XIC ic;
  XKeyPressedEvent *event;
  wchar_t *w_buffer;
  int num_wchars;
  KeySym *keysym;
  Status *status;
```

ic	specifies the input context.
event	specifies the key event being processed. If an event other than a `KeyPress` event is passed in, the results of this function are undefined.
buffer	pointer to your buffer where the character(s) composed by the input method are returned.
w_buffer	pointer to a buffer of wide characters where a wide character representation of the character(s) composed by the input method are returned.
bytes_buffer	size (in bytes) of the `buffer` your software supplies.
num_wchars	number of wide characters in the `w_buffer` your software supplies.
keysym	pointer to the location where the keysym associated with the event is returned. If you are not interested in processing keysyms, your software can pass NULL for this argument.
status	indicates the kind of data returned by the routine.

   `XmbLookupString()` returns the *number of bytes* copied into *buffer*.
`XwcLookupString()` returns the *number of wide characters* copied into *w_buffer*.
   Be sure to examine *status* before using any of the values returned by these routines.
status indicates if an error occurred and indicates which of the return parameters contains
valid data. The possible values for *status* are described below.

XBufferOverflow	The input string was too large to copy into the supplied buffer. The routine returns the required size of the buffer (in bytes); the content of the supplied buffer and *keysym* are not modified. Your software should call this function again with the same event once you can provide a buffer of sufficient size.

`XLookupNone`	No input composed yet. The buffer and *keysym* returned are not modified; the function returns zero.
`XLookupChars`	Characters have been composed and were copied into the supplied buffer. The content of *keysym* is not modified.
`XLookupKeySym`	No characters have been composed. However, a keysym for the event is returned in *keysym*. The routine returns zero.
`XLookupBoth`	A string of one or more characters was generated by the input method and copied into the supplied buffer. A keysym for the keycode in the event was copied into keysym; the keysym returned does not necessarily correspond to the string returned in the buffer.

7.8 Setting and Querying XIC Data Values

Once you have created the XIC, your software can modify the value of XIC values by calling `XSetICValues()`. The syntax of this routine is

```
char * XSetICValues(ic, ...)
  XIC ic;
```

Your software can obtain the current settings of XIC values by calling `XGetICValues()`. The syntax of `XGetICValues()` is

```
char * XGetICValues(ic, ...)
  XIC ic;
```

`ic` specifies the input context. The ellipses (...) in the syntax indicate a variable length argument list; the list must be null-terminated. When querying for XIC values, you must pass as an argument to each XIC value, a pointer to the location where the value should be stored. For example, the `XNFilterEvents` XIC value takes an argument of type `unsigned long`. If you are querying the input context for `XNFilterEvents`, you would pass as argument `unsigned long*`. When the argument of the XIC value is already a pointer type, then the X library allocates memory to contain the returned value. In this case, your software should free the memory allocated by calling `XFree()`. For example, suppose your software queries for the current resource name:

```
char *res_name, *ret_val;
...
ret_val = XGetICValues(ic, XNResourceName, &res_name, NULL);
if (!ret_val){
  printf(catgets(msg_fd, 1, 1,
                "The resource name is: %s\n", res_name));
  XFree(res_name);
}
```

When querying for an XIC value whose data type is XVaNestedList, the data type you must pass is XVaNestedList. For each element of the nested list, you must pass a pointer to a location for storing the returned value. As in the cases above, if the data type of the XIC value is already a pointer, then the X library allocates memory to contain the returned value; your software must free that allocated memory by calling XFree(). For example,

```
char *ret_val;
XRectangle *area_needed;
unsigned long background;
int dummy = 0;
XVaNestedList list;
...
list = XVaCreateNestedList(dummy,
                           XNBackground, &background,
                           XnAreaNeeded, &area_needed,
                           NULL);
XGetICValues(ic, XNPreeditAttributes, list, NULL);
printf(catgets(msg_fd, 1, 2,
            "The background pixel value is: %d\n"), background);
printf(catgets(msg_fd, 1, 3,
            "The area needed (height x width) is %d x %d\n"),
        area_needed->height, area_needed->width);
XFree(area_needed);
XFree(list);
...
```

7.8.1   Which Attributes Should You Set?

You will probably write your software to support a variety of preedit and status styles. Because the X library ignores attributes that are not appropriate for the current style, you should set the union of all attributes needed for all styles your software supports.

7.9 Tell the Input Method When Keyboard Focus Is Gained or Lost

Your software needs to notify the input method any time it gains or loses keyboard focus. The input method needs this information to give a visual indication of the ability to perform keyboard input and to update any filters it has registered.

To notify the input method about focus changes, use the following routines:

```
void XSetICFocus(ic)
   XIC ic;
```

```
    void XUnsetICFocus(ic)
      XIC ic;
```

7.10 Example: Putting It All Together

It's time to gather all the concepts in this book and look at an example showing how the pieces fit together. The "Hello World!" program from section 4.5 on page 81 has been modified and renamed `simple_input.c`. The greeting kept in a message catalog has been changed to a prompt. And the size of the window has been enlarged to accommodate two lines of text — the first line contains a prompt for the user to type their name, and the second is a blank line allowing the user to enter their name. The program uses the `Select-Style()` and `BestStyle()` routines introduced in section 7.3.1 on page 119. To keep the size of the program manageable, the code for those routines is not duplicated here.

After prompting the user to enter their name, the program uses the routines described earlier in this chapter to generate characters from the keyboard. Software that allows keyboard entry usually allows the user to correct the characters entered. To help you see how this can be done, this program allows the user to erase a character entered by pressing the backspace key. The program terminates when the user presses the return key.

The new key changes to look for in the example are *highlighted by change bars* in the margin. Those sections are discussed in detail following the program listing.

```
/* simple_input.c demonstrates how to connect to input methods
 * using root preedit and status styles.
 */
#include <stdio.h>
#include <X11/Xlib.h>
#include <X11/keysym.h>
#include <locale.h>
#include <limits.h>
#include <nl_types.h>

#define PROMPTS 1
#define ERR_SET 2
#define DEFAULTS 3
#define MARGIN_X 10
#define MARGIN_Y 10
#define WNAME_MAX 1024

main(argc, argv)
  int argc;
  char *argv[];
{
  Display *dpy;
```

```
    int screen;
    Window win;
    GC gc;
    XGCValues gcv;
    unsigned long gcv_mask;
    XEvent event;
    XFontSet fs;
    char *program_name = argv[0];
    char greeting[NL_TEXTMAX+1];
    char def_basename[] = "-*-medium-r-normal-*-24-*";
    char *basename;
    char **missing_charsets;
    int num_missing_charsets = 0, i = 0;
    char *default_string;
    int x_start, y_start, width, height, line_height, descent;
    XRectangle ink_return, logical_return;
    nl_catd my_cat;
    XFontSetExtents *fs_metrics;
    int char_width;
    XIMStyle my_style, style;
    XIM im;
    XIC ic;
    long im_event_mask;
    long event_mask;
    wchar_t *winput_buf;
    int buf_size = 128;
    int wname_len = 0;
    XGCValues gcv_inverse;
    int len;
    KeySym keysym;
    Status status;
    Bool redraw = False;
    Bool need_erase = False;
    wchar_t wname[WNAME_MAX];


    (void)setlocale(LC_ALL, "");
    my_cat = catopen("simple_input", NL_CAT_LOCALE);
    if ((dpy = XOpenDisplay(NULL)) == NULL) {
      (void) fprintf(stderr, catgets(my_cat, ERR_SET, 1,
                          "%s: cannot open Display.\n"),
                    program_name);
      exit(1);
    }
```

```
   (void)XSetLocaleModifiers("");

   basename=catgets(my_cat, DEFAULTS, 1, def_basename);
   fs = XCreateFontSet(dpy, basename,  &missing_charsets,
                       &num_missing_charsets, &default_string);

   if (!fs){
      fprintf(stderr, catgets(my_cat, ERR_SET, 2,
                              "No font set! Exiting....\n"));
      exit(1);
   }
   if(num_missing_charsets > 0){
      fprintf(stderr, catgets(my_cat, ERR_SET, 3,
             "Incomplete font set!  Missing characters set:\n"));
      for (i=0; i< num_missing_charsets; i++){
         fprintf(stderr, catgets(my_cat, ERR_SET, 4, "\t%s\n"),
              missing_charsets[i]);


      }
      XFreeStringList(missing_charsets);
   }
   (void)sprintf(greeting, catgets(my_cat, PROMPTS, 1,
                           "Please enter your name:"));
   fs_metrics = XExtentsOfFontSet(fs);
   line_height = fs_metrics->max_logical_extent.height;
   char_width = fs_metrics->max_logical_extent.width;
   width = (char_width *
           mbstowcs(NULL, greeting, strlen(greeting))) +
           (2 * MARGIN_X);
   height = (2*line_height) + (2*MARGIN_Y);
   x_start = MARGIN_X;
   y_start = MARGIN_Y - fs_metrics->max_logical_extent.y;
   descent = line_height + fs_metrics->max_logical_extent.y;

   screen = DefaultScreen(dpy);
   win = XCreateSimpleWindow(dpy, RootWindow(dpy, screen), 0, 0,
                             width, height, 2,
                             BlackPixel(dpy,screen),
                             WhitePixel(dpy,screen));

   gcv.foreground = BlackPixel(dpy,screen);
   gcv.background = WhitePixel(dpy,screen);
   gcv_inverse.foreground = gcv.background;
```

```
 gcv_inverse.background = gcv.foreground;
 gcv_mask = GCForeground | GCBackground;
 gc = XCreateGC(dpy, win, gcv_mask, &gcv);

/* Open the input method and select styles. */
 if ((im = XOpenIM(dpy, NULL, NULL, NULL)) == NULL) {
    (void) fprintf(stderr, catgets(my_cat, ERR_SET, 5,
                                   "Couldn't open IM\n"));
    exit(1);
 }

 my_style = XIMPreeditNothing | XIMPreeditNone;
 my_style |= XIMStatusNothing | XIMStatusNone;
 style = SelectStyle(im, my_style);
 if (!style)
    fprintf(stderr, catgets(my_cat, ERR_SET, 6,
                            "IM doesn't support my styles!\n"));

 ic = XCreateIC(im, XNInputStyle, style,
                XNClientWindow, win,
                XNPreeditAttributes, NULL,
                XNStatusAttributes, NULL,
                NULL);

 if (ic == NULL) {
    (void)fprintf(stderr, catgets(my_cat, ERR_SET, 7,
                            "Cannot create input context.\n"));
    exit(1);
 }

XGetICValues(ic, XNFilterEvents, &im_event_mask, NULL);

event_mask = KeyPressMask | FocusChangeMask | ExposureMask;
event_mask |= im_event_mask;
XSelectInput(dpy, win, event_mask);

winput_buf = (wchar_t*)malloc((buf_size + 1) *
                              sizeof(wchar_t));

XMapWindow(dpy, win);

while(1) {

   XNextEvent(dpy, &event);
```

```
    if (XFilterEvent(&event, None))
      continue;


switch (event.type) {
  case Expose:
    if (event.xexpose.count == 0)
      XmbDrawString(dpy, win, fs, gc, x_start, y_start,
                    greeting, strlen(greeting));
      XwcDrawString(dpy, win, fs, gc,
                    x_start, y_start + line_height,
                    wname, wname_len);
      break;
  case KeyPress:
    len = XwcLookupString(ic, (XKeyPressedEvent*)&event,
                          winput_buf, buf_size,
                          &keysym, &status);
    if (status == XBufferOverflow){
      buf_size = len;
      winput_buf = (wchar_t*)realloc((char*)winput_buf,
                          (buf_size + 1) * sizeof(wchar_t));
      len = XwcLookupString(ic, (XKeyPressedEvent*)&event,
                          winput_buf, buf_size,
                          &keysym, &status);
    }
    redraw = False;

    switch (status) {
      case XLookupNone:
        break;
      case XLookupKeySym:
      case XLookupBoth:
        if (keysym == XK_BackSpace){
          if (wname_len > 0) wname_len --;
          redraw = True;
          need_erase = True;
          break;
        }
        if (keysym == XK_Return) exit(0);
        if (status == XLookupKeySym) break;
      case XLookupChars:
        for (i = 0;(i < len) && (wname_len < WNAME_MAX);
            i++)
          wname[wname_len++] = winput_buf[i];
```

```
                    redraw = True;
                    break;
            }
        if (redraw) {
          if (need_erase){
            XChangeGC(dpy, gc, gcv_mask, &gcv_inverse);
            XFillRectangle(dpy, win, gc,
                            x_start, y_start + descent,
                            width - MARGIN_X, line_height);
            XChangeGC(dpy, gc, gcv_mask, &gcv);
            need_erase = False;
          }
        XwcDrawString(dpy, win, fs, gc,
                        x_start, y_start + line_height,
                        wname, wname_len);
        }
        break;
      case FocusIn:
        XSetICFocus(ic);
        break;
      case FocusOut:
        XUnsetICFocus(ic);
        break;
    }
  }
}
```

The following code is the source for `simple_input.c`'s message catalog file. It is provided here to give you an idea of how the message catalog should be formatted and how comments can be used to aid the translator. By convention, the message catalog source is stored in a separate file. The name of the message catalog source file is usually the same as the application source file, with a suffix ".msg". So for this example, the message catalog source file is named `simple_input.msg`.

```
$ Set number 1 corresponds to #define PROMPTS in the application
$ source code. It is used to group prompts and labels together in
$ the message catalog.
$set 1
$ Message 1 is a prompt. It should direct the user to type his or
$ her name into the window.
1 Please enter your name:
$
$ Set number 2 corresponds to #define ERR_SET in the application
```

```
$ source code. It is used to group error messages together in
$ the catalog.
$set 2
$ Note to the translator - %s is a format specifier that will be
$ replaced with the name of the application.
1 %s: cannot open Display.\n
$
$ Message 2 is displayed when a font set cannot be generated using
$ the basename supplied in set 3, message 1.
2 No font set! Exiting....\n
$
$ Messages 3 and 4 together identify a list of fonts that cannot
$ be located. Message three states that the following list of
$ CHARSET_REGISTERY and CHARSET_ENCODING could not be found.
$ Message 4 is the %s string format specifier that will be replaced
$ with each CHARSET_REGISTRY-CHARSET_ENCODING pair that could not
$ be found. The %s format uses tab to indent and newline to
$ separate entries - you can reformat these are appropriate for
$ your language and customs.
3 Incomplete font set!  Missing characters set:\n
4 \t%s\n
$ Message 5 warns the user that an input method could not be
$ opened. The program exits because no keyboard input is possible.
$ This may be caused by a bad setting for XMODIFIERS. Or the user
$ may have failed to start the input method before starting the
$ application.
5 Couldn't open IM\n
$
$ Message 6 warns the user that the input method does not support
$ any styles that the application can support. The program exits
$ when this message is displayed. The user should set XMODIFIERS
$ to identify a different input method.
6 IM doesn't support my styles!\n
$
$ Message 7 warns the user that a connection to the input method
$ failed. The reasons for this are unknown. The input method was
$ present, and XMODIFIERS was set so that the application found
$ the input method. And the input method and application support
$ a common preedit and status style. The user should check that
$ the input method is functioning correctly. If the message is
$ still displayed, there is a possible bug in the application; the
$ user should file a bug report.
7 Cannot create input context.\n
$ Set number 3 corresponds to #define DEFAULTS in the application
```

```
$ source code. It is used to group defaults (file names, paths,
$ font set names, ...) together in the message catalog.
$set 3
$ Message 1 is the basename used to create the font set.
1 -*-medium-r-normal-*-24-*
$
$ END OF CATALOG
```

The first major change between "Hello World!" and `simple_input.c` is in the way font metrics are calculated.

```
fs_metrics = XExtentsOfFontSet(fs);
line_height = fs_metrics->max_logical_extent.height;
char_width = fs_metrics->max_logical_extent.width;
width = (char_width *
          mbstowcs(NULL, greeting, strlen(greeting))) +
          (2 * MARGIN_X);
height = (2*line_height) + (2*MARGIN_Y);
x_start = MARGIN_X;
y_start = MARGIN_Y - fs_metrics->max_logical_extent.y;
descent = line_height + fs_metrics->max_logical_extent.y;
```

Notice that this program calls `XExtentsOfFontSet()` instead of `XmbTextExtents()`. This is done because `XmbTextExtents()` requires that you pass in the string to be measured. However, two lines of text are displayed by the program. Until the user has generated the second string from the keyboard, you don't have the string to measure. So, in the absence of the second string, the program calls `XExtentsOfFontSet()` which returns a metric for the largest and smallest possible characters displayed with the font set. Multiplying the length of the prompt string (in characters) times the maximum width of a character displayed with font set `fs` provides a reasonable estimate for the width of the window. Notice the use of `mbstowcs(NULL, ...)`. When called with a NULL argument for the wide character buffer, `mbstowcs()` returns the number of characters (not bytes) in the multibyte string. In this case, the program uses it to count the number of characters in the prompt.

Notice also this version of the program changes from using ink metrics to using logical metrics. Section 4.5 on page 81 mentioned that logical metrics included calculations for interline spacing. Since the window now contains two lines of text, it is appropriate to use logical metrics for calculating the height of the window and for calculating the y location for each line of text.

Next, a set of GC values are defined. These are used to exchange the foreground and background colors in the GC when erasing characters (when the user presses the backspace key).

```
gcv_inverse.foreground = gcv.background;
gcv_inverse.background = gcv.foreground;
```

The next major change to the program is that it now opens an input method.

```
if ((im = XOpenIM(dpy, NULL, NULL, NULL)) == NULL) {
...
  }


my_style = XIMPreeditNothing | XIMPreeditNone;
my_style |= XIMStatusNothing | XIMStatusNone;
style = SelectStyle(im, my_style);
  ...


ic = XCreateIC(im, XNInputStyle, style,
               XNClientWindow, win,
               XNPreeditAttributes, NULL,
               XNStatusAttributes, NULL,
               NULL);
```

To keep things relatively simple, `simple_input.c` supports only root styles (designated by XIMPreeditNothing and XIMStatusNothing). To work correctly with input methods that require no preedit or status feedback, it also designates XIMPreeditNone and XIMStatusNone in the set of styles it is willing to support. Again, to keep the program small, it allows the X library to supply defaults for all XIM data values and all preedit and status attributes that do not require a value to be supplied by the application. If this were a real application instead of an example, the program would have at least built preedit and status attributes that included the font set and the foreground and background colors. These are values that were already available when creating the XIC.

The program calls `SelectStyle()` to choose the best style supported by both the input method and the program. Finally, the program creates the XIC, passing along the client window as the only required XIC data value. All other values are set to their default values by the X library.

The next significant change from "Hello World!" is that `simple_input.c` queries the input method to see what events the input method needs to know about. The program then tells the X server that it wants to select for those events plus the events that the program knows it is interested in. Notice that the program now selects for FocusChange events. This is needed in order to tell the input method when focus is gained or lost.

Finally, the program allocates a block of memory to store characters typed from the keyboard. The text is stored as wide character since this makes it easier to process backspace, deleting the last character in the buffer.

```
XGetICValues(ic, XNFilterEvents, &im_event_mask, NULL);
event_mask = KeyPressMask | FocusChangeMask | ExposureMask;
```

```
event_mask |= im_event_mask;
XSelectInput(dpy, win, event_mask);
winput_buf = (wchar_t*)malloc((buf_size + 1) *
                               sizeof(wchar_t));
```

The next important change in the program is the call to XFilterEvent() during the event loop. This allows an input method to examine (and optionally consume) an event before software processes the event — this is critical correct operation of some types of input methods.

```
XNextEvent(dpy, &event);
  if (XFilterEvent(&event, None))
    continue;
```

The event processing loop of the program contains the bulk of the remaining changes made to "Hello World!" in creating simple_input.c. The Expose event block was modified to redraw both the prompt and any characters typed in by the user.

```
if (event.xexpose.count == 0)
  XmbDrawString(dpy, win, fs, gc, x_start, y_start,
                greeting, strlen(greeting));
  XwcDrawString(dpy, win, fs, gc,
                x_start, y_start + line_height,
                wname, wname_len);
```

As you would expect for keyboard input, there is a significant block of code associated with KeyPress events in the event processing block. First, the program attempts to convert the event into a character. If XwcLookupString() finds that it needs more memory to store the characters returned from the input method, it places the value XBufferOverFlow in the status variable and returns the required buffer size. In this case, the program reallocates the buffer and calls XwcLookupString() again.

```
len = XwcLookupString(ic, (XKeyPressedEvent*)&event,
                      winput_buf, buf_size,
                      &keysym, &status);
if (status == XBufferOverflow){
  buf_size = len;
  winput_buf = (wchar_t*)realloc((char*)winput_buf,
                      (buf_size + 1) * sizeof(wchar_t));
  len = XwcLookupString(ic, (XKeyPressedEvent*)&event,
                      winput_buf, buf_size,
                      &keysym, &status);
```

The program now uses the status returned by XwcLookupString() to decide what action to take. If the status is XLookupNone, the input method did not return any data that requires action. If the status is XLookupKeySym or XLookupBoth, then the input method returned a keysym. The program must examine the keysym to decide if it identifies the backspace key (indicating that the user wants to delete the character previously typed) or the return key, indicating that the user has finished typing in her name. If the backspace key was pressed, the program sets a boolean indicating that the data typed in so far must be erased before redrawing. If the status is XLookupBoth or XLookupChars, then the input method returned characters in the buffer passed to XwcLookupString().

```
switch (status) {
  case XLookupNone:
    break;
  case XLookupKeySym:
  case XLookupBoth:
    if (keysym == XK_BackSpace){
      if (wname_len > 0) wname_len --;
      redraw = True;
      need_erase = True;
      break;
    }
    if (keysym == XK_Return) exit(0);
    if (status == XLookupKeySym) break;
  case XLookupChars:
    for (i = 0;(i < len) && (wname_len < WNAME_MAX);
        i++)
      wname[wname_len++] = winput_buf[i];
    redraw = True;
    break;
}
```

Next the program updates the contents of the window to reflect the latest character(s) typed by the user. The program uses XFillRectangle() to erase the current input string if the user presses the backspace key.

```
if (redraw) {
  if (need_erase){
    XChangeGC(dpy, gc, gcv_mask, &gcv_inverse);
    XFillRectangle(dpy, win, gc,
                    x_start, y_start + descent,
                    width - MARGIN_X, line_height);
    XChangeGC(dpy, gc, gcv_mask, &gcv);
    need_erase = False;
  }
```

```
XwcDrawString(dpy, win, fs, gc,
              x_start, y_start + line_height,
              wname, wname_len);
}
```

Finally, the program notifies the input method when focus is gained or lost.

```
case FocusIn:
  XSetICFocus(ic);
  break;
case FocusOut:
  XUnsetICFocus(ic);
  break;
```

7.11 Summary: Internationalized Keyboard Input with X11R5

1.   Open a connection to the input method.
2.   Ask the input method which preedit styles and which status styles it supports.
3.   Choose a preedit style and status style that the input method supports and that you are
      willing to support.
4.   Create an *input context*, specifying the chosen styles and any initial data required by
      those styles. An input context is an object used for all communication between your
      software and the input method.
5.   Identify which events the input method needs to know about. Combine those events
      with the events your software is interested in when selecting for input.
6.   Allow the input method to examine events before your software processes them. You
      do this by calling `XFilterEvent()` immediately after calling `XNextEvent()`.
7.   Process `KeyPress` events by calling `XmbLookupString()` or
      `XwcLookupString()`, depending on whether your software wants multibyte char-
      acters or wide characters returned. Both routines pass the event to the input method,
      which eventually converts `KeyPress` events into characters coded in the code set of
      the current locale.
8.   Tell the input method anytime data required by the chosen styles changes.
9.   Tell the input method when keyboard focus is gained or lost.

7.12 Frequently Asked Questions

Question: Simple input methods work fine, but I'm having trouble getting characters
back from a complex input method.

Answer: This could be any number of problems. Try the following list of suggestions.

1. Make sure that your X library supports complex input methods. The X library specification doesn't require that complex input methods be supported.

2. Make sure that the complex input method software is installed and configured correctly on your system. For some vendors, this software is purchased separately from the operating system. For example, with Hewlett-Packard's HP-UX, Asian input methods for a language are bundled together with the fonts for that language and are sold separately. If the complex input method runs as a separate process, make sure that the input method is running before starting your software.

3. Make sure that the operating system's locale for the language is installed on your system. You will need to consult the operating system installation and configuration documentation to help.

4. Check the documentation from your X library supplier to find out the correct values for setting XMODIFIERS. Sometimes this is documented with the complex input method. Remember, the value of the modifier is vendor dependent.

5. Make sure the locale is specified correctly. If you are using the LANG or LC_* environment variables to announce the locale, make sure they are set correctly.

6. Make sure that your software calls setlocale(LC_ALL, "") before it calls XSetLocaleModifiers(), XOpenIM(), or any of the other X library I18N routines described in this book. Ideally, setlocale() should be the first call made by your software.

7. Check the return from XOpenIM(). If you are connecting to an input method, XOpenIM() returns a non-NULL value.

8. Check the return from XCreateIC(). If you are connecting to an input method, XCreateIC() returns a non-NULL value.

9. Verify that you are selecting for KeyPress events and focus events, along with the events indicated by the input method when you queried for the XNFilterEvents IC value.

10. Make sure that you are calling XFilterEvent() immediately after the XNextEvent() in your software's event loop.

Question: I'm getting the wrong character from the input method! I press a-diaeresis (ä) and get o-grave (ò) displayed instead. What's going on?

Answer: There is a good chance you have a mismatch between the character set generated by the input method and the font used to display the text. For example, you generate an ISO 8859.1 character but display it with an ISO 8859.2 font. Make sure your software is using font sets to display the data. Then double-check the base name you specify when creating the font set. Make sure it does not include CHARSET_REGISTRY and CHARSET_ENCODING fields.

Question: I've opened my connection to the input method and created the XIC. And I'm able to input characters successfully. But I don't seem to be able to generate some characters in the character set from the keyboard.

Answer: If the input method is a complex input method, such as a Kanji input method, and you are able to generate at least some complex characters, then there is a good chance that the problem is in the input method. There isn't much you can do in this case except talk to the input method supplier.

However, if the input method is a simple method, such as an ISO 8859.* or other eight-bit character set input method, the problem may be caused by the lack of appropriate *keysym* in the server's *keymap*. The following few paragraphs explain exactly what a keysym is and what a keymap is, and how they are involved in the generation of characters from the keyboard.

Warning: Boring text alert. The following paragraphs describe the X server's keymap. An understanding of keymaps is *not* necessary for an initial understanding of how to generate characters from the keyboard. At your first reading of this chapter, you may want to skim or even ignore these paragraphs. However, at some point you will find yourself wondering why you can't enter character FOO from your keyboard, even though FOO is a valid character in the code set of the locale. In such a case, there is a good chance that FOO's keysym isn't present in the server's keymap. At that time you will need an understanding of the structure of the keymap and the function of modifiers so that you can add the needed keysym.

The X server provides one additional piece of information to help identify the character associated with the `KeyPress`. When your software opens the display [e.g., by calling `XOpenDisplay()`] the X library fills in a `Display` data structure for your application. Part of this structure is a copy of the X server's *keymap*. A keymap is a table mapping a device dependent key code to a code set independent *keysym* (data type is `KeySym`). A keysym is a symbolic representation of a character. It is not a coded character value. For example, the keysym `XK_a` only identifies the character "a". The coded character value of "a" must be generated in some other (locale specific) manner — this is the function of the input method. The X Consortium has a registry of keysyms that are guaranteed to have the same value across all platforms. Some example keysyms are `XK_b`, `XK_Z`, `XK_comma`, and `XK_dollar`. These keysyms are defined on your system in header file `<X11/keysymdef.h>` or `<X11/keysym.h>`. The keysym for a given `KeyPress` event is generated by calling any of several X library routines, passing the `KeyPress` event as a parameter.

The X server's keymap provides a mapping between each keycode on the keyboard and a set of keysyms.[1] Each keycode has four keysyms, referred to here as KS1, KS2, KS3 and KS4, associated with it. The collection of key codes and their associated keysyms form a four-column keymap. Further, the four columns are separated into two groups. Group 1 contains the first two keysyms, KS1 and KS2. Group 2 contains the next two keysyms, KS3 and KS4. Which of these four keysyms is the keysym associated with the keycode of a KeyPress event is determined by the modifiers of the event. If the `MODE SWITCH` modifier is set, the

---

1. To examine your X server's keymap, execute the command `xmodmap -pk` from the command line of a terminal emulator running on your X server.

keysym associated with the keycode comes from Group 2; otherwise the keysym comes from Group 1. The keysym within the group is also determined by the modifier. If Shift is one of the modifiers in the modifier value, then the associated keysym is the second keysym within the group; otherwise, the keysym is the first keysym in the group.

For example, assume MODE SWITCH is assigned to the Alt key. Consider the following keymap entry:

```
53  XK_a  XK_A  XK_aring  XK_Aring
```

This keymap entry says, for the key whose keycode is 53, pressing this key without any modifiers should cause an XK_a keysym to be generated. Pressing the key at the same time the Shift key is held down should cause an XK_A keysym to be generated. Pressing the key at the same time the Alt key is held down should cause XK_aring (keysym for å) to be generated. Pressing the key at the same time that both Shift and Alt are held down should cause the XK_Aring (keysym for Å) to be generated.

Keyboard Input: Supporting Over-the-Spot and Off-the-Spot Preedit and Status Styles

T he previous chapter described the general architecture of keyboard input in internationalized X-based software. The chapter showed how to support relatively simply preedit and status styles. This chapter builds on these concepts, showing how to support over-the-spot preedit style and off-the-spot preedit and status styles. The steps presented in the previous chapter are still valid. However, when supporting these additional styles, your software needs to provide additional data to the input method — when creating the XIC and in response to specific events.

To illustrate support for the additional styles, the program introduced in the previous chapter, `simple_input.c`, is expanded. With its new abilities to support over-the-spot and off-the-spot styles, the program is renamed `offnover_spot.c`, and its source is presented at the end of this chapter. A complete example, supporting root, off-the-spot, over-the-spot, and on-the-spot styles, is provided in Appendix C.

8.1 Supporting Over-the-Spot Style

Adding support for over-the-spot preedit style is relatively easy. The table titled Table B.2 on page 294 shows that most values can be left to default for this style. The only additional attributes that you must specify when creating the XIC are the font set and the initial spot location. Then, the only thing you need to do is notify the input method whenever the spot location changes. To do this, you need to understand exactly what the spot location is. You can think of it as the x,y position where the character generated by the input method will be placed, as is illustrated in Figure 8.1.

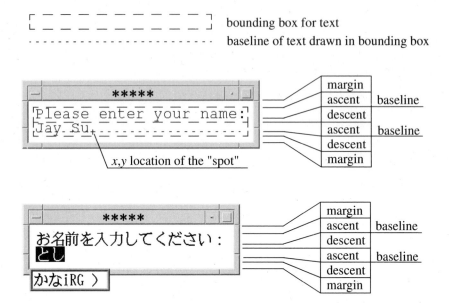

Figure 8.1

The spot location is the x,y position of the character to be entered. The first window shows how that position is determined. The second window shows the preedit window when the spot location is x_start, y_start; preediting is in process with two Hiragana characters in the over-the-spot feedback area.

Building on the example code `simple_input.c`, over-the-spot preedit style is supported by making the following code modifications.

Prior to creating the XIC, add the following lines:

```
XVaNestedList preedit_att;
int dummy;
XPoint spot;
...
my_style |= XIMPreeditPosition;
...
spot.x = x_start;
spot.y = y_start + line_height;
preedit_att = XVaCreateNestedList(dummy,
                      XNForeground, gcv.foreground,
                      XNBackground, gcv.background,
                      XNFontSet, fs,
                      XNSpotLocation, &spot, NULL);
...
```

The initial position of the spot location is the *x,y* position of the first character of the second line of text. So it has the same *x* position as the first line (the prompt), but its *y* position is the *y* position of the first line of text, plus the height of the line.

By passing the new preedit attribute in when creating the XIC, you have done most of the work required to support over-the-spot preedit style. All that remains is to notify the input method any time the spot location changes. Because the program forces the cursor position to be at the end of the offnover_spot.c's buffer, the spot location only can change when the content of wname changes. This can happen either due to additional characters being typed, or due to characters being deleted with the backspace key. When the text is redrawn inside the part of the event loop processing KeyPress events, you know the content of the buffer reflects the result of whatever changes have been made to wname. And, since you know that the location of the next character to be typed is always at the end of the current buffer, you can update the spot location immediately after the XwcDrawString() call by adding this code:

```
if (redraw) {
    ...
}
XwcDrawString(dpy, win, fs, gc, x_start,
                    y_start + line_height, wname, wname_len);
spot.x = x_start +
            XwcTextEscapement(fs, wname, wname_len);
spot.y = y_start + line_height;
preedit_att = XVaCreateNestedList(dummy,
                                XNSpotLocation, &spot, NULL);
XSetICValues(ic, XNPreeditAttributes,
                preedit_att, NULL);
XFree(preedit_att);
```

With these few additions, the example program now supports over-the-spot preedit style.

8.2 Adding Support for Off-the-Spot Preedit and Status Styles

When supporting off-the-spot style, your software reserves a portion of its window for use by the input method. The input method uses this space to display preedit or status feedback information. To support this style, your software must do the following:

1. Provide the XIC data required for off-the-spot style when creating the XIC. At a minimum, you must at least include the font set in the list of preedit and status attributes.

2. When calling XSelectInput(), be sure to include StructureNotifyMask to indicate that your software wants to know whenever the window changes size.

3.   After creating the window and the XIC, negotiate with the input method to find out the size window it needs to display feedback information. Grow (resize) your software's window to make room for the feedback information.

4.   When your software's window is resized (for example, if the user stretches or shrinks the window), notify the input method of the new size and location of the feedback area.

8.2.1   Provide Required Data When Creating the XIC

To support `XIMPreeditArea` and `XIMStatusArea`, look at Table B.2 on page 294 to see what XIC data values you must specify when creating the XIC. From the table you can see that you need not supply additional XIC data values; the X library provides default values for all XIC data values used by these styles. Next, look at Table B.5 on page 299 to see what additional preedit attributes you should pass to the input method. From the table you can see that you must at least specify the font set when creating the XIC. Similarly, looking at Table B.6 on page 299 you find that the font set is the only additional status attribute you must pass to the input method. The following code shows the additions made to the example program `simple_input.c` when creating the XIC and supporting off-the-spot styles. The sample shows specification of the foreground and background colors in the preedit and status attributes. These are included here since it is good form to provide the input method with this information. This lets the input method match its colors to the colors of your software's window, giving the user a visual association between the feedback information and the window with keyboard focus.

```
XVaNestedList preedit_att, status_att;
int dummy;
...
  my_style |= XIMStatusArea | XIMPreeditArea;
...
  preedit_att = XVaCreateNextedList(dummy,
                              XNForeground, gcv.foreground,
                              XNBackground, gcv.background,
                              XNFontSet, fs, NULL);
  status_att = XVaCreateNextedList(dummy,
                              XNForeground, gcv.foreground,
                              XNBackground, gcv.background,
                              XNFontSet, fs, NULL);
  ic = XCreateIC(im, XNInputStyle, style,
                 XNClientWindow, win,
                 XNPreeditAttributes, preedit_att,
                 XNStatusAttributes, status_att,
                 NULL);
XFree(preedit_att);
XFree(status_att);
```

8.2.2   Select for Window Size Change Events

If your software allows its window to be resized, you need to be notified any time the window size changes. This enables you to notify the input method that the area it has available to display feedback information has changed. To be notified when the window size changes, include `StructureNotifyMask` when selecting input.

```
. . .
   event_mask = KeyPressMask | FocusChangeMask | ExposureMask;
   event_mask |= StructureNotifyMask | im_event_mask;
   XSelectInput(dpy, win, event_mask);
. . .
```

8.2.3   Negotiate with the Input Method for the Geometry Needed

Using `XIMPreeditArea` or `XIMStatusArea` styles means that your software must negotiate with the input method about the size and location of the area where feedback information will be displayed by the input method. With these styles, your software is responsible for providing an area for the input method to display feedback information; the input method then displays its feedback data in that area. The input method can suggest the size of the feedback area needed, but not the location. Your software is not obligated to honor the input method's size request.

A typical geometry negotiation follows this sequence:

1.   Your software suggests an initial size and location for the feedback information by using the `XNAreaNeeded` attribute and calling `XSetICValues()`. If you have no constraints on the feedback area size, set the width and height of the `XRectangle` argument to zero.
2.   Next, your software asks the input method what size it would like to be by using the `XNAreaNeeded` attribute and calling `XGetICValues()`. The input method returns in the `XRectangle` argument the width and height it would like to have to display input method feedback information.
3.   Finally, your software tells the input method your decision about the geometry for the feedback information by using the `XNArea` attribute and calling `XSetICValues()`. The `XRectangle` argument you pass indicates the feedback area's height and width, as well as its *x,y* location (relative to the client window).

8.2.3.1   IM initiated geometry negotiations

On occasion, the input method may have reason to change the size of its status or preedit area. For example, the input method might have a graphical user interface allowing the user to select the font used to display preedit and status information. When the font changes, the input method needs to change the size of the preedit or status window.

To support input method initiated geometry negotiations, you should include a geometry callback procedure as an XIC data value. If you do not provide this callback, the X library provides default callback for you. The default callback ignores the input method initiated geometry request, telling the IM to use the geometry it already has.

A geometry callback is always called with a NULL call data argument. Data is not passed between the input method and your software via the callback interface. Instead, the callback is a way for the input method to trigger a geometry negotiation.

The form of the geometry callback is

```
void GeometryCallback(xic, client_data, call_data)
    XIC xic;
    XPointer client_data;
    XPointer call_data;
```

The content of the callback should be similar to the three-step negotiation described above. The input method will cause your geometry callback to be called when it wants to change the size of its feedback area. Your callback will need to query the input method for XNAreaNeeded. You then have to decide if you want to honor the size requested by the input method. The input method must abide by the size you specify when setting XNArea.

8.2.3.2   When should you negotiate the geometry?

- immediately after creating the input context,
- any time the geometry of your software's window changes,
- any time you change one of the XIC data values, preedit attributes, or status attributes that affects the input method's geometry: XNFocusWindow, XNAreaNeeded, XNFontSet, or XNLineSpace.
- When the input method initiates a geometry negotiation.

8.2.3.3   Example of geometry negotiation

For this example, assume you have already called setlocale(), created your window, created your font set, queried the input method for supported styles, and created the XIC specifying XIMPreeditPosition and XIMStatusArea styles. The initial size of the window is 200x200. Finally, for this example the application dictates the status area width but changes its window size to accommodate the status area height wanted by the IM.

```
. . .
Arg var_list[MAXVARG];
int win_width = 200;
int win_height = 200;
XRectangle status_area;
XRectangle *desired_geometry;
int im_height = 0; /* To keep track of the IM's height. */
. . .
/* Suggest an width to the input method. Let the IM suggest
 * a height. */
```

```
status_area.width = win_width;
status_area.height = 0;
var_list[0].name = XNAreaNeeded;
var_list[0].value = &status_area;
XSetICValues(my_ic, XNStatusAttributes, &var_list[0], NULL);

/* Now ask the IM how big it wants to be. */
var_list[0].name = XNAreaNeeded;
var_list[0].value = &desired_status;
XGetICValues(my_ic, XNStatusAttributes, &var_list[0], NULL);
win_height += desired_geometry->height;
im_height = desired_geometry->height;
XFree(desired_geometry);

/* The application changes it's window's height to include
 * the height of the status window. Then, it tells the IM the
 * geometry to be used for the status feedback area. */
...
status_area.width = win_width;
status_area.height = im_height;
status_area.x = 0;
status_area.y = win_height - im_height;
var_list[0].name = XNAreaNeeded;
var_list[0].value = &status_area;
XSetICValues(my_ic, XNStatusAttributes, &valr_list[0], NULL);
...
```

8.2.3.4   Convenience routines for negotiating geometry and their usage

Once you decide on the size for your software's window, you need to negotiate with the input method to see how much space the input method wants to display feedback information. To aid in the process, here are two utility routines; they will come in handy in the repeated negotiations. The example program's in the rest of the book make use of these routines.

```
void GetPreferredGeometry(ic, name, limits, area)
  XIC ic;
  char *name;
  XRectangle *limits;
  XRectangle **area;
{
  XVaNestedList list;
  int dummy = 0;
```

```
   /* Tell the input method any limits on geometry before
    * asking it for its preferred size. */
   list = XVaCreateNestedList(dummy, XNAreaNeeded, limits,
                              NULL);
   XSetICValues(ic, name, list, NULL);
   XFree(list);
   list = XVaCreateNestedList(dummy, XNAreaNeeded, area, NULL);
   XGetICValues(ic, name, list, NULL);
   XFree(list);
}

void SetGeometry(ic, name, area)
   XIC ic;
   char *name;
   XRectangle *area;
{
   XVaNestedList list;
   int dummy = 0;

   list = XVaCreateNestedList(dummy, XNArea, area, NULL);
   XSetICValues(ic, name, list, NULL);
   XFree(list);
}
```

Now consider how you might use these routines in offnover_spot.c to negotiate geometry. To do this, you must first decide where to allocate space to display the feedback information. For this example, if only one feedback area is needed, it is displayed directly below the offnover_spot.c application window. If two feedback areas are needed (one for preedit information and one for status information), the feedback areas are stacked below the application data, as shown in Figure 8.2. In either case, the application must resize the window to display the feedback information.

Before beginning to process events, the example program queries the input method to determine how much space is needed for status and preedit feedback areas. The program uses the variables preedit_height and status_height to keep track of the size of the off-the-spot feedback areas. Note that the program never changes its own window size except to make room for the feedback areas. So this is the only time it negotiates for the geometry and changes its window size to accommodate the input method geometry. If the program changed its window size (for example, because the size of the font used changed or the number of lines displayed in the window changed), it would renegotiate geometry with the input method and resize its window again.

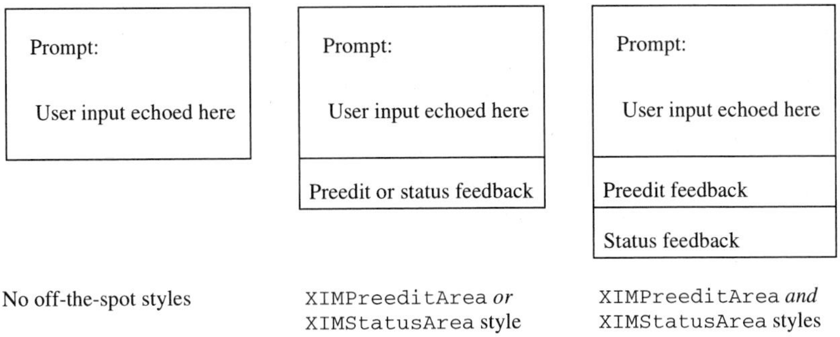

Prompt:

User input echoed here

Prompt:

User input echoed here

Preedit or status feedback

Prompt:

User input echoed here

Preedit feedback

Status feedback

No off-the-spot styles   `XIMPreeditArea` *or*   `XIMPreeditArea` *and*
                                `XIMStatusArea` style   `XIMStatusArea` styles

Figure 8.2
Location of off-the-spot feedback areas for the example program.

To keep the example easier to understand, only the window height is changed to accommodate the off-the-spot feedback areas. In your own software, you will want to resize the width of the window (if possible) when the input method indicates it needs a wider area to display the feedback information.

```
XRectangle limits;
XRectangle status_area, *status_area_ptr;
XRectangle preedit_area, *preedit_area_ptr;
int status_height = 0;
int preedit_height = 0;
...
  if (style & XIMPreeditArea){
    limits.width = 0;
    limits.height = 0;
    GetPreferredGeometry(ic, XNPreeditAttributes, &limits,
                         &preedit_area_ptr);
    if (preedit_area_ptr->height > 0) {
      preedit_height = preedit_area_ptr->height;
      XResizeWindow(dpy, win, width, height + preedit_height);
    }
    if (width >= preedit_area_ptr->width)
      preedit_area.width = preedit_area_ptr->width;
    else
      preedit_area.width = width;
    preedit_area.x = x_start;
    preedit_area.y = (2 * line_height) + (2 * MARGIN_Y);
    preedit_area.height = preedit_height;
    SetGeometry(ic, XNPreeditAttributes, &preedit_area);
  }
```

```
if (style & XIMStatusArea){
  limits.width = 0;
  limits.height = 0;
  GetPreferredGeometry(ic, XNStatusAttributes, &limits,
              &status_area_ptr);
  if (status_area_ptr->height > 0) {
    status_height = status_area_ptr->height;
    XResizeWindow(dpy, win, width,
              height + status_height + preedit_height);
  }
  if (width >= status_area_ptr->width)
    status_area.width = status_area_ptr->width;
  else
    status_area.width = width;
  status_area.x = x_start;
 /* Place the status area below the preedit area, if it
  * exists; if it doesn't exist, preedit_height == 0.
  */
  status_area.y = (2 * line_height) + (2 * MARGIN_Y) +
              preedit_height;
  status_area.height = status_height;
  SetGeometry(ic, XNStatusAttributes, &status_area);
}
```

8.2.4   Notify the Input Method When the Window is Resized

Any time the window size changes, you must notify the input method of the new size, telling the input method how much space you are providing it. This can be done by adding code handling ConfigureNotify events to your software's event loop. You can see an example of how this is done by looking at the event handler in the source for overnoff_input provided in section 8.3. Because a ConfigureNotify event can be generated by actions other than a change in size of the window, overnoff_input com-pares the current size of the window to the size indicated by the event. If the window hasn't changed size, the program breaks out of handling the ConfigureNotify event. Other-wise, the size of the window has changed, and the program allocates the new geometry between the application and the input method feedback areas.

Regardless of the input method styles in use, the overnoff_input always first uses the window space it needs to display its prompt and input string. Any space left over it allo-cates to the feedback areas. If both preedit and status off-the-spot styles are in use, the overnoff_input allocates the extra space equally to the preedit and status areas. Other-wise, if there is only one off-the-spot style in use, the extra space is allocated to displaying the feedback information for that style.

8.3 Example

The following example is the complete source code for `overnoff_input.c`. This example combines support for root, off-the-spot, and over-the-spot preedit styles, along with support for root and off-the-spot status styles. Because the source for the message catalog has not changed significantly from that used by `simple_input.c`, its source is not reproduced here.

```
/* overnoff_input.c demonstrates how to connect to input methods
 * using the preedit styles: root, off-the-spot, and over-the-spot.
 * It also shows support for root and off-the-spot status styles.
 */
#include <stdio.h>
#include <X11/Xlib.h>
#include <X11/keysym.h>
#include <locale.h>
#include <limits.h>
#include <nl_types.h>

#define PROMPTS 1
#define ERR_SET 2
#define DEFAULTS 3
#define MARGIN_X 10
#define MARGIN_Y 10
#define WNAME_MAX 1024

main(argc, argv)
  int argc;
  char *argv[];
{
  Display *dpy;
  int screen;
  Window win;
  GC gc;
  XGCValues gcv;
  unsigned long gcv_mask;
  XEvent event;
  XFontSet fs;
  char *program_name = argv[0];
  char greeting[NL_TEXTMAX+1];
  char def_basename[] = "-*-medium-r-normal-*-24-*";
  char *basename;
  char **missing_charsets;
  int num_missing_charsets = 0, i = 0;
```

```
char *default_string;
int x_start, y_start, width, height, line_height, descent;
XRectangle ink_return, logical_return;
nl_catd my_cat;
XFontSetExtents *fs_metrics;
int char_width;
XIMStyle my_style, style;
XIM im;
XIC ic;
long im_event_mask;
long event_mask;
wchar_t *winput_buf;
int buf_size = 128;
int wname_len = 0;
XGCValues gcv_inverse;
int len;
KeySym keysym;
Status status;
Bool redraw = False;
Bool need_erase = False;
wchar_t wname[WNAME_MAX];
XVaNestedList preedit_att, status_att;
int dummy;
XPoint spot;
XRectangle *status_area_ptr, status_area;
XRectangle *preedit_area_ptr, preedit_area;
XRectangle limits;
int status_height = 0;
int preedit_height = 0;
int height_avail;

(void)setlocale(LC_ALL, "");
my_cat = catopen("overnoff_input", NL_CAT_LOCALE);
if ((dpy = XOpenDisplay(NULL)) == NULL) {
  (void) fprintf(stderr, catgets(my_cat, ERR_SET, 1,
                        "%s: cannot open Display.\n"),
              program_name);
  exit(1);
}

(void)XSetLocaleModifiers("");

basename=catgets(my_cat, DEFAULTS, 1, def_basename);
```

```
fs = XCreateFontSet(dpy, basename,  &missing_charsets,
                    &num_missing_charsets, &default_string);

if (!fs){
  fprintf(stderr, catgets(my_cat, ERR_SET, 2,
                          "No font set!  Exiting....\n"));
  exit(1);
}
if(num_missing_charsets > 0){
  fprintf(stderr, catgets(my_cat, ERR_SET, 3,
          "Incomplete font set!  Missing characters set:\n"));
  for (i=0; i< num_missing_charsets; i++){
    fprintf(stderr, catgets(my_cat, ERR_SET, 4, "\t%s\n"),
            missing_charsets[i]);


  }
  XFreeStringList(missing_charsets);
}
(void)sprintf(greeting, catgets(my_cat, PROMPTS, 1,
                        "Please enter your name:"));
fs_metrics = XExtentsOfFontSet(fs);
line_height = fs_metrics->max_logical_extent.height;
char_width = fs_metrics->max_logical_extent.width;
width = (char_width * mbstowcs(NULL,greeting, strlen(greeting)))
        + (2 * MARGIN_X);
height = (2*line_height) + (2*MARGIN_Y);
x_start = MARGIN_X;
y_start = MARGIN_Y - fs_metrics->max_logical_extent.y;
descent = line_height + fs_metrics->max_logical_extent.y;

screen = DefaultScreen(dpy);
win = XCreateSimpleWindow(dpy, RootWindow(dpy, screen), 0, 0,
                          width, height, 2,
                          BlackPixel(dpy,screen),
                          WhitePixel(dpy,screen));

gcv.foreground = BlackPixel(dpy,screen);
gcv.background = WhitePixel(dpy,screen);
gcv_inverse.foreground = gcv.background;
gcv_inverse.background = gcv.foreground;
gcv_mask = GCForeground | GCBackground;
gc = XCreateGC(dpy, win, gcv_mask, &gcv);

/* Open the input method and select styles. */
```

```
if ((im = XOpenIM(dpy, NULL, NULL, NULL)) == NULL) {
  (void) fprintf(stderr, catgets(my_cat, ERR_SET, 5,
                                "Couldn't open IM\n"));
  exit(1);
}

my_style = XIMPreeditNothing | XIMPreeditNone;
my_style |= XIMStatusNothing | XIMStatusNone;
my_style |= XIMPreeditPosition;
my_style |= XIMStatusArea | XIMPreeditArea;
style = SelectStyle(im, my_style);
if (!style)
  fprintf(stderr, catgets(my_cat, ERR_SET, 6,
                          "IM doesn't support my styles!\n"));

spot.x = x_start;
spot.y = y_start + line_height;
preedit_att = XVaCreateNestedList(dummy,
                                  XNForeground, gcv.foreground,
                                  XNBackground, gcv.background,
                                  XNFontSet, fs,
                                  XNSpotLocation, &spot, NULL);
status_att = XVaCreateNestedList(dummy,
                                 XNForeground, gcv.foreground,
                                 XNBackground, gcv.background,
                                 XNFontSet, fs, NULL);
ic = XCreateIC(im, XNInputStyle, style,
               XNClientWindow, win,
               XNFocusWindow, win,
               XNPreeditAttributes, preedit_att,
               XNStatusAttributes, status_att,
               NULL);
XFree(preedit_att);
XFree(status_att);

if (ic == NULL) {
  (void)fprintf(stderr, catgets(my_cat, ERR_SET, 7,
                               "Cannot create input context.\n"));
  exit(1);
}

XGetICValues(ic, XNFilterEvents, &im_event_mask, NULL);

event_mask = KeyPressMask | FocusChangeMask | ExposureMask;
```

```
event_mask |= StructureNotifyMask | im_event_mask;
XSelectInput(dpy, win, event_mask);

winput_buf = (wchar_t*)malloc((buf_size + 1) *
                              sizeof(wchar_t));


XMapWindow(dpy,win);

if (style & XIMPreeditArea){
  limits.width = 0;
  limits.height = 0;
  GetPreferredGeometry(ic, XNPreeditAttributes, &limits,
                       &preedit_area_ptr);
  if (preedit_area_ptr->height > 0) {
    preedit_height = preedit_area_ptr->height;
    XResizeWindow(dpy, win, width, height + preedit_height);
  }
  if (width >= preedit_area_ptr->width)
    preedit_area.width = preedit_area_ptr->width;
  else
    preedit_area.width = width;
  preedit_area.x = x_start;
  preedit_area.y = (2 * line_height) + (2 * MARGIN_Y);
  preedit_area.height = preedit_height;
  SetGeometry(ic, XNPreeditAttributes, &preedit_area);
}
if (style & XIMStatusArea){
  limits.width = 0;
  limits.height = 0;
  GetPreferredGeometry(ic, XNStatusAttributes, &limits,
                       &status_area_ptr);
  if (status_area_ptr->height > 0) {
    status_height = status_area_ptr->height;
    XResizeWindow(dpy, win, width,
                  height + status_height + preedit_height);
  }
  if (width >= status_area_ptr->width)
    status_area.width = status_area_ptr->width;
  else
    status_area.width = width;
  status_area.x = x_start;
 /* Place the status area below the preedit area, if it exists;
  * if it doesn't exist, preedit_height == 0.
  */
```

```
    status_area.y = (2 * line_height) + (2 * MARGIN_Y) +
                    preedit_height;
    status_area.height = status_height;
    SetGeometry(ic, XNStatusAttributes, &status_area);
}

while(1) {
  XNextEvent(dpy, &event);
    if (XFilterEvent(&event, None))
      continue;

  switch (event.type) {
    case Expose:
      if (event.xexpose.count == 0)
        XmbDrawString(dpy, win, fs, gc, x_start, y_start,
                      greeting, strlen(greeting));
        XwcDrawString(dpy, win, fs, gc, x_start,
                      y_start + line_height,
                      wname, wname_len);
      break;
    case KeyPress:
      len = XwcLookupString(ic, (XKeyPressedEvent*)&event,
                            winput_buf, buf_size, &keysym, &status);
      if (status == XBufferOverflow){
        buf_size = len;
        winput_buf = (wchar_t*)realloc((char*)winput_buf,
                              (buf_size + 1) * sizeof(wchar_t));
        len = XwcLookupString(ic, (XKeyPressedEvent*)&event,
                              winput_buf, buf_size,
                              &keysym, &status);
      }
      redraw = False;

      switch (status) {
        case XLookupNone:
          break;
        case XLookupKeySym:
        case XLookupBoth:
          if ((keysym == XK_Delete) || (keysym == XK_BackSpace)){
            if (wname_len > 0) wname_len --;
            redraw = True;
            need_erase = True;
            break;
          }
```

```
            if (keysym == XK_Return) exit(0);
            if (status == XLookupKeySym) break;
        case XLookupChars:
            for (i = 0;(i < len) && (wname_len < WNAME_MAX); i++)
                wname[wname_len++] = winput_buf[i];
            redraw = True;
            break;
        }
        if (redraw) {
            if (need_erase){
                XChangeGC(dpy, gc, gcv_mask, &gcv_inverse);
                XFillRectangle(dpy, win, gc,
                                x_start, y_start + descent,
                                width - MARGIN_X, line_height);
                XChangeGC(dpy, gc, gcv_mask, &gcv);
                need_erase = False;
            }
            XwcDrawString(dpy, win, fs, gc, x_start,
                                y_start + line_height, wname, wname_len);
            if (style & XIMPreeditPosition){
                spot.x = x_start +
                                XwcTextEscapement(fs, wname, wname_len);
                spot.y = y_start + line_height;
                preedit_att = XVaCreateNestedList(dummy,
                                        XNSpotLocation, &spot, NULL);
                XSetICValues(ic, XNPreeditAttributes,
                                preedit_att, NULL);
                XFree(preedit_att);
            }
        }
        break;
    case FocusIn:
        XSetICFocus(ic);
        break;
    case FocusOut:
        XUnsetICFocus(ic);
        break;
    case ConfigureNotify:
        /* If the window size hasn't changed, there is no new
         * geometry to communicate to the input method. */
        if ((width == event.xconfigure.width) &&
            ((height + preedit_height + status_height) ==
                event.xconfigure.height))
            break;
```

```
width = event.xconfigure.width;
if ((style & XIMPreeditArea) && (style & XIMStatusArea)){
  XRectangle preedit_limits, status_limits;
  preedit_limits.width = width;
  status_limits.width = width;
  height_avail = event.xconfigure.height -
                      ((2 * line_height) + (2 * MARGIN_Y));
  if (height_avail < 0) {
    preedit_limits.height = 0;
    status_limits.height = 0;
  } else {
    status_limits.height = .5 * height_avail;
    preedit_limits.height =
                      height_avail - status_limits.height;
  }

/* Tell the input method its geometry constraints and
 * ask for the preferred size for each. */
GetPreferredGeometry(ic, XNPreeditAttributes,
                        &preedit_limits,
                        &preedit_area_ptr);
GetPreferredGeometry(ic, XNStatusAttributes,
                        &status_limits, &status_area_ptr);

/* It is purely a style choice in deciding how to
 * allocate geometry for the preedit and status areas.
 * For this example program, if the input method wants
 * less than half of the area available to display the
 * status feedback, give it the geometry it asks for.
 * Otherwise, give it half of what's available. Give
 * any remaining geometry (at least half of the extra
 * space in the window) to the input method to display
 * the preedit feedback data. */
if (height_avail > 0 &&
      (.5 * height_avail) >= status_area_ptr->height)
  status_height = status_area_ptr->height;
else if (height_avail >= 0)
  status_height = .5 * height_avail;
else
  status_height = 0;
height_avail -= status_height;
if (height_avail > 0 &&
      height_avail >= preedit_area_ptr->height)
  preedit_height = preedit_area_ptr->height;
```

```
      else if (height_avail >= 0)
        preedit_height = height_avail;
      else
        preedit_height = 0;
      preedit_area.x = x_start;
      preedit_area.y = (2 * line_height) + (2 * MARGIN_Y);
      preedit_area.height = preedit_height;
      preedit_area.width = width;
      status_area.x = x_start;
      status_area.y = preedit_area.y + preedit_height;
      status_area.height = status_height;
      status_area.width = width;
      SetGeometry(ic, XNStatusAttributes, &status_area);
      SetGeometry(ic, XNPreeditAttributes, &preedit_area);
      height = event.xconfigure.height -
                  (preedit_height + status_height);
      break;
  }
  /* If there is only one off-the-spot feedback area,
   * give it all the extra space in the window. */
  if (style & XIMPreeditArea){
    limits.width = width;
    height_avail = event.xconfigure.height -
                        ((2 * line_height) + (2 * MARGIN_Y));
    if (height_avail < 0)
      limits.height = 0;
    else
      limits.height = height_avail;
    GetPreferredGeometry(ic, XNPreeditAttributes,
                          &limits, &preedit_area_ptr);
    if (preedit_area_ptr->height <= height_avail)
      preedit_height = preedit_area_ptr->height;
    else if (height_avail >= 0)
      preedit_height = height_avail;
    else
      preedit_height = 0;
    if (preedit_height < 0)
      preedit_height = 0;
    preedit_area.x = x_start;
    preedit_area.y = (2 * line_height) + (2 * MARGIN_Y);
    preedit_area.height = preedit_height;
    preedit_area.width = width;
    SetGeometry(ic, XNPreeditAttributes, &preedit_area);
    height = event.xconfigure.height - preedit_height;
```

```
      break;
    }
  /* Identical to the XIMPreeditArea style code above, but
   * using XNStatusAttributes instead. */
  if (style & XIMStatusArea){
    limits.width = width;
    height_avail = event.xconfigure.height -
                    ((2 * line_height) + (2 * MARGIN_Y));
    if (height_avail < 0)
      limits.height = 0;
    else
      limits.height = height_avail;
    GetPreferredGeometry(ic, XNStatusAttributes,
                         &limits, &status_area_ptr);
    if (status_area_ptr->height <= height_avail)
      status_height = status_area_ptr->height;
    else if (height_avail >= 0)
      status_height = height_avail;
    else
      status_height = 0;
    if (status_height < 0)
      status_height = 0;
    status_area.x = x_start;
    status_area.y = (2*line_height) + (2*MARGIN_Y);
    status_area.height = status_height;
    status_area.width = width;
    SetGeometry(ic, XNStatusAttributes, &status_area);
    height = event.xconfigure.height - status_height;
    break;
  }
  break;
}
}
}
```

Keyboard Input with On-the-Spot Preedit and Status Styles

T his chapter describes the details of supporting on-the-spot preedit and status styles. It describes the various callbacks you must write to support this style and provides examples of each of the callbacks. The examples build on the example program `overnoff_input.c` in the previous chapter. The new example created is listed in its entirety in Appendix C.

This chapter also tries to fill in the gaps in the X11R5 and X11R6 specifications for on-the-spot style. In many places the specification is vague or ambiguous. Discussions with the X11R5 and X11R6 design teams brought out the intent of the specification; that information is included here and is noted as "outside the formal specifications." The X Consortium plans to update the specification with the release 6.1 of the X Window System, including the clarifications that resulted from these discussions.

9.1 Adding support for On-the-Spot Preedit and Status Styles

When supporting on-the-spot feedback style, your software is responsible for rendering preedit and status feedback information to the user. This includes echoing keystrokes as the user types as well as displaying and highlighting preedit and status data. From a human factors standpoint, on-the-spot preedit style is arguably the best style, since it places preedit feedback exactly where the eventually composed character will be placed. It also allows the user to see the preedit feedback data without obscuring any exiting characters.

However, these advantages come at a cost to you, the software developer. To support on-the-spot preedit and status styles, you must essentially write a small text editor and include it with your software. You do this by writing and registering callbacks that render the preedit and status information. As the preedit and status information changes, the X library calls your software's callbacks, passing to them the latest changes to the contents of the preedit and status feedback information along with indications of how the data should be displayed. Your software must keep track of the cumulative affects of these changes and display the result to the user.

The callbacks you must create and register are listed and described in Table 9.1.

Table 9.1 Description of Callbacks Required for On-the-Spot Input Style

Callback name	Description
PreeditStartCallback	Called when preediting begins.
PreeditDoneCallback	Called when preediting completes.
PreeditDrawCallback	Called when the input method wants to update the data in its buffer or when it wants to change the way the data in its buffer is highlighted.
PreeditCaretCallback	Called when the input method wants to move the location of the insert or caret cursor within the preedit data.
StatusStartCallback	Called when the input context is created and when the input context is notified that focus is gained.
StatusDoneCallback	Called when the input context is destroyed and when the input context is notified that focus is lost.
StatusDrawCallback	Called when the input method wants to change the status information displayed to the user

Callbacks have the general form

```
void CallbackProc(ic, client_data, call_data)
   XIC ic;
   XPointer client_data;
   CallbackSpecificType call_data;
```

ic is the input context for communicating with the input method. *client_data* is data passed to the callback from the software that registered the callback. It is a way for you to pass data into the callback. *call_data* is a structure specific to the function of the callback. It contains the data needed by the callback to perform its task. If the callback needs no data to perform its task, *call_data* is NULL. The data type for *call_data* depends on the type of callback.

9.1.1   PreeditStartCallback

The X library calls the PreeditStartCallback when input method preediting begins. This gives your software the opportunity to prepare for drawing preedit feedback information when the PreeditDrawCallback is called. This includes setting up temporary storage to contain the preedit data to be displayed as well as initializing any data (such as creation of additional graphics contexts for visual highlights of feedback data and creation of the *caret cursor*) needed to display the preedit data. The `PreeditStartCallback` your software registers must return the maximum size (in bytes) of the preedit data that your software is willing to support. If your software places no limit on the size of the preedit data, it should return −1. The syntax of the `PreeditStartCallback` is

```
int PreeditStartCallback(ic, client_data, call_data)
  XIC ic;
  XPointer client_data;
  XPointer call_data;
```

`ic` identifies the input context for which preedit has started; `call_data` is always NULL for the `PreeditStartCallback`. Once called, the `PreeditStartCallback` will not be called again until after the `PreeditDoneCallback` has been called.

9.1.2 PreeditDoneCallback

The X library calls your software's `PreeditDoneCallback` when the user completes preediting. This gives your software the opportunity to clean up after preedit. This might include freeing the buffer your software uses to store preedit data and erasing any currently displayed preedit data.

The syntax for the `PreeditDoneCallback` is

```
void PreeditDoneCallback(ic, client_data, call_data)
  XIC ic;
  XPointer client_data;
  XPointer call_data;
```

`ic` identifies the input context for which preedit has completed. `call_data` is always NULL for the `PreeditDoneCallback`.

Though the X11R5 specification suggests that the `PreeditDoneCallback` can be used to free memory used to store the preedit data, your software should avoid freeing the preedit buffer. It is reasonable to assume that if the software user has performed a preedit operation once, he will do so again. Repeated calls to `malloc()` and `free()` fragments memory and hurts your software's performance.

9.1.3 PreeditDrawCallback

The X library calls the `PreeditDrawCallback` whenever the input method wants to change the contents of the preedit data or the way the preedit data is being displayed. Each time the `PreeditDrawCallback` is called, the X library identifies only the changes to the preedit data; it does not pass the callback the entire preedit string when it is called. (The designers at the X Consortium felt that passing only changes to the contents of the preedit buffer would allow the `PreeditDrawCallback` to be optimized, redrawing only data that changed during that callback.) The result of this decision is that when you write a

`PreeditDrawCallback`, you are essentially implementing a small text editor, allowing new characters to be inserted into the preedit buffer and existing characters to be deleted or replaced in the preedit buffer.

The syntax of the `PreeditDrawCallback` is

```
void PreeditDrawCallback(ic, client_data, call_data)
    XIC ic;
    XPointer client_data;
    XIMPreeditDrawCallbackStruct *call_data;
```

ic identifies the input context associated with the preedit operation. *call_data* identifies the change to the preedit data, allowing your software to correctly render it. *call_data* is a pointer to `XIMPreeditDrawCallbackStruct`, which is defined

```
typedef struct _XIMPreeditDrawCallbackStruct{
    int caret;
    int chg_first;
    int chg_length;
    XIMText *text;
}XIMPreeditDrawCallbackStruct;
```

Some input methods use a visual indicator to show the user where the next keystroke will be placed in the preedit buffer. This visual indicator is referred to as the *caret* or *caret cursor*. Often, the user can use the mouse or arrow keys to place the caret somewhere other than the end of the preedit buffer. `caret` in the `XIMPreeditDrawCallbackStruct` identifies the character position where the caret should be placed after the changes identified by the rest of the structure have been applied. For example, assume that after applying the changes indicated by the `XIMPreeditDrawCallbackStruct`, the contents of the preedit buffer are `abcdef`. Figure 9.1 shows how the caret is placed for various values of `caret` in the `XIMPreeditDrawCallbackStruct`.

chg_first identifies the first character in the current preedit buffer that is affected by this call to the callback. Like *caret*, the value of *chg_first* is a character position, with zero identifying the position immediately before the first character in the buffer.

chg_length identifies the number of characters already present in the preedit buffer affected by this call to the callback.

text is a pointer to a structure of type `XIMText` and identifies the textual change to the preedit buffer; *chg_first* and *chg_length* tell your software how much of the existing preedit buffer is being modified by text. The elements of the `XIMPreeditDrawCallbackStruct` basically tell your software: "Beginning with the character at *chg_first*, replace *chg_length* characters in the preedit buffer with the characters contained in *text*." If *text* is NULL, the input method is directing you to delete *chg_length* characters from the preedit buffer. If *chg_length* is zero, the input method is directing you to insert the characters in *text* into the preedit buffer, beginning at the character position *chg_first*.

```
Preedit caret cursor: ∧
XIMPreeditDrawCallbackStruct *pedcb;


This is the preedit buffer: abcdef   pedcb->caret == 0;
                            ∧


This is the preedit buffer: abcdef   pedcb->caret == 1;
                             ∧


This is the preedit buffer: abcdef   pedcb->caret == 5;
                                 ∧
```

Figure 9.1
Placement of the caret cursor at completion of a `PreeditDrawCallback`.

The structure `XIMText` is defined

```
typedef struct _XIMText{
    unsigned short length;
    XIMFeedback *feedback;
    Bool encoding_is_wchar;
    union{
      char *multi_byte;
      wchar_t *wide_char;
    }string;
}XIMText;
```

The `XIMText` structure identifies the new characters your software must place in the preedit buffer. `length` identifies the number of characters (not bytes) contained in `string`. The X library may pass these characters to your software either as multibyte or as wide character; your software has no control over which data type is passed in the `XIMText` structure. The X library tells your software whether `string` contains multibyte or wide characters by means of the `encoding_is_wchar` element of the structure.[1] This means that your `PreeditDrawCallback` must be written to accept both multibyte and wide characters passed through in the `XIMText` structure.

---

1. The members of the X Consortium recognize this as a much less than elegant design. But support for on-the-spot style was added late in the X11R5 design process, and Consortium members could not agree on a single data type for the character data passed in the XIMText structure.

The `XIMText` structure also identifies the way the preedit data should be rendered. The input method may specify any of six ways that a character in the preedit buffer should be rendered. These are identified by the type `XIMFeedback`, which is defined as

```
typedef unsigned long XIMFeedback;
#define XIMReverse     1L
#define XIMUnderline   (1L<<1)
#define XIMHighlight   (1L<<2)
#define XIMPrimary     (1L<<5)
#define XIMSecondary   (1L<<6)
#define XIMTertiary    (1L<<7)
```

The `feedback` field of the `XIMText` structure is a pointer to an array of `XIMFeedback`. The `length` field identifies the number of elements in the feedback array. If `string` is NULL, `feedback` identifies a change to `length` elements of feedback information for the existing preedit buffer, beginning at `chg_first`. If `string` is not NULL, `feedback` identifies the way each character in `string` should be drawn. If `feedback` is NULL and `string` is not NULL, the application should use the feedback style of the nearest character in the existing preedit buffer for the feedback style of the new data in `string`.

Of the six defined feedback highlights, only two have specific semantics. `XIMReverse` means that the character should be drawn with the background color and foreground color of the graphics context swapped — this is sometimes called inverse video. `XIMUnderline` means that the character should be drawn with an underline. The semantics of the remaining highlights are not specified. Therefore, you may choose any means you like to render with these highlights. The X11 specifications state only that text rendered with `XIMPrimary` must be visually distinguishable from text rendered with `XIMSecondary`.

Though the X11 specification does not say so, the intent of the six defined feedback highlights was that the input method could give either specific highlight instructions (`XIMReverse`, `XIMUnderline` and `XIMHighlight`) or generic highlight instructions (`XIMPrimary`, `XIMSecondary` and `XIMTertiary`). So at most, only three feedback highlights would be used for any single connection to an input method. However, since it wasn't explicitly stated in the X11R5 specifications, it is possible that your software may connect to an input method that makes use of all six highlights for a single connection.

> **Note**
>
> Since you do not know what information the input method wants to impart to your user by any of the highlights, your software's documentation cannot explain to the user the semantics of each of these highlights. Similarly, since the input method creators have no idea how your software will render XIMHighlight, XIMPrimary, XIMSecondary, and XIMTertiary, the input method's documentation cannot describe to the end user how a particular semantic will be displayed. In short, these four highlights cannot be reasonably used to convey information to the input method user. This is not one of the more well thought out parts of the X11R5 specification.

9.1.4   PreeditCaretCallback

The caret cursor indicates the location in the displayed preedit data where keyboard input will be placed. Some input methods allow the user to move the caret position within the preedit data. For on-the-spot preedit style, this means that the input method needs some means to tell your software to move the caret cursor location. The PreeditCaretCallback serves this purpose. Its syntax is

```
void PreeditCaretCallback(ic, client_data, call_data)
    XIC ic;
    XPointer client_data
    XIMPreeditCaretCallbackStruct *call_data
```

call_data is a pointer to XIMPreeditCaretCallbackStruct, which is defined as

```
typedef struct_XIMPPreeditCaretCallbackStruct{
    int position;
    XIMCaretDirection direction;
    XIMCaretStyle style;
} XIMPreeditCaretCallbackStruct;
```

The direction field identifies how the caret cursor should be repositioned while the style field specifies how the caret cursor should be rendered. Your software must calculate the new caret cursor position (character offset within the preedit buffer) and return that value in the position field. The XIMCaretStyle and XIMCaretDirection data types are defined below. Table 9.2 and Table 9.3 describe the meaning and use of each value.

```
typedef enum{
  XIMIsInvisible,
  XIMIsPrimary,
  XIMIsSecondary
} XIMCaretStyle;
```

Table 9.2 Description of XIMCaretStyle Values

XIMStyle value	Description
`XIMIsInvisible`	Turn off display of the caret cursor; make it invisible.
`XIMIsPrimary`	Display the caret cursor using an application defined style.
`XIMIsSecondary`	Display the caret cursor using an application defined style that is both visible and is different from `XIMIsPrimary`.

Note

Since you do not know what information the input method wants to impart to your user by changing the caret style between `XIMIsPrimary` and `XIMIsSecondary`, your software's documentation cannot explain to the user the semantics of each of these styles. Similarly, since the input method creators have no idea how your software will render `XIMIsPrimary` and `XIMIsSecondary`, the input method's documentation cannot describe to the end user what visual indicator is associated with a particular semantic. Like the `XIMFeedback` highlights, the styles of `XIMCaretStyle` are not among the more well thought out parts of the X11R5 specification.

`XIMCaretDirection` describes how the caret cursor should be repositioned. It is defined as

```
typedef enum{
  XIMForwardChar, XIMBackwardChar,
  XIMForwardWord, XIMBackwardWord,
  XIMCaretUp, XIMCaretDown,
  XIMNextLine, XIMPreviousLine,
  XIMLineStart, XIMLineEnd,
  XIMAbsolutePosition,
  XIMDontChange
} XIMCaretDirection;
```

Table 9.3 Description of XIMCaretDirection Values

XIMCaretDirection value	Description
`XIMForwardChar`	Move the caret cursor forward one character position in the preedit buffer.
`XIMBackwardChar`	Move the caret cursor backward one character position in the preedit buffer.
`XIMForwardWord`	Move the caret cursor to the character position at the beginning of the next word[†] in the preedit buffer.
`XIMBackwardWord`	Move the caret cursor to the character position at the beginning of the current word.[†] If the caret is already positioned at the beginning of a word, move it to the character position at the beginning of the previous word in the preedit buffer.
`XIMCaretUp`	Move the caret cursor to the previous line in the preedit data, keeping the current offset.[††]
`XIMCaretDown`	Move the caret cursor to the next line in the preedit data, keeping the current offset.[††]
`XIMPreviousLine`	Move the caret cursor up one line in the preedit data, if possible.[†††]
`XIMNextLine`	Move the caret cursor down one line in the preedit data, if possible.[†††]
`XIMLineStart`	Move the caret cursor to the character position at the beginning of the current line of preedit data.
`XIMLineEnd`	Move the caret cursor to the character position at the end of the current line.
`XIMAbsolutePosition`	Move the caret cursor to the character position `position` in the preedit buffer.
`XIMDontChange`	Do not change the caret position. This value will be sent when only the `XIMCaretStyle` should be changed.

†. The X11 specification does not define *word* in this context. The languages of the Americas and Europe tend to use white space and punctuation marks to identify word boundaries. Asian languages use other guidelines. Unfortunately, no standard internationalization tools exist for identifying word boundaries in a string.

††. The X11 specification does not say whether this offset is a character position offset or a pixel offset. Therefore, you are free to implement whichever you feel is a better user interface.

†††. The X11 specification does not say *where* in the line you must place the caret cursor. However, discussions with the X Consortium indicate that the intent is that the caret should be placed at the beginning of the line. The next revision of the specification will more clearly state this.

9.1.5   StatusStartCallback

The `StatusStartCallback` is called when the input context is created or when the input context gains focus. Your implementation of the `StatusStartCallback` should initialize any data that is needed to render status information. This includes creation or initialization of graphics context for rendering status information with different highlights. Once the `StatusStartCallback` has been called, it will not be called again until after the `StatusDoneCallback` has been called. The syntax of the `StatusStartCallback` is

```
void StatusStartCallback(ic, client_data, call_data)
  XIC ic;
  XPointer client_data;
  XPointer call_data;
```

`ic` is the input context associated with the status information. The input method does not pass any information into this callback; `call_data` is always NULL.

9.1.6   StatusDoneCallback

The `StatusDoneCallback` is called when the input context is destroyed or when the input context loses focus. It is used to free any resources allocated during the `StatusStartCallback` and `StatusDrawCallback`. Its syntax is

```
void StatusDoneCallback(ic, client_data, call_data)
  XIC ic;
  XPointer client_data;
  XPointer call_data;
```

`ic` is the input context that has been destroyed or has lost focus. The input method does not pass any information into this callback; `call_data` is always NULL.

9.1.7   StatusDrawCallback

The `StatusDrawCallback` is called whenever the contents of the status information changes. The syntax of the `StatusDrawCallback` is

```
void StatusDrawCallback(ic, client_data, call_data)
  XIC ic;
  Xpointer client_data;
  XIMStatusDrawCallbackStruct *call_data;
```

`ic` is the input context for which the status information has changed. `call_data` points to the status information, which is a structure of type `XIMStatusDrawCallbackStruct`. This structure is defined as

```
typedef struct _XIMStatusDrawCallbackStruct{
  XIMStatusDataType type;
  union {
    XIMText *text;
    Pixmap bitmap;
  }data;
}XIMStatusDrawCallbackStruct;
```

The type element of the structure specifies whether the status information is a bitmap or whether it is textual information. `XIMStatusDataType` is defined as

```
typedef enum {
  XIMTextType,
  XIMBitmapType
}XIMStatusDataType;
```

When the status information is textual, its type is `XIMText`. This is the same type as is used in the `PreeditDrawCallback`. When used with the `StatusDrawCallback`, the `feedback` field of the `XIMText` structure identifies the highlight for each character in the `string` field; `length` identifies both the number of characters in the `string` field of the `XIMText` structure as well as the number of elements in `feedback` field.

9.2 Example: Using On-the-Spot Style

The example in this chapter continues to build on the example program presented in the previous chapter. First, an example implementation of each of the callbacks is listed and described. Then, at the end of the chapter, program fragments are used to show how to integrate the callbacks into the sample application.

9.2.1   Initial Design Decisions

Before creating the callbacks, some basic design decisions must be made. For example, you must decide how much memory you will use to store the preedit data. Is the memory for the preedit buffer fixed in size or will you resize the preedit buffer to accommodate any request from the input method? How will the various highlights needed for the `PreeditDrawCallback`, `PreeditCaretCallback`, and `StatusDrawCallback` be represented? How will you store the highlight information for each character in the preedit buffer? How about highlights for the caret cursor?

For this example, the following design decisions were made:

• The callbacks for on-the-spot status style are similar to the callbacks for on-the-spot preedit style, only simpler. Also, few examples of input methods using on-the-spot status style exist. For these reasons, on-the-spot status style is not included in the example.

Including its code would only add to the size of the example without providing any new information.

- The preedit buffer data is stored as wide character. This makes it easy to map text positions directly to buffer offsets.

- The size of the preedit buffer is initially zero bytes and is reallocated larger (in blocks of 64 wide characters) as needed.

- Several existing program variables become global variables, allowing the callbacks to share them. For example, the graphics context used to draw text in the application is also used to draw XIMUnderline and XIMSecondary highlights as well as the caret cursor. Similarly, the display variable dpy and the window ID variable win are needed in many rendering calls.

- The application declares a global pointer for the preedit buffer. This way, the main body of the application, the PreeditStartCallback, the PreeditDrawCallback, and the PreeditDoneCallback, can all share the preedit buffer without passing it via *client_data* pointer.

- The PreeditStartCallback creates two graphics contexts to be used to render the XIMReverse and XIMHighlight. (XIMUnderline highlight uses the same graphics context as normal text in the application but adds a line drawn at the text baseline for highlight.) Because the X11 specification does not prohibit it, the example uses the same highlight for XIMPrimary as it does for XIMReverse. Similarly, the XIMSecondary highlight is rendered in the same way as XIMUnderline. And XIMTertiary is rendered with the same highlight as XIMHighlight. Reusing the highlights keeps the example simple and easier to understand.

- The PreeditStartCallback allocates an array that contains the highlight specification for each character in the preedit buffer. A more elegant design might use a linked list of highlight records, where a highlight record contains the starting character position for the highlight and an XIMFeedback element identifying the highlight. However, since this would require more complex code to implement, and since the purpose of the example is to illustrate use of the callbacks, the simpler approach is used here.

- The PreeditStartCallback creates a caret cursor used to display the caret cursor position, as directed by the PreeditCaretCallback and the PreeditDrawCallback. The caret cursor is shaped like the circumflex (^) character, drawn at the text baseline. The caret cursor is drawn by filling a rectangle using the caret cursor pixmap as a stencil through which the rectangle is filled, as is shown in Figure 9.2. This design allows additional pixmaps to be used to provide various highlights for the caret cursor, though in this example secondary highlight is achieved by drawing the caret cursor in a different color.

Painting this rectangle... through this stencil... produces a caret cursor.

Figure 9.2
Drawing the caret cursor using a pixmap "stencil."

- The `PreeditStartCallback` creates two highlights for the caret cursor. Drawing the caret cursor with the normal highlight causes it to be drawn with the text foreground color. Drawing the caret cursor with the secondary highlight causes it to be drawn with the highlight color. The `XIMIsInvisible` highlight is achieved by overwriting the existing caret cursor using the graphics context for the `XIMReverse` highlight. This causes the caret to be painted with the background color, erasing it from the display.
- Your software needs to draw the preedit area not only when told to do so by the callbacks, but also when exposure events occur. For this reason, the sample creates the new routine `MyDrawPreedit()`. It is called in the `PreeditDrawCallback` and in the program's event loop for handling exposure events. The sample program also adds the new routine `MyErasePreedit()` which is used to erase any preedit data currently displayed. The caret cursor needs to be erased and drawn when its position changes in the `PreeditDrawCallback`, the `PreeditCaretCallback`, and when an exposure event occurs. The program creates the routine `MyPaintCaret()` to perform these functions.
- To keep the example simple, the `PreeditDrawCallback` redraws the entire preedit buffer at the completion of each call. A more elegant implementation would redraw only those portions of the preedit buffer that were changed by the `XIMPreeditDrawCallbackStruct` data.
- Since the example program has only one line of input, many of the navigation requests in the `PreeditCaretCallback` can be safely ignored. Only requests to move the caret to an absolute character position, or to move the caret ahead or back a specified number of positions are supported in the example program.
- Another simplifying design decision is to allow text input only at the end of the current line. That is, the program does not allow the user to edit a character in the middle of the line without backspacing (and deleting) all the characters that follow the character to be edited. Therefore, the *x,y* position of the preedit buffer is the same as the *x,y* position of the last character in the line.
- If the preedit buffer grows such that it cannot be contained by the application window, the window is not resized. A well-written application would either resize the window

or scroll the existing data within the current window to make room for the new data. But adding the code to do this would complicate the example without providing any additional understanding of how to use on-the-spot style.

9.2.2   Example: Accessing Application Data in the Callbacks

Many values currently used by the program `overnoff_input.c` are needed in the callbacks as support for on-the-spot preedit style is added. This data is usually passed through the `client_data` argument of the callback. However, this would complicate the example and detract from illustrating how the callbacks are actually used. To keep the example simple, global variables are used to allow the callbacks to share data with the main application.

The following block of code shows the global data, #defines, and #includes added to `overnoff_input.c` to support on-the-spot feedback style in the new program `allstyles_input.c`.

```
...
#include <stdlib.h>
...
#define MARGIN_X 10
#define MARGIN_Y 10
#define WNAME_MAX 1024
#define CARET_HEIGHT 10
#define CARET_WIDTH 10
#define CARET_THICKNESS 2
#define BUFFER_BLOCK 64

/* Application global variables needed by preedit callbacks. */
Display *dpy;
Window win;
GC gc;
int screen;
XFontSet fs;
int x_start, y_start, line_height;
wchar_t wname[WNAME_MAX];
int wname_len = 0;

/* New global variables for on-the-spot feedback style. */
wchar_t *pe_buf = NULL;          /* preedit buffer */
XIMFeedback *pe_highlight;        /* array of highlights;
                                  * 1 per pe_buf[i]*/
unsigned int pe_buf_size = 0;     /* alloc'ed size of pe_buf */
unsigned int num_pe_chars = 0;    /* number of characters
                                  * in pe_buf */
GC reverse_gc;     /* XIMReverse and XIMPrimary highlights */
```

```
GC highlight_gc;   /* XIMHighlight and XIMTertiary highlights */
                   /* XIMUnderline and XIMSecondary highlights
                    * use the application's normal GC, but add
                    * underlining through XDrawLine. */
GC caret_gc;       /* GC used to paint the caret cursor */
XIMCaretStyle cur_caret_style;   /* Keep track of the
                                  * current caret style. */
int caret_pos;     /* Current caret character position. */
unsigned long app_foreground;    /* Application foreground. */
unsigned long app_background;    /* Application background. */
unsigned long highlight_pixel;   /* XIMHighlight color. */
```

9.2.3   Example: PreeditStartCallback

The `PreeditStartCallback` is responsible for preparing the application for future preediting. For this particular example, the `PreeditStartCallback` allocates memory for storing the preedit characters and associated highlight information, creates the caret cursor, and creates the graphics contexts used to display the various highlights. In this example callback, these operations are done only once — the first time the `PreeditStartCallback` is called. When the `PreeditDoneCallback` is called, the memory for the preedit buffer and memory for preedit highlights are not freed. Similarly, the graphics contexts are not destroyed and the caret cursor is not destroyed. It would be wasteful and slow to create and destroy these objects each time preedit is performed. To ensure that these operations are performed only once, the example callback uses the local static boolean `initialized` to indicate that the information needed for preediting has been created.

Also, since the example `PreeditStartCallback` procedure dynamically allocates memory to hold the preedit data, it returns –1 to indicate that there is no limit to the size of the preedit buffer.

```
int MyPreeditStartCallback(ic, client_data, call_data)
  XIC ic;
  XPointer client_data;
  XPointer call_data;
{
  GC fillGC;                    /* GC for creating the caret cursor. */
  XGCValues values;
  Pixmap clip_mask;
  Pixmap caret_cursor;   /* Stencil used to paint the
                          * caret cursor. */
  XRectangle clip;
  XSegment segments[2]; /* For drawing the caret cursor. */
  unsigned long vmask;
```

```
static Bool initialized = False;  /* Create buffers, cursors,
                                   * GCs, etc. only once in
                                   * the life of the program. */
XColor xcolor;
Status status;

if (!initialized){
  initialized = True;

 /* Allocate memory for preedit buffer and highlight
  * buffer. */
  pe_buf_size = BUFFER_BLOCK;
  pe_buf = (wchar_t*)
                  malloc(pe_buf_size * sizeof(wchar_t));
  pe_highlight = (XIMFeedback*)
                    malloc(pe_buf_size * sizeof(XIMFeedback));

 /* Temporarily use caret_gc to hold a GC that will be
  * used to construct the stencil. Later, we'll free this
  * temporary GC and create a new one to contain the
  * stencil and use it to paint the caret cursor. */

  caret_cursor = XCreatePixmap(dpy, win, CARET_HEIGHT,
                               CARET_WIDTH, 1);
  caret_gc = XCreateGC(dpy, caret_cursor, 0,
                     (XGCValues *)NULL);

 /* Fill in the pixmap with a solid in preparation to
  * "cut out" the caret. */
  XFillRectangle(dpy, caret_cursor, caret_gc, 0, 0,
                 CARET_WIDTH, CARET_HEIGHT);

 /* Change the GC for use in "cutting out" the caret shape. */
  values.foreground = 1;
  values.line_width = CARET_THICKNESS;
  XChangeGC(dpy, caret_gc, GCForeground | GCLineWidth,
            &values);

  clip.width = CARET_WIDTH;
  clip.height = CARET_HEIGHT;
  clip.x = 0;
  clip.y = 0;
  XSetClipRectangles(dpy, caret_gc, 0, 0, &clip,
                     1, Unsorted);
```

```
/* Cut out the caret shape in the stencil. */
segments[0].x1 = 0;
segments[0].y1 = CARET_HEIGHT;
segments[0].x2 = CARET_WIDTH/2;
segments[0].y2 = 0;

segments[1].x1 = CARET_WIDTH/2;
segments[1].y1 = 0;
segments[1].x2 = CARET_WIDTH;
segments[1].y2 = CARET_HEIGHT;

XDrawSegments(dpy, caret_cursor, caret_gc, segments, 2);

XFreeGC(dpy, caret_gc);
clip_mask = XCreatePixmap(dpy, RootWindow(dpy, screen),
                        CARET_HEIGHT, CARET_WIDTH, 1);
values.foreground = 1;
values.background = 0;
caret_gc = XCreateGC(dpy, clip_mask,
                    GCForeground | GCBackground, &values);
XFillRectangle(dpy, clip_mask, caret_gc, 0, 0, CARET_WIDTH,
              CARET_HEIGHT);
XFreeGC(dpy, caret_gc);

vmask = (GCFunction | GCClilpMask | GCStipple |
        GCForeground | GCBackground | GCFillStyle);
values.function = GXcopy;
values.clip_mask = clip_mask;
values.stipple = caret_cursor;
values.fill_style = FillStippled;
values.foreground = app_foreground;
values.background = app_background;
caret_gc = XCreateGC(dpy, win, vmask, &values);

/* Create the GC for rendering XIMReverse/XIMPrimary
 * highlights. */
values.foreground = app_background;
values.background = app_foreground;
reverse_gc = XCreateGC(dpy, win,
                        GCForeground | GCBackground,
                        &values);
```

```
/* Create the GC for rendering XIMHighlight/XIMTertiary
 * highlights. */
xcolor.red = 65535;
xcolor.green = 0;
xcolor.blue = 0;
xcolor.flags = DoRed;
status = XAllocColor(dpy, DefaultColormap(dpy,screen),
                     &xcolor);
if (status)
  values.foreground = highlight_pixel = xcolor.pixel;
else
  values.foreground = app_background;
values.background = app_foreground;
highlight_gc = XCreateGC(dpy, win,
                         GCForeground | GCBackground,
                         &values);
caret_pos = 0;
    }


  return (-1);
}
```

9.2.4   Example: PreeditDoneCallback

The `PreeditDoneCallback` cleans up when preediting finishes. Because of design decisions made on page 175, this example `PreeditDoneCallback` is fairly simple. It erases any currently displayed preedit data, erases the caret cursor, and resets the counters to indicate that there are zero characters in the preedit buffer.

Because other parts of the application also need to draw and erase the preedit buffer and caret cursor, the example creates three new routines: `MyDrawPreedit()`, `MyErasePreedit()`, and `MyPaintCursor()`. `MyDrawPreedit()` draws the contents of the preedit buffer using the highlights specified in a highlight array (maintained by the `PreeditDrawCallback`). `MyErasePreedit()` erases any currently displayed preedit data. `MyPaintCursor()` draws the caret cursor using a highlight passed as an argument. For example, when the application wants to erase the caret, it calls `MyPaintCursor(XIMIsInvisible)`.

```
void
MyDrawPreedit()
{
  int x, y;           /* Location of character to be drawn. */
  int i, char_width;
```

```
/* Initialize x,y to end of current data in wname buffer;
 * since we decided to allow data entry only at the end of
 * the line, this is where preedit should be displayed. */

x = x_start + XwcTextEscapement(fs, wname, wname_len);
y = y_start + line_height;

for (i = 0; i < num_pe_chars; i++){
  char_width = XwcTextEscapement(fs, &pe_buf[i], 1);
  if (pe_highlight[i] == XIMPrimary ||
      pe_highlight[i] == XIMReverse){
    XwcDrawImageString(dpy, win, fs, reverse_gc,
                    x, y, &pe_buf[i], 1);
  } else if (pe_highlight[i] == XIMSecondary ||
             pe_highlight[i] == XIMUnderline){
    XwcDrawImageString(dpy, win, fs, gc, x, y,
                          &pe_buf[i], 1);
    XDrawLine(dpy, win, gc, x, y, x + char_width, y);
  } else { /* XIMTertiary || XIMHighlight */
    XwcDrawImageString(dpy, win, fs, highlight_gc,
                    x, y, &pe_buf[i], 1);
  }
  x += char_width;
}
}

/* Erase the current contents of the preedit area being
 * displayed. */

void
MyErasePreedit()
{
  XRectangle ink, logical;
  int x, y;

  /* Initialize x,y to end of current data in wname buffer;
   * since we decided to allow data entry only at the end of
   * the line, this is where preedit should be displayed. */

  x = x_start + XwcTextEscapement(fs, wname, wname_len);
  y = y_start + line_height;

  (void) XwcTextExtents(fs, pe_buf, num_pe_chars, &ink,
                     &logical);
```

```c
    XFillRectangle(dpy, win, reverse_gc,
                    x + logical.x, y + logical.y,
                    logical.width, logical.height);
}

void
MyPaintCaret(feedback)
  XIMFeedback feedback;
{
    int x, y; /* Location of 1st character in pe_buf. */
    int i;
    unsigned long vmask = GCForeground | GCBackground;
    XGCValues values;
    static Bool is_erased = True;

    if (feedback == XIMIsInvisible) {
     /* Paint with reverse GC to erase the caret by painting
      * with background. */
      if (is_erased) return;
      values.foreground = app_background;
      values.background = app_foreground;
      is_erased = True;
      }
    } else if (feedback == XIMIsPrimary) {
      values.foreground = app_foreground;
      values.background = app_background;
      is_erased = False;
    } else { /* must be XIMIsSecondary */
      values.foreground = highlight_pixel;
      values.background = app_background;
      is_erased = False;
    }

    x = x_start + XwcTextEscapement(fs, wname, wname_len) +
        XwcTextEscapement(fs, pe_buf, caret_pos);
    y = y_start + line_height;

    XSetClipOrigin(dpy, caret_gc, x - (CARET_WIDTH >> 1), y);
    XSetTSOrigin(dpy, caret_gc, x - (CARET_WIDTH >> 1), y);
    XChangeGC(dpy, caret_gc, vmask, &values);
    XFillRectangle(dpy, win, caret_gc, x, y,
                    CARET_WIDTH, CARET_HEIGHT);
}
```

```
void
MyPreeditDoneCallback(ic, client_data, call_data)
  XIC ic;
  XPointer client_data;
  XPointer call_data;
{
  XRectangle ink, logical;

 /* Since there is a good chance the user will preedit
  * data again in the future, the existing preedit and
  * highlight buffers are not freed. However, the
  * variable indicating the amount of the buffer used must
  * be reset since there is no more useful data in the
  * preedit buffer at this time.
  *
  * Similarly, there is no need to destroy the GCs or caret
  * cursor, since they will be needed for the next preedit
  * session. They will remain allocated until the program
  * terminates. */

 /* Erase the caret cursor; reset the caret highlight
  * to XIMIsInvisible. */

  MyPaintCaret(XIMIsInvisible);
  cur_caret_style = XIMIsInvisible;

 /* Reset the preedit buffer length and the caret position
  * in preparation for the next preedit session. */
  num_pe_chars = 0;
  caret_pos = 0;
}
```

9.2.5   Example: PreeditDrawCallback

The `PreeditDrawCallback` is responsible for keeping track of and displaying the current contents of the preedit buffer. In essence, the `PreeditDrawCallback` is a small text editor.

This example `PreeditDrawCallback` does not try to minimize the amount of drawing it does. A more elegant implementation would attempt to draw only the portions of the preedit buffer that change with each call to the callback.

This example `PreeditDrawCallback` is written around the following design. Each time the callback is called, it

1.   Erases all preedit data currently displayed.
2.   Checks the currently allocated size of the preedit buffer. If the preedit buffer is not large
     enough to contain the results of the requested update, the callback calculates a new size
     for the preedit buffer and reallocates it. Similarly, the callback reallocates memory used
     to store highlight information for each character in the preedit buffer.
3.   Moves preedit data unaffected by this call to the callback to its new location in the pre-
     edit buffer, making room for the new data being inserted.
4.   Copies any new preedit data from the XIMPreeditDrawCallbackStruct into
     the callback's preedit buffer.
5.   Repeats steps 3 and 4 for the preedit highlight information stored by the callback.
6.   Updates num_pe_chars, the variable used to keep track of the current number of
     characters in the preedit buffer.
7.   Draws the entire contents of the preedit buffer by calling the routine
     MyDrawPreedit().
8.   Checks to see if the caret cursor location has changed. If it has, erases the caret at its
     current location by calling MyPaintCaret(XIMIsInvisible). Next, it updates
     the caret location as directed by the XIMPreeditDrawCallbackStruct and
     draws it using the current caret highlight style.

```
void
MyPreeditDrawCallback(ic, client_data, call_data)
  XIC ic;
  XPointer client_data;
  XIMPreeditDrawCallbackStruct *call_data;
{
  XIMPreeditDrawCallbackStruct *draw_data = call_data;
  int delta = 0;
  int insert_length = 0;
  int chg_length = 0;
  int chg_first = 0;
  XIMText *text = draw_data->text;
  wchar_t *src_wptr, *dst_wptr;
  char *src_ptr;
  XIMFeedback *src_hlite, *dst_hlite;
  int i, num_bytes;

 /* Though not prohibited by the spec, these cases indicate
  * the IM made an error, so ignore the request. */
  if (draw_data->caret < 0 || draw_data->chg_length < 0
      || draw_data->chg_first < 0)
    return;
 /* Before modifying the contents of the preedit buffer, erase
  * the current display of the contents of the preedit buffer;
```

```
 * the new contents will be displayed by a call to
 * MyDrawPreedit() at the end of this routine. */

MyErasePreedit();

/* Make sure there is room for preedit buffer that results from
 * this call. "delta" identifies the change to the total
 * number of characters in the preedit buffer. It is
 * calculated as:
 *   delta = number of characters inserted -
 *                                 number of characters deleted
 */

if (text)
   insert_length = text->length;

chg_length = draw_data->chg_length;
chg_first = draw_data->chg_first;

delta = insert_length - chg_length;

if (num_pe_chars + delta >= pe_buf_size) {
   while (pe_buf_size <= num_pe_chars + delta)
     pe_buf_size += BUFFER_BLOCK;
   pe_buf = (wchar_t*)realloc(pe_buf,
                                   pe_buf_size * sizeof(wchar_t));
   pe_highlight = (XIMFeedback*)realloc(pe_highlight,
                       pe_buf_size * sizeof(XIMFeedback));
   if (!pe_buf || !pe_highlight)
     exit(1);  /* insufficient memory; exit */
}

/* Shift the contents of the pe_buf and the highlight_buf to
 * make room for the new data. */
if (delta < 0){
  /* Shift characters to the left in the buffer. */

   for(src_wptr = pe_buf + (chg_first + chg_length),
       dst_wptr = src_wptr + delta,
       src_hlite = pe_highlight + (chg_first + chg_length),
       dst_hlite = src_hlite + delta,
       i = num_pe_chars - (chg_first + chg_length);
       i > 0;
       ++src_wptr, ++src_hlite, ++dst_wptr, ++dst_hlite, --i){
```

```
            *dst_wptr = *src_wptr;
            *dst_hlite = *src_hlite;
        }
    } else if (delta > 0 && num_pe_chars > 0) {
      /* Shift characters to the right in the buffer. */
        for(src_wptr = pe_buf + (num_pe_chars - 1),
            dst_wptr = src_wptr + delta,
            src_hlite = pe_highlight + (num_pe_chars - 1),
            dst_hlite = src_hlite + delta,
            i = num_pe_chars - (chg_first + chg_length);
            i > 0;
            ++src_wptr, ++src_hlite, ++dst_wptr, ++dst_hlite,
            --i){
          *dst_wptr = *src_wptr;
          *dst_hlite = *src_hlite;
        }
    }


/* Update pe_buf to reflect the new data. */
 if ((text->encoding_is_wchar && text->string.wide_char) ||
        (!text->encoding_is_wchar && text->string.multi_byte)){
    if (insert_length != 0){
      /* If data is wchar_t, just copy from the callback data
       * into the buffer, now that text is moved out of the
       * way for the new data. */
        if (text->encoding_is_wchar){
          for (src_wptr = text->string.wide_char,
              dst_wptr = pe_buf + chg_first,
              i = insert_length;
              i > 0; ++src_wptr, ++dst_wptr, --i)
            *dst_wptr = *src_wptr;
        } else {
        /* Data is char* and must be converted into wchar_t
         * as it is copied. */
          for (src_ptr = text->string.multi_byte,
              dst_wptr = pe_buf + chg_first,
              i = insert_length; i > 0; ++dst_wptr, --i){
            num_bytes = mbtowc(dst_wptr, src_ptr, MB_CUR_MAX);
            if (num_bytes == 0)
              break;
            if (num_bytes < 0) /* error: exit */
              exit(1);
            src_ptr += num_bytes;
          }
```

```
       }
     }
   }
/* Update highlight_buf to reflect the new data. */
 if (text->feedback){
    if (insert_length != 0){
     /* If data is wchar_t, just copy from the callback
      * data into the buffer, now that text is moved out of
      * the way for the new data. */
     for (src_hlite = text->feedback,
          dst_hlite = pe_highlight + chg_first,
          i = insert_length;
          i > 0; ++src_hlite, ++dst_hlite, --i)
        *dst_hlite = *src_hlite;
    }
  } else {
   /* Feedback is NULL; assign feedback of new characters
    * to be that of existing surrounding characters in the
    * preedit buffer. */
   XIMFeedback newfeedback;
   if (chg_first > 0)
    /* Take the highlight from the character to the left
     * of chg_first. */
    newfeedback = pe_highlight[chg_first - 1];
   else
    /* Take the highlight from the characters following
     * the change. */
    newfeedback = pe_highlight[chg_first + insert_length];
   for (dst_hlite = pe_highlight + chg_first,
        i = insert_length;
        i > 0; ++dst_hlite, --i)
      *dst_hlite = newfeedback;
 }

/* Update num_pe_chars to reflect new pe_buf contents. */
 num_pe_chars += delta;

/* Draw the updated preedit buffer. */
 MyDrawPreedit();

/* Erase the current caret cursor and move it to the location
  * specified by the input method. */
 MyPaintCaret(XIMIsInvisible);   /* Erase the caret. */
 caret_pos = draw_data->caret;
```

```
  /* Draw the caret at new position. */
  MyPaintCaret(cur_caret_style);
}
```

9.2.6   Example: PreeditCaretCallback

The `PreeditCaretCallback` is called when the input method wants to update the location or highlight of the caret cursor. Because this is a simple example, allowing only keyboard input for a single line of text data — and only at the end of the input line — only a few of the many caret cursor position commands are dealt with. This example callback determines the new caret position and new feedback style for displaying the caret, erases the old caret, and then draws the caret at the new location using the new feedback style. The caret position and style are maintained in the global variables `caret_pos` and `cur_caret_style`.

```
void
MyPreeditCaretCallback(ic, client_data, call_data)
  XIC ic;
  XPointer client_data;
  XIMPreeditCaretCallbackStruct *call_data;
{
  XIMPreeditCaretCallbackStruct *caret_data = call_data;
  XIMCaretStyle newstyle = cur_caret_style;
  int newpos = caret_pos;

 /* Design decision: ignore any movement of the caret except
  * XIMForwardChar, XIMBackwardChar, XIMLineStart, XIMLineEnd,
  * XIMAbsolutePosition, and XIMDontChange. */

  switch (caret_data->direction){
    case XIMForwardChar:
      if (caret_pos < num_pe_chars){
        newpos = caret_pos + 1;
        newstyle = caret_data->style;
      }
      break;
    case XIMBackwardChar:
      if (caret_pos > 0){
        newpos = caret_pos - 1;
        newstyle = caret_data->style;
      }
      break;
    case XIMLineStart:
      newpos = 0;
```

```
        newstyle = caret_data->style;
        break;
     case XIMLineEnd:
        newpos = num_pe_chars;
        newstyle = caret_data->style;
        break;
     case XIMAbsolutePosition:
        newpos = caret_data->position;
        newstyle = caret_data->style;
        break;
     case XIMDontChange:
        newstyle = caret_data->style;
        break;
   }
   if (newstyle != cur_caret_style || newpos != caret_pos){
    /* Erase the old caret cursor. */
    MyPaintCaret(XIMIsInvisible);
    cur_caret_style = newstyle;
    caret_pos = newpos;
    /* Paint the caret and set cur_caret_style to the new style. */
    MyPaintCaret(newstyle);   }
}
```

9.2.7   Example: Using the Callbacks in an Application

Once the callbacks are coded and designed, they need to be passed as attributes when creating the input context. In addition, the program's event loop needs to be modified to accommodate on-the-spot style. The preedit buffer and caret cursor need to be redrawn during expose events. Because of the asynchronous nature of events, it is possible that a KeyPress event generated by the input method[2] may arrive at the application before the PreeditDoneCallback has been called. In this situation, the preedit buffer is still displayed as the application processes the KeyPress event, which will cause the newly entered data to be drawn over the top of the now defunct (but not yet erased) preedit data. In anticipation of this, the KeyPress event handler needs to erase the preedit data and the caret cursor.

The changes required when adding on-the-spot preedit style are indicated in the following code fragments by change bars in the margin:

```
...
/* Open the input method and select styles. */
   if ((im = XOpenIM(dpy, NULL, NULL, NULL)) == NULL) {
```

---

2. Input methods sometimes generate artificial key press events, passing the results of preediting to the application when it calls XmbLookupString() or XwcLookupString() while processing the KeyPress event.

```
  (void) fprintf(stderr, catgets(my_cat, ERR_SET, 5,
                                 "Couldn't open IM\n"));
  exit(1);
}

my_style = XIMPreeditNothing | XIMPreeditNone;
my_style |= XIMStatusNothing | XIMStatusNone;
my_style |= XIMStatusArea | XIMPreeditArea;
my_style |= XIMPreeditPosition;
my_style |= XIMPreeditCallbacks;
style = SelectStyle(im, my_style);
if (!style)
  fprintf(stderr, "IM doesn't support my styles!\n");

spot.x = x_start;
spot.y = y_start + line_height;
if (my_style & XIMPreeditCallbacks){
  pe_start.callback = (XIMProc)MyPreeditStartCallback;
  pe_start.client_data = (XPointer)NULL;
  pe_done.callback = (XIMProc)MyPreeditDoneCallback;
  pe_done.client_data = (XPointer)NULL;
  pe_draw.callback = (XIMProc)MyPreeditDrawCallback;
  pe_draw.client_data = (XPointer)NULL;
  pe_caret.callback = (XIMProc)MyPreeditCaretCallback;
  pe_caret.client_data = (XPointer)NULL;
  preedit_att = XVaCreateNestedList(dummy,
                    XNPreeditStartCallback, &pe_start,
                    XNPreeditDoneCallback, &pe_done,
                    XNPreeditDrawCallback, &pe_draw,
                    XNPreeditCaretCallback, &pe_caret,
                    NULL);
} else {
  preedit_att = XVaCreateNestedList(dummy,
                      XNForeground, gcv.foreground,
                      XNBackground, gcv.background,
                      XNFontSet, fs,
                      XNSpotLocation, &spot, NULL);
}
status_att = XVaCreateNestedList(dummy,
                    XNForeground, gcv.foreground,
                    XNBackground, gcv.background,
                    XNFontSet, fs, NULL);
```

```
ic = XCreateIC(im, XNInputStyle, style,
               XNClientWindow, win,
               XNFocusWindow, win,
               XNPreeditAttributes, preedit_att,
               XNStatusAttributes, status_att,
               NULL);
...

    switch (event.type) {
      case Expose:
        if (event.xexpose.count == 0){
          XmbDrawString(dpy, win, fs, gc, x_start, y_start,
                        greeting, strlen(greeting));
          XwcDrawString(dpy, win, fs, gc, x_start,
                        y_start + line_height,
                        wname, wname_len);
          if (num_pe_chars > 0)
            MyDrawPreedit();
          MyPaintCaret(cur_caret_style);
        }
        break;
      case KeyPress:
        len = XwcLookupString(ic, (XKeyPressedEvent*)&event,
                              winput_buf, buf_size,
                              &keysym, &status);
        if (status == XBufferOverflow){
          buf_size = len;
          winput_buf = (wchar_t*)realloc((char*)winput_buf,
                              (buf_size + 1) * sizeof(wchar_t));
          len = XwcLookupString(ic,
                              (XKeyPressedEvent*)&event,
                              winput_buf, buf_size,
                              &keysym, &status);
        }
        redraw = False;

        switch (status) {
          case XLookupNone:
            break;
          case XLookupKeySym:
          case XLookupBoth:
            if (num_pe_chars > 0)
              MyErasePreedit();
```

```
      if ((keysym == XK_Delete) ||
                          (keysym == XK_BackSpace)){
        if (wname_len > 0) wname_len --;
        redraw = True;
        need_erase = True;
        break;
      }
      if (keysym == XK_Return) exit(0);
      if (status == XLookupKeySym) break;
    case XLookupChars:
      if (num_pe_chars > 0)
        MyErasePreedit();
      for (i = 0;
           (i < len) && (wname_len < WNAME_MAX); i++)
        wname[wname_len++] = winput_buf[i];
      redraw = True;
      break;
    }
    if (redraw) {
      if (need_erase){
        XChangeGC(dpy, gc, gcv_mask, &gcv_inverse);
        XFillRectangle(dpy, win, gc,
                       x_start, y_start + descent,
                       width - MARGIN_X, line_height);
        XChangeGC(dpy, gc, gcv_mask, &gcv);
        need_erase = False;
      }
      if (num_pe_chars > 0)
        MyDrawPreedit();
      XwcDrawString(dpy, win, fs, gc, x_start,
                    y_start + line_height, wname, wname_len);
      if (style & XIMPreeditPosition){
        spot.x = x_start +
              XwcTextEscapement(fs, wname, wname_len);
        spot.y = y_start + line_height;
        preedit_att = XVaCreateNestedList(dummy,
                          XNSpotLocation, &spot, NULL);
        XSetICValues(ic, XNPreeditAttributes, preedit_att,
                    NULL);
        XFree(preedit_att);
      }
    }
    break;
  ...
```

C H A P T E R

10

Keyboard Input with X11R6

X11R6 extends the keyboard input capabilities
described in Chapters 6 through 9, providing several new routines, input method values (XIM
values), and input context values (XIC values). These routines and values provide the following new features:

- a new routine for setting input method values, `XSetIMValues()`, and new memory
  management techniques for using `XGetIMValues()`.
- a new callback that allows an application to be notified when connection to an input
  method is broken (for example, the input method crashes).
- a new callback that allows an application to be notified when an input method is finally
  ready to accept connections from clients.
- capability to query and programmatically control the input method preedit state.
- capability to reset the input context (XIC) and control the preedit state in the reset input
  context.
- new XIC data values allowing the application to specify a set of keys that the input
  method must ignore, allowing the application to process these keys directly.
- new XIC data values allowing an application to pass a string to the input method to initialize the preedit buffer.
- a new callback that allows the input method to request a copy of some of the application's text data. This is typically used by the input method to initialize the preedit area
  to a string that already exists in the application's data.
- a standard protocol between the implementation of the X library and a complex input
  method. This makes it possible to implement an input method that is portable to any
  platform supporting X11R6.

Each of these new capabilities is described in the sections that follow. At the end of this chapter you will find a summary of the new XIM values and new XIC values introduced with X11R6.

Many of these new features are optional — input methods are not required to provide the functionality that the new functions and values allow you to access. This makes it difficult for you to provide consistent functionality to your software user and makes it almost impossible to document your software's behavior to your user. If your software takes advantage of these optional features, the best you can do is document your software's capabilities to support the features while pointing the user to the documentation for the input method.

10.1   Setting Input Method Values

X11R6 provides a new function for setting XIM values. Its syntax is

```
char * XSetIMValues(im, ...)
   XIM im;
```

The ellipses (. . .) in the syntax indicate that the routine accepts a variable length argument list. The routine returns NULL if it succeeds in setting the IM values for the input method *im*; otherwise, it returns the name of the first argument that could not be set.

If XSetIMValues() fails, the X11R6 specification does not say whether any of the XIM values supplied were successfully set to the input method. For example, consider the following block of code:

```
extern void MyDestroyCallback();
XIMCallback im_destroy_cb;
Bool use_R6 = True;
char* ret_val;
...
im_destroy_cb.callback = (XIMProc)MyDestroyCallback;
im_destroy_cb.client_data = (XPointer)NULL;
ret_val = XSetIMValues(my_im,
                    XNDestroyCallback, &im_destroy_cb,
                    XNR6PreeditCallbackBehavior, &use_R6, NULL);
...
```

Suppose that after the call to XSetIMValues(), ret_val points to the string XNR6PreeditCallbackBehavior. This means that the call to XSetIMValues() was unable to set this value. Because of the way the X11R6 specification is written, you have no way of knowing if the DestroyCallback was successfully set for the input method; you only know that passing that value did not cause XSetIMValues() to fail. In this case, the application should again call XSetIMValues() to set the DestroyCallback value. The only way to ensure that an XIM value is successfully set is when XSetIMValues() returns NULL.

10.2   Managing Memory with XGetIMValues()

X11R6 introduces a number of new XIM values which your software can query. When querying for an XIM value, the argument (following the XIM value name) must point to a location where the XIM value is to be stored. If the XIM value is of type `Foo`, then the argument passed in `XGetIMValues()` must be `Foo*`. If `Foo` itself is a pointer, then `XGetIMValues()` allocates memory to store the actual data; in this case, your software must free this memory by calling `XFree()` with the returned pointer.

10.3   When Input Methods Start Up

There are many situations in which your software would like to know that an input method has started. For example, suppose your software starts before the input method is available. In this case, when your software calls `XOpenIM()`, no input method is available. This can happen if the user forgets to start the input method before starting your software. Similarly, this can happen if a session manager starts or restores your software before the input method is ready to accept connections.

If your user wants to change the input method being used, your software needs to know when the new input method starts. For example, the user might first kill the current input method (breaking the connection between your software and the input method) and then start the new input method. In this case, your software also wants to know that the original input method quit functioning (see section 10.4 on page 202).

X11R6 provides the capability for your software to be notified when an input method becomes available. If your software calls the new X11R6 routine `XRegisterIMInstantiateCallback()`, the callback you pass to this routine is called when an input method is available for connection. The syntax for this routine is

```
Bool XRegisterIMInstantiateCallback(dpy, db, res_name,
                             res_class, callback, client_data)
        Display *dpy;
        XrmDatabase db;
        char *res_name;
        char *res_class;
        XIMProc callback;
        XPointer *client_data;
```

dpy	identifies the connection to the X server.
db	a pointer to the resource database.
res_name	the complete resource name for the application.
res_class	the complete class name for the application.
callback	a pointer to the input method reconnect or instantiate callback.
client_data	additional client data you want to pass into the callback when called.

XRegisterIMInstantiateCallback() returns True if it succeeds; otherwise, it returns False. The syntax of the instantiate or reconnect callback is

```
void IMInstantiateCallback(dpy, client_data, call_data)
    Display *dpy;
    XPointer client_data;
    XPointer call_data;
```

dpy   identifies the connection to the X server.

client_data   additional client data passed into the callback by the client.

call_data   not used — always pass as NULL.

The callback you register with XRegisterIMInstantiateCallback() is called when an input method becomes available. When your software no longer needs the IMInstantiateCallback, call XUnregisterIMInstantiateCallback() to unregister the callback. The syntax for this routine is

```
Bool XUnregisterIMInstantiateCallback(dpy, db, res_name,
                            res_class, callback, client_data)
    Display *dpy;
    XrmDatabase db;
    char *res_name;
    char *res_class;
    XIMProc callback;
    XPointer *client_data;
```

dpy   identifies the connection to the X server.

db   a pointer to the resource database passed when registering the callback.

res_name   the complete resource name for the application passed when registering the callback.

res_class   the complete class name for the application passed when registering the callback.

callback   a pointer to the currently registered input method reconnect or instantiate callback.

client_data   pointer to the additional client data specified when registering the instantiate callback.

XUnregisterIMInstantiateCallback() returns True if it succeeds; otherwise, it returns False.

10.3.1 Example Usage

The following is a typical scenario for using the `IMInstantiateCallback`:

1. During initialization, your software attempts to open an input method calling
    `XOpenIM()`, as described in section 7.1 on page 116. If the input method is not yet
    running, `XOpenIM()` returns NULL. Your software has some options at this point:
    * exit because no local language character can be entered from the keyboard.
    * register an `IMInstantiateCallback` and wait for the input method to come up.
    * register an `IMInstantiateCallback` and continue using `XLookupString()`[1]
       to process key events until the local language input method is available. This provides
       the user the most flexibility and is the option used for the remainder of this scenario.
2. Set a flag indicating that the local language input method is not in use, such as

    ```
    Bool im_avail = False
    ```

3. Call `XRegisterIMInstantiateCallback()` to allow connection to the local
    language input method when it comes up.

4. In the `IMInstantiateCallback`,
    * Call `XOpenIM()`.
    * If `XOpenIM()` succeeds, negotiate for the styles to be used and create an input con-
       text.
    * If the input context can also be created, clear the flag that indicates the local language
       input method is not available, for example, `im_avail = True`.
    * Register a destroy callback for the input method (see section 10.4 on page 202). In the
       destroy callback, call `XRegisterIMInstantiateCallback()` to allow connec-
       tion to the local language input method when it comes up — and set a flag indicating
       that the local language input method is not in use: `im_avail = False`.

5. In the software's event loop, if `im_avail == True`, call `XmbLookupString()`
    or `XwcLookupString()` as normal. If `im_avail == False`, call
    `XLookupString()` to process key events.

6. Make sure the input method is available (in this example, by checking `im_avail`)
    before attempting to send information to the input method, such as setting XIC values
    or negotiating geometry with the input method.

The following is an example of an `IMInstantiateCallback` and fragments of a
program that show its use in a scenario such as the one above.

---

1. Using `XLookupString()` to process key events allows the user to at least enter characters from the X Portable
   Character Set from the keyboard.

```
XIM my_im = NULL; /* If input method is not available, im
                   * is NULL; otherwise, it holds the
                   * input method XIM value. */
void
MyDestroyCB(reconnect_ximCB)
  XIMCallback *reconnect_ximCB
{
  my_im = NULL;
  XRegisterIMInstantiateCallback(dpy, NULL, NULL, NULL,
                                 reconnect_ximCB->callback,
                                 reconnect_ximCB);
 /* If using PreeditCallbacks or StatusCallbacks, clean
  * up display of preedit/status info... */
  ...
}
void
MyReconnectCB(reconnect_ximCB)
  XIMCallback *reconnect_ximCB
{
  XIMCallback my_destroy;
  my_im = XOpenIM(dpy, NULL, NULL, NULL);
  if (!my_im) return;
  ...
 /* Renegotiate for supported styles; the new input method
  * may support different styles than the previous input
  * method. */
  ic = XCreateIC(my_im, XNInputStyle, style,
                 XNClientWindow, win,
                 XNFocusWindow, win,
                 XNPreeditAttributes, preedit_att,
                 XNStatusAttributes, status_att, NULL);
  ...
  if (!ic){
    XCloseIM(my_im);
    my_im = NULL;
    return;
  }

  XUnregisterIMInstantiateCallback(dpy, NULL, NULL, NULL,
                                   reconnect_ximCB->callback,
                                   reconnect_ximCB);
  my_destroy.client_data = NULL;
  my_destroy.callback = (XIMProc)MyDestroyCB;
```

```
    XSetIMValues(my_im,
                XNDestroyCallback, &my_destroy, NULL);
}
main(){
  XIMCallback reconnect_ximCB;
  XIMCallback my_destroy;
  Bool need_reconnect = False;
  ...
  reconnect_ximCB.callback = (XIMProc)MyReconnectCB;
  reconnect_ximCB.client_data = NULL;
  ...
  my_im = XOpenIM(dpy, NULL, NULL, NULL);
  if (!my_im) {
    need_reconnect = True;
  } else {
    ...
    ic = XCreateIC(my_im, XNInputStyle, style,
                   XNClientWindow, win,
                   XNFocusWindow, win,
                   XNPreeditAttributes, preedit_att,
                   XNStatusAttributes, status_att, NULL);
    ...
    }
    if (!ic){
      if (need_reconnect)
        XRegisterIMInstantiateCallback(dpy, NULL, NULL, NULL,
                                       (XIMProc)MyReconnectCB,
                                       &reconnect_ximCB);
      XCloseIM(my_im);
      my_im = NULL;
    }
  /* The rest of setting up the input method, such as
   * geometry negotiations, should happen here.
   */
    ...
  }
  ...
/* For KeyPress events, only call input method or input context
 * functions if im is non-NULL. */
    switch (event.type) {
      ...
      case KeyPress:
        if (!im){
```

```
        len = XLookupString((XKeyEvent *) &event, buf,
                            buf_size, &keysym,
                            &comp_status);

        ...
    } else {
        len = XwcLookupString(ic,
                            (XKeyPressedEvent*)&event,
                            winput_buf, buf_size,
                            &keysym, &status);

        ...
    }
    ...
case FocusIn:
    if(my_im) XSetICFocus(ic);
    break;
case FocusOut:
    if(my_im) XUnsetICFocus(ic);
    break;
```

10.4   When Input Methods Stop Working

Once your software connects to a complex input method, it is possible that the input method will be unable to continue functioning. This may happen for any number of reasons. For example, the input method my stop functioning because

- the user terminates the input method,
- the system on which the input method is running crashes,
- there is a bug in the input method, or
- a server (such as a font server) needed by the input method becomes unavailable.

With X11R5, if the input method quit functioning, your software had no way of knowing this had happened. This could cause your software to hang trying to process a KeyPress event, or could even cause it to crash.

X11R6 allows your software to register a callback that is called when, for any reason, the input method stops functioning. The X library automatically closes the input method after calling the callback and destroys the input contexts associated with the input method; your software does not need to call XCloseIM() or XDestroyIC() when the destroy callback is called.

The syntax of the DestroyCallback is

```
void DestroyCallback(im, client_data, call_data)
   XIM im;
   XPointer client_data;
   XPointer call_data;
```

im   identifies the input method that is no longer working.

client_data   additional client data passed into the callback by the client.

call_data   not used — always pass as NULL.

The destroy callback can be set as an XIM value as well as an XIC value. In each case, the callback allows your software to clean up when the input method stops functioning. For example, suppose your software creates two XICs for a single connection to the input method. It uses one of the XICs to perform on-the-spot preediting. In this case, you might use the XIM destroy callback to register your IMInstantiateCallback, allowing your software to reconnect to an input method when it becomes available. Your software might also register an XIC destroy callback for the XIC used for on-the-spot preediting. In the XIC's destroy callback, you would free the memory allocated for storing the preedit buffer and highlight information, as well as destroy the GCs used to display the caret cursor. In this case, the XIC's destroy callback would also make sure to erase any currently displayed pre-edit data.

X11R6 defines the XIM value XNDestroyCallback and the XIC value XNDestroyCallback. The XIM value is set with XSetIMValues(); the XIC value is set with XSetICValues(). In each case, the argument to XNDestroyCallback is pointer to an XIMCallback structure.

In the destroy callback, you should decide how to handle keyboard input in your software. In most situations, the best strategy is to take advantage of the reconnect capabilities of X11R6 (see section 10.3 on page 197). However, if it is critical that your software have the ability to enter keyboard data at all times, then you may elect to display a dialog allowing the user to select a different input method. For example, your dialog might display alternative X modifiers, allowing the user to choose one with the mouse. Another option might be to display a dialog notifying the user that the input method is not available. The dialog asks if the user wants to terminate the software or wait for the input method to restart.

10.5   Finding and Controlling the Input Method's Preedit State

X11R6 provides the capability for your software to determine if the input method is currently in preedit mode or not. It also allows your software to programmatically turn preedit mode on or off. Finally, X11R6 provides a mechanism that allows your software to be notified whenever the input method's preedit mode changes.

10.5.1 Does the Input Method Support Setting/Querying Preedit Mode?

Not all input methods support the ability to query or set preedit mode. Before attempting to do so, your software should query for the XIM value XNQueryICValuesList, passing a pointer to an XIMValuesList as an argument, where XIMValuesList is defined:

```
typedef struct {
  unsigned short count_values;
  char **supported_values;
} XIMValuesList;
```

The X library returns in the pointer a list of all XIC values supported by the input method. Your software can examine the list to see if the string XNPreeditState is present. If the string is present, then the input method supports the ability to query and set the preedit mode. Similarly, your software should look for the string XNPreeditStateCallback. If the string is present, then the input method supports the ability to notify your software when the preedit mode changes.

When you have finished examining the list of values returned by querying for XNQueryICValuesList, you should free the XIMValuesList structure by calling XFree().

The following example shows how your software can determine if the input method supports the ability to query and set the preedit mode:

```
XIM my_im;
XIC my_ic;
XIMValuesList vlist;
Bool support_query_and_set = False;
Bool support_notify = False;
int i;
char *ret_val;
...
ret_val = XGetIMValues(my_im,
                      XNQueryICValuesList, &vlist, NULL);
if (!ret_val){
  for (i=0; i < vlist.count_values; i++){
    if(!strcmp(vlist[i], "XNPreeditState"))
      supports_query_and_set = True;
    else if(!strcmp(vlist[i], "XNPreeditStateCallback"))
      supports_notify = True;
  }
  XFree(vlist);
}
```

10.5.2 Querying the Input Method's Preedit State

X11R6 introduces the XIC preedit attribute, XNPreeditState. You can use this attribute together with XGetICValues() to determine the input method's current preedit mode. When querying for the preedit mode, XNPreeditState takes an argument of XIMPreeditState, which is defined as

```
typedef unsigned long XIMPreeditState;
```

The currently defined XIMPreeditState values are

```
#define XIMPreeditUnknown 0L
#define XIMPreeditEnable  1L
#define XIMPreeditDisable (1L<<1)
```

The following code fragment builds on the example in the previous section. The boolean supports_query_and_set indicates if the input method supports query and set operations for preedit state.

```
XVaNestedList preedit_att;
int dummy;
...
if (supports_query_and_set){
  preedit_att = XVaCreateNestedList(dummy,
                        XNPreeditState, &current_state,
                        NULL);
  XGetICValues(my_ic,
              XNPreeditAttributes, preedit_att, NULL);
  XFree(preedit_att);
  if (current_state == XIMPreeditEnable){
    /* Preedit mode is on! */
    ...
  } else if (current_state == XIMPreeditDisable){
    /* Preedit mode is off! */
    ...
  } else {
    /* Preedit mode is unknown! */
    ...
  }
}
```

10.5.3 Setting the Input Method's Preedit State

If the input method allows you to set the preedit state, your software can set the initial preedit state of the input method when creating the input context, or it can set the preedit state of the input method after the input context is in use. When creating the input context, you can

set the initial preedit mode by passing XNPreeditState to XCreateIC(). After the
input context has been created, you can set the preedit mode by passing XNPreeditState
to XSetICValues(). In each case, XNPreeditState takes an argument of
XIMPreeditState.

10.5.4 Controlling the Input Method's Default Preedit State

Your software can use the routines XmbResetIC() or XwcResetIC() to reset the
input context to its initial state (and initial preedit mode).

With X11R6, your software can control the preedit state of the input context when it is
reset. If the input method allows you to set the preedit state, your software can set the
XNResetState XIC value to an XIMResetState. X11R6 defines the following
XIMResetState values:

```
typedef unsigned long XIMResetState;
#define XIMInitialState    (1L)
#define XIMPreserveState   (1L<<1)
```

Setting the XNResetState to XIMInitialState causes the reset input context to
use the initial preedit state of the input context. If you set the initial preedit state with
XNPreeditState when creating the input context, this is the preedit state of the reset
input context. Otherwise, the preedit state of the reset context is determined by the input
method.

If you set XNResetState to XIMPreserveState, resetting the input context pre-
serves the current preedit state of the input context.

10.5.5 Finding Out When the Input Method's Preedit State Changes

If the input method allows you to set the preedit state, your software can ask to be notified any time that state changes by setting the XNPreeditStateNotifyCallback XIC
value. XNPreeditStateNotifyCallback requires a pointer to XIMCallback as the
accompanying argument. The syntax of the callback is

```
void PreeditStateNotifyCallback(ic, client_data, call_data)
   XIM ic;
   XPointer client_data;
   XIMPreeditStateNotifyCallbackStruct *call_data;
```

ic   identifies the input context for which the preedit state has changed.

client_data   additional client data passed into the callback by the client.

call_data   identifies the preedit state of the input context.

The XIMPreeditStateNotifyCallbackStruct is defined as

```
typedef struct _XIMPreeditStateNotifyCallbackStruct {
    XIMPreeditState;
} XIMPreeditStateNotifyCallbackStruct;
```

10.6   Forcing the Input Method to Ignore Keys

There may some keys on the keyboard that you want the input method not to process. For example, your software may define a function key to be an interrupt key, a help key, or a quit key. In this case you may not want the input method to process the keystrokes. X11R6 provides a mechanism that allows your software to specify a list of *hot keys* that should not be interpreted by the input method; key events for hot keys are ignored by the input method and passed directly to your software.

Hot keys are set using `XSetICValues()` and the `XNHotKey` XIC value. The argument to `XNHotKey` is a pointer to a structure of type `XIMHotKeyTriggers`. This structure identifies the events which your software wants the input method to ignore. The `XIMHotKeyTriggers` structure is defined as

```
typedef struct {
    KeySym keysym;
    unsigned int modifier;
    unsigned int modifier_mask;
} XIMHotKeyTrigger;
```

keysym	keysym of the key that you want the input method to ignore.
modifier	a set of bits for modifier keys (such as `ShiftMask` and `Mod5Mask`)
modifier_mask	identifies which modifier bits are actually relevant. If a bit is set to 1, the corresponding modifier must be set for the key to be hot; otherwise, the corresponding modifier is not considered when determining if the key is hot.

```
typedef struct {
    int num_hot_keys;
    XIMHotKeyTrigger *key;
} XIMHotKeyTriggers;
```

For example, suppose that you want to make sure that function key 8 is not processed by the input method. You want the key to be "hot," but only when the Shift modifier is used, and only when the Shift modifier is used and the Control modifier is not used. Your code to set up the hot key structures might be as follows:

```
XIMHotKeyTrigger hot;
XIMHotKeyTriggers hot_list;
...
```

```
  hot.keysym = XK_f8;
/* hot.modifier_mask lists all the modifiers we care about.
 * Any other modifier encountered is treated as "don't care". */
  hot.modifier_mask = ShiftMask | ControlMask;
/* hot.modifier says which of the modifiers listed in hot.modifier
 * must be set in the key event for the key to be "hot". Any
 * modifier listed in hot.modifier_mask that does not have a
 * corresponding entry in hot.modifier, must not be present in
 * the key event for the key to be hot. */
  hot.modifier = ShiftMask;
  hot_list.num_hot_keys = 1;
  hot_list.key = &hot;
```

Once you set a list of hot keys, you can tell the input method when to ignore the hot keys and when it is OK for the input method to process hot keys. You can use the `XNHotKeyState` input context value to set the hot key state. The argument to `XNHot-KeyState` is a pointer to `XIMHotKeyState`, which is defined as

```
typedef unsigned long XIMHotKeyState;

#define XIMHotKeyStateON  (0x0001L) /* ignore hot keys */
#define XIMHotKeyStateOFF (0x0002L) /* OK for IM to process
                                     * hot keys */
```

Not all input methods support the ability to set hot keys. Before your software attempts to set a hot key list or to set the hot key state, you should query the input method with `XNQueryICValuesList` — if the strings "`XNHotKey`" and "`XNHotKeysState`" are present in the list of XIC values, your software can safely set the hot key list and hot key state.

<u>Note</u>

It is not good internationalization design technique to attempt to outguess the input method as to which keys it needs. For example, if your software decides that `f8` (function key eight) must be the application's interrupt key, there is probably an input method out there somewhere for which `f8` has critical importance and must be seen by the input method.

If your software absolutely needs to have hot keys, then use some mechanism that allows the hot key associated with each action to be changed by the user. In this way, if the user picks an input method that absolutely must have access to certain keys, your software allows the user make sure your software's hot keys don't conflict with those the input method needs.

10.7   Asking the Input Method to Perform String Conversions

During a typical preediting session, the user types a series of keys which are interpreted by the input method until the input method is capable of producing the final character(s) the user desires. In some rare cases, you may want to perform preediting by sending a string of characters to the input method directly from your software. For example, suppose your software is a text editor. And suppose that a user just finished typing a sequence of 20 keystrokes during preedit to generate a sequence of characters. While typing, the user made a mistake, causing the input method to send the wrong sequence of characters to your software. Ideally, you would like to offer the user an "undo" function, allowing your software to restore the input method's preedit buffer to its contents just before the user caused the wrong characters to be sent to your software. X11R6 provides the capability for your software to send a string of characters to the input method, telling the input method to set the preedit buffer to a state that would allow those characters to be generated. This capability is called *string conversion*.

Note

Input methods are not required to support program-initiated string conversion. Further, string conversion is a meaningful operation in only certain languages. It is your software's responsibility to decide what actions cause your software to initiate string conversion, what to do with the data in your application that you send back to the input method (e.g., do you delete it from the buffer or leave it there?), and how much data to send to the input method.

For all of these reasons, performing string conversion from your internationalized software provides a questionable benefit. It places a large burden on your software and, because the functionality is optional for the input method, makes it difficult for you to document to your software's user the actions and results that should be expected when performing string conversion.

Your software passes the string to be converted to the input method using the XNStringConversion XIC value. The argument to this value is a structure of type XIMStringConversionText, which is defined as

```
typedef struct _XIMStringConversionText {
    unsigned short length;
    XIMStringConversionFeedback *feedback;
    Bool encoding_is_wchar;
    union {
        char *mbs;
        wchar_t *wcs;
```

```
    } string;
  } XIMStringConversionText;

  typedef unsigned long XIMStringConversionFeedback;
```

`length`	number of characters of data stored in string. If `encoding_is_wchar` is `True`, `length` identifies the number of wide characters stored in `string.wcs`; otherwise, `length` identifies the number of multibyte characters stored in `string.mbs`.
`feedback`	currently unused — reserved for future use. Your software should set this to NULL to avoid potential memory problems when freeing the structure.
`encoding_is_wchar`	`True` if data you pass in `string` is wide character; `False` otherwise.
`string`	data your software passes to the input method.

Before setting the `XNStringConversion` XIC value, you must make sure that the input method supports the ability to perform program initiated string conversions. You do this by calling `XGetIMValues()` and querying the input method for `XNQueryICValuesList`. If the list of strings returned by `XGetIMValues()` contains the string `XNStringConversion`, the input method supports software initiated string conversion.

10.8   Allowing the Input Method to Request String Conversions

Section 10.7 on page 209 described situations when it might be useful for your software to ask the input method to perform a string conversion — to initialize the preedit buffer with a string. In some cases, the input method may want to initiate string conversion. For example, the input method may want to provide a feature such that when the user performs a certain action (such as pressing a function key), the input method sets the contents of its preedit buffer to a string that would result in the characters preceding the cursor. This would be a useful feature for a user typing several similar, but not identical, strings into your software. The input method initiated string conversion could save the user many keystrokes in this situation.

Your software can support input method initiated string conversion by setting the `XNStringConversionCallback` XIC value, passing a pointer to a structure of type `XIMCallback`. The `callback` element of the `XIMCallback` must be a callback whose syntax is

```
  void StringConversionCallback(ic, client_data, call_data)
    XIM ic;
    XPointer client_data;
    XIMStringConversionCallbackStruct *call_data;
```

ic   identifies the input context for which the preedit state has changed.

client_data   additional client data passed into the callback by the client.

call_data   identifies data the input method needs from your software, and potentially directs
                   you to delete the data from your software's buffer once you pass it to the input
                   method.

   call_data is a pointer to `XIMStringConversionCallbackStruct`, which
along with the new data types it uses, is defined and described as follows:

```
typedef struct _XIMStringConversionCallbackStruct {
    XIMStringConversionPosition position;
    XIMCaretDirection direction;
    short factor;
    XIMStringConversionOperation operation;
    XIMStringConversionText *text;
} XIMStringConversionCallbackStruct;

typedef short XIMStringConversionPosition;
typedef unsigned short XIMStringConversionOperation
#define XIMStringConversionSubstitution  (0x0001)
#define XIMStringConversionRetrieval     (0x0002)
```

position   specifies the starting position of the data you should copy into `text`. This is a
              character position relative to the current text insertion point in your software.

direction   combined with `factor`, identifies the ending character of the data your soft-
              ware should copy into text. If direction is `XIMLineEnd` and `factor` is 1, your
              software should copy into `text` all characters from the current insert position
              + `position`, through the end of the current line of data. If direction is
              `XIMLineEnd` and factor is 2, your software should copy into `text` all charac-
              ters from the current insert position + `position`, through the end of the next
              line of data.

factor   multiplier for `direction`. For example, if direction is `XIMForwardChar`
              and `factor` is 5, the input method is requesting the next five characters for-
              ward from the current insert position + `position`.

operation   specifies whether data should be copied into text or moved into text. If data is
              moved (`operation` is `XIMStringConversionSubstitution`), your
              software should delete the data from your buffer after copying it into `text`. If
              data is copied (`operation` is `XIMStringConversionRetrieval`), your
              software should not delete the data from your buffer after copying it into `text`.

text   structure to contain the data requested by the input method.

The `text` element in the `XIMStringConversionCallbackStruct` is a pointer to a new structure of type `XIMStringConversionText`. That structure is defined and described as

```
typedef struct _XIMStringConversionText {
    unsigned short length;
    XIMStringConversionFeedback *feedback;
    Bool encoding_is_wchar;
    union {
        char *mbs;
        wchar_t *wcs;
    } string;
} XIMStringConversionText;

typedef unsigned long XIMStringConversionFeedback;
```

`length`	number of characters of data stored in string. If `encoding_is_wchar` is `True`, `length` identifies the number of wide characters stored in `string.wcs`; otherwise, `length` identifies the number of multibyte characters stored in `string.mbs`.
`feedback`	currently unused — reserved for future use.
`encoding_is_wchar`	`True` if data you pass in `string` is wide character; `False` otherwise.
`string`	data your software passes to the input method. This should be dynamically allocated memory with contents copied from your software's data buffer; the input method calls `XFree()` to free `string` upon completion of the callback.

Before setting the `XNStringConversionCallback` XIC value, you must make sure that the input method supports the ability to perform input method initiated string conversions.

10.9   Standard Protocol for Input Method Implementers

X11R5 defines standard application program interfaces allowing internationalized software to communicate with whatever input methods an implementation of the X library happens to support. Software written with these interfaces is portable to any platform that implements X11R5. However, X11R5 does not define how input methods communicate with the X library. This means that, unlike internationalized applications, it is impossible to write an input method for X11R5 that is portable to different platforms. This also means that applications are dependent on the platform's X library supplier for which input methods (if any) are available on that platform.

X11R6 defines a standard protocol for communications between the X library and the input method. This makes it possible for input method developers to develop a single version of an input method and be sure that the input method works with all X11R6 libraries.

Since the standard protocol is useful only for developing language specific input methods (and not internationalized software), the input method protocol is not covered in this book. Readers interested in more details on the protocol can obtain the specifications for it in the sources available from the X Consortium.

10.10 Summary: New Input Method Values

X11R5 defines only one XIM value, `XNQueryInputStyle`. X11R6 introduces several new input method values. Table 10.1 summarizes the XIM values that are valid with X11R6. Each of the new XIM values is explained in the sections that follow the table. Table 10.2 shows the applicability of each XIM value for each preedit and style.

Table 10.1 XIM Values: Description

XIC Value	Data Type	Description
`XNInputStyle`	`XIMStyle`	Identifies the preedit style and status style that you may use for this connections to this input method.
`XNResourceName` `XNResourceClass`	`char*`	The names used by the input method when obtaining resources; used when looking up input method specific resources. XIM values should not be set as resources.
`XNDestroyCallback`	`XIMCallback*`	Specifies a callback to be called when an input method stops working.
`XNQueryIMValuesList`	`XIMValuesList*`	Used to query for a list of IM values supported by the input method; many IM values defined in R6 are optional.
`XNQueryICValuesList`	`XIMValuesList*`	Used to query for a list of IC values supported by the input method; many IC values defined in R6 are optional.
`XNVisiblePosition`	`Bool`	Used to find out if the input method is capable of sending hints in the `XIMFeedback` element of `XIMText` structures during preedit callbacks. This value is optional. Before using it, you must query for the list of support IM values. If the string `XNVisiblePosition` is not present in the list returned, then the input method will not send display hints.

Table 10.1 XIM Values: Description (Continued)

XIC Value	Data Type	Description
`XNR6PreeditCallback-Behavior`	`Bool*`	Controls whether the preedit callbacks have X11R5 or X11R6 semanitcs. Since the only difference between R5 and R6 semantics is that an input method can send hints for drawing preedit and status information, and since the input methods support for hints is indicated by the `XNVisiblePosition` XIM value, the `XNR6PreeditCallbackBehavior` XIC data value was deprecated with release 6.1.

Table 10.2 Description of X11R6 XIM Values

XIM Value	D-R-S	Description
`XNQueryInputStyle`	R	Query for the preedit and status styles supported by the input method.[1]
`XNResourceName`	D-R-S	Used to specify resources for the input method.
`XNResourceClass`	D-R-S	Used to specify resources for the input method.
`XNDestroyCallback`	D-R-S	Called when the input method ceases operation, regardless of the reason.
`XNQueryIMValuesList`	R	Returns the list of XIM values supported by the input method. Some values are optional — an input method is not required to support an optional value.
`XNQueryICValuesList`	R	Returns the list of XIC values supported by the input method. Some values are optional — an input method is not required to support an optional value.
`XNVisiblePosition`	R†	Returns a boolean indicating whether or not the input method supplies hints to help software understand how to display preedit/status feedback information when there is not enough room to display all of the feedback information.
`XNR6PreeditCallback-Behavior`	D-R-S†	Indicates whether the contents of `XIMPreeditDrawCallbackStruct` values follow X11R5 or X11R6 semantics.

1. See section 7.2 on page 117 for a complete description of this XIM value.

Key	Description
D	If not set with `XSetIMValues()`, a default value is provided.
R	Value may be retrieved or read with `XGetIMValues()`.
S	Value may be set by calling `XSetIMValues()`.
†	Value is optional — the input method may or may not support the value. Software should query the input method to see if the value is in the list of supported values before using this value.

10.10.1 XNResourceName and XNResourceClass

These values are strings that specify the resource name and resource class for the input method. The input method uses these names to identify resources meant for it when connecting to your software. This allows the input method to identify input method specific resource values from your software and differentiate them from the same input method resources being set by other software. The input method's documentation identifies what input method specific resources can be set.

10.10.2 XNDestroyCallback

X11R6 allows your software to register a callback that is called when the input method stops functioning. The X library automatically closes the input method and destroys the associated input contexts after calling the callback; your software does not need to call `XCloseIM()` or `XDestroyIC()` when the `DestroyCallback` is called.

The `XNDestroyCallback` argument is a structure of type `XIMCallback` (see section 9.1 on page 165 for a description of the callback structure). The `DestroyCallback` is always called with a NULL *client_data* argument.

10.10.3 XNQueryIMValuesList and XNQueryICValuesList

Several of the XIM values and XIC values new with X11R6 are optional — an input method is not required to support optional values. Before your software relies on such optional functionality, it should query the input method to find out if it supports the optional value. The `XNQueryIMValuesList`, in combination with `XGetIMValues()`, allows you to query the input method for a list of the XIM values supported by the input method. Similarly, `XNQueryICValuesList`, in combination with `XGetIMValues()`, allows you to obtain a list of the XIC values supported by the input method.

In each case, the argument passed is a pointer to an `XIMValuesList` structure, which is defined as

```
typedef struct {
    unsigned short count_values;
    char **supported_values;
} XIMValuesList;
```

After obtaining the list of values, your software must free the memory associated with the `XIMValuesList` structure by calling `XFree()`.

10.10.4 XNVisiblePosition

When supporting on-the-spot preedit style, it is possible that the area your software has available to display the feedback information is not large enough to contain the data to be displayed. With X11R5, your software had to decide how to display the feedback information in this situation. X11R6 provides a mechanism for the input method to provide hints for displaying feedback information when there is insufficient room to display the entire feedback data. X11R6 does not require input methods to provide this information — it is optional for input methods to support this feature.

The `XNVisiblePosition` XIM value allows you to query the input method to find out if it supplies hints on how to display feedback information when geometry is constrained. The argument supplied with `XNVisiblePosition` must be a pointer to type `Bool`. If the returned value is `True`, the input method is capable of providing hints for displaying feedback information. If the input method is capable of providing these hints, your software must[2] tell it to send the hints by setting the `XNR6PreeditCallbackBehavior` XIM value (see section 10.10.5 on page 218).

Hints for displaying feedback information are passed by the input method as new feedback styles in the `XIMText` structure used in the `PreeditDrawCallback` and the `StatusDrawCallback`. The following list shows the values possible with X11R6 for `XIMFeedback` elements in an `XIMText` structure. The change bar in the margin highlights the new or changed feedback elements for X11R6. The new feedback styles, `XIMVisibleTo*`, describe how your software should display feedback information when the window geometry doesn't allow the entire feedback information to be displayed.

```
typedef unsigned long XIMFeedback;
#define XIMReverse        1L
#define XIMUnderline      (1L<<1)
#define XIMHighlight      (1L<<2)
#define XIMPrimary        (1L<<5)
#define XIMSecondary      (1L<<6)
#define XIMTertiary       (1L<<7)
```

---

2. Release X11R6.1 obsoletes `XNR6PreeditCallbackBehavior`. You should assume that an input method will always send a visible position hint. It is possible that a X11R6 implementation may require `XNR6PreeditCallbackBehavior` to be set before supplying display hints.

```
#define XIMVisibleToForward   (1L<<8)
#define XIMVisibleToBackward  (1L<<9)
#define XIMVisibleToCenter    (1L<<10)
```

These new feedback styles are described in Table 10.3.

Table 10.3 XIMFeedback Hints

XIMFeedback style	When geometry is constrained
XIMVisibleToForward	Draw feedback information such that at least feedback information from the insertion point or caret position forward is visible.
XIMVisibleToBackward	Draw feedback information such that at least feedback information from the insertion point or caret position backward is visible.
XIMVisibleToCenter	Draw feedback information such that the feedback information at the insertion point or caret position is centered in the available display space.

Note

The X11R6 value of the XIMPrimary, XIMSecondary, and XIMTertiary highlights differ from the values specified in X11R5. There was a bug in the X11R5 specification. The sample implementation of X11R5 defined the values of XIMPrimary, XIMSecondary, and XIMTertiary correctly — that is, not as erroneously stated in the X11R5 specification. The X11R6 specification and sample implementation define and implement the value of these feedback highlights correctly. The values defined in X11R6 match the values assigned to these highlights in the X11R5 sample implementation.

It is possible that a vendor of the X library modified the values of the X11R5 feedbacks to match the R5 specification, and not the X11R5 sample implementation. In this case, your software may not correctly handle XIMReverse, XIMUnderline, and XIMHighlight feedbacks.

When an input method supplies the new feedback styles XIMVisibleToForward, XIMVisibleToBackward, and XIMVisibleToCenter, the value is OR'd together with a feedback style dictating the physical rendering of that character. When your software tells the input method to send these new rendering hints, your software must check each feedback element to see if one of the visibility hints is set. For example,

```
XIMText *text;
XIMFeedback visible_hint = 0;
```

```
Bool use_R6_style; /* Query the IM to see if it supports
                    * XNVisiblePosition and XNR6Preedit-
                    * CallbackBehavior XIM values. If it does, set
                    * XNR6PreeditCallbackBehavior to True;
                    * set use_R6_style to True to flag that visible
                    * hints are in use. Note that this is not needed
                    * as of release 6.1. */
...
/* In the PreeditDrawCallback, as the software copies
 * each new feedback element into the software's preedit
 * buffer highlight array (pe_highlight), check to see
 * if any of the visibility hints are set. If so, set
 * a global flag to indicate the preferred visibility. */
if (text->feedback){
  if (text->length != 0){
    if (use_R6_style){
      for (i = insert_length; i > 0; --i){
        if (text->feedback[i] & XIMVisibleToForward)
          visible_hint = XIMVisibleToForward;
        else if (text->feedback[i] & XIMVisibleToBackward)
          visible_hint = XIMVisibleToBackward;
        else if (text->feedback[i] & XIMVisibleToCenter)
          visible_hint = XIMVisibleToCenter;
      }
    }...
```

10.10.5 XNR6PreeditCallbackBehavior

X11R6 changed the semantics of the `PreeditDrawCallback` in one minor way. The difference between the X11R5 `PreeditDrawCallback` semantics and those defined in X11R6 is the addition of hints for drawing the preedit buffer when window geometry does not allow you to display the entire preedit buffer.

X11R6 based software does not supply the display hints unless the software set the optional `XNR6PreeditCallbackBehaivor` XIM value to `True`. The default behavior for the `PreeditCallback` is to provide the identical behavior as that in X11R5.

> **Note**
>
> Release 6.1 deprecates the `XNR6PreeditCallback-Behavior` XIM value. Your software should use the `XNVisiblePosition` value to determine if an input method will send display hints in the highlights passed to the `PreeditDrawCallback`.

10.11 Summary: New XIC Values

X11R6 introduces several new input context values. Table 10.4 summarizes the XIC values that are added with X11R6. Each of these new XIC values is explained in the sections that follow the table.

Note

With the exception of `XNDestroyCallback`, all of the new X11R6 XIC values are optional — an input method is not required to support these values. Before setting or querying any of these values, you must query the input method with `XGetIMValues()` and the `XNQueryICValuesList` XIM value to make sure the XIC value is supported by the input method.

Table 10.4 XIC Values: Description

XIC Value	Data Type	Description
XNDestroyCallback	XIMCallback	Specifies a callback to be called when an input methods stops working.
XNPreeditState	XIMPreeditState	Specifies whether or not the input method is currently preediting.
XNPreeditStateNotifyCallack	XIMCallback*	Specifies a callback to be called whenever the input method's preedit state changes.
XNResetState	XIMResetState	Specifies the state of the input method's preedit mode after `XmbResetIC()` or `XwcResetIC()` are called.
XNHotKey	XIMHotKeyTriggers*	Specifies a list of keysyms that should not be interpreted by the input method; the hot keys are passed to your software without modification.
XNHotKeyState	XIMHotKeyState*	Specifies whether the current list of hot keys are active or inactive.
XNStringConversion	XIMStringConversionText	Specifies a string to be converted by the input method, initializing its preedit buffer.
XNStringConversionCallback	XIMCallback	Specifies a callback that the input method can caused to be called, allowing the input method to request a string to be used to initialize its preedit buffer.

X11R6 extends X11R5's XIC values that can be used to communicate with the input method. Similarly, X11R6 extends the preedit attributes defined by X11R5. Table 10.5 lists the XIC values added by X11R6. Table 10.6 lists the new preedit attributes added by X11R6. Each of the new XIC values and preedit attributes is described in the paragraphs following Table 10.6.

Table 10.5 New X11R6 XIC Values

XIC Value	Preedit Style				
	Preedit None	Preedit Nothing	Preedit Area	Preedit Position	Preedit Callbacks
XNDestroyCallback	D-R-S	D-R-S	D-R-S	D-R-S	D-R-S
XNResetState	Ignored	D-R-S	D-R-S	D-R-S	D-R-S
XNHotKey	Ignored	R-S†	R-S†	R-S†	R-S†
XNHotKeyState	Ignored	D-R-S†	D-R-S†	D-R-S†	D-R-S†
XNStringConversion	D-R-S†	D-R-S†	D-R-S†	D-R-S†	D-R-S†
XNStringConversionCallback	R-S†	R-S†	R-S†	R-S†	R-S†

Table 10.6 New X11R6 Preedit Attribute Values

Preedit Attribute	Preedit Style				
	Preedit None	Preedit Nothing	Preedit Area	Preedit Position	Preedit Callbacks
XNPreeditState	Ignored	D-R-S†	D-R-S†	D-R-S†	D-R-S†
XNPreeditStateNotifyCallback	Ignored	R-S†	R-S†	R-S†	R-S†

Key	Description
D	If not set with XCreateIC() or XSetICValues(), a default value is provided.
R	Value may be retrieved or read with XGetICValues().
S	Value may be set by calling XSetICValues().
†	Value is optional — the input method may or may not support the value. Software should query the input method to see if the value is in the list of supported XIC values before using this value.

10.11.1 XNDestroyCallback

The `XNDestroyCallback` XIC value is identical in form and function to the XIM value of the same name (see section 10.10.2 on page 215 for more information). The XIC version of the callback allows your software to perform any XIC specific cleanup when the input method quits functioning. For example, it allows you to free memory or graphics context you may have allocated to support on-the-spot preedit style.

10.11.2 XNResetState

This XIC value allows your software to control the preedit state of the input method once `XmbResetIC()` or `XwcResetIC()` is called. The `XNResetState` XIC value takes an argument of type `XIMResetState`, which is defined as

```
typedef unsigned long XIMResetState;
#define XIMInitialState  (1L)    /* Use initial state. */
#define XIMPreserveState (1L<<1) /* Retain current state. */
```

10.11.3 XNHotKey

This optional XIC values allows your software to provide a list of keys that the input method should not process. Normally, the input method has the option to use any key event for preediting or control of the input method. The `XNHotKey` XIC value forces the input method to ignore the keys identified in the supplied list of hot keys, allowing your software to then process the events in its event loop.

The argument for `XNHotKey` XIC value is a pointer to `XIMHotKeyTrigger`, which is defined as

```
typedef struct {
  KeySym keysym;
  unsigned int modifier;
  unsigned int modifier_mask;
}XIMHotKeyTrigger;
```

10.11.4 XNHotKeyState

This optional XIC value allows your software to toggle on and off use of the list of hot keys supplied with the `XNHotKey` XIC value. The `XNHotKeyState` XIC value requires as an argument a pointer to `XIMHotKeyState`, which is defined as

```
typedef unsigned long XIMHotKeyState;
#define XIMHotKeyStateON  (0x0001L)
#define XIMHotKeyStateOFF (0x0002L)
```

10.11.5 XNStringConversion

This optional XIC value allows your software to send a string to the input method. The string passed to the input method is used to initialize its preedit buffer to a content that would cause the string passed in to be generated. The `XNStringConversion` XIC value requires an argument of type `XIMStringConversionText`, which is defined as

```
typedef struct _XIMStringConversionText{
  unsigned short length;
  XIMStringConversionFeedback *feedback;
  Bool encoding_is_wchar;
  union {
    char *mbs;
    wchar_t *wcs;
  } string;
}XIMStringConversionText;
typedef unsigned long XIMStringConversionFeeback;
```

The `feedback` element is not currently used; it is reserved for definition in a future X11 specification.

10.11.6 XNStateConversionCallback

This optional XIC value specifies a callback that the input method can call when it wants to request a portion of your software's current text buffer. Typically it does this to initialize its own preedit buffer. The input method can request a copy of the data or can direct your software to delete the data once you have provided it with a copy.

The `XNStateConversionCallback` requires an argument of type `XIMCallback`. For a detailed description of the callbacks form and that structures passed between your software and the input method, see section 10.8 on page 210.

10.11.7 XNPreeditState

This option XIC value allows your software to control and query the preedit state of the input method. The `XNPreeditState` XIC value requires an argument of type `XIMPreeditState`, which is defined as

```
typedef unsigned long XIMPreeditState;
#define XIMPreeditUnknown   0L
#define XIMPreeditEnable    1L
#define XIMPreeditDisable   (1L<<1)
```

10.11.8 XNPreeditStateNotifyCallback

This optional XIC value allows your software to be notified whenever the preedit state of the input method changes. The `XNPreeditStateNotifyCallback` XIC value requires an argument of a pointer to `XIMCallback`. For a detailed description of the callback and the structure passed to the callback by the input method, see section 10.5.5 on page 206.

Data Interchange and Internationalization

W hen your software exchanges information with other software using the Inter-Client Communications Conventions, internationalization isn't really an issue. The problems of data interchange are the same whether the software exchanging data are internationalized or not. However, when two internationalized applications exchange data, there is a much higher likelihood that the code set of the data owner is different from that of the receiver. This chapter describes how your software uses the capabilities of X11R5 to correctly interchange text data with other internationalized software.

Note that this chapter does not attempt to teach the general principals of data interchange. There are many books available that explain the general data interchange model. For example, the X11R5 ICCCM[1] (Inter-Client Communications Conventions Manual) available from the X Consortium or *X Window System*[2] are good sources of information for learning about data interchange. This chapter assumes you already understand ICCCM-based data interchange. It focuses on the changes you must make to your software to successfully interchange text data with other software that may be using a different coded character set than the one your software is currently using.

This chapter uses the primary selection mechanism to illustrate data interchange in an environment where the code set of the data owner may be different than that of the data receiver. You should be aware that data interchange can be done in many different ways. For example, setting the window title by calling XSetWMName() or setting your software's icon name by calling XSetWMIconName() are forms of data interchange. The concepts presented in this chapter are valid for these types of exchange as well.

---

1. Available from the X Consortium, the ICCCM is delivered as part of the X11R5 and X11R6 sources from the X Consortium as well.

2. *X Window System*, 3rd ed., by Robert W. Scheifler and James Gettys — published by Digital Press, DP ISBN 1-55558-088-2, PH ISBN 0-13-971201-1.

One note of caution: You should not use X11's cut buffers to exchange data in internationalized software. The cut buffers support exchange of ISO 8859.1 encoded character data only.

11.1   A Typical Data Exchange

Selections are the primary mechanism that X11-based applications use for exchanging text data. For example, cut and paste is the exchange of the *primary selection* (Atom PRIMARY) between two pieces of software. When exchanging text data using selections, a series of communications typically takes place between the selection requestor and the selection owner. The following is an example of this communication flow during a paste operation where the requestor asks for a copy of the current primary selection:

Requestor: Who has the primary selection?
Owner: I have the primary selection!
Requestor: In what types (TARGETS) can you pass the selection?[3]
Owner: Here is a list of the types (TARGETS) I support.
Requestor: Send me a copy of the primary selection in this type (one of the TARGETS previously obtained).
Owner: OK! Here is an XTextProperty containing a copy of the primary selection, with the data formatted as you requested.

11.2   Exchanging Text Data with Internationalized Software

The Atom XA_STRING is a predefined Atom specifying that text data is encoded as ISO 8859.1. Prior to X11R5, the X Window System officially supported only ISO 8859.1 encoded characters — a request for TARGETS would result in a target list that contained XA_STRING as the only encoding in which the selection could be returned.

With X11R5, it became likely that text data was no longer encoded in ISO 8859.1. It also became possible that the coded character set used by the selection owner was not the same as the coded character set used by the requestor. As a solution, X11R5 introduced Compound Text, a new type for representing text data. Compound Text is a way of representing text data such that the data contained is tagged, with the tag identifying the coded character set of the data. It is based on the ISO/IEC 2022 standard for data representation. Because text data is tagged, Compound Text allows data encoded in many different coded character sets to be mixed together. As a software developer, you do not need to know or understand Compound Text data representation; you only need to know the following:

---

3. The ICCCM requires that selection owners must support a target with Atom TARGETS. When requested for TARGETS, the selection owner must return a list of Atoms representing the targets for which an attempt to convert the current selection will succeed (barring unforeseeable problems).

- The X library provides tools for converting data encoded in the code set of the current locale into Compound Text.
- The X library provides tools for converting data encoded as Compound Text into data encoded in the code set of the current locale.
- When exchanging data with other software, the safest way to represent or request text data is as Compound Text.
- When asked for a list of TARGETS, include an Atom for COMPOUND_TEXT. You can generate this atom by calling

```
XInternAtom(display, "COMPOUND_TEXT", False);
```

- When you request a list of TARGETS from the selection owner, search for the Atom COMPOUND_TEXT. If it exists, request the selection with that type.

To convert text data encoded in the code set of the current locale into Compound Text, use XmbTextListToTextProperty() or XwcTextListToTextProperty(). The syntax for these routines is

```
int XmbTextListToTextProperty(dpy, list, count, style,
                                prop_return)
    Display *dpy;
    char **list;
    int count;
    XICCEncodingStyle style;
    XTextProperty *prop_return;

int XwcTextListToTextProperty(dpy, list, count, style.
                                prop_return)
    Display *dpy;
    wchar_t **list;
    int count;
    XICCEncodingStyle style;
    XTextProperty *prop_return;
```

dpy	identifies the connection to the X server.
list	a list of null-terminated character strings. Data is assumed to be encoded in the code set of the current locale.
count	number of null-terminated strings in list.
style	specifies the conversion to be performed.
prop_return	a pointer to a text property that contains the converted string along with an Atom identifying the encoding of the data.

The data type `XICCEncodingStyle` is defined as

```
typedef enum {
  XStringStyle,
  XCompoundTextStyle,
  XTextStyle,
  XStdICCTextStyle
} XICCEncodingStyle;
```

Table 11.1 describes each of the `XICCEncodingStyle` values defined by X11R5 and X11R6.

Table 11.1 Description of XICCEncodingStyle

XiCCEncodingStyle	Description
`XStringStyle`	Convert the data to ISO 8859.1 if possible. Data not convertible to ISO 8859.1 is ignored. The Atom placed in the encoding field of the text property is `XA_STRING`.
`XCompoundTextStyle`	Convert the data to Compound Text. The Atom placed in the encoding field of the text property is `COMPOUND_TEXT`. The X library guarantees that all data encoded in the code set of the locale can be converted into Compound Text — as long as the current locale is supported by the X library.
`XTextStyle`	Perform no conversion. Place data in the text property using the code set of the current locale. Generates a unique Atom for code set of the current locale, placing that Atom in the encoding field of the text property.
`XStdICCTextStyle`	Convert the data using `XStringStyle` if possible. If not fully convertible using `XStringStyle`, convert the data using `XCompoundTextStyle`.

The routines return `XNoMemory` (a negative value) if there is insufficient memory for the `XTextProperty`. The routines return `XLocaleNotSupported` (a negative value) if the X library does not support the current locale. If one or more characters could not be converted to the requested encoding, the routines return the number of inconvertible characters. Otherwise, the routines return `Success`.

These routines allocate memory to contain the encoded data in the `XTextProperty`. When you are finished with the property, you should free the memory associated with the property's value field by calling `XFree()`.

Because pre-X11R5 software knows only about `TARGETS` of type `XA_STRING` (ISO 8859.1), your software should use `XStdICCTextStyle` if you want the ability to exchange data with such pre-X11R5 software. The `XStdICCTextStyle` attempts to convert your software's data into ISO 8859.1 encoded data. If all the data can successfully be converted to ISO 8859.1, then the encoding field for the `XTextProperty` is `XA_STRING`.

Pre-X11R5 software is capable of processing selections with type XA_STRING. If the data cannot be fully converted to ISO 8859.1, then data is converted to Compound Text.

When your software receives a selection encoded as Compound Text, it can use the XmbTextPropertyToTextList() or XwcTextPropertyToTextList() routines to convert the XTextProperty containing the selection into data encoded in the code set of the current locale. The syntax for these routines is

```
int XmbTextPropertyToTextList(dpy, prop, list_return,
                                        count_return)
    Display *dpy;
    XTextProperty *prop;
    char ***list_return;
    int *count_return;


int XwcTextListToTextProperty(dpy, prop, list_return,
                                        count_return)
    Display *dpy;
    XTextProperty *prop;
    wchar_t ***list_return;
    int *count_return;
```

dpy	identifies the connection to the X server.
prop	text property containing the data to be converted.
list_return	list of null-terminated strings, encoded in the code set of the current locale.
count_return	number of null-terminated strings in list_return.

If there is insufficient memory to create the list of converted strings, the routines return XNoMemory (a negative value). If the current locale is not supported by the X library, the routines return XLocaleNotSupported (a negative value). If the encoding field of prop is not convertible to the code set of the current locale, the routines return XConverterNotFound (a negative value). If one or more characters in prop could not be converted into the code set of the current locale, the routines return the number of characters that could not be converted. Each inconvertible character is replaced with a locale-specific default string.[4] If the routines complete without error, they return Success.

The strings returned in list_return are null-terminated; the number of null-terminated strings is specified by count_return. XmbTextPropertyToTextList() allocates memory to hold the list of strings returned in list_return. To free this memory, call XFreeStringList(). To free the memory allocated by

---

4. To get a copy of the locale's default string, call XDefaultString().

`XwcTextListToTextProperty()`   associated   with   *list_return,*   call
`XwcFreeStringList().`

11.3   Performance Hints for Text Data Interchange

In many cases, it is likely that your software's user wants to transfer text data within the same application or between two applications running in the same locale. In either case, passing the data using Compound Text works — the data is converted and transferred successfully. However, in such cases the conversion from code set of the locale to Compound Text and back are wasted operations that only serve to slow down data transfer. With a little additional work, your software can ensure the highest possible performance when the code set of the selection owner is the same as that of the selection requestor.

If the code set of the selection owner is the same as that of the selection requestor, and if the requestor is aware of this, the requestor can ask for the selection *as is*, with no conversion performed at all. This results in the fastest possible transfer of the selection. To enable this, your software should generate an Atom for the code set of the current locale. By including this Atom in the list of TARGETS it advertises to selection requestors, your software allows the selection requestor to know the code set of your current locale. Similarly, if your software finds this Atom in the list of TARGETS provided by selection owner, your software knows that the selection owner and your software are using the same coded character set. In this case, your software can ask for data encoded in this type.

It's simple to generate an Atom for the code set of the current locale. The I18N capabilities of X require that all locales supported by the X library have the same value for a group of characters known as the *X Portable Character Set* (XPCS). The characters of the XPCS must have the same coded values in every coded character set supported on a system by the X library. The XPCS includes the characters A–Z and a–z. This means that the encoded value of the character "A" must be the same in every locale supported by the X library. With this bit of knowledge, you can then create an Atom for the code set of the current locale as follows:

```
char *tmp = "A"; /* The character is an XPCS character */
XTextProperty tmp_prop;
Atom CS_OF_LOCALE;
int ret_status;

ret_status = XmbTextListToTextProperty(dpy, &tmp, 1,
                (XICCEncodingStyle)XTextStyle, &tmp_prop);
if (ret_status == Success){
  CS_OF_LOCALE = tmp_prop.encoding;
  XFree((char*)tmp_prop.value);
}
```

When you request a conversion to XTextProperty using XTextStyle,
XmbTextListToTextProperty() copies into the properties value field the existing
data without conversion (encoded in the code set of the current locale) and places in the properties encoding field an Atom that identifies the encoding of the data. In the preceding example, the Atom CS_OF_LOCALE is assigned a value that uniquely identifies the code set of
the current locale.

11.4   Example

The following example consists of code fragments. This is because the complete code
to support data interchange using the selection model is large, and because the portions of
that code impacted by the routines and techniques described in this chapter are small. To keep
the program as easy to understand as possible, it uses the Xt toolkit for selection handling.

Assume you are working on an application in which you support data transfer using the
primary selection. Your application includes code allowing the user to specify the primary
selection, for example by dragging the mouse with button one down. Your application
includes code allowing the user to request that the primary selection be pasted at a particular
location, for example by pressing mouse button two.

This example is broken into two pieces. The first shows the I18N changes required to
support being the selection owner. The second shows the I18N changes required when you
request the selection from the selection owner.

11.4.1   Selection Owner

This example assumes you have already written the routines to interact with the user,
allowing them to specify the primary selection. Assuming that you know what text the user
wants as the primary selection, you are ready to tell the toolkit that you want to *own the primary selection*. You do this by calling XtOwnSelection(). In the call to
XtOwnSelection(), you specify three procedure pointers:

- a procedure pointer to a routine that is called whenever anyone asks for a copy of the
  current value of the selection from the selection owner. In this example, this routine is
  called MySelectionConvert().
- a procedure pointer to a routine that is called when other software takes ownership of
  the selection, causing your software to lose ownership. In this example, this routine is
  called MyLoseSelection(). Since this routine is not affected by I18N, its implementation is not included here.
- a procedure pointer to a routine that is called when the requestor has received the selection. Since this is not affected by I18N and the implementation of
  MySelectionConvert() has no clean up required, the routine is NULL in the
  example.

The call to own the selection, looks like this:

```
Boolean got_it = False;
Time event_time; /* Initialize to the time the user completes
                  * specification of the selection. */
...
got_it = XtOwnSelection(my_widget, XA_PRIMARY, event_time,
                        MySelectionConvert,
                        MyLoseSelection,
                        (XtSelectionDoneProc)NULL);
```

The only work remaining as selection owner now is to update `MySelectionConvert()` to handle requests for the primary selection. `MySelectionConvert()` is an `XtConvertSelectionProc` procedure. As such, it is defined to have a specific set of parameters. Since this book is not trying to teach general selection mechanisms, only the parameters used for I18N support are explained in detail. The comments beside the declarations describe the use of the others.

```
Boolean MySelectionConvert(widget, selection, target, type,
                           value, length, format)
  Widget widget;    /* Widget that currently owns selection. */
  Atom *selection; /* Atom name of the selection requested. */
  Atom *target;    /* Specifies the target type of the requested
                    * selection; this proc attempts to convert the
                    * selection to this type, if possible. */
  Atom *type;      /* Used to return the type the selection was
                    * converted into. */
  XtPointer *value; /* Return the converted selection here. */
  unsigned long *length; /* Return the number of format sized
                          * elements that were copied into
                          * value. */
  int *format;         /* Returns the size in bits of the data
                        * elements written into value. */
{

  Atom TARGETS = XInternAtom(XtDisplay(widget), "TARGETS", False);
  Atom TEXT = XInternAtom(XtDisplay(widget), "TEXT", False);
  Atom COMPOUND_TEXT = XInternAtom(XtDisplay(w), "COMPOUND_TEXT",
                                   False);
  Atom CS_OF_LOCALE; /* Initialize later for use in the
                      * performance saving techniques described
                      * earlier in this chapter. */
  XTextProperty tmp_prop;
  char *tmp_string = "A";
```

```
  int ret_status;
  int MAX_TARGETS = 8; /* Maximum number of targets I'll return
                        * when requestor asks for a list of
                        * targets I support. */

...
/* Build a tmp property to obtain an Atom for the code set of the
 * current locale. */
  ret_status = XmbTextListToTextProperty(XtDisplay(widget),
                  &tmp_string, 1, (XICCEncodingStyle)XTextStyle,
                  &tmp_prop);
  if (ret_status) == Success) {
    CS_OF_LOCALE = tmp_prop.encoding;
    XFree((char*)tmp_prop.value);
  } else
    CS_OF_LOCALE = (Atom)NULL;

/* Assume the value of the primary selection is stored in my local
 * variable: char *my_selection. */

  if (*selection == XA_PRIMARY) {
    if (*targets == TARGETS) {
      unsigned int target_count = 0;
      Atom *targets = (Atom *)XtMalloc((unsigned)
                                   (MAX_TARGETS * sizeof(Atom)));
      *value = (XtPointer) targets;
      *targets++ = CS_OF_LOCALE; target_count++;
      *targets++ = TARGETS; target_count++;
      *targets++ = COMPOUND_TEXT; target_count++;
      *targets++ = TEXT; target_count++;
      *targets++ = XA_STRING; target_count++;
      *type = XA_ATOM;
      *length = (target_count * sizeof(Atom)) >> 2;
      *format = 32;
    } else if (*target == CS_OF_LOCALE || *target == TEXT) {
      /* CS_OF_LOCALE: the requestor has asked for the primary
       * selection in the encoding I already am using.
       *
       * TEXT: the requestor has asked for the primary selection
       * in what ever encoding is convenient for me.  CS_OF_LOCALE
       * is about as convenient as it gets. */

      /* ICCCM says that if the requestor asks for TEXT, I must
       * return a type indicating the encoding of the data I
```

```
      * return; the value returned cannot be TEXT. So, return
      * CS_OF_LOCALE in this case since it identifies the
      * encoding. */

     *type = CS_OF_LOCALE;
     *format = 8;
   /* Since we are returning a string, length is a byte count. */
     *length = strlen(my_selection);
     *value = XtMalloc((unsigned) *length + 1);
     (void)strcpy((char*)*value, my_selection);
   } else if (*target == COMPOUND_TEXT) {
     *type = COMPOUND_TEXT;
     *format = 8;
     ret_status = XmbTextListToTextProperty(XtDisplay(widget),
                        &my_selection, 1,
                        (XICCEncodingStyle)XCompoundTextStyle,
                        &tmp_prop);
     if (ret_status == Success || ret_status > 0) {
      /* We were fully successful, or at least converted some
       * characters to compound text. */
       *length = tmp_prop.nitems;
       *value = (XtPointer)tmp_prop.value;
     } else {
      /* Couldn't convert to compound text. */
       *length = 0;
       *value = NULL;
       return (False);
     }
   } else if (*target == XA_STRING) {
    /* The requestor wants only ISO 8859.1 encoded characters.
     * Convert as much of my_selection as possible to 8859.1.
     * Ignore anything that can't be converted. */
     *type = XA_STRING;
     *format = 8;
     ret_status = XmbTextListToTextProperty(XtDisplay(widget),
                          my_selection, 1,
                          (XICCEncodingStyle)XStringStyle,
                          &tmp_prop);
     if (ret_status == Success || ret_status > 0) {
      /* We were fully successful, or at least converted some
       * characters to ISO 8859.1. */
       *length = tmp_prop.nitems;
       *value = (XtPointer)tmp_prop.value;
     } else {
```

```
          /* Couldn't convert to ISO 8859.1. */
          *length = 0;
          *value = NULL;
          return (False);
      }
    } else {
     /* Unknown request; return false. */
      *length = 0;
      *value = NULL;
      return (False);
    }
    return (True);
  }
}
```

11.4.2 Selection Requestor

When the user indicates that the primary selection should be transferred into your software, your software performs a few basic steps. The first is to ask Xt to return a list of supported targets from the owner of the primary selection. Your software does this by calling `XtGetSelectionValue()`. One of the parameters you must supply to `XtGetSelectionValue()` is a pointer to a routine that processes the list targets requested. In this example, the routine `ProcessTargets()` performs this function.

```
XtGetSelectionValue(widget, XA_PRIMARY,
              XInternAtom(XtDisplay(widget), "TARGETS", False),
              ProcessTargets, NULL, event_time);
```

`ProcessTargets()` must examine the list of targets returned by the selection owner and decide which would be best for obtaining a copy of the primary selection. It then calls `XtGetSelectionValue()` to request a copy of the primary selection, formatted according to a specific target type, and passes a pointer to `ProcessPrimary()`. The routine `ProcessPrimary()` converts the primary selection into something usable by the application. For the purposes of this example, `ProcessPrimary()` converts the primary selection into the code set of the locale and stores it in the `char*` variable `my_prime_copy`.

A real example would handle more than just the primary selection in its version of `ProcessPrimary()` and `ProcessTargets()`. However, to keep this example relatively simple, these sample routines process only the primary selection.

The specification for `XtGetSelectionValue()` requires that the procedure pointer passed be of type `XtSelectionCallbackProc`, which is defined to have a specific set of parameters. Since this book is not trying to teach general selection mechanisms, only the parameters used for I18N support are explained in detail. The comments beside the declarations describe the use of the other parameters.

```
void ProcessTargets(widget, client_data, selection, type, value
                    length, format)
  Widget widget;              /* Widget that requested selection. */
  XtPointer client_data;      /* NULL for this example. */
  Atom *selection;            /* Name of the selection requested. */
  Atom *type;                 /* Representation type of the selection
                               * value. */
  XtPointer value;            /* Points to the selection value. */
  unsigned long *length;      /* Number of format sized elements
                               * in value. */
  int *format;                /* size in bits of the data elements
                               * in value. */
{
  Atom TEXT = XInternAtom(XtDisplay(widget), "TEXT, False);
  Atom COMPOUND_TEXT = XInternAtom(XtDisplay(widget),
                                   "COMPOUND_TEXT", False);
  Atom CS_OF_LOCALE; /* Initialize later for use in the
                      * performance saving techniques described
                      * earlier in this chapter. */
  Atom *atom_ptr, target;
  XTextProperty tmp_prop;
  char *tmp_string = "A";
  int ret_status, index;
  Boolean use_CT = False;
  Boolean use_CS = False;
  Boolean use_STRING = False;
  Boolean use_TEXT = False;

  if (!length){
    XtFree((char *)value);
    value = NULL;
    return;
  }
...
  ret_status = XmbTextListToTextProperty(XtDisplay(widget),
                                         &tmp_string, 1,
                                         (XICCEncodingStyle)XTextStyle,
                                         &tmp_prop);
  if (ret_status == Success){
    CS_OF_LOCALE = tmp_prop.encoding;
    XFree((char*)tmp_prop.value);
```

```
    } else
      CS_OF_LOCALE = (Atom)NULL;

    /* Walk the list of TARGETS to decide the best type for
     * transferring the primary selection.
     * - Use CS_OF_LOCALE, if possible.
     * - If CS_OF_LOCALE is not available, use compound text.
     * - If compound text is not supported, use ISO 8859.1.
     * - If ISO 8859.1 (XA_STRING) is not available, request text
     *   and take your chances. */

  atom_ptr = (Atom *)value;
  for (index = 0; index < *length; index++, atom_ptr++){
    if (*atom_ptr == CS_OF_LOCALE){
      use_CS = True;
      break;
    } else if (*atom_ptr == COMPOUND_TEXT){
      use_CT = True;
    } else if (*atom_ptr == XA_STRING){
      use_STRING = True;
    } else if (*atom_ptr == TEXT){
      use_TEXT = True;
    }
  }

  if (use_CS)
    target = CS_OF_LOCALE;
  else if (use_CT)
    target = COMPOUND_TEXT;
  else if (use_STRING)
    target = XA_STRING;
  else if (use_text)
    target = TEXT;
  else
    return; /* Owner doesn't support any targets I can process. */

  XtGetSelectionValue(widget, XA_PRIMARY, target, ProcessPrimary,
                      (XtPointer)NULL, event_time);

  XtFree((char*)value);
  value = NULL;
}
```

```
void ProcessPrimary(widget, client_data, selection, type,
                    value, length, format)
  Widget widget;          /* Widget that requested selection. */
  XtPointer client_data;  /* NULL for this example. */
  Atom *selection;        /* Name of the selection requested. */
  Atom *type;             /* Representation type of the selection
                           * value. */
  XtPointer value;        /* Points to the selection value. */
  unsigned long *length;  /* Number of format sized elements
                           * in value. */
  int *format;            /* size in bits of the data elements
                           * in value. */
{
  Atom CS_OF_LOCALE;    /* Initialize later for use in the
                         * performance saving techniques described
                         * earlier in this chapter. */
  char *my_prime_copy;  /* Use to store the primary selection
                         * value retrieved. */
  XTextProperty tmp_prop; /* Use this property convert the
                           * selection value into code set of the
                           * locale. */
  int ret_status, count;
  int num_values;  /* Number of strings in list returned. */
  int size_needed; /* Calculate size needed for my_prime_copy. */
  char *tmp_string = "A";
  char *tmp;

  ret_status = XmbTextListToTextProperty(XtDisplay(widget),
                                    &tmp_string, 1,
                                    (XICCEncodingStyle)XTextStyle,
                                    &tmp_prop);
  if (ret_status == Success){
    CS_OF_LOCALE = tmp_prop.encoding;
    XFree((char*)tmp_prop.value);
  } else
    CS_OF_LOCALE = (Atom)NULL;

  if (*type == XInternAtom(XtDisplay(widget),
                      "COMPOUND_TEXT", False) ||
      *type == XA_STRING){

    /* Copy value and type into tmp_prop and convert the data
     * into code set of the locale using the X11R5 I18N
     * routine XmbTextPropertyToTextList(). */
```

```
      tmp_prop.value = (unsigned char*) value;
      tmp_prop.encoding = *type;
      tmp_prop.format = *format;
      tmp_prop.nitems = *length;
      num_values = 0;
      ret_status = XmbTextPropertyToTextList(XtDisplay(widget),
                                 &tmp_prop, &tmp, &num_values);
      if (num_values && (ret_status == Success || ret_status > 0)){
        for (count = 0, size_needed = 1;
             count < num_values; count++)
          size_needed += strlen(tmp[count]);
        my_prime_copy = XtMalloc((unsigned) size_needed);
        my_prime_copy[0] = '\0';
        for (count = 0; count < num_values; count++)
          strcat(my_prime_copy, tmp[count]);
        XFreeStringList(tmp);
    } else if (*type == CS_OF_LOCALE) {
     /* If data is in CS_OF_LOCALE, it's already in the code set of
      * the current locale - so just copy it in. */
      my_prime_copy = XtMalloc((unsigned)*length + 1);
      strncpy(my_prime_copy, value, *length);
      my_prime_copy[*length] = '\0';
    }

   /* Note: If I asked for TEXT in ProcessTargets(), ICCCM says that
    * the selection will be returned in a form convenient for the
    * owner. Whatever that form is, it must have a type that
    * identifies the encoding; the value of type cannot be TEXT.
    * So, I'll handle the types I know about (COMPOUND_TEXT,
    * CS_OF_LOCALE, and XA_STRING), hoping that the owner will
    * send it as one of those.  If it doesn't come in tagged as
    * one of those three, I don't know how to handle it anyway,
    * so ignore the selection value passed in this case. */

    XFree((char *)value);
    value = NULL;
}
```

11.5 Summary: Data Interchange for Internationalized Software

Assuming you have already written your software to enable data interchange using the conventions of ICCCM, the following summarizes the changes you must make to your software to enable data interchange with software running in a locale different from your own.

When your software is the selection owner,

1. Add an Atom for COMPOUND_TEXT to the list of TARGETS your software generates.
2. Generate an Atom for the code set of the current locale. Add that Atom to the list of TARGETS your software generates.
3. When the requester asks for the selection and the type specified matches the Atom you generated for code set of the current locale, copy the text data directly from your application without conversion. If the data is encoded as wide character, you must either first convert it to multibyte by calling wcstombs() or you can use XwcTextListToTextProperty() with encoding style XTextStyle. Do *not* pass the selection in its wide character representation. For details on why not to pass wide characters, see section 2.3.1 on page 32.
4. When the requestor asks for the selection and requests conversion to type COMPOUND_TEXT, call XmbTextListToTextProperty() or XwcTextListToTextProperty() to create the XTextProperty needed. Use XCompoundTextStyle as the XICCEncodingStyle parameter for either routine.

When your software is the selection requestor,

1. Generate an Atom for the code set of the current locale.
2. Search the list of TARGETS provided by the selection owner for the Atom that matches the Atom you generated for code set of the current locale. If it exists, request the selection using the Atom for code set of the current locale as type.
3. If TARGETS does not contain an entry that matches the Atom for the code set of the current locale, search the list of TARGETS for the Atom COMPOUND_TEXT. If it exists, request the selection with type COMPOUND_TEXT.
4. When the selection owner provides the selection with type COMPOUND_TEXT, use XmbTextPropertyToTextList() or XwcTextPropertyToTextList() to convert the data into your locale's coded character set. You can use these same routines to convert the data if the selection owner provides the selection in ISO 8859.1 (type XA_STRING).

Using Resources and the Xt Toolkit with Your Internationalized Software

$\mathbf{X}$11R5 modified the X resource manager (Xrm) to allow use of localized resource values; the string value of a resource is now assumed to be encoded in the code set of the current locale. (Prior to X11R5, all strings were assumed to be encoded in ISO 8859.1 — the only code set that X officially supported.) Though no code changes are needed to use these localized resource values, this chapter provides the background you need to define the resources and enable their translation. It also describes new features of the Xt toolkit that allow your software to find localized resources based on the user's current locale.

In addition to aiding you in finding localized resource files, the X11R5 Xt toolkit provides some additional functionality to help when developing internationalized software:

- provides an additional way to initialize the software's locale: `XtSetLanguageProc()`. This routine also helps enable the display of localized titles and icon names by the window manager.
- adds a command line option and a resource for specifying the locale.
- provides tools that help you find files containing locale-specific information. For example, your software might want to allow the bitmap used to label a push button to be changed based on the current locale. A German might expect to see one bitmap while a Japanese user might expect a different bitmap. Xt provides tools that allow you to place such locale-specific data in separate files, one per locale. The tools then find the correct file at run time, based on the user's current locale.
- provides a resource converter for creating font sets.
- modifies the convenience routine `XtDispatchEvent()` to automatically call to `XFilterEvent()`.

12.1   Localized Resources

The X11R5 X resource manager supports localized resource values. This means that a string resource value is assumed to be encoded in the code set of the current locale. However, resource names must consist only of characters from the X Portable Character Set (XPCS).

The XPCS is a set of 97 characters that must exist in every locale supported by Xlib on a system. The characters of the XPCS are

```
abcdefghijklmnopqrstuvwxyz
ABCDEFGHIJKLMNOPQRSTUVWXYZ0123456789
!"#$%&'()*+,-./:;<=>?@[]&_`{|}~
<space>, <tab>, and <newline>
```

X11R5 does not specify the encoded value of these characters, but it does require that the coded value of each character in the XPCS be identical in every locale supported by Xlib on a system. (The encoding of the XPCS is called the Host Portable Character Encoding.)

For example, suppose that your software wants to use the `title` resource. Further suppose that you want the title translated for the language of the user. The resource specification might look like this:

```
*TopLevelShell.title: local_language_title_string
```

The resource name, `TopLevelShell.title`, is represented in XPCS. However, the value of that resource may contain any character in the code set of the current locale.

12.2   Initializing the Locale of Xt-Based Software

If you are writing software that uses Xt or a toolkit built on top of Xt (such as Motif), your internationalized software must change the way it initializes the locale. Xt requires that prior to opening the display, your software must call `XtSetLanguageProc()`. This routine provides Xt with a locale initialization procedure which Xt calls when opening the display and initializing the toolkit. The syntax of this routine is

```
XtLanguageProc XtSetLanguageProc(app_context, proc,
                                 client_data)
   XtAppContext app_context;
   XtLanguageProc proc;
   XtPointer client_data;
```

app_context   specifies the application context where the language procedure *proc* will be used. If this value is NULL, *proc* will be used in all application contexts.

proc   specifies the language procedure. If this value is NULL, a default language procedure (described below) is used.

client_data   allows you to pass additional data to the language procedure.

The syntax of the language procedure is

```
typedef String (*XtLanguageProc)(Display*, String, XtPointer);
  Display *dpy;
  String locale;
  XtPointer client_data;
```

dpy   passes the connection to the X server.

locale   passes the string identifying the locale. This string is obtained from the command line or server per display resource specifications.

client_data   passes the additional data specified in the call to XtSetLanguageProc().

XtSetLanguageProc() returns a pointer to the previous language procedure.

Unless you have very unusual circumstances and cannot use the default language procedure, your software should always call XtSetLanguageProc() as follows:

```
(void) XtSetLanguageProc(NULL, NULL, NULL);
```

Remember, calling XtSetLanguageProc() initializes a procedure pointer; the procedure doesn't actually get called until Xt opens the display and initializes the toolkit. Your software should not perform locale-sensitive operations until after it has initialized the language procedure, opened the display, and initialized the toolkit. If for some reason you cannot open the display prior to performing locale-sensitive operations and you know the locale is specified using the LANG or LC_* environment variables,[1] then call setlocale(LC_ALL, "") prior to performing the locale-sensitive operations.

12.2.1 Locale Command Line Option and Locale Resource

Xt adds support for the user to specify the locale either via a command line option or via a resource. The command line option is specified as

```
-xnlLanguage locale_string
```

The locale resource is specified as:

```
-xrm "*.xnlLanguage: locale_name", or
-xrm "*.XnlLanguage: locale_name"
```

These values are evaluated by XtDisplayInitialize(), which first checks to see if either the -xnlLanguage command line option has been specified or if the -xrm "*XnlLanguage" resource has been specified on the command line. If neither exists, XtDisplayInitialize() queries the server resource database for the

---

1. Do this only if you are willing to risk that the value of these environment variables may be different from the values of the locale command line option or locale resource.

app_name.xnlLanguage and *app_class*.XnlLanguage resources, where *app_name* is the application name and *app_class* is the application class passed to XtDisplayInitialize(). The value for the locale name that results from this search is the value passed as the locale name to the language procedure set with XtSetLanguageProc().

12.2.2 Default Language Procedure

The default language procedure

- calls setlocale(LC_ALL, *locale*), where *locale* is the value of the locale Xt obtains from the -xnlLanguage command line option or from the xnlLanguage or XnlLanguage locale resource, if set. If the locale command line option or locale resource are not set, locale is replaced with " " causing setlocale() to use the LANG and LC_* environment variables as described in section 2.1.1 on page 17. If an error occurs, Xt issues a warning message by calling XtWarning. Otherwise, the default language procedure returns the value returned by setlocale().
- calls XSupportsLocale() to make sure that the X library supports the requested locale. If the locale is not supported, the locale is initialized to the C locale; Xt issues a warning message by calling XtWarning.
- calls XSetLocaleModifiers("") causing X to use the modifiers set in the XMODIFIERS environment variable.

As you can see, the default language procedure does all the operations internationalized X-based GUI software should do to initialize the locale.

12.3   Finding Locale-Specific Files

The design of internationalized software emphasizes placing locale-specific data external to the software and reading that data into the software at run time. For example, message catalogs contain the translated strings used by your software. You create a different catalog for each locale your software supports. At software start-up, catopen() finds the correct message catalog for the current locale using, in part, the NLSPATH environment variable. NLSPATH allows inclusion of wild cards (such as %L for the current locale) that are expanded at run time based on current conditions.

To find all the locale-specific files (such as resource files) that it needs, your software needs a generic equivalent of catopen(), capable of finding any kind of locale-specific file. Fortunately, Xt provides this functionality with the routine XtResolvePathname(). The routine takes a generic path description which, like catopen(), allows the embedding of wild cards for the locale name. It then searches the file system, expanding the wild cards based on current conditions, and returns a full path name to the first file found that matches the generic path description.

The syntax of `XtResolvePathname()` is provided below:

```
String XtResolvePathname(dpy, type, filename, suffix,
                         path, subs, num_subs, predicate)
   Display *dpy,
   String type, filename, suffix, path;
   Substitution subs;
   Cardinal num_subs;
   XtFilePredicate predicate;
typedef struct {
   char match; /* Character to parse for: %<match>. */
   String Substitution; /* Replacement for %<match> in path.*/
}SubstitutionRec, *Substitution;
```

`dpy`	identifies the connection to the X server.
`type`	specifies value to be substituted for the `%T` wild card when it appears in `path`.
`filename`	specifies the value to be substituted for the `%N` wild card when it appears in `path`.
`suffix`	specifies the value to be substituted for the `%S` wild card when it appears in `path`.
`path`	specifies a series of colon (`":"`) separated path names that are searched. If path is NULL, the value of the `XFILESEARCHPATH` environment variable is used as a search path. If `XFILESEARCHPATH` is not defined, an implementation default path is searched.
`subs`	specifies a series of additional application defined substitutions that `XtResolvePathname()` should perform.
`num_subs`	specifies the number of additional substitutions defined in `subs`.
`predicate`	specifies a procedure that is called for each potential file name. If `predicate` is NULL, a default procedure is used. The default procedure makes sure the file exists, the file is readable, and the file is not a directory.

The file name evaluation is handled by the operating system via an `XtFilePredicate` procedure, which is defined as follows:

```
typedef struct {
   char match; /* Character to parse for: %<match>. */
   String Substitution; /* Replacement for %<match> in path.*/
}SubstitutionRec, *Substitution;
typedef Boolean (*XtFilePredicate)(String);
     String filename;
```

`filename`	identifies a potential file name.

The wild cards that `XtResolvePathname()` can expand are shown in Table 12.1.

Table 12.1 Description of Wild Cards Used by XtResolvePathname()

Wild card	XtResolvePathname() replaces the wild card with...
%N	the value of the *filename* parameter, or the application's class name if *filename* is NULL.
%T	the value of the *type* parameter. This typically indicates a class of files and maps to a directory name. Examples include "app-defaults", "help", "bitmap" and "fonts".
%S	the value of the *suffix* parameter. This typically indicates the kind of data in the file. Examples include ".txt", ".bm", and ".dat".
%L	the locale of the display, as initialized by the language procedure set with `XtSetLanguageProc()`.
%l	the language component of the locale of the display.
%t	the territory component of the locale of the display.
%c	the code set component of the locale of the display.
%C	the customization string retrieved from the resource database associated with the display *dpy*.

It is up to the implementation of Xlib to determine how to replace the %l, %t, and %c wild cards. The intent was to support systems where the locale was defined to identify a language, a territory where that language is spoken, and the code set used to encode characters of that language. For example, French as spoken in Canada, with data encoded in ISO 8859.1, might have %l replaced with "fr", %t replaced with "CA", and %c replaced with "iso88591". This maps well to operating systems that define the locale name as *language_territory.codeset* (such as LANG=fr_CA.iso88591).

12.3.1 Finding Locale-Specific Resource Files

Xt makes the following call to find resource files when initializing the display:

```
XtResolvePathname(dpy, NULL, NULL, NULL, path, NULL, 0, NULL);
```

The *path* used to find the resources is controlled by the XUSERFILESEARCHPATH environment variable. If XUSERFILESEARCHPATH is not defined, an implementation defined system default search path is used. The implementation defined default must include the APPLRESDIR environment if it is defined. This means that you or the user can control where resources are found by setting the XUSERFILESEARCHPATH or XAPPLRESDIR environment variables.

Before completing the initialization of the resource database, the display initialize routine searches for the application class resource file by calling

```
XtResolvePathname(dpy, "app-defaults", NULL, NULL, NULL, NULL,
                  0, NULL).
```

Because the path parameter in this call is null, the XFILESEARCHPATH environment variable can control where Xt searches for the app-defaults file.

12.4   Font Set Resource Converter

Xt provides a predefined resource for internationalized software: XtRFontSet. The associated resource converter is XtCvtStringToFontSet, which converts a string to a font set. XtCvtStringToFontSet recognizes the constant XtDefaultFontSet, which can be used as a default when using the font set resource converter in your software. For example,

```
...
typedef struct {
  XFontSet fontset;
  char *foo;
}AppData, *AppDataPtr;
static XtResource my_resources[] = {
  {XtNfontSet, XtCFontSet, XtRFontSet, sizeof(XFontSet),
   XtOffset(AppDataPtr, fontset), XtRString,
   XtDefaultFontSet}
}
...
XFontSet fontset;
AppData data;
...
XtSetLanguageProc(NULL, NULL, NULL);
toplevel = XtInitialize(...
XtGetApplicationResources(toplevel, &data, my_resources,
                          XtNumber(my_resources), NULL, 0);
fontset = data.fontset;
```

The default font set created when XtDefaultFontSet is used is determined using the following procedure:

1. Xt queries the resource database for a resource whose full name is
    xtDefaultFontSet and whose full class name is XtDefaultFontSet; there
    can be no widget name or widget class prefixes. If one of these names exists and a font
    set can be created from the resource, that font set is returned as the default font set.

2.   If Xt could not create a default font set using the `xtDefaultFontSet` or `XtDefaultFontSet` resources, an implementation defined default resource is returned.

3.   If a font set could not be created using the implementation defined method, Xt issues a warning and the converter returns `False`.

If the resource converter could create only a partially complete font set (for example, `XCreateFontSet()` indicates that there are some missing charsets with the font set created), the resource converter returns the partial font set and issues a warning.

12.5   Event Loops, I18N, and Xt

As you discovered in section 7.7 on page 125, your internationalized software needs to call `XFilterEvent()` to work properly with different input methods. However, few applications really dispatch their own events. Instead, they rely on the toolkit to dispatch events for them.

Beginning with X11R5, `XtDispatchEvent()` calls `XFilterEvent()` as its first action on an event. `XtDispatchEvent()` is called by both `XtMainLoop()` and `XtAppMainLoop()`. If you use either of these functions to process and dispatch events in your software, there is no need to call `XFilterEvent()`.

Developing Internationalized Software with Motif

$\mathbf{M}$otif 1.2 is based on X11R5. It is the first release of Motif that officially supports developing internationalized Motif software.

The problems you must address when developing internationalized software with Motif are largely the same problems you must address when developing internationalized software with X:

- correctly displaying local language characters to the user,
- obtaining coded characters from the keyboard, and
- interchanging text data with other software.

If you are developing software using existing Motif widgets, these problems are easily solved. If you are writing your own widgets, these problems require more detailed explanation. Since most Motif software developers use only existing Motif widgets, this chapter focuses on writing internationalized software with existing widgets. This helps keep the material focused on topics that are of interest and use to most readers. If you are writing your own widgets, or if you want to display or input local language characters in the `XmDrawingArea` widget, Chapter 14 provides the additional information you need.

13.1 Displaying Local Language Characters with Motif

Motif uses two forms of text data:

- normal string data (data stored and passed as `char*` or `wchar_t*`) — `Text` and `TextField` widgets store their data this way.
- compound string (data stored and passed as `XmString`). All widgets except `Text` and `TextField` widgets use compound string data.

In both cases, Motif uses a font list (data type `XmFontList`) to identify the font to display character data. Prior to Motif 1.2, a font list could contain only font structures (data type `XFontStruct`). With Motif 1.2, the definition of `fontList` expanded, allowing it to contain both font structures and font sets. When a Motif widget draws text with a font list entry that is a font set, the widget uses the X11R5 internationalized rendering routines; local language characters are displayed correctly.

13.1.1   Motif Font Lists and fontList Resources

The Motif 1.2 `fontList` resource is a list of any combination of `XFontStruct` and `XFontSet`. Each element of a font list can be associated with a tag. You assign a tag to an element of a font list if you want to direct Motif to draw a segment of a compound string with the font or font set associated with that tag.

Internationalized software should use font structures in font lists only when the characters needed are not part of the code set of the locale. For example, you would use a font struct in a font list if your software needed a special math symbol from a math font.

The easiest way to create a font list is by specifying the `fontList` resource for a widget, allowing Motif's font list resource converter to do the work for you. A `fontList` resource specification consists of a series of comma separated entries; each entry identifies either a font structure or a font set. You specify a font list entry as shown by the following single element `fontList` resource specifications:

```
*fontList: font_name
*fontList: font_name=font_tag
*fontList: base_name:
*fontList: base_name:font_tag
```

`font_name`	a font alias or an XLFD that identifies a font; a `XFontStruct` is created with this specification by passing `font_name` to `XLoadQueryFont()`.
`font_tag`	tag used with compound strings. When a compound string includes this tag, the associated segment is drawn with the font or font struct in the font list that has the matching tag. If no tag is supplied, Motif automatically assigns the tag `XmFONTLIST_DEFAULT_TAG`.
`base_name`	base name used to create a font set. If multiple XLFDs are used in the base name, semi-colons (";") separate the base names.
:	a colon (":") embedded in the `fontList` resource specification is a signal to Motif's string-to-fontList resource converter that it should create a font set for this entry. The colon (":") and optional tag are stripped, and any embedded semi-colons (";") are replaced with commas (",") before passing `base_name` to `XCreateFontSet()`.

13.1.1.1   Example font list specifications

The following are some examples of font list resource specifications in a command line:

```
foo -xrm "foo*XmPushButton*fontList: *-24-*:bar, *-18-*:"
```

This command line resource specification says to create a font list containing two font sets. The first font set has the base name `*-24-*` and has the tag `bar`. The tag `bar` will be used by a compound string in the application to access that particular font set from the font list. The second font set in the font list has the base name `*-18-*`. It uses the default font tag `XmFONTLIST_DEFAULT_TAG`.

The next example might be taken from the Japanese EUC app-defaults file for application `foo`:

```
foo*fontList: \
  *-medium-r-normal--18-150-75-75-m-80-jisx0201.1976-0;\
  *-medium-r-normal--18-150-75-75-c-160-jisx0208.1983-0;\
  *-medium-r-normal--18-180-75-75-c-160-jisx0212.1990-0:
```

In this example, the font list contains a single font set, consisting of three base names. Each base name tightly specifies one of the fonts needed for the font set.

13.1.2 Compound Strings

Compound strings are a way of encoding strings such that a specific font and a drawing direction can be associated with that string. All widgets except `Text` and `TextField` widgets use compound strings to display text data. The description of font lists showed how you associate a specific font or font set in the font set with a tag. When you create a compound string, you specify a tag and a drawing direction to be associated with that compound string. Then, when Motif renders the compound string using a font list, it searches the font list for a font list entry with a tag that matches the tag of the compound string and renders the text in the direction indicated.

There are many ways to create the compound strings used by Motif widgets. Some let you specify your own font tag while others provide a default tag for you. Similarly, some let you specify a drawing direction while others provide a default drawing direction. Perhaps the easiest way to provide a compound string to a widget is by specifying a normal multibyte string in a resource file and letting Motif's String-to-XmString resource converter do the work for you. If you need to provide a compound string programmatically, use the routines listed in Table 13.1.

In most cases, programs call only `XmStringCreateLocalized()` or `XmStringCreate()`. The other routines aren't needed unless you need to control the direction of drawing. Call `XmStringCreateLocalized()` if you don't need to associate a font tag with the compound string; otherwise, call `XmStringCreate()`.

Table 13.1 Routines for Creating Compound Strings

Routine	Description
XmStringCreate(*text*, *tag*)	Create a compound string and associate the tag *tag* with it.
XmStringCreateLocalized(*text*)	Identical to XmStringCreate() with *tag* set to XmFONTLIST_DEFAULT_TAG.
XmStringCreateLtoR(*text*, *tag*)	Create a compound string that is drawn left to right and associate the tag *tag* with it.
XmStringSegmentCreate(*text*, *tag*, *dir*, *separator*)	Create a compound string that is drawn in direction *dir* and associate the tag *tag* with it.
XmCvtCTToXmString(*text*)	Creates a compound string from the compound text data passed in *text*.
XmCvtXmStringToCT(*xm_string*)	Creates compound text from the compound string passed in *xm_string*.

Note that early implementations of XmStringCreateLocalized() contained a bug in that the routine did not handle embedded newlines in the string argument. If your system exhibits this problem and you want a multiline compound string, you either need to get a patch from your Motif supplier, or use XmStringCreateLtoR() (which did not have this problem).

13.2   Obtaining Local Language Characters from the Keyboard

Obtaining local language characters from the keyboard with Motif is simple. Both the Text and TextField widgets call the XmIm* Motif routines; for more information on these routines, refer to the description of these routines in section 14.3 on page 274. These functions establish a connection to the input method, create and manage the input context, and notify the input method when values change (for example, when the font list changes, or when focus changes). All your software needs to do is to call XtSetLanguageProc() prior to initializing the display and the toolkit and make sure you specify a font set for the widget's font list resource. The Text and TextField widgets (and all dialogs that use these widgets) correctly interact with the input method to produce local language characters encoded in the code set of the user's locale.

Note that both the Text and TextField widgets accept and produce both multibyte and wide character data; these widgets do not accept or produce compound string data. You can even use multibyte and wide character data with the same Text or TextField widget. The following example shows how an application might chose to interact with TextField using multibyte for one call, and wide character in the next. This is not typical application usage, but Text and TextField have this flexibility.

```
XmTextField tf;
char string[] = "Initial string value";
char new_str[] = "New";
wchar_t wcstmp[4];
wchar_t *new_wcsval;
...
XmTextFieldSetString(tf, string);
mbstowcs(wcstmp, new_str, 4);
XmTextFieldReplaceStringWcs(tf, 0, strlen("Initial"), wcstmp);
new_wcsval = XmTextFieldGetStringWcs(tf);
...
XtFree(new_wcsval);
```

The initial call to `XmTextFieldSetString()` sets a multibyte string as the TextField value. The call to `XmTextFieldReplaceStringWcs()` tells the widget to replace the characters from position 0 through position 7 with the wide character string `wcstmp`, which contain a wide character representation of the string "New." Finally, the call to `XmTextFieldGetStringWcs()` returns a wide character representation of the modified string into `new_wcsval`; `new_wcsval` now points to the wide character representation of the string "New string value."

The Text and TextField widgets support root, off-the-spot, and over-the-spot preedit and status styles; they do not support on-the-spot style. Geometry management for off-the-spot style is handled by Motif's VendorShell. It negotiates with the input method to determine how much area is needed for the off-the-spot preedit and status areas and then allocates and manages that space. If the size of the VendorShell changes, or if an attribute of the Text or TextField widgets that affects the geometry (such as the font set used by the widget) changes, VendorShell renegotiates the geometry with the input method.

13.2.1 Controlling Input with Motif

Motif provides resources that allow you or your software's user to control which input method is used by the Text and TextField widgets, as well as which input styles are preferred.

The VendorShell resource XmNinputMethod can be used to specify the modifier to the input method. This is a supplement to the XMODIFIERS environment variable. VendorShell uses the XmIm* routines, which call XSetLocaleModifiers() with the value of the XmNinputMethod resource. The X library automatically appends the value of the XMODIFIERS environment variable to the end of the list of modifiers passed in via XSetLocaleModifiers(). The values for the XmNinputMethod resource are dependent on the implementation of the X library.

The VendorShell resource XmNpreeditType allows you or your software's user to control which preedit style (among the many supported by an input method) is used for all keyboard input managed by VendorShell. XmNpreeditType is an ordered list of preedit styles. VendorShell uses the first style in the list of values that the input method supports. If the input method does not support any of the styles listed in the resource, *no connection to the input method occurs*. For this reason, you should always specify a complete list of preedit styles when setting this resource. The specification says that the syntax, possible values, and defaults for this resource are implementation dependent. However, the implementation of Motif 1.2.* shipped by OSF and the implementation of Motif used by, and shipped with, CDE specify the values as those contained in the default setting for XmNpreeditType:

> "OverTheSpot,OffTheSpot,Root"

Further, the next revision of the Motif specs removes the "implementation dependent" wording, explicitly stating that the value of XmNpreeditType is a string of comma separated values, where the possible values are OverTheSpot, OffTheSpot, and Root.

13.3   Data Interchange Using Motif

The Motif 1.2 widgets implement selections and drag and drop using the techniques described in section 11.2 on page 226 and section 11.3 on page 230. This means that when your software uses the existing Motif 1.2 widgets, a user can cut and paste or drag and drop local language characters between the widgets in your software, or between your software and other internationalized Motif software — even if the other software is running in a different locale.

In addition, the Text and TextField widgets provide routines, such as XmText[Field]Copy() and XmText[Field]Paste(), that copy text data to and from the Motif clipboard. These routines use Compound Text to make sure data can correctly be exchanged via the clipboard.

13.4   Setting Localized Titles and Icon Names

There is really nothing special about setting localized titles and icon names for internationalized software. But for some reason, this task seems to cause programmers and users much more trouble than it should. Setting localized titles and icons is simple if you remember these basic points:

- Setting a title or an icon name is really "data interchange" with another application (the window manager).
- To work properly, both your software and the window manager must be internationalized, with the locale set properly for each. Both must call XtSetLanguageProc() prior to initializing the display and the toolkit.
- The font list used by the window manager to display the title and the icon name must contain a font set.

- The resource for the title, and icon name (XmNtitle and XmNiconName) is data type String, not XmString. Simply pass a multibyte string encoded in the code set of the current locale when setting these resources. Under no circumstance should you pass a compound string representation to the window manager for these resources.
- The resource for dialog titles (XmNdialogTitle) is data type XmString, not String.
- Do not set or change the XmNtitleEncoding or XmNiconNameEncoding resources. The only reason to do this is if you want to force a specific representation to be sent to the window manager, and this is almost never a good idea. When your software calls XtSetLanguageProc() it determines the correct setting for XmNtitleEncoding and XmNiconNameEncoding and converts these resources appropriately before communicating them to the window manager.

13.5   Locale Sensitive Motif Resources

Many of the resources defined by the Motif widgets specify values that may need to be changed based on the locale of the user. Examples include font lists, button labels, and initial Text widget values. These localizable resources are listed in tables in Appendix E.

13.5.1   Which to Use: Resources or Message Catalogs?

When you write Motif-based software, you have at least two mechanisms available to you to separate localizable text from your software: message catalogs and resource files.

When should you use message catalogs and when should you use resource files? The answer is subjective. Each call to a message catalog is a round trip to the file system. Each string defined in a resource data base is loaded at application start-up and occupies memory whether that string is ever actually used or not.

Two general rules many software organizations use are

1. If a string has to be loaded and displayed by the user interface, place it in a resource file. Examples include initial Text widget values, labels, and frequently used dialogs.
2. If a string may be displayed only on occasion, or is large, then place it in a message catalog. Examples include error messages and text in infrequently used dialogs.

One additional consideration is that it can be confusing for the persons actually translating text to have some text in message catalogs while other text is in resource files.

13.6   Locale Sensitive Pixmaps

If your software uses pixmaps that may vary from locale to locale, the pixmaps should be stored in files external to your software. You can then use Motif's XmGetPixmap() routine to load the pixmap that is correct for the user's current locale. The syntax for the routine is

```
#include <Xm/Xm.h>
Pixmap XmGetPixmap(screen, image, foreground, background)
  Screen *screen;
  char *image;
  Pixel foreground;
  Pixel background;
```

screen   Specifies the display screen on which the pixmap will be drawn.

image   Specifies the name of the image to be loaded.

foreground   If the image is a bit-per-pixel image, the routine combines the image with the
                foreground color to create the pixmap.

background   If the image is a bit-per-pixel image, the routine combines the image with the
                background color to create the pixmap.

XmGetPixmap() attempts to locate the named image in the image cache. If it cannot
find it there, it loads the named image from a file. If the first character in image is /, it
assumes image specifies a full path name and attempts to load the image from that file. Otherwise, XmGetPixmap() searches a series of paths searching for the named file. The search
paths are controlled by the XBMLANGPATH and XAPPLRESDIR environment variables, as
well as the current locale.

In evaluating the paths searched by XmGetPixmap(), it allows the same substitutions as are used by XtResolvePathname(). In addition, the following substitutions are
made:

%B   replaced with the image name — the image argument to XmGetPixmap().

%N   replaced with the class name of the application.

%L   replaced with the display's locale string — same as XtResolvePathname().

%l   replaced with the language component of the display's locale string — same as
     XtResolvePathname().

%T   XtResolvePathname() substitution field — always replaced with bitmaps in this case.

%S   XtResolvePathname() substitution field — always replaced with NULL in this case.

The XBMLANGPATH environment variable can be set to specify a search path for bitmap files. If XMBLANGPATH is not set but the environment variable XAPPLRESDIR is set,
the following path names are searched:

```
%B
$XAPPLRESDIR/%L/bitmaps/%N/%B
$XAPPLRESDIR/%l/bitmaps/%N/%B
$XAPPLRESDIR/bitmaps/%N/%B
$XAPPLRESDIR/%L/bitmaps/%B
$XAPPLRESDIR/%l/bitmaps/%B
```

```
$XAPPLRESDIR/bitmaps/%B
$HOME/bitmaps/%B
$HOME/%B
/usr/lib/X11/%L/bitmaps/%N/%B
/usr/lib/X11/%l/bitmaps/%N/%B
/usr/lib/X11/bitmaps/%N/%B
/usr/lib/X11/%L/bitmaps/%B
/usr/lib/X11/%l/bitmaps/%B
/usr/lib/X11/bitmaps/%B
/usr/include/X11/bitmaps/%B
```

If neither XBMLANGPATH nor XAPPLRESDIR is set, the following path names are searched:

```
%B
$HOME/%L/bitmaps/%N/%B
$HOME/%l/bitmaps/%N/%B
$HOME/bitmaps/%N/%B
$HOME/%L/bitmaps/%B
$HOME/%l/bitmaps/%B
$HOME/bitmaps/%B
$HOME/%B
/usr/lib/X11/%L/bitmaps/%N/%B
/usr/lib/X11/%l/bitmaps/%N/%B
/usr/lib/X11/bitmaps/%N/%B
/usr/lib/X11/%L/bitmaps/%B
/usr/lib/X11/%l/bitmaps/%B
/usr/lib/X11/bitmaps/%B
/usr/include/X11/bitmaps/%B
```

A Motif vendor may override or change these default path locations.

13.7   Limits of Motif I18N Support

Motif 1.2 support for internationalization is limited to the I18N capabilities of the operating system and the X11R5 library on which it is built. If the operating system doesn't support a locale or the X library doesn't support a locale, then Motif cannot support that locale. Motif 1.2 does not support rendering of complex text languages nor does it fully support rendering of bidirectional languages. Motif compound strings allow you to specify some strings as drawn from left to right and others from right to left. However, you must specify which strings are drawn in which directions. And because Text and TextField widgets do not use compound strings, Motif 1.2 does not provide an edit widget for bidirectional text.

13.8   Example Internationalized Motif Program

The following program is i18n_motif.c, an example internationalized Motif application. Like the example X11R5 programs input_allstyles.c and overnoff_input.c introduced in previous chapters, this program prompts the user to enter his or her name. i18n_motif.c shows use of both message catalogs and resource files. The sources for the message catalog and app-defaults file follow the main application.

```
/*
 * This is a sample program that illustrates use of
 * internationalization with Motif 1.2.*.
 *
 * The program prompts the user to enter his or her name
 * by displaying a label above a TextField widget. A dialog
 * instructs the user on the programs use. Pressing the return
 * key causes the application to display a confirmation dialog
 * to the user. At that point the user can press the OK button
 * indicating that the value entered is acceptable, or press
 * the Cancel button (labeled "Oops" by default) to try again.
 *
 * The program sets its title by setting the XmNtitle resource.
 * This could have been done using resources in a resource file,
 * taking advantage of Motif's string-to-title resource
 * converter.  It is included here since this seems to be a
 * common source of problems for developers creating inter-
 * nationalized Motif applications.
 *
 * NOTE: For the localized title to be displayed correctly, all
 * the characters of the title must be present in the locale of
 * the window manager.  It is the window manager's job to display
 * the title that is passed by the application; the characters in
 * that title string must be fully convertible (by the window
 * manager) to the codeset of the window manager's locale.
 *
 * The program uses XPG4 (X/Open Portability Guide Version 4)
 * defined internationalization routines.
 */


/*
 * Message catalog messages can be grouped into sets of like or
 * similar messages.  Each set is identified by an integer set
 * number.  To make the message catalog access calls more
 * readible, create a macro for the message set number.
 */
```

```
#define VALUE_SET 1
#define LABEL_SET 2
#define ERR_SET 3

#include <stdio.h>
#include <limits.h>
#include <X11/Xlib.h>
#include <X11/StringDefs.h>
#include <X11/Xatom.h>
/* nl_types.h is needed for message catalog use. */
#include <nl_types.h>
#include <Xm/Xm.h>
#include <Xm/BulletinB.h>
#include <Xm/Form.h>
#include <Xm/Label.h>
#include <Xm/TextF.h>
#include <Xm/PushB.h>
#include <Xm/MainW.h>
#include <Xm/RowColumn.h>
#include <Xm/MenuShell.h>
#include <Xm/CascadeB.h>
#include <Xm/MessageB.h>

typedef struct {
   Widget textfield;
   Widget resultwidget;
} WidgetData, *WidgetDataPtr;

nl_catd   cat_fd;
char ok_msg[128], try_again_msg[128];

static XtCallbackProc ExitProg(w, client_data, call_data)
Widget w;
XtPointer client_data;
XtPointer call_data;
{
  exit(0);
}

static XtCallbackProc OopsCallback(w, client_data, call_data)
Widget w;
WidgetDataPtr client_data;
XtPointer call_data;
```

```
{
  Widget TextF1 = (Widget) client_data->textfield;

/* Select the current contents of the widget, so that when the
 * user sets focus in the widget the first keystroke causes
 * the current contents of the TextField to be deleted.
 */
  XmTextFieldSetSelection(TextF1, 0,
                     XmTextFieldGetLastPosition(TextF1),
                     XtLastTimestampProcessed(XtDisplay(TextF1)));
}

static XtCallbackProc ReadData(w, client_data, call_data)
Widget w;
WidgetDataPtr client_data;
XtPointer call_data;
{
  WidgetData widget_pair = *client_data;
  Widget TextF = (Widget) client_data->textfield;
  Widget ResultDialog = (Widget) client_data->resultwidget;
  XmString result_label;
  char tmp[NL_TEXTMAX];          /* Maximum size of a message,
                                  * defined in <limits.h>. */
  char result_fmt[256], result_msg[512];
  Arg args[20];
  int num_args;

/* This callback simply prints/displays the string value of
 * the widget. In a real application, the widget's value is
 * typically retrieved because the application wants to do
 * something with it. For example, the application might
 * parse the value, it might use the value as a key for a
 * sort operation, it might want to "normalize" the data by
 * converting it to all upper- or lowercase characters.
 * Regardless, internationalization does not stop with
 * Text[Field]'s properly generating local language characters.
 * The application must then use the appropriate C library
 * internationalization routines when processing the data.
 * Examples of these routines include strcoll(), mblen(),
 * mbtowc(), wcscspn(), wcspbrk(), and wcstok().
 */
```

```
    strcpy(result_fmt, catgets(cat_fd, VALUE_SET, 2,
                            "The name entered was %1$s.\n\n\
Press %2$s if this is acceptable.\n\n\
Otherwise, press %3$s to enter the name again."));

    sprintf(result_msg, result_fmt, XmTextFieldGetString(TextF),
            ok_msg, try_again_msg);
    result_label = XmStringCreateLocalized(result_msg);

    num_args = 0;
    XtSetArg(args[num_args], XmNmessageString,
            result_label);   num_args++;
    XtSetValues(ResultDialog, args, num_args);
    XtManageChild(ResultDialog);

    XmStringFree(result_label);
}


void main (argc, argv)
int argc;
char **argv;
{
  Arg args[20];
  int num_args;
  Display        *display;
  Widget Shell1, TextF1, ExitButton;
  Widget RowColumn1, MenuBar, MainWindow, CascadeWidget;
  Widget PullDown, PromptLabel, ResultDialog, MessageBox1;
  XtAppContext   app_context;
  XTextProperty prop;
  char * localized_title;
  XmString prompt, button_label, result;
  XmString exit_label, instructions;
  XmString ok_label, try_again_label, menu_label;
  WidgetData widget_pair;

  XtSetLanguageProc(NULL,NULL,NULL);

  /* Initializing the toolkit forces it to call the language
   * proc initialized by XtSetLanguageProc(). Any I18N routine
   * (such as catopen() that is called prior to the language
   * proc being called will not operate in the correct locale.
   */
```

```
XtToolkitInitialize();

/* Open the message catalog for this application.  Passing
 * the argument "i18n_motif" causes "i18n_motif" to be
 * substituted for the wildcard %N wherever it occurs in the
 * message catalog search path. NL_CAT_LOCALE is a standard
 * argument that tells catopen() to use the value of the
 * LC_MESSAGES category when substituting for %L in the
 * message catalog search path.
 */

cat_fd = catopen("i18n_motif", NL_CAT_LOCALE);

/* If no message catalog can be found, catopen() returns a
 * negative value. */

if (cat_fd < 0) {
   printf("No message catalog found! \
Continuing with default messages.\n");
 }

app_context = XtCreateApplicationContext();
display = XtOpenDisplay(app_context, NULL, argv[0],
                       "XMclient", NULL, 0, &argc, argv);

/* Error messages are placed in message catalogs. */
if (!display){
   printf(catgets(cat_fd, ERR_SET, 1,
               "Unable to open display!\n"));
   exit(0);
 }


/* create top level shell */
num_args = 0;
XtSetArg (args[num_args], XmNallowShellResize,
          True); num_args++;
Shell1 = XtAppCreateShell(argv[0], NULL,
                          applicationShellWidgetClass,
                          display, args, num_args);

/* Set the title for the application. */
```

```
  /* The title can most easily be set by setting a resource
   * in the application's app-default's file:
   *
   *     motif_i18n*title: <localized string data>
   *
   * However, some programs want tighter control and set
   * the title from the application.  There are (at least)
   * two different ways to do this: by passing the title
   * resource as a String (not  an XmString) or by passing the
   * title resource as CompoundText. The choice impacts what
   * you should do with the titleEncoding resource.
   *
   * When setting the title resource in the program by passing
   * a String, you should allow the titleEncoding to default.
   * Alternatively, the title should be passed as CompoundText,
   * with the titleEncoding resource set appropriately.
   *
   * The following example shows how to set the title both
   * ways. Regardless of which you choose, *NEVER* pass a
   * compound string (XmString) as the title.  This is probably
   * the most common cause of errors in setting the title.
   */

  localized_title = catgets(cat_fd, LABEL_SET, 1,
                            "Example I18N Motif App");
#ifdef USE_COMPOUND_TEXT
  XmbTextListToTextProperty(XtDisplay(Shell1), &localized_title,
                            1, XCompoundTextStyle, &prop);
  num_args = 0;
  XtSetArg(args[num_args], XmNtitle, prop.value); num_args++;
  XtSetArg(args[num_args], XmNtitleEncoding,
           prop.encoding); num_args++;
  XtSetValues(Shell1, args, num_args);

  /* Free the memory associated with the CompoundText value
   * now that it is no longer needed.
   */
  XFree((char*)prop.value);
#else /* Pass title as String. */
  num_args = 0;
  XtSetArg(args[num_args], XmNtitle,
           localized_title); num_args++;
  XtSetValues(Shell1, args, num_args);
#endif /* USE_COMPOUND_TEXT */
```

```
/* Create the menubar and pulldown menus for the exit
 * button. */
num_args = 0;
MainWindow = XmCreateMainWindow(Shell1, "MainWindow",
                                args, num_args);
XtManageChild(MainWindow);
num_args = 0;
MenuBar = XmCreateMenuBar(MainWindow, "MenuBar",
                          (ArgList)args, num_args);
XtManageChild(MenuBar);
num_args = 0;
PullDown = XmCreatePulldownMenu(MenuBar, "PullDown",
                                (ArgList)args, num_args);
/* Create the menu button's label. */
menu_label = XmStringCreateLocalized(catgets(cat_fd,
                             LABEL_SET, 2, "File"));
num_args = 0;
XtSetArg(args[num_args], XmNlabelString,
        menu_label);  num_args++;
XtSetArg(args[num_args], XmNsubMenuId,
        PullDown); num_args++;
CascadeWidget = XmCreateCascadeButton(MenuBar, "File",
                                      args, num_args);
XtManageChild(CascadeWidget);
XmStringFree(menu_label);


/* Create the exit button in the menu bar. Retrieve its
 * label from the message catalog. */
exit_label = XmStringCreateLocalized(catgets(cat_fd,
                             LABEL_SET, 3, "Exit"));
num_args = 0;
XtSetArg(args[num_args], XmNlabelString,
        exit_label);  num_args++;
ExitButton = XmCreatePushButton(PullDown, "ExitButton",
                                args, num_args);
XtManageChild(ExitButton);
XmStringFree(exit_label);


XtAddCallback(ExitButton, XmNactivateCallback,
              (XtCallbackProc) ExitProg, (XtPointer) NULL);
```

```
num_args = 0;
XtSetArg(args[num_args], XmNentryVerticalAlignment,
        XmALIGNMENT_BASELINE_BOTTOM); num_args++;
XtSetArg(args[num_args], XmNnumColumns, 2); num_args++;
XtSetArg(args[num_args], XmNorientation,
        XmHORIZONTAL); num_args++;
XtSetArg(args[num_args], XmNpacking,
        XmPACK_TIGHT); num_args++;
RowColumn1 = XmCreateRowColumn(MainWindow, "RowColumn1",
                                args, num_args);
XtManageChild(RowColumn1);

/* For widgets that need CompoundStrings (XmString), you
 * need to create these strings starting with localized
 * text. Use the function XmStringCreateLocalized() to create
 * the XmString.
 */
prompt = XmStringCreateLocalized(catgets(cat_fd,
                                LABEL_SET, 4, "Name: "));
XtSetArg(args[num_args], XmNlabelString,
        prompt); num_args++;
PromptLabel = XmCreateLabel(RowColumn1, "Prompt", args,
                            num_args);
XtManageChild(PromptLabel);
XmStringFree(prompt);

/* The widget's initial value can be set either in the
 * localized app-defaults file:
 *    *XmTextField.value: <initial_value>
 * Alternatively, the value can be read from a message catalog
 * and passed in programmatically.
 */

num_args = 0;
XtSetArg(args[num_args], XmNvalue,
        catgets(cat_fd, VALUE_SET, 1,
                "Your name")); num_args++;
TextF1 = XmCreateTextField(RowColumn1, "TextF1",
                            args, num_args);
XtManageChild (TextF1);

/* Create the message dialog that displays the results of
 * the data entered in the text field widget.
 *
```

```
 * If the user likes the value entered, they press the OK
 * button. If the user wants to enter the name again, they
 * press the Cancel button.
 *
 * The label for both buttons are read from a message
 * catalog and copied into global variables. This is done
 * because the labels are needed in the dialog displayed to
 * the user in the text fields activate callback, ReadData().
 */

strcpy(ok_msg, catgets(cat_fd, LABEL_SET, 5, "OK!"));
strcpy(try_again_msg, catgets(cat_fd, LABEL_SET, 6, "Oops!"));
ok_label = XmStringCreateLocalized(ok_msg);
try_again_label = XmStringCreateLocalized(try_again_msg);

num_args = 0;
XtSetArg(args[num_args], XmNokLabelString,
         ok_label);  num_args++;
XtSetArg(args[num_args], XmNcancelLabelString,
         try_again_label);  num_args++;
ResultDialog = XmCreateMessageDialog(MainWindow,
                          "ResultDialog", args, num_args);
XtAddCallback(ResultDialog, XmNokCallback,
              (XtCallbackProc)ExitProg, NULL);
widget_pair.textfield = TextF1;
XtAddCallback(ResultDialog, XmNcancelCallback,
              (XtCallbackProc) OopsCallback,
              (XtPointer) &widget_pair);
XmStringFree(ok_label);
XmStringFree(try_again_label);

/* Now that the ResultDialog is created, I can set the text
 * field's activate callback. (The ResultDialog ID was needed
 * for the  call_data passed to the callback.)
 */
widget_pair.textfield = TextF1;
widget_pair.resultwidget = ResultDialog;
XtAddCallback(TextF1, XmNactivateCallback,
         (XtCallbackProc) ReadData, (XtPointer) &widget_pair);

XmMainWindowSetAreas(MainWindow, MenuBar, NULL, NULL,
                      NULL, RowColumn1);

XtRealizeWidget(Shell1);
```

```
   XmTextFieldSetSelection(TextF1, 0,
                   XmTextFieldGetLastPosition(TextF1),
                   XtLastTimestampProcessed(XtDisplay(TextF1))));

   instructions = XmStringCreateLocalized(catgets(cat_fd,
                   LABEL_SET, 7, "Please enter your name.\n\n\
Then press <Return>."));

   num_args = 0;
   XtSetArg(args[num_args], XmNmessageString,
           instructions);  num_args++;
   MessageBox1 = XmCreateMessageDialog(MainWindow, "Instructions",
                                       args, num_args);
   XtManageChild(MessageBox1);


   XtAppMainLoop(app_context);
}
```

The following is the source for i18n_motif.c's message catalog. The comments illustrate how you can embed documentation directly in the message catalog source to aid the translator.

```
$ set 1 corresponds to #define VALUE_SET in the application
$ source code.
$set 1

$ Message 1 is the initial value of the text widget in the
$ dialog presented to the user. This value will be selected
$ (highlighted) when presented to the user.

1 Your name

$ Message 2 formats the message to be displayed in the results
$ dialog. It shows the user the value entered, offering a
$ chance to use the value entered, or try again. If the user
$ elects to try again, the current value entered by the user
$ will be selected (hence, highlighted), making for easy
$ replacement. The strings substituted for %s, the string format
$ specifier, are:
$
$    %1$s = name entered into the text widget.
$    %2$s = PushButton label from $set2, message 5 (indicating that
```

```
$          the entry should be accepted0.
$   %3$s = PushButton label from $set2, message 6 (indicating that
$          the entry is not correct — the user would like to try
$          again).
$
$ These strings are substituted using the XPG4 sprintf() routine.
$ This means that you can change the order of the strings by
$ changing "n" in the %n$ format.

2 The name entered was %s.\n\n\
Press %s if this is acceptable.\n\n\
Otherwise, press %s to enter the name again.

$ set 2 corresponds to #define LABEL_SET in the application
$ source code.
$set 2

$ Message 1 is the title displayed by the window manager in the
$ title bar.

1 Example I18N Motif App

$ Messages 2 and 3 are displayed in the pull-down menu. There is
$ currently no action tied to the "File" entry in the menu. When
$ the user selects the menu entry labeled with message 3, the
$ program exits.

2 File
3 Exit

$ Message 4 is the label displayed immediately to the left of the
$ TextField widget where the user will enter his/her name.

4 Name:

$ Message 5 is the label for the OK button in the dialog. The
$ user should press this button if the value entered into the
$ TextField widget is acceptable.

5 OK!

$ Message 6 is the label for the Cancel button in the dialog. The
$ user should press this button if the value entered into the
$ TextField widget needs to be modified.
```

```
6 Oops!
```

```
$ Message 7 is the prompt displayed in the instructional dialog
$ for the application.
```

```
7 Please enter your name.\n\nThen press <Return>.
```

```
$ set 3 corresponds to #define ERR_SET in the application source.
```

```
$set 3
```

```
$ Message 1 is displayed if the system is unable to open the
$ display. The program will exit immediately after this is
$ displayed. The user should check the value of the DISPLAY
$ environment variable or the -display command line argument and
$ try again.
```

```
1 Unable to open display!\n
```

In the sample app-defaults file, only the application's font list resource is specified. If this application were a real application to be used on systems with desktops (such as the CDE — the Common Desktop Environment), the font list resource would not be set in the resource file. Instead, the application would allow the desktop's font list resources to control the application's fonts.

```
! The application's resource file is normally used to specify many
! resources used by the application, such as color, labels, and
! font lists.  In this example, the labels have been set using
! message catalog calls. And we are leaving color choice to the
! desktop's resource controller, giving our application a common
! color scheme with other application's on the desktop.  This
! leaves only the font list resource to be specified and localized.
```

```
! Use an 18 point font set for all widget's in the application
! except the TextField. For TextField, use a 24 point font set.
! When localized, the translator should replace these base names
! with names appropriate for the fonts needed in their locale.
```

```
i18n_motif*fontList: *-medium-r-normal-*-18-*:
i18n_motif*XmTextField: *-medium-r-normal-*-24-*:
```

13.9 Summary

Creating internationalized software with Motif is simple, assuming you need only standard Motif widgets.

1. Use the internationalization routines for the non-graphical user interface parts of your software.
2. Call `XtSetLanguageProc(NULL, NULL, NULL)` immediately after the opening main brace of your software. Open the display and initialize the toolkit before performing any locale sensitive operations (for example, before opening a message catalog).
3. Call `XtAppMainLoop()` or `XtMainLoop()` to process events in your software. This ensures that input methods have the opportunity to filter events.
4. Make text, data formats, bitmaps, and localizable resources external to your software by placing them in message catalogs, resource files, and pixmap files. Use the internationalized routines (such `catopen()` and `XmGetPixmap()`) to load them at run time.
5. Use `Text` or `TextField` widgets to obtain characters from the keyboard. Make sure the `VendorShell` resources `XmNpreeditType` and `XmNinputMethod` are not hard coded into your software.
6. When creating compound strings, use the font tag XmFONTLIST_DEFAULT_TAG if you do not need a specific font tag. If you do need a font tag, be sure the font list entry that corresponds to that tag is a font set.
7. Always specify font sets in font list resources unless you specifically need access to a glyph that is not present in the code set of the user's locale. When specifying the font list via a resource, this means that you should make sure each font list entry ends with a colon (`:`). To make sure the font list can be localized, do not hard code font lists in your software.
8. When setting the `XmNtitle` or `XmNiconName` resources, do *not* pass `XmString` for the value and do *not* set the `XmNtitleEncoding` resource.
9. Make sure that either the `xnlLanguage` resource is set or that the `LANG` (or `LC_*`) environment variables are set before running the software.

Advanced Topics: I18N for the Motif Widget Writer

T he previous chapter described how to develop internationalized Motif applications using existing widgets. If you want to write your own internationalized Motif widgets, or want to use the `XmDrawingArea` to display and input localized character data, you need more in-depth knowledge than the previous chapter provided. This chapter describes

- how to programmatically create Motif font lists that contain font sets.
- how to extract a font set from a Motif font list so that you can render localized character data.
- how to use Motif's `XmIm*` functions to obtain local language characters from the keyboard.

Each of these topics is described in the sections that follow.

14.1 Creating Font Lists

To create a font list programmatically,

- Create a font list entry.
  - If you already have a font set or a font structure, use `XmFontListEntryCreate()`.
  - If you have not yet created a font set or opened a font structure, use `XmFontListEntryLoad()`.
- Create a new font list and append the font list entry to it by calling `XmFontListAppendEntry()`.
  - If you already have an existing font list, append the font list entry to it by calling `XmFontListAppendEntry()`.

- After appending your font list entry to the font list, free the font list entry by calling `XmFontListEntryFree()`.

Both `XmFontListEntryCreate()` and `XmFontListEntryLoad()` allow you to specify if the new entry in the font list is a font structure or a font set. This is specified with an `XmFontType` argument. If the argument is `XmFONT_IS_FONTSET`, the accompanying argument is assumed to specify a font set; if the argument is `XmFONT_IS_FONT`, the accompanying argument is assumed to specify a font structure.

The following code fragment is an example of creating a font list with multiple font sets:

```
...
typedef struct {
  XFontSet fontset;
  char *foo;
}AppData, *AppDataPtr;
static XtResource my_resources[] = {
  {XtNfontSet, XtCFontSet, XtRFontSet, sizeof(XFontSet),
   XtOffset(AppDataPtr, fontset), XtRString,
   XtDefaultFontSet}
}
...
XFontSet fontset;
AppData data;
XmFontListEntry fontlistEntry;
XmFontList fontlist;


...
XtSetLanguageProc(NULL, NULL, NULL);
toplevel = XtAppInitialize(...);

/* Use Xt's string-to-fontset resource converter to create
 * one font set. */
XtGetApplicationResources(toplevel, &data, my_resources,
                          XtNumber(my_resources), NULL, 0);
fontset = data.fontset;
fontlistEntry = XmFontListEntryCreate("ApplFontSet",
                          XmFONT_IS_FONTSET, fontset);
fontlist = XmFontListAppendEntry(NULL, fontListEntry);
XmFontListEntryFree(&fontlistEntry);

/* base_name contains a user supplied base name for a font
 * set, acquired from a dialog. */
```

```
fontlistEntry = XmFontListEntryLoad(XtDisplay(toplevel),
                            base_name, XmFONT_IS_FONTSET,
                            "UserFontSet");
fontlist = XmFontListAppendEntry(fontlist, fontListEntry);
XmFontListEntryFree(&fontlistEntry);
fontlistEntry = XmFontListEntryLoad(XtDisplay(toplevel),
                            "*-18-*", XmFONT_IS_FONTSET,
                            XmFONTLIST_DEFAULT_TAG);
fontlist = XmFontListAppendEntry(fontlist, fontListEntry);
XmFontListEntryFree(&fontlistEntry);
/* fontlist now contains three font sets, one with tag
 * "ApplFontSet" (created from application resources),
 * one with tag "UserFontSet" created from a user supplied
 * base font name, and one with the default tag
 * XmFONTLIST_DEFAULT_TAG. */
```

14.2   Extracting Font Sets from Font Lists

You may find it necessary to parse a font list to extract a font set from the font list. For example, if you are writing a new widget and that widget has a font list, you will need to parse the font list to find out what it contains — hopefully it contains a font set so that you can render local language text data for the user. The following code fragment illustrates how you extract font list entries from a font list, checking to see if the entry is a font set or a font struct.

```
...
XmFontContext context;
XmFontListEntry entry;
XmFontType font_type = XmFONT_IS_FONT;
XmFontList my_fontlist;
XmFontSet first_font_set = NULL;
XtPointer font;
char *tag = NULL;

...
/* Assume my_fontlist contains a valid font list. */
(void)XmFontListInitFontContext(&context, my_fontlist);

for (entry = XmFontListNextEntry(context);
     entry != NULL;
     entry = XmFontListNextEntry(context)){
  font = XmFontListEntryGetFont(entry, &font_type);
  if (type == XmFONT_IS_FONTSET){
    first_font_set = (XmFontSet) font;
```

```
        tag = XmFontListEntryGetTag(entry);
        break;
    }
}
XmFontListFreeFontContext(context);
...
```

14.3   Obtaining Local Language Characters from the Keyboard

Occasionally, you may need to obtain local language characters from the keyboard without using a `Text` or a `TextField` widget. For example, you need this capability if you are writing a new text editor widget or a terminal emulator widget. Even if you are not writing a new widget, this capability may be useful. For example, if you are using a `DrawingArea` widget to allow a user to draw a diagram, you probably want to allow the user to label the parts on the diagram and enter a name for the diagram.

Beginning with Motif 1.2, you can obtain local language characters from the keyboard without the hassles involved in using the low level X11R5 calls to open and manage input methods and input contexts. The collection of routines referred to as the `XmIm*` routines are supplied with Motif 1.2. Motif's `Text` and `TextField` widgets use these routines internally to manage keyboard input.

When releasing Motif 1.2, OSF was not certain that the `XmIm*` routines provided the correct set of keyboard input functionality. Therefore, it did not document these routines in the public documentation. (However, the function definitions are included in the public header file `Xm.h` with Motif 1.2.) Most of the `XmIm*` functions were made public and documented with the next major release of Motif.

This section documents the `XmIm*` routines that are distributed in and available for use with Motif 1.2 and that are also public, documented functions in later releases of Motif. This gives you the ability to use these functions in your Motif 1.2-based software with the confidence that the software can compile and work properly with future releases of Motif.

14.3.1   Overview: XmIm* Routines

The `XmIm*` routines provide a high-level interface to obtain coded characters from the keyboard. The routines eliminate the need for details of using the low-level X11R5 input method routines. For example, with `XmIm*` your software does not need to open the input method, negotiate for a common input style, or create the input context. And as long as the widget calling `XmIm*` has a Motif `VendorShell` in its widget hierarchy, the `VendorShell` takes care of geometry management for off-the-spot feedback styles.

The `XmIm*` routines support all preedit and status styles supported by X11R5 except "on-the-spot" style. If your software needs on-the-spot preedit or status style, you will have to use the X11R5 X library calls directly.

To obtain keyboard input using XmIm*, your software performs the following steps.

1. Initialize the locale by calling XtSetLanguageProc(NULL, NULL, NULL), and then initialize the display and the toolkit.

2. Establish a connection between your software and an input method by calling XmImRegister().

3. Pass a small list of values of interest to the input method (such as font list, location of the input cursor, foreground color and background color) by calling either XmImSetValues() or XmImVaSetValues().

4. Notify the input method when your software gains focus by calling XmImSetFocusValues() or XmImVaSetFocusValues(); you may pass additional or changed input method values at the same time.

5. Notify the input method any time a value of interest to the input method changes. For example, if your software changed the font list it uses or the location of the input cursor, it would notify the input method of this change with XmImSetValues() or XmImVaSetValues().

6. When your software loses focus, notify the input method by calling XmImUnsetFocus().

7. In your software's event loop, call XmImMbLookupString() to convert key events into characters encoded in the code set of the current locale.

8. When your software no longer needs to talk to an input method, call XmImUnregister() to break the connection.

The syntax for each of these routines is provided in the following pages. Appendix D contains a complete example program showing how to use the XmIm* routines to obtain keyboard input in a DrawingArea widget.

14.3.2 Connecting to the Input Method: XmImRegister()

The XmImRegister() routine establishes a connection between the input method and the widget where keyboard input will occur. Only one input method is opened per locale. If multiple widgets call XmImRegister(), they all use the same input method connection; each widget may get its own input context or they may share an input context, depending on the implementation. If VendorShell is not yet managing an input method connection, it opens an input method. The input method opened is determined by the VendorShell resource XmNinputMethod. If XmNinputMethod is not set, the input method opened depends on the value of the XMODIFIERS environment variable and the default input method for the current locale.

The syntax of this routine is

```
#include <Xm/XmIm.h>
void XmImRegister(w, reserved)
```

```
Widget w;
unsigned int reserved;
```

w   specifies the widget interested in processing keyboard input.

reserved   reserved for future use. This argument is ignored.

The Text, TextField, and List widgets already call this function when they are created. You should not pass a Text, TextField, or List widget to this function.

14.3.3 Sending Values to the Input Method: XmIm[Va]SetValues()

Once your software has a connection to the input method, it needs to pass input context attributes to the input method; these are needed for the input method to function properly. Your software can use either XmImSetValues() or XmImVaSetValues() to do this. The routines are identical except that XmImVaSetValues() uses a variable length argument list.

The syntax for each of these routines is as follows:

```
#include <Xm/XmIm.h>
void XmImSetValues(w, arglist, num_args)
   Widget w;
   ArgList arglist;
   Cardinal num_args;
```

w   specifies the widget interested in processing keyboard input.

arglist   list of input context attribute values to be passed to the input method.

num_args   number of values provided in arglist.

```
   void XmImVaSetValues(w, ...)
      Widget w;
```

w   specifies the widget interested in processing keyboard input.

...   specifies that a null terminates list of arguments follows.

Table 14.1 shows which attributes you should set with XmIm[Va]SetValues(). It also shows what arguments you must pass for each attribute.

Table 14.1 Description of Input Method Attributes Used with XmIm[Va]SetValues

Attribute name	Data type	Description
XmNfontList	XmFontList	specifies the font list the widget uses to render data.
XmNbackground	Pixel	specifies the background color (pixel) of the widget.
XmNbackgroundPixmap	Pixmap	specifies the background pixmap of the widget.

Table 14.1 Description of Input Method Attributes Used with XmIm[Va]SetValues (Continued)

Attribute name	Data type	Description
XmNforeground	Pixel	specifies the foreground color (pixmap) of the widget.
XmNspotLocation	XPoint*	specifies the *x,y* location of where the next character input will be drawn. This is the cursor location.
XmNlineSpace	int	specifies the number of pixels between the baselines of consecutive lines of text in the widget.

When setting the XmNfontList attribute, XmIm[Va]SetValues() passes the first font set in the font list that has the tag XmFONTLIST_DEFAULT_TAG to the input method. If no font set has that tag, then it passes the first font set in the font list to the input method. If the font list does not contain a font set, the behavior is input method implementation defined.

14.3.4 Gaining Focus: XmIm[Va]SetFocusValues()

When your software's window that is using XmIm* gains focus, you must notify the input method so it can update its status information and correctly filter events. The XmIm* routines combine focus notification with the ability to send new or changed attributes to the input method into a single call. To do this, use either XmImSetFocusValues() or XmImVaSetFocusValues(). If you only need to notify the input method that the window has gained focus, call the routine without passing any attribute to the input method.

The syntax for these routines is

```
#include <Xm/XmIm.h>
void XmImSetFocusValues(w, arglist, num_args)
   Widget w;
   ArgList arglist;
   Cardinal num_args;
```

w   specifies the widget interested in processing keyboard input.

arglist   list of input context attribute values to be passed to the input method. Valid arguments are the same as those used with XmIm[Va]SetValues().

num_args   number of values provided in *arglist*.

```
   void XmImVaSetValues(w, ...)
      Widget w;
```

w   specifies the widget interested in processing keyboard input.

. . .   specifies that a null terminates list of arguments follows. Valid arguments are the same as those used with XmIm[Va]SetValues().

14.3.5 Losing Focus: XmImUnsetFocus()

When your software's window that is using XmIm* loses focus, you must notify the input method so it can update its status information. To do this, call XmImUnsetFocus(). The syntax for the routine is

```
void XmImUnsetFocus(w)
    Widget w;
```

w   identifies the widget that has lost focus.

14.3.6 Handling Key Events: XmImMbLookupString()

When processing events in your software's event loop, call XmImMbLookupString() when your software receives a KeyPress event. XmImMbLookupString() copies the characters generated by the input method into a buffer you supply. It operates identically to XmbLookupString(). The syntax for XmImMbLookupString() is

```
int XmImMbLookupString(w, event, buffer, bytes_buffer,
                            keysym, status);
    Widget w;
    XKeyPressedEvent *event;
    char *buffer;
    int bytes_buffer;
    KeySym *keysym;
    Status *status;
```

w   specifies the widget where input occurred.

event   specifies the key event being processed. If an event other than a KeyPress event is passed in, the results of this function are undefined.

buffer   pointer to your buffer where the character(s) composed by the input method are returned.

bytes_buffer   size (in bytes) of the buffer your software supplies.

keysym   pointer to the location where the keysym associated with the event is returned.

status   indicates the kind of data is returned by the routine.

XmImMbLookupString() returns the number of bytes copied into *buffer*.

Be sure to examine *status* before using any of the values returned by this routine. *status* indicates if an error has occurred and which of the return parameters contains valid data. The possible values for *status* are described in Table 14.2..

Table 14.2 Status Values for XmImMbLookupString()

Status	Description
XBufferOverflow	The input string was too large to copy into the supplied buffer. The routine returns the required size of the buffer (in bytes); the contents of the supplied buffer and *keysym* are not modified. Your software should call this function again with the same event once you can provide a buffer of sufficient size.
XLookupNone	No input composed yet. The buffer and *keysym* returned are not modified; the function returns zero.
XLookupChars	Characters have been composed and were copied into the supplied buffer. The content of *keysym* is not modified.
XLookupKeySym	No characters have been composed. However, a keysym for the event is returned in *keysym*. The routine returns zero.
XLookupBoth	A string of one or more characters was generated by the input method and copied into the supplied buffer. And a keysym for the keycode in the event was copied into keysym; the keysym returned does not necessarily correspond to the string returned in the buffer.

14.3.7   Breaking Connection with the Input Method: XmImUnregister()

When your software no longer needs to process key events into coded characters, break the connection to the input method by calling XmImUnregister(). The syntax for this routine is

```
void XmImUnsetFocus(w)
   Widget w;
```

w   specifies the previously registered widget for which connection to the input method should be discontinued.

I18N and the Common Desktop Environment (CDE 1.0)

C DE 1.0 is built using the I18N concepts described throughout this book. The various CDE components use the C library I18N routines described in Chapters 2 and 3 to parse and manipulate text data. They are built with CDE Motif, which is based on Motif 1.2.5; all CDE Motif components are internationalized to the same extent as OSF Motif 1.2.5. Where Motif `Text` and `TextField` widgets could not be used for keyboard input (for example, in the terminal emulator widget), either the X11R5 XIM routines are used or the `XmIm*` routines are used. So why does this book include a chapter on CDE? The answer is that as a software developer, you may want to integrate your internationalized software with the Common Desktop Environment. And CDE 1.0 has a few features that you will want to be aware of and take advantage of to make your software integrate more smoothly. These features are

- a font alias mechanism that allows the fonts of all CDE software to be controlled by a simple, user accessible client — `dtstyle`. You need to understand how CDE font resources are set and evaluated in order to correctly localize the font resources for your software.
- a mechanism for setting the `LANG` environment variable and exporting to all clients run under CDE.
- a mechanism for automatically starting an input method when a user logs in and setting and exporting `XMODIFIERS` such that all internationalized clients started (including those started by the session manager) connect to that input method.
- local language customized menus. To integrate your software into CDE's default menus, you need to know where they are defined and how they are localized.

This chapter does not attempt to teach you about using CDE or general programming design for CDE; if you are reading this chapter, you are probably already familiar with these topics. If not, there are many books on these subjects available. Instead, this chapter discusses only those items necessary for you to integrate your internationalized software into the Common Desktop Environment. Additionally, this chapter describes how CDE's international behavior can impact your software's behavior.

15.1   Setting Font Resources with CDE

The CDE style manager (`dtstyle`) allows a user to control which styles of fonts are used by CDE conforming software. `Dtstyle` presents the user with a choice of seven different sizes of fonts. When the user makes a selection, `dtstyle` sets a collection of resources into the window manager's RESOURCE_MANAGER property; if you want your software's fonts to be controllable with `dtstyle`, you must avoid setting these resources either programmatically or in an application specific resource file.

When setting `SystemFont`, the style manager sets each of the following resources to the user specified value:

```
*fontList:
*systemFont:
```

The `SystemFont` is used for system areas, such as menu bars, push buttons, and labels. When setting `UserFont`, the style manager sets each of the following resources to the user specified value:

```
*Font:
*FontList:
*FontSet:
*XmText*FontList:
*XmTextField*FontList:
*DtEditor*textFontList:
*userFont:
```

In each case, the resources are set to a generic XLFD. For font structure resources, the ":" is stripped from the end to ensure that the resource converter produces a font structure. The generic XLFDs for `SystemFont` and `UserFont` are specified in `/usr/dt/app-defaults/`*locale*`/Dtstyle`, where *locale* is the locale of the display, as set by `XtSetLanguageProc()`. Up to seven different sizes can be specified. By default, the `SystemFont` values are

```
-dt-interface system-medium-r-normal-xxs*-*-*-*-*-*-*-*-*:
-dt-interface system-medium-r-normal-xs*-*-*-*-*-*-*-*-*:
-dt-interface system-medium-r-normal-s*-*-*-*-*-*-*-*-*:
-dt-interface system-medium-r-normal-m*-*-*-*-*-*-*-*-*:
-dt-interface system-medium-r-normal-l*-*-*-*-*-*-*-*-*:
-dt-interface system-medium-r-normal-xl*-*-*-*-*-*-*-*-*:
-dt-interface system-medium-r-normal-xxl*-*-*-*-*-*-*-*-*:
```

Similarly, the `UserFont` values are

```
-dt-interface user-medium-r-normal-xxs*-*-*-*-*-*-*-*-*:
-dt-interface user-medium-r-normal-xs*-*-*-*-*-*-*-*-*:
-dt-interface user-medium-r-normal-s*-*-*-*-*-*-*-*-*:
-dt-interface user-medium-r-normal-m*-*-*-*-*-*-*-*-*:
-dt-interface user-medium-r-normal-l*-*-*-*-*-*-*-*-*:
-dt-interface user-medium-r-normal-xl*-*-*-*-*-*-*-*-*:
-dt-interface user-medium-r-normal-xxl*-*-*-*-*-*-*-*-*:
```

These font list XLFD values are commonly referred to as *Tee Shirt Size aliases*. This is because each value is identical to a clothing style size indicator commonly used for tee shirts. For example, `xs` specifies "extra small," `m` specifies "medium," `l` specifies "large," and `xl` specifies "extra large." Each font directory containing fonts used by CDE should contain aliases mapping the Tee Shirt Size aliases to real fonts.

When you combine the CDE Tee Shirt Size aliases with the X library's font set mechanism, it is sometimes hard to figure out exactly which fonts are (or should be) loaded for your software. Consider an example where a Japanese user (example locale name: `ja_JP.eucJP`) selects the following `UserFont`:

```
-dt-interface user-medium-r-normal-m*-*-*-*-*-*-*-*-*:
```

Also suppose that your software uses a `TextField` widget, whose font list is controlled by the `UserFont` resource `*XmTextField*FontList`. What font or font set does your software's `TextField` widget use?

Since the resource ends in ":", Motif's string to font list resource convert calls `XCreateFontSet()` with the string:

```
-dt-interface user-medium-r-normal-m*-*-*-*-*-*-*-*-*
```

`XCreateFontSet()` asks the X server for a list of all fonts that match this alias. It also looks at the X library's locale data base for data for the `ja_JP.eucJP` locale. In that database, it finds that to create a font set for the specified locale, it must have at least three fonts. The `CHARSET_REGISTRY-CHARSET_ENCODING` fields (on this example system) for these fonts must be

```
JISX0201.1976-0
JISX0208.1990-0
JISX0212.1990-0
```

`XCreateFontSet()` searches the list of fonts given to it by the X server for fonts with `CHARSET_REGISTRY-CHARSET_ENCODING` fields that match. Then, the first match for each `CHARSET_REGISTRY-CHARSET_ENCODING` is used in the font set.

Assume that the supplier of the Japanese fonts for the system included Tee Shirt Size aliases in the `fonts.alias` file in the directory containing Japanese fonts. For example, the `fonts.alias` file in the Japanese fonts directory probably contains entries like the following:

```
...
"-dt-interface   user-medium-r-normal-m   gothic-16-116-100-100-m-80-
jisx0201.1976-0"\
"-hp-gothic-medium-r-normal--16-116-100-100-c-80-jisx0201.1976-0"

"-dt-interface   user-medium-r-normal-m   gothic-16-116-100-100-m-160-
jisx0208.1990-0"\
"-hp-gothic-medium-r-normal--16-116-100-100-c-160-jisx0208.1990-0"

"-dt-interface   user-medium-r-normal-m   gothic-16-116-100-100-m-160-
jisx0212.1990-0"\
"-hp-gothic-medium-r-normal--16-116-100-100-c-160-jisx0212.1990-0"
...
```

In this case, the Tee Shirt Size alias

```
-dt-interface user-medium-r-normal-m*-*-*-*-*-*-*-*-*
```

combined with the three required CHARSET_REGISTRY-CHARSET_ENCODING XLFD fields cause the following fonts to be used for the font set:

```
-hp-gothic-medium-r-normal--16-116-100-100-c-80-jisx0201.1976-0
-hp-gothic-medium-r-normal--16-116-100-100-c-160-jisx0208.1990-0
-hp-gothic-medium-r-normal--16-116-100-100-c-160-jisx0212.1990-0
```

What if the supplier of the Japanese fonts does not provide these Tee Shirt Size aliases? Each system vendor that ships CDE provides a set of backup aliases that are used if no other aliases are provided. These backup aliases are located in

```
/usr/dt/config/xfonts/locale/
```

In this directory you will find both a `fonts.alias` file and an empty `fonts.dir` file. At login, the CDE login client (`dtlogin`) automatically appends to the end of the X server's font search path `/usr/dt/config/xfonts/locale/` and `/usr/dt/config/xfonts/C/`. In the `fonts.alias` file, the system vendor defines Tee Shirt Size aliases for the fonts most commonly used on that system for that locale.

15.2   Controlling Locale and Input Method Selection with CDE

Your software's user has four different mechanisms to select the preferred locale:

• The user may select the locale from the Options menu in the login screen.

- The locale may be set as a resource in the Xconfig file. The system default Xconfig file is located at /usr/dt/config/Xconfig. If it is modified, it is copied to /etc/dt/config/Xconfig, where the value of LANG can be set for all users.
- The system administrator can create a a shell script in /usr/dt/config/Xsession.d/ where the value of LANG can be set.
- Users can set their preferred value of LANG in their $HOME/.dtprofile file.

Regardless of how it is set, it is exported and used by all clients managed by CDE. The user specified locale controls the following CDE resources and values:

```
/usr/dt/palettes/desc.locale
/usr/dt/backdrops/desc.locale
/usr/dt/config/locale/Xresources
/usr/dt/config/locale/sys.font
/usr/dt/config/locale/sys.resources
/usr/dt/config/locale/sys.session
/usr/dt/config/locale/sys.dtwmrc
/usr/dt/appconfig/types/locale/dtwm.fp
```

It also controls the replacement of the %L wild card in CDE search path environment variables, such as NLSPATH, XFILESEARCHPATH, DTAPPSEARCHPATH, and DTDATABASESEARCHPATH.

15.2.1   Controlling the choice of input method

When a user logs in to CDE, the CDE session manager executes a series of shell scripts located in /usr/dt/config/Xsession.d/. One of the default shell scripts shipped with CDE is the 0020.dtims shell script. This shell script is a vendor dependent shell script that examines the currently selected locale and, if appropriate,

- either starts an input method or offers the user a choice among several input methods appropriate for the selected locale.
- sets the XMODIFIERS environment variable so that clients started by the session manager connect to the input method.

15.3   Integrating Your Software with the CDE Workspace Menu

When integrating your software with CDE, you may decide that you want the software selectable from the CDE's workspace menu. In this case, you need to know where the menus are defined and where the local language menus are defined.

A user's workspace menu is controlled by the following files. When the workspace manager searches for its configuration files, it uses the first of the following files that it finds:

```
$HOME/.dt/dtwmrc
/etc/dt/config/locale/sys.dtwmrc
/usr/dt/config/locale/sys.dtwmrc
```

To integrate your software with the workspace manager, modify either the $HOME/.dt.dtwmrc file or /etc/dt/config/*locale*/sys.dtwmrc, depending on whether you want your change to affect only one user or all users of locale *locale* on the system. When parsing these files, the workspace manager assumes that text for the button names are encoded in the code set of the current locale.

15.4   Integrating Your Software with the Application Manager

The application manager is a container for applications available to the user. The applications offered by the application manager are gathered from the following locations:

```
/usr/dt/appconfig/appmanager/locale/
/etc/dt/appconfig/appmanager/locale/
$HOME/.dt/appmanager
```

You can add your software to the application manager by registering the software or by adding an icon to the application manager without registering the software. The CDE documentation covers both procedures well. The reason it is mentioned here is to point out that you can control which software is available via the application manager to users of a given *locale*. Your localizers may tell you that for locale X the user would find it very useful to have your software as its own application group, while the localizers for locale Y say that their users would prefer to have the software available in a different work group.

Quick Reference: C Library Internationalization Routines

T he following tables give you a summary of the different C library I18N routines you may need when developing your internationalized software. It also identifies which tool is defined by which standard. All tools available in ISO C are also available in ANSI C.

A.1 Tools for Converting between Multibyte and Wide Character

Table A.1 identifies the tools you can use to convert between multibyte and wide character.

Table A.1 Routines for Converting between Multibyte and Wide Character

Routine	XPG4	ISO C	ISO C + MSE
btowc(c)	no	no	yes
fgetwc(stream)	yes	no	yes
fgetws(ws, n, stream)	yes	no	yes
fprintf(stream, fmt, ...)	yes[†]	no	yes[†]
fputwc(wc, stream)	yes	no	yes
fputws(ws, stream)	yes	no	yes
fscanf(stream, fmt, ...)	yes[†]	no	yes[†]
fwprintf(stream, wfmt, ...)	no	no	yes
fwscanf(stream, wfmt, ...)	no	no	yes
getwc(stream)	yes	no	yes
getwchar()	yes	no	yes

Table A.1 Routines for Converting between Multibyte and Wide Character (Continued)

Routine	XPG4	ISO C	ISO C + MSE
mbrtowc(*ws, s, ps*)	no	no	yes
mbsrtowcs(*ws, s, n, ps*)	no	no	yes
mbstowcs(*ws, s, n*)	yes	yes	yes
mbtowc(*ws, s*)	yes	yes	yes
printf(*fmt, ...*)	yes[†]	no	yes[†]
putwc(*wc, stream*)	yes	no	yes
putwchar(*wc*)	yes	no	yes
scanf(*fmt, ...*)	yes[†]	no	yes[†]
sprintf(*s, fmt, ...*)	yes[†]	no	yes[†]
sscanf(*s, fmt, ...*)	yes[†]	no	yes[†]
swprintf(*ws, n, wfmt, ...*)	no	no	yes
swscanf(*ws, wfmt, ...*)	no	no	yes
ungetwc(*wc, stream*)	yes	no	yes
vfprintf(*stream, fmt, varg_list*)	yes[†]	no	yes[†]
vfwprintf(*stream, wfmt, varg_list*)	no	no	yes
vprintf(*fmt, varg_list*)	yes[†]	no	yes[†]
vsprintf(*s, fmt, varg_list*)	yes[†]	no	yes[†]
vswprintf(*s, n, wfmt, varg_list*)	no	no	yes
vwprintf(*wfmt, varg_list*)	no	no	yes
wcrtomb(*s, wc, ps*)	no	no	yes
wcsrtombs(*s, ws, n, ps*)	no	no	yes
wcstombs(*s, ws, n*)	yes	yes	yes
wctob(*c*)	no	no	yes
wctomb(*s, wc*)	yes	yes	yes
wprintf(*wfmt, ...*)	no	no	yes
wscanf(*wfmt, ...*)	no	no	yes

†. XPG4 and the MSE both use this routine to convert between multibyte and wide character. However, they use a different format string for doing so.

A.2 Tools for Parsing and Scanning

The tools listed in Table A.2 aid in parsing and scanning operations. Some help by identifying the size of a multibyte character. Others actually locate characters or substrings within a string.

Table A.2 Routines That Aid in Parsing and Scanning

Routine	XPG4	ISO C	ISO C + MSE
MB_CUR_MAX	yes	yes	yes
MB_MAX_LEN	yes	yes	yes
mblen(*s*, *n*)	yes	yes	yes
mbrlen(*s*, *n*, *ps*)	no	no	yes
mbrtowc(*w*, *s*, *n*, *ps*)	no	no	yes
mbsrtowcs(*w*, *s*, *n*, *ps*)	yes	yes	yes
mbstowcs(*w*, *s*, *n*)	no	no	yes
mbtowc(*w*, *s*, *n*)	yes	yes	yes
wcschr(*wcs*, *wc*)	no	no	yes
wcscspn(*wcs1*, *wcs2*)	no	no	yes
wcspbrk(*wcs1*, *wcs2*)	no	no	yes
wcsrchr(*wcs*, *wc*)	no	no	yes
wcsspn(*wcs1*, *wcs2*)	no	no	yes
wcsstr(*wcs1*, *wcs2*)	no	no	yes
wcstok(*wcs1*, *wcs2*, *ptr*)	no	no	yes
wmemchr(*wcs*, *wc*, *n*)	no	no	yes

A.3 Tools for Character Classification

Table A.3 identifies the C library routines that help you identify or classify an individual character.

Table A.3 Character Classification Routines

Routine	XPG4	ISO C	ISO C + MSE
iswalnum(*wc*)	yes	no	yes
iswalpha(*wc*)	yes	no	yes
iswcntrl(*wc*)	yes	no	yes

Table A.3 Character Classification Routines (Continued)

Routine	XPG4	ISO C	ISO C + MSE
iswctype(*wc, cl*)	yes	no	yes
iswdigit(*wc*)	yes	no	yes
iswgraph(*wc*)	yes	no	yes
iswlower(*wc*)	yes	no	yes
iswprint(*wc*)	yes	no	yes
iswpunct(*wc*)	yes	no	yes
iswspace(*wc*)	yes	no	yes
iswupper(*wc*)	yes	no	yes
iswxdigit(*wc*)	yes	no	yes
wctype(*ch_class*)	yes	no	yes

A.4 Tools for Case Conversion

Table A.4 identifies the routines you can use to convert characters between uppercase representation and lowercase representation. If the concept of case does not apply (for example, the percent sign % is neither uppercase nor lowercase), the character is unaffected by the routine.

Table A.4 Case Conversion Routines

Routine	XPG4	ISO C	ISO C + MSE
towlower(*wc*)	yes	no	yes
towupper(*wc*)	yes	no	yes

A.5 Tools for Sorting

Table A.5 identifies the routines you can use to order two strings according to rules and customs of the user's locale. When comparing only for string equality, you can avoid any performance overhead of these routines and simply call strcmp(). The routine strncmp() should be avoided unless you can guarantee that you are comparing complete characters.

Table A.5 Routines for Sorting Strings

Routine	XPG4	ISO C	ISO C + MSE
strcoll(*s1*, *s2*)	yes	yes	yes
strxfrm(*s1*, *s2*, *n*)	yes	yes	yes
wcscoll(*ws1*, *ws2*)	yes	no	yes
wcsxfrm(*ws1*, *ws2*, *n*)	yes	no	yes

A.6 Tools for Converting between Code Sets

Table A.6 identifies the standard tools you can use to convert data from one code set to another.

Table A.6 Code Set Conversion Routines

Routine	XPG4	ISO C	ISO C + MSE
iconv_open(*to*, *from*)	yes	no	no
iconv_close(*cd*)	yes	no	no
iconv(*cd*, *in*, *m*, *out*, *n*)	yes	no	no
iconv -f *from* -t *to* [*file*...]	yes	no	no

X11R5: XIC Values, Preedit Attributes, and Status Attributes

XIC values are used to pass information between your software and the input method. Some XIC values are relevant only for certain preedit or status styles. Some values must be set when creating the XIC; some values default if not set when creating the XIC. This appendix describes each XIC value and its associated data type. It also describes how and when the value should be used when communicating with the input method.

B.1 XIC Data Values

XIC data values are values used to pass information between your software and the input method. Table B.1 describes each XIC data value defined by X11R5

Table B.1 XIC Data Values: Description

XIC Value	Data Type	Description
XNClientWindow	Window	Identifies the window in which the input method can display its preedit/status data. The input method may create subwindows for this purpose.
XNFocusWindow	Window	Identifies the window that will receive key events. The input method may send events to this window, modify its properties, grab the keyboard when focus is in the focus window, and select for events on the focus window. If not specified, the default is the XNClientWindow.

Table B.1 XIC Data Values: Description (Continued)

XIC Value	Data Type	Description
XNResourceName XNResourceClass	char*	These are the names used by your software when obtaining resources for the client window. They should be used when looking up resources that may vary depending on the XIC. XIC values should not be set as resources.
XNGeometryCallback	XIMCallback	Callback provided by you that allows the input method to initiate or negotiate a change in geometry. You need set this value only if you want to allow the input method to dynamically change its input method window.
XNFilterEvents	unsigned long	When querying for this value, the input method returns an event mask indicating which events on the client window it needs to receive. Your software should select for events identified by event mask as well as any events your software is interested in. The input method then examines these events when your software calls XFilterEvent().
XNPreeditAttributes XNStatusAttributes	variable length list	Communicates a variable length list of preedit attributes and status attributes between the input method and your software.

With the exception of XNPreeditAttributes and XNStatusAttributes, the XIC data values apply equally to the preedit style and the status style. They identify information that is needed for displaying both preedit and status information. Table B.2 shows how the XIC data values affect the different preedit and status styles.

Table B.2 XIC Data Values

	XIC Data Values				
Style	Client Window	Focus Window[†]	Resource Name/Class	Geometry Callback	Filter Events
XIMPreeditNone	Ignored	Ignored	Ignored	Ignored	Ignored
XIMPreeditNothing	Ignored	D-R-S	D-R-S	Ignored	R
XIMPreeditArea	O-R	D-R-S	D-R-S	D-R-S	R
XIMPreeditPosition	O-R	D-R-S	D-R-S	Ignored	R
XIMPreeditCallbacks	O-R	D-R-S	Ignored	Ignored	R
XIMStatusNone	Ignored	Ignored	Ignored	Ignored	R

Table B.2 XIC Data Values (Continued)

Style	XIC Data Values				
	Client Window	Focus Window†	Resource Name/Class	Geometry Callback	Filter Events
XIMStatusNothing	O-R	D-R-S	D-R-S	Ignored	R
XIMStatusArea	O-R	D-R-S	D-R-S	D-R-S	R
XIMStatusCallbacks	O-R	D-R-S	Ignored	Ignored	R

†. Setting this value may force geometry negotiations with the input method.

Key	Description
C	Value must be specified when creating the XIC.
D	If not set when creating the XIC, a default value is provided.
O	Value must be set only once. It need not be set when creating the XIC.
R	Value may be retrieved or read with XGetICValues().
S	Value may be set by calling XSetICValues().
Ignored	Value is not used by the input method for the specified style; if set, it is ignored.

B.1.1   Preedit and Status Attributes

XNPreeditAttributes is an XIC data value used to pass preedit *attributes* to the input method; preedit attributes are collections of data needed to display preedit feedback information to the user. Similarly, XNStatusAttributes is an XIC data value used to pass status *attributes* to the input method; status attributes are collections of data needed to display status feedback information. X11R5 defines 14 preedit attributes and 12 status attributes. Not all attributes are relevant for every preedit style and status style. You will use XNPreeditAttributes and XNStatusAttributes to pass attributes needed for your chosen preedit and status style. Table B.3 and Table B.4 describe each preedit attribute and each status attribute. Table B.5 and Table B.6 show for each style which attributes must be set when creating the XIC, which can be queried, which can be set after creating the XIC and which attributes are ignored.

Table B.3 Preedit Attributes Description

Attribute name	Data type	Description
XNArea	XRectangle*	For `XIMPreeditArea` style, this specifies the geometry of the area your software provides for the IM's use; the IM must abide by this geometry. For `XIMPreeditPosition` style, this is the clipping region for displaying preedit feedback information.
XNAreaNeeded	XRectangle*	Specifies a value used in geometry negotiations when using `XIMPreeditArea` style. When setting this value, your software tells the IM the geometry you are willing to allocate for its use. When queried for this attribute, the IM identifies the area it wants. Only the width and height values of the `XRectangle` are significant; the *x* and *y* values are ignored.
XNSpotLocation	XPoint*	Specifies the location for placement of the preedit feedback information when using `XIMPreeditPosition` style. The *x* value specifies the location of the next character to be inserted; the *y* value specifies the baseline of the line to contain the inserted character. The points are relative to the focus window if set; otherwise they are relative to the client window.
XNColormap	Colormap	Specifies the colormap ID from which the IM should allocate colors. If unspecified, the client window's colormap is used as the default colormap. If both `XNColormap` and `XNStdColormap` are specified, the results are undefined.
XNStdColormap	Atom	Specifies the name of the standard colormap from which the IM should allocate colors. The argument should be retrieved by calling `XGetRGBColormaps()`. If unspecified, the client window's colormap is used as the default colormap. If both `XNColormap` and `XNStdColormap` are specified, the results are undefined.
XNBackground	unsigned long	Specifies the background pixel for the preedit feedback information. If unspecified, the default is determined by the IM.
XNForeground	unsigned long	Specifies the foreground pixel for the preedit feedback information. If unspecified, the default is determined by the IM.
XNBackground-Pixmap	Pixmap	Specifies the pixmap displayed in the background of preedit feedback information. If unspecified, the default is determined by the IM.

Table B.3 Preedit Attributes Description (Continued)

Attribute name	Data type	Description
`XNFontSet`	`XFontSet`	Specifies the font set used to display preedit feedback information. If unspecified, the input method selects a default font set.
`XNLineSpace`	`int`	Specifies the number of pixels between baselines when multiple lines are displayed in the preedit feedback information. If unspecified, the input method selects a default for this attribute.
`XNCursor`	`Cursor`	Specifies the cursor to be used in the preedit feedback window. If unspecified, the input method selects a default for this attribute.
`XNPreeditStart-Callback`	`XIMCallback`	Specifies a procedure called when the IM begins preedit and `XIMPreeditCallback` style is used.
`XNPreeditDone-Callback`	`XIMCallback`	Specifies a procedure called when the IM stops preedit and `XIMPreeditCallback` style is used.
`XNPreeditDraw-Callback`	`XIMCallback`	Specifies a procedure called when the IM has preedit feedback information to be displayed and `XIMPreeditCallback` style is used.
`XNPreeditCaret-Callback`	`XIMCallback`	Specifies a procedure called when the IM wants to move the preedit position within the preedit feedback information displayed and `XIMPreeditCallback` style is used.

Table B.4 Status Attributes Description

Attribute name	Data type	Description
`XNArea`	`XRectangle*`	Specifies the geometry of the area provided by the client for the IM's use; the IM must abide by this geometry. This value is used only with `XIMStatusArea` style.
`XNAreaNeeded`	`XRectangle*`	Specifies a value used in geometry negotiations. This value is used only with `XIMStatusArea` style. When setting this value, your software tells the IM the geometry you are willing to allocate for its use. When queried for this attribute, the IM identifies the area it wants. Only the width and height values of the `XRectangle` are significant; the x and y values are ignored.

Table B.4 Status Attributes Description (Continued)

Attribute name	Data type	Description
XNColormap	Colormap	Specifies the colormap ID from which the IM should allocate colors. If unspecified, the client window's colormap is used as the default colormap. If both XNColormap and XNStdColormap are specified, the results are undefined.
XNStdColormap	Atom	Specifies the name of the standard colormap from which the IM should allocate colors. The argument should be retrieved by calling XGetRGBColormaps(). If unspecified, the client window's colormap is used as the default colormap. If both XNColormap and XNStdColormap are specified, the results are undefined.
XNBackground	unsigned long	Specifies the background pixel for the status feedback information. If unspecified, the default is determined by the IM.
XNForeground	unsigned long	Specifies the foreground pixel for the status feedback information. If unspecified, the default is determined by the IM.
XNBackground-Pixmap	Pixmap	Specifies the pixmap displayed in background of the status feedback information. If unspecified, the default is determined by the IM.
XNFontSet	XFontSet	Specifies the font set used to display the status feedback information. If unspecified, the input method selects a default font set.
XNLineSpace	int	Specifies the number of pixels between baselines when multiple lines are displayed in the status feedback information. If unspecified, the input method selects a default for this attribute.
XNCursor	Cursor	Specifies the cursor to be used in the status feedback window. If unspecified, the input method selects a default for this attribute.
XNStatusStart-Callback	XIMCallback	Specifies a procedure called when the IM initializes the status area and XIMStatusCallback style is used.
XNStatusDone-Callback	XIMCallback	Specifies a procedure called when the IM no longer needs to display status feedback information and XIMStatusCallback style is used.
XNStatusDraw-Callback	XIMCallback	Specifies a procedure called when the IM has status feedback information to be displayed and XIMStatusCallback style is used.

Which preedit attributes are used with which preedit styles? And which status attributes are used with which status styles? Table B.5 and Table B.6 show which attributes are applicable to each style, and when each may be used.

Table B.5 Preedit Attributes

Preedit Attribute	Preedit Style				
	Preedit None	Preedit Nothing	Preedit Area	Preedit Position	Preedit Callbacks
XNArea[†]	Ignored	Ignored	D-R-S	D-R-S	Ignored
XNAreaNeeded[††]	Ignored	Ignored	R-S	Ignored	Ignored
XNSpotLocation	Ignored	Ignored	Ignored	C-R-S	Ignored
XNColormap XNStdColormap	Ignored	D-R-S	D-R-S	D-R-S	Ignored
XNForeground	Ignored	D-R-S	D-R-S	D-R-S	Ignored
XNBackground	Ignored	D-R-S	D-R-S	D-R-S	Ignored
XNBackgroundPixmap	Ignored	D-R-S	D-R-S	D-R-S	Ignored
XNFontSet[†††]	Ignored	D-R-S	C-R-S	C-R-S	Ignored
XNLineSpace[†††]	Ignored	D-R-S	D-R-S	D-R-S	Ignored
XNCursor	Ignored	D-R-S	D-R-S	D-R-S	Ignored
Preedit Callbacks	Ignored	Ignored	Ignored	Ignored	C-R-S

†. Setting XNArea causes the geometry of the input method to be set.

††. Setting XNAreaNeeded forces geometry negotiations with the input method. When negotiating geometry with an input method, the input method indicates its preferred geometry via the XNAreaNeeded attribute.

†††. If you set this attribute while using XIMPreeditArea style, you should renegotiate geometry.

Table B.6 Status Attributes

Status Attribute	Status Style			
	Status None	Status Nothing	Status Area	Status Callbacks
XNArea[†]	Ignored	Ignored	D-R-S	Ignored
XNAreaNeeded[††]	Ignored	Ignored	R-S	Ignored
XNColormap XNStdColormap	Ignored	D-R-S	D-R-S	Ignored

Table B.6 Status Attributes (Continued)

	Status Style			
Status Attribute	Status None	Status Nothing	Status Area	Status Callbacks
XNForeground	Ignored	D-R-S	D-R-S	Ignored
XNBackground	Ignored	D-R-S	D-R-S	Ignored
XNBackgroundPixmap	Ignored	D-R-S	D-R-S	Ignored
XNFontSet[†††]	Ignored	D-R-S	C-R-S	Ignored
XNLineSpace[†††]	Ignored	D-R-S	D-R-S	Ignored
XNCursor	Ignored	D-R-S	D-R-S	Ignored
Status Callbacks	Ignored	Ignored	Ignored	C-R-S

†. Setting XNArea causes the geometry of the input method to be set.

††. Setting XNAreaNeeded forces geometry negotiations with the input method. When negotiating geometry with an input method, the input method indicates its preferred geometry via the XNAreaNeeded attribute.

†††. Setting this attribute forces geometry negotiations for XIMStatusArea style.

Key	Description
C	Value must be specified when creating the XIC.
D	If not set when creating the XIC, a default value is provided.
O	Value must be set only once. It need not be set when creating the XIC.
R	Value may be retrieved or read with XGetICValues().
S	Value may be set by calling XSetICValues().
Ignored	Value is not used by the input method for the specified style; if set, it is ignored.

Example Program: Keyboard Input with X11R5

The following example shows how to use the various preedit styles and status styles with X11R5 to obtain coded characters from the keyboard. This program, allstyles_input.c, started out as the "Hello World!" program introduced in Chapter 4. "Hello World!" grew into simple_input.c in Chapter 7 as support was added for root preedit and status styles. This chapter also introduced and provided the sources for the routines GetPreferredGeometry(), SetGeometry(), Best-Style(), and SelectStyle(). In Chapter 8, simple_input.c was modified to add support for over-the-spot preedit style and off-the-spot preedit and status style. The modified program was renamed overnoff_input.c. Finally, in Chapter 9, overnoff_input.c was modified to add support for on-the-spot preedit style. The resulting program, allstyles_input.c, is listed below.

```
/* allstyles_input.c demonstrates how to connect to input methods
 * using the preedit styles: root, off-the-spot, over-the-spot,
 * and on-the-spot.  It also shows support for root and
 * off-the-spot status styles.
 */

#include <stdio.h>
#include <X11/Xlib.h>
#include <X11/keysym.h>
#include <locale.h>
#include <limits.h>
#include <nl_types.h>
#include <stdlib.h>

#define PROMPTS 1
#define ERR_SET 2
```

```
#define DEFAULTS 3
#define MARGIN_X 10
#define MARGIN_Y 10
#define WNAME_MAX 1024
#define CARET_HEIGHT 10
#define CARET_WIDTH 10
#define CARET_THICKNESS 2
#define BUFFER_BLOCK 64

/* Application global variables needed by preedit callbacks. */
Display *dpy;
Window win;
GC gc;
int screen;
XFontSet fs;
int x_start, y_start, line_height;
wchar_t wname[WNAME_MAX];
int wname_len = 0;


/* New global variables for on-the-spot feedback style. */
wchar_t *pe_buf = NULL;          /* preedit buffer */
XIMFeedback *pe_highlight;       /* array of highlights;
                                    1 per pe_buf[i]*/
unsigned int pe_buf_size = 0;    /* current alloc'ed size of pe_buf */
unsigned int num_pe_chars = 0;   /* number of characters in pe_buf */
GC reverse_gc;        /* XIMReverse and XIMPrimary highlights */
GC highlight_gc;      /* XIMHighlight and XIMTertiary highlights */
                      /* XIMUnderline and XIMSecondary highlights
                       * use the applications normal GC, but add
                       * underlining through XDrawLine. */
GC caret_gc;          /* GC used to paint the caret cursor. */
XIMCaretStyle cur_caret_style; /* keep track of the caret style */
int caret_pos;                 /* current caret position */
unsigned long app_foreground;  /* Application foreground */
unsigned long app_background;  /* Application background */
unsigned long highlight_pixel; /* Highlight color */


void
MyDrawPreedit()
{
  int x, y; /* x,y location of character in preedit buffer
           * to be drawn. */
```

```
    int i, char_width;

 /* Initialize x,y to end of current data in wname buffer; since
  * we decided to allow data entry only at the end of the
  * line, this is where preedit should be displayed. */

  x = x_start + XwcTextEscapement(fs, wname, wname_len);
  y = y_start + line_height;

  for (i = 0; i < num_pe_chars; i++){
    char_width = XwcTextEscapement(fs, &pe_buf[i], 1);
    if (pe_highlight[i] == XIMPrimary ||
        pe_highlight[i] == XIMReverse){
      XwcDrawImageString(dpy, win, fs, reverse_gc, x, y,
                         &pe_buf[i], 1);
    } else if (pe_highlight[i] == XIMSecondary ||
               pe_highlight[i] == XIMUnderline){
      XwcDrawImageString(dpy, win, fs, gc, x, y, &pe_buf[i], 1);
      XDrawLine(dpy, win, gc, x, y, x + char_width, y);
    } else { /* XIMFeedbackTertiery || XIMHighlight */
      XwcDrawImageString(dpy, win, fs, highlight_gc, x, y,
                         &pe_buf[i], 1);
    }
    x += char_width;
  }
}


/* Erase the current contents of the preedit area being displayed. */

void
MyErasePreedit()
{
  XRectangle ink, logical;
  int x, y;

 /* Initialize x,y to end of current data in wname buffer; since
  * we decided to allow data entry only at the end of the
  * line, this is where preedit should be displayed. */

  x = x_start + XwcTextEscapement(fs, wname, wname_len);
  y = y_start + line_height;
  (void) XwcTextExtents(fs, pe_buf, num_pe_chars, &ink, &logical);
```

```
    XFillRectangle(dpy, win, reverse_gc,
                    x + logical.x, y + logical.y,
                    logical.width, logical.height);
}

void
MyPaintCaret(feedback)
  XIMFeedback feedback;
{
    int x, y; /* x,y location of 1st character of the
               * preedit buffer. */
    int i;
    unsigned long vmask = GCForeground | GCBackground;
    XGCValues values;
    static Bool is_erased = True;

    if (feedback == XIMIsInvisible) {
     /* Paint with reverse GC to erase the caret by painting
      * with background. */
      if (is_erased) return;
      values.foreground = app_background;
      values.background = app_foreground;
      is_erased = True;
    } else if (feedback == XIMIsPrimary) {
      values.foreground = app_foreground;
      values.background = app_background;
      is_erased = False;
    } else { /* must be XIMIsSecondary */
      values.foreground = highlight_pixel;
      values.background = app_background;
      is_erased = False;
    }

    x = x_start + XwcTextEscapement(fs, wname, wname_len) +
        XwcTextEscapement(fs, pe_buf, caret_pos);
    y = y_start + line_height;

    XSetClipOrigin(dpy, caret_gc, x - ((CARET_WIDTH >> 1)), y);
    XSetTSOrigin(dpy, caret_gc, x - ((CARET_WIDTH >> 1)), y);
    XChangeGC(dpy, caret_gc, vmask, &values);
    XFillRectangle(dpy, win, caret_gc,
                    x - ((CARET_WIDTH >> 1)), y,
                    CARET_WIDTH, CARET_HEIGHT);
}
```

```
int MyPreeditStartCallback(ic, client_data, call_data)
  XIC ic;
  XPointer client_data;
  XPointer call_data;
{
  GC fillGC;                /* GC for creating the caret cursor */
  XGCValues values;
  Pixmap clip_mask;
  Pixmap caret_cursor; /* stencil for painting the caret cursor */
  XRectangle clip;
  XSegment segments[2]; /* segments for drawing the caret cursor */
  unsigned long vmask;
  static Bool initialized = False;  /* create buffers, cursors,
                                     * GCs, etc., only once in
                                     * life of program. */
  XColor xcolor;
  Status status;

  if (!initialized){

    initialized = True;

   /* Allocate memory for preedit buffer and highlight buffer. */
    pe_buf_size = BUFFER_BLOCK;
    pe_buf = (wchar_t*)malloc(pe_buf_size * sizeof(wchar_t));
    pe_highlight = (XIMFeedback*)malloc(
                            pe_buf_size * sizeof(XIMFeedback));

   /* Temporarily use caret_gc to hold a GC that will be used to
    * construct the stencil. Later, we'll free this temporary GC
    * and create a new one to contain the stencil and use it to
    * paint the caret cursor. */

    caret_cursor = XCreatePixmap(dpy, win,
                               CARET_WIDTH, CARET_HEIGHT, 1);
    caret_gc = XCreateGC(dpy, caret_cursor, 0,
                        (XGCValues *)NULL);

   /* Fill in the pixmap with a solid in preparation to
    * "cut out" the caret. */
    XFillRectangle(dpy, caret_cursor, caret_gc, 0, 0,
                 CARET_WIDTH, CARET_HEIGHT);
```

```
/* Change the GC for use in "cutting out" the caret shape. */
 values.foreground = 1;
 values.background = 0;
 values.line_width = CARET_THICKNESS;
 XChangeGC(dpy, caret_gc,
            GCForeground | GCLineWidth, &values);

 clip.width = CARET_WIDTH;
 clip.height = CARET_HEIGHT;
 clip.x = 0;
 clip.y = 0;
 XSetClipRectangles(dpy, caret_gc, 0, 0, &clip, 1, Unsorted);

/* Cut out the caret shape in the stencil. */
 segments[0].x1 = 0;
 segments[0].y1 = CARET_HEIGHT;
 segments[0].x2 = CARET_WIDTH/2;
 segments[0].y2 = 0;

 segments[1].x1 = CARET_WIDTH/2;
 segments[1].y1 = 0;
 segments[1].x2 = CARET_WIDTH;
 segments[1].y2 = CARET_HEIGHT;

 XDrawSegments(dpy, caret_cursor, caret_gc, segments, 2);

 XFreeGC(dpy, caret_gc);
 clip_mask = XCreatePixmap(dpy, RootWindow(dpy, screen),
                           CARET_WIDTH, CARET_HEIGHT, 1);
 values.foreground = 1;
 values.background = 0;
 caret_gc = XCreateGC(dpy, clip_mask,
                        GCForeground | GCBackground, &values);

 XFillRectangle(dpy, clip_mask, caret_gc, 0, 0,
                 CARET_WIDTH, CARET_HEIGHT);
 XFreeGC(dpy, caret_gc);

 vmask = (GCFunction | GCClipMask | GCStipple | GCForeground |
          GCBackground | GCFillStyle);
 values.function = GXcopy;
 values.clip_mask = clip_mask;
 values.stipple = caret_cursor;
```

```
    values.fill_style = FillStippled;
    values.foreground = app_foreground;
    values.background = app_background;
    caret_gc = XCreateGC(dpy, win, vmask, &values);

  /* Create the GC for rendering XIMReverse/XIMPrimary
   * highlights. */
    values.foreground = app_background;
    values.background = app_foreground ;
    reverse_gc = XCreateGC(dpy, win,
                           GCForeground | GCBackground, &values);

  /* Create the GC for rendering XIMHighlight/XIMTertiary
   * highlights. */
    xcolor.red = 65535;
    xcolor.green = 0;
    xcolor.blue = 0;
    xcolor.flags = DoRed;
    status = XAllocColor(dpy, DefaultColormap(dpy,screen),
                         &xcolor);
    if (status)
      values.foreground = highlight_pixel = xcolor.pixel;
    else
      values.foreground = app_background;
    values.background = app_foreground;
    highlight_gc = XCreateGC(dpy, win,
                             GCForeground | GCBackground, &values);

    caret_pos = 0;
  }

  return (-1);
}

void
MyPreeditDoneCallback(ic, client_data, call_data)
  XIC ic;
  XPointer client_data;
  XPointer call_data;
{
  XRectangle ink, logical;

  /* Since there is a good chance the user will preedit data
   * again in the future, the existing preedit and highlight
   * buffers are not freed. However, the variable indicating the
```

```
 * amount of the buffer used must  be reset since there is no
 * more useful data in the preedit buffer  at this time.
 *
 * Similarly, there is no need to destroy the GCs or caret
 * cursor, since they will be needed for the next preedit
 * session. They will remain allocated until the program
 * terminates. */

/* Erase the caret cursor; reset the caret highlight to
 * XIMIsInvisible. */

MyPaintCaret(XIMIsInvisible);
cur_caret_style = XIMIsInvisible;

/* Reset the preedit buffer length and the caret position in
 * preparation for the next preedit session. */
num_pe_chars = 0;
caret_pos = 0;
}

void
MyPreeditDrawCallback(ic, client_data, call_data)
  XIC ic;
  XPointer client_data;
  XIMPreeditDrawCallbackStruct *call_data;
{
  XIMPreeditDrawCallbackStruct *draw_data = call_data;
  int delta = 0;
  int insert_length = 0;
  int chg_length = 0;
  int chg_first = 0;
  XIMText *text = draw_data->text;
  wchar_t *src_wptr, *dst_wptr;
  char *src_ptr;
  XIMFeedback *src_hlite, *dst_hlite;
  int i, num_bytes;

  if (draw_data->caret < 0 || draw_data->chg_length < 0
      || draw_data->chg_first < 0)
    return; /* Though not prohibited by the spec, these cases
             * indicate the IM made an error, so ignore the
             * request. */

  /* Before modifying the contents of the preedit buffer, erase
```

```
 * the current display of the contents of the preedit buffer;
 * the new contents will be displayed by a call to
 * MyDrawPreedit() at the end of this routine. */

MyErasePreedit();

/* Make sure the is room for preedit buffer that results from
 * this call. delta identifies the change to the total number
 * of characters in the preedit buffer. It is calculated as:
 *   delta = number of characters inserted -
 *                             number of characters deleted
 */

if (text)
   insert_length = text->length;

chg_length = draw_data->chg_length;
chg_first = draw_data->chg_first;

delta = insert_length - chg_length;

if (num_pe_chars + delta >= pe_buf_size) {
   while (pe_buf_size <= num_pe_chars + delta)
     pe_buf_size += BUFFER_BLOCK;
   pe_buf = (wchar_t*)realloc(pe_buf,
                           pe_buf_size * sizeof(wchar_t));
   pe_highlight = (XIMFeedback*)realloc(pe_highlight,
                           pe_buf_size * sizeof(XIMFeedback));
   if (!pe_buf || !pe_highlight)
     exit(1);  /* Insufficient memory; exit. */
}

/* Shift the contents of the pe_buf and the highlight_buf to
 * make room for the new data. */
if (delta < 0){
  /* Shift characters to the left in the buffer. */
   for(src_wptr = pe_buf + (chg_first + chg_length),
       dst_wptr = src_wptr + delta,
       src_hlite = pe_highlight + (chg_first + chg_length),
       dst_hlite = src_hlite + delta,
       i = num_pe_chars - (chg_first + chg_length);
       i > 0;
       ++src_wptr, ++src_hlite, ++dst_wptr, ++dst_hlite,  --i){
     *dst_wptr = *src_wptr;
```

```
        *dst_hlite = *src_hlite;
    }
  } else if (delta > 0 && num_pe_chars > 0) {
    /* Shift characters to the right in the buffer. */
    for(src_wptr = pe_buf + (num_pe_chars - 1),
        dst_wptr = src_wptr + delta,
        src_hlite = pe_highlight + (num_pe_chars - 1),
        dst_hlite = src_hlite + delta,
        i = num_pe_chars - (chg_first + chg_length);
        i > 0;
        ++src_wptr, ++src_hlite, ++dst_wptr, ++dst_hlite, --i){
      *dst_wptr = *src_wptr;
      *dst_hlite = *src_hlite;
    }
  }
/* Update pe_buf to reflect the new data. */
  if ((text->encoding_is_wchar && text->string.wide_char) ||
      (!text->encoding_is_wchar && text->string.multi_byte)){
    if (insert_length != 0){
      /* If data is wchar_t, just copy from the callback data
       * into the buffer, now that text is moved out of the way
       * for the new data. */
      if (text->encoding_is_wchar){
        for (src_wptr = text->string.wide_char,
             dst_wptr = pe_buf + chg_first,
             i = insert_length;
             i > 0; ++src_wptr, ++dst_wptr, --i)
          *dst_wptr = *src_wptr;
      } else {
       /* Data is char* and must be converted into wchar_t as
        * it is copied. */
        for (src_ptr = text->string.multi_byte,
             dst_wptr = pe_buf + chg_first,
             i = insert_length; i > 0; ++dst_wptr, --i){
          num_bytes = mbtowc(dst_wptr, src_ptr, MB_CUR_MAX);
          if (num_bytes == 0)
            break;
          if (num_bytes < 0) /* error: exit */
            exit(1);
          src_ptr += num_bytes;
        }
      }
    }
  }
}
```

```
    /* Update highlight_buf to reflect the new data. */
     if (text->feedback){ /* Non-NULL if there is feedback array. */
       if (insert_length != 0){
         /* If data is wchar_t, just copy from the callback data
          * into the buffer, now that text is moved out of the way
          * for the new data. */
         for (src_hlite = text->feedback,
              dst_hlite = pe_highlight + chg_first,
              i = insert_length;
              i > 0; ++src_hlite, ++dst_hlite, --i)
           *dst_hlite = *src_hlite;
       }
     } else { /* Feedback is NULL; assign feedback of new characters
              * to be that of existing surrounding characters in
              * the preedit buffer. */
       XIMFeedback newfeedback;
       if (chg_first > 0)
       /* Take the highlight from the character to the
        * left of chg_first. */
         newfeedback = pe_highlight[chg_first - 1];
       else
       /* Take the highlight from the characters following
        * the change. */
         newfeedback = pe_highlight[chg_first + insert_length];
       for (dst_hlite = pe_highlight + chg_first, i = insert_length;
            i > 0; ++dst_hlite, --i)
         *dst_hlite = newfeedback;
     }


    /* Update num_pe_chars to reflect new pe_buf contents. */

     num_pe_chars += delta;

    /* Draw the updated preedit buffer. */

     MyDrawPreedit();

    /* Erase the current caret cursor and move it to the location
     * specified by the input method. */
     MyPaintCaret(XIMIsInvisible); /* Erase the current caret. */
     caret_pos = draw_data->caret;
     MyPaintCaret(cur_caret_style);
 }
```

```
void
MyPreeditCaretCallback(ic, client_data, call_data)
  XIC ic;
  XPointer client_data;
  XIMPreeditCaretCallbackStruct *call_data;
{
  XIMPreeditCaretCallbackStruct *caret_data = call_data;
  XIMCaretStyle newstyle = cur_caret_style;
  int newpos = caret_pos;

 /* Design decision - ignore any movement of the caret except:
  * XIMForwardChar, XIMBackwardChar, XIMLineStart, XIMLineEnd,
  * XIMAbsolutePosition, and XIMDontChange. */

  switch (caret_data->direction){
    case XIMForwardChar:
      if (caret_pos < num_pe_chars){
        newpos = caret_pos + 1;
        newstyle = caret_data->style;
      }
      break;
    case XIMBackwardChar:
      if (caret_pos > 0){
        newpos = caret_pos - 1;
        newstyle = caret_data->style;
      }
      break;
    case XIMLineStart:
      newpos = 0;
      newstyle = caret_data->style;
      break;
    case XIMLineEnd:
      newpos = num_pe_chars;
      newstyle = caret_data->style;
      break;
    case XIMAbsolutePosition:
      newpos = caret_data->position;
      newstyle = caret_data->style;
      break;
    case XIMDontChange:
      newstyle = caret_data->style;
      break;
  }
```

```
  if (newstyle != cur_caret_style || newpos != caret_pos){
   /* Erase the old caret cursor. */
    MyPaintCaret(XIMIsInvisible);
    cur_caret_style = newstyle;
    caret_pos = newpos;
   /* Draw the caret in the new style. */
    MyPaintCaret(cur_caret_style);
  }
}

main(argc, argv)
  int argc;
  char*argv[];
{
  XGCValues gcv;
  unsigned long gcv_mask;
  XEvent event;
  char *program_name = argv[0];
  char greeting[NL_TEXTMAX+1];
  char def_basename[] = "-*-medium-r-normal-*-24-*";
  char *basename;
  char **missing_charsets;
  int num_missing_charsets = 0, i = 0;
  char *default_string;
  int width, height, descent;
  XRectangle ink_return, logical_return;
  XRectangle *status_area_ptr, status_area;
  XRectangle *preedit_area_ptr, preedit_area;
  XRectangle limits;
  int status_height = 0;
  int preedit_height = 0;
  nl_catd my_cat;
  XFontSetExtents *fs_metrics;
  int char_width;
  XIMStyle my_style, style;
  XIM im;
  XIC ic;
  long im_event_mask;
  long event_mask;
  wchar_t *winput_buf;
  int buf_size = 128;
  XGCValues gcv_inverse;
  int len;
  KeySym keysym;
```

```
Status status;
Bool redraw = False;
Bool need_erase = False;
XVaNestedList preedit_att, status_att;
int dummy;
int height_avail;
XPoint spot;
XIMCallback pe_start, pe_done, pe_draw, pe_caret;


(void)setlocale(LC_ALL, "");
my_cat = catopen("allstyles_input", NL_CAT_LOCALE);
if ((dpy = XOpenDisplay(NULL)) == NULL) {
   (void) fprintf(stderr, catgets(my_cat, ERR_SET, 1,
                           "%s: cannot open Display.\n"),
                 program_name);
   exit(1);
}


(void)XSetLocaleModifiers("");

basename=catgets(my_cat, DEFAULTS, 1, def_basename);
fs = XCreateFontSet(dpy, basename,  &missing_charsets,
                    &num_missing_charsets, &default_string);

if (!fs){
   fprintf(stderr, catgets(my_cat, ERR_SET, 2,
                           "No font set!  Exiting....\n"));
   exit(1);
}
if(num_missing_charsets > 0){
   fprintf(stderr, catgets(my_cat, ERR_SET, 3,
           "Incomplete font set!  Missing characters set:\n"));
   for (i=0; i< num_missing_charsets; i++){
     fprintf(stderr, catgets(my_cat, ERR_SET, 4, "\t%s\n"),
             missing_charsets[i]);

   }
   XFreeStringList(missing_charsets);
}
(void)sprintf(greeting, catgets(my_cat, PROMPTS, 1,
                       "Please enter your name:"));
fs_metrics = XExtentsOfFontSet(fs);
line_height = fs_metrics->max_logical_extent.height;
```

```
char_width = fs_metrics->max_logical_extent.width;
width = (char_width * mbstowcs(NULL, greeting,
                              strlen(greeting))) +
        (2 * MARGIN_X);
height = (2 * line_height) + (2 * MARGIN_Y);
x_start = MARGIN_X;
y_start = MARGIN_Y - fs_metrics->max_logical_extent.y;
descent = line_height + fs_metrics->max_logical_extent.y;

screen = DefaultScreen(dpy);
win = XCreateSimpleWindow(dpy, RootWindow(dpy, screen), 0, 0,
                          width, height, 2,
                          BlackPixel(dpy,screen),
                          WhitePixel(dpy,screen));

gcv.foreground = app_foreground = BlackPixel(dpy,screen);
gcv.background = app_background = WhitePixel(dpy,screen);
gcv_inverse.foreground = gcv.background;
gcv_inverse.background = gcv.foreground;
gcv_mask = GCForeground | GCBackground;
gc = XCreateGC(dpy, win, gcv_mask, &gcv);

/* Open the input method and select styles. */
if ((im = XOpenIM(dpy, NULL, NULL, NULL)) == NULL) {
   (void) fprintf(stderr, catgets(my_cat, ERR_SET, 5,
                           "Couldn't open IM\n"));
   exit(1);
}

my_style = XIMPreeditNothing | XIMPreeditNone;
my_style |= XIMStatusNothing | XIMStatusNone;
my_style |= XIMStatusArea | XIMPreeditArea;
my_style |= XIMPreeditPosition;
my_style |= XIMPreeditCallbacks;
style = SelectStyle(im, my_style);
if (!style)
   fprintf(stderr, catgets(my_cat, ERR_SET, 6,
                     "IM doesn't support my styles!\n"));

spot.x = x_start;
spot.y = y_start + line_height;
if (my_style & XIMPreeditCallbacks){
  pe_start.callback = (XIMProc)MyPreeditStartCallback;
  pe_start.client_data = (XPointer)NULL;
```

```
    pe_done.callback = (XIMProc)MyPreeditDoneCallback;
    pe_done.client_data = (XPointer)NULL;
    pe_draw.callback = (XIMProc)MyPreeditDrawCallback;
    pe_draw.client_data = (XPointer)NULL;
    pe_caret.callback = (XIMProc)MyPreeditCaretCallback;
    pe_caret.client_data = (XPointer)NULL;
    preedit_att = XVaCreateNestedList(dummy,
                              XNPreeditStartCallback, &pe_start,
                              XNPreeditDoneCallback, &pe_done,
                              XNPreeditDrawCallback, &pe_draw,
                              XNPreeditCaretCallback, &pe_caret,
                              NULL);
  } else {
    preedit_att = XVaCreateNestedList(dummy,
                                XNForeground, gcv.foreground,
                                XNBackground, gcv.background,
                                XNFontSet, fs,
                                XNSpotLocation, &spot, NULL);
  }
  status_att = XVaCreateNestedList(dummy,
                                XNForeground, gcv.foreground,
                                XNBackground, gcv.background,
                                XNFontSet, fs, NULL);
  ic = XCreateIC(im, XNInputStyle, style,
                 XNClientWindow, win,
                 XNFocusWindow, win,
                 XNPreeditAttributes, preedit_att,
                 XNStatusAttributes, status_att,
                 NULL);

XFree(preedit_att);
XFree(status_att);
if (ic == NULL) {
  (void)fprintf(stderr, catgets(my_cat, ERR_SET, 7,
                      "Cannot create input context.\n"));
  exit(1);
}
XGetICValues(ic, XNFilterEvents, &im_event_mask, NULL);

event_mask = KeyPressMask | FocusChangeMask | ExposureMask;
event_mask |= StructureNotifyMask | im_event_mask;
XSelectInput(dpy, win, event_mask);
```

```
winput_buf = (wchar_t*)malloc((buf_size + 1) *
                               sizeof(wchar_t));
XMapWindow(dpy,win);
if (style & XIMPreeditArea){
  limits.width = 0;
  limits.height = 0;
  GetPreferredGeometry(ic, XNPreeditAttributes, &limits,
                       &preedit_area_ptr);
  if (preedit_area_ptr->height > 0) {
    preedit_height = preedit_area_ptr->height;
    XResizeWindow(dpy, win, width, height + preedit_height);
  }
  if (width >= preedit_area_ptr->width)
    preedit_area.width = preedit_area_ptr->width;
  else
    preedit_area.width = width;
  preedit_area.x = x_start;
  preedit_area.y = (2 * line_height) + (2 * MARGIN_Y);
  preedit_area.height = preedit_height;
  SetGeometry(ic, XNPreeditAttributes, &preedit_area);
}
if (style & XIMStatusArea){
  limits.width = 0;
  limits.height = 0;
  GetPreferredGeometry(ic, XNStatusAttributes, &limits,
                       &status_area_ptr);
  if (status_area_ptr->height > 0) {
    status_height = status_area_ptr->height;
    XResizeWindow(dpy, win, width,
                  height + status_height + preedit_height);
  }
  if (width >= status_area_ptr->width)
    status_area.width = status_area_ptr->width;
  else
    status_area.width = width;
  status_area.x = x_start;
  /* Place the status area below the preedit area, if it exists;
   * if it doesn't exist, preedit_height == 0.
   */
  status_area.y = (2 * line_height) + (2 * MARGIN_Y) +
                  preedit_height;
  status_area.height = status_height;
  SetGeometry(ic, XNStatusAttributes, &status_area);
}
```

```
while(1) {
  XNextEvent(dpy, &event);
    if (XFilterEvent(&event, None))
      continue;

  switch (event.type) {
    case Expose:
      if (event.xexpose.count == 0) {
        XmbDrawString(dpy, win, fs, gc, x_start, y_start,
                      greeting, strlen(greeting));
        XwcDrawString(dpy, win, fs, gc,
                      x_start, y_start + line_height,
                      wname, wname_len);
        if (num_pe_chars > 0)
          MyDrawPreedit();
        MyPaintCaret(cur_caret_style);
      }
      break;
    case KeyPress:
      len = XwcLookupString(ic, (XKeyPressedEvent*)&event,
                            winput_buf, buf_size,
                            &keysym, &status);
      if (status == XBufferOverflow){
        buf_size = len;
        winput_buf = (wchar_t*)realloc((char*)winput_buf,
                             (buf_size + 1) * sizeof(wchar_t));
        len = XwcLookupString(ic, (XKeyPressedEvent*)&event,
                      winput_buf, buf_size, &keysym, &status);
      }
      redraw = False;

      switch (status) {
        case XLookupNone:
          break;
        case XLookupKeySym:
        case XLookupBoth:
          if (num_pe_chars > 0)
            MyErasePreedit();
          if ((keysym == XK_Delete) ||
              (keysym == XK_BackSpace)){
            if (wname_len > 0) wname_len --;
            redraw = True;
            need_erase = True;
```

```
          break;
      }
      if (keysym == XK_Return) exit(0);
      if (status == XLookupKeySym) break;
    case XLookupChars:
      if (num_pe_chars > 0)
        MyErasePreedit();
      for (i = 0;(i < len) && (wname_len < WNAME_MAX); i++)
        wname[wname_len++] = winput_buf[i];
      redraw = True;
      break;
  }
  if (redraw) {
    if (need_erase){
      XChangeGC(dpy, gc, gcv_mask, &gcv_inverse);
      XFillRectangle(dpy, win, gc,
                     x_start, y_start + descent,
                     width - MARGIN_X, line_height);
      XChangeGC(dpy, gc, gcv_mask, &gcv);
      need_erase = False;
    }
    if (num_pe_chars > 0)
      MyDrawPreedit();
    XwcDrawString(dpy, win, fs, gc, x_start,
                  y_start + line_height, wname, wname_len);
    if (style & XIMPreeditPosition){
      spot.x = x_start +
                  XwcTextEscapement(fs, wname, wname_len);
      spot.y = y_start + line_height;
      preedit_att = XVaCreateNestedList(dummy,
                              XNSpotLocation, &spot, NULL);
      XSetICValues(ic,
                  XNPreeditAttributes, preedit_att, NULL);
      XFree(preedit_att);
    }
  }
  break;
case FocusIn:
  XSetICFocus(ic);
  break;
case FocusOut:
  XUnsetICFocus(ic);
  break;
case ConfigureNotify:
```

```
/* If the window size hasn't changed, there is no new
 * geometry to communicate to the input method. */
if ((width == event.xconfigure.width) &&
     ((height + preedit_height + status_height) ==
      event.xconfigure.height))
  break;
width = event.xconfigure.width;
if ((style & XIMPreeditArea) &&
     (style & XIMStatusArea)){
  XRectangle preedit_limits, status_limits;
  preedit_limits.width = width;
  status_limits.width = width;
  height_avail = event.xconfigure.height -
                   ((2 * line_height) + (2 * MARGIN_Y));
  if (height_avail < 0){
    preedit_limits.height = 0;
    status_limits.height = 0;
  } else {
    status_limits.height = .5 * height_avail;
    preedit_limits.height =
                   height_avail - status_limits.height;
  }
  /* Tell the input method its geometry constraints and
   * ask for the preferred size for each. */
  GetPreferredGeometry(ic, XNPreeditAttributes,
                   &preedit_limits, &preedit_area_ptr);
  GetPreferredGeometry(ic, XNStatusAttributes,
                    &status_limits, &status_area_ptr);
  /* If the input method wants less than half of the area
   * available to display the status feedback, give it the
   * geometry it asks for.  Otherwise, give it half of
   * what's available. Give any remaining geometry (at
   * least half of the extra space in the window) to the
   * input method to display the preedit feedback data. */
  if (height_avail > 0 &&
        (.5 * height_avail) >= status_area_ptr->height)
    status_height = status_area_ptr->height;
  else if (height_avail >= 0)
    status_height = .5 * height_avail;
  else
    status_height = 0;
  height_avail -= status_height;
  if (height_avail > 0 &&
        height_avail >= preedit_area_ptr->height)
```

```
        preedit_height = preedit_area_ptr->height;
      else if (height_avail >= 0)
        preedit_height = height_avail;
      else
        preedit_height = 0;
      preedit_area.x = x_start;
      preedit_area.y = (2 * line_height) + (2 * MARGIN_Y);
      preedit_area.height = preedit_height;
      preedit_area.width = width;
      status_area.x = x_start;
      status_area.y = preedit_area.y + preedit_height;
      status_area.height = status_height;
      status_area.width = width;
      SetGeometry(ic, XNStatusAttributes, &status_area);
      SetGeometry(ic, XNPreeditAttributes, &preedit_area);
      height = event.xconfigure.height -
               (preedit_height + status_height);
      break;
  }
  /* If there is only one off-the-spot feedback area,
   * give it all the extra space in the window. */
  if (style & XIMPreeditArea){
    limits.width = width;
    height_avail = event.xconfigure.height -
                   ((2 * line_height) + (2 * MARGIN_Y));
    if (height_avail < 0)
      limits.height = 0;
    else
      limits.height = height_avail;
    GetPreferredGeometry(ic, XNPreeditAttributes,
                         &limits, &preedit_area_ptr);
    if (preedit_area_ptr->height <= height_avail)
      preedit_height = preedit_area_ptr->height;
    else if (height_avail >= 0)
      preedit_height = height_avail;
    else
      preedit_height = 0;
    if (preedit_height < 0)
      preedit_height = 0;
    preedit_area.x = x_start;
    preedit_area.y = (2 * line_height) + (2 * MARGIN_Y);
    preedit_area.height = preedit_height;
    preedit_area.width = width;
    SetGeometry(ic, XNPreeditAttributes, &preedit_area);
```

```
      height = event.xconfigure.height - preedit_height;
      break;
    }
  /* Identical to the XIMPreeditArea style code above, but
   * using XNStatusAttributes instead. */
   if (style & XIMStatusArea){
     limits.width = width;
     height_avail = event.xconfigure.height -
                       ((2 * line_height) + (2 * MARGIN_Y));
     if (height_avail < 0)
       limits.height = 0;
     else
       limits.height = height_avail;
     GetPreferredGeometry(ic, XNStatusAttributes, &limits,
                            &status_area_ptr);
     if (status_area_ptr->height <= height_avail)
       status_height = status_area_ptr->height;
     else if (height_avail >= 0)
       status_height = height_avail;
     else
       status_height = 0;
     if (status_height < 0)
       status_height = 0;
     status_area.x = x_start;
     status_area.y = (2*line_height) + (2*MARGIN_Y);
     status_area.height = status_height;
     status_area.width = width;
     SetGeometry(ic, XNStatusAttributes, &status_area);
     height = event.xconfigure.height - status_height;
   }
   break;
  }
 }
}
```

Example: Keyboard Input
Using XmIm*

The following example shows how you might use XmIm* to obtain keyboard input in a Motif DrawingArea widget. To help you find the calls to XmIm* and see how they are used, the lines relevant to keyboard input are marked with *change bars* in the margin. Comments in the code describe the specific actions taken. However, in general the program does the following:

- creates a DrawingArea widget and uses it as a simple text editor.
- creates three procedures (plus supporting routines) and registers these for the DrawingArea widget's XmNexposeCallback procedure, XmNinputCallback procedure, and XmNdestroyCallback procedure.
- allows up to 100 lines of text to be entered and displayed, though in the interest of simplicity, the program does not perform robust error checking. Multiple lines of text were needed to illustrate use of XmNlineSpace. Since this is an example to illustrate use of XmIm*, the program uses the simplifying assumption of fixed length lines and a fixed number of lines. To help see lines of text in the output, every other line reverses the foreground and background colors.
- stores data as multibyte when the largest character in the current locale requires only one byte; otherwise, it stores the data as wide character. This shows a common practice of coding for minimum memory use. It also has the side benefit of demonstrating use of XmIm* with both multibyte and wide character I18N models.
- processes the Backspace key and the Return key to illustrate how to use the different status return values from XmImMbLookupString(). Each time the users presses the Return key, the widget swaps its foreground and background colors. While no reasonable application would ever do this, the example shows how to notify the input method when these values change.
- attempts to support both use of font sets and use of font structures. However, the program isn't robust about making sure that a font set is used when one is needed. Support

for both font structures and font sets provides an opportunity to demonstrate the font
list manipulation routines described in section 14.2 on page 273.

```c
#include <stdio.h>
#include <locale.h>
#include <nl_types.h>
#include <string.h>
#include <stdlib.h> /* Needed for MB_CUR_MAX. */
#include <X11/keysym.h>
#include <X11/Intrinsic.h>
#include <X11/Shell.h>
#include <Xm/Xm.h>
#include <Xm/DrawingA.h>
#include <Xm/BulletinB.h>

/* Defines for symbolic set identifiers; to be used with
 * catalogs. */

#define VALUE_SET 1  /* Set number text widget value strings. */
#define ERROR_SET 2  /* Set number for error messages. */

#define MAXLINESIZE      256
#define MAXLINES         100
#define TEXT_MAX_INSERT_SIZE   80

typedef struct {
  XPoint         location;
  char           text[MAXLINESIZE];
  wchar_t        wc_text[MAXLINESIZE];
  int            num_chars;
} MyLineRec, *MyLineRecPtr;

typedef struct {
  int            line_height;
  int            ascent;
  int            descent;
  Widget         widget;
  MyLineRec      lines[MAXLINES];
  int            num_lines;
  int            active_line;   /* Line# for current I/O */
  XmFontList     fontlist;
  XFontSet       fontset;
  XFontStruct    *font;
} DrawData, *DrawDataPtr;
```

```
XtAppContext  app_context;

void DA_Expose();
void DA_Input();
void DA_Destroy();

static XtResource resources [] = {
    {XmNfontList, XmCFontList, XmRFontList, sizeof(XmFontList),
     XtOffset(DrawDataPtr, fontlist), XmRString, "*-18-*:"},
};

/* Global variables needed by the application. */

static char initial_string[512];
nl_catd my_fd; /* Message catalog file descriptor. */
Widget Shell1;
Widget DrawArea;
GC my_gc = NULL;

void InitializeDrawStruct(widget, data_ptr)
  DrawData *data_ptr;
  Widget widget;
{
  Boolean have_font_struct = False;
  XmFontContext context;
  XmFontListEntry next_entry;
  XmFontType type_return = XmFONT_IS_FONT;
  char* font_tag = NULL;
  XtPointer tmp_font;
  int ascent = 0, descent = 0;
  XFontSetExtents *fs_extents;

  data_ptr->widget = widget;

 /* If we have one byte per character, store the data in
  * the char* portion of the structure; initialize the
  * wchar_t portion to NULL. */

  if (MB_CUR_MAX == 1){
    strcpy(data_ptr->lines[0].text, initial_string);
    data_ptr->lines[0].num_chars =
      strlen(data_ptr->lines[0].text);
    data_ptr->lines[0].wc_text[0] = (wchar_t) NULL;
```

```
  } else {
/* We need wchar_t to store one character per storage element
 * (eases character manipulation, such as processing
 * backspace.  Use the ANSI-C function mbstowcs() to convert
 * and store the data. */
  data_ptr->lines[0].num_chars =
    mbstowcs(data_ptr->lines[0].wc_text,
             initial_string, MAXLINESIZE);
 /* If an error occurs in conversion, the initial value
  * must be bad. so we'll just ignore the initial value
  * and initialize to the empty string, terminated with
  * a wide character NULL.   */
  if (data_ptr->lines[0].num_chars < 0) {
    data_ptr->lines[0].num_chars = 0;
    data_ptr->lines[0].wc_text[0] = (wchar_t) NULL;
  }
  data_ptr->lines[0].text[0] = (char) NULL;
}
/* For this example, we'll assume a single line in the
 * initial text. If this was a real application, we would
 * check and count the number of lines, filling out lines
 * in the structure as appropriate. */
data_ptr->num_lines = 1;
data_ptr->active_line = 0;
data_ptr->fontset = NULL;
data_ptr->font = NULL;

/* Find the first fontset in the font list.  If there is no
 * fontset, use the first font struct in the font list. */

if (!XmFontListInitFontContext(&context,
                               data_ptr->fontlist)){
  printf(catgets(my_fd, ERROR_SET, 2,
                "Uh oh, no font list!\n"));
  exit(1);
}

do {
  next_entry = XmFontListNextEntry(context);
  if (next_entry) {
    tmp_font =
      XmFontListEntryGetFont(next_entry, &type_return);
    if (type_return == XmFONT_IS_FONTSET) {
      data_ptr->fontset = (XFontSet) tmp_font;
```

```
         break; /* We've found the one we want. */
      } else if (!have_font_struct){
       /* Value of return_type must be XmFONT_IS_FONT. */
       /* Save the first font struct in case no font
        * set is found. */
        data_ptr->font = (XFontStruct *)tmp_font;
        have_font_struct = True;
      }
    }
  } while(next_entry != NULL);

  XmFontListFreeFontContext(context);

 /* Determine metrics of the font[set] to be used. */
  if (data_ptr->fontset){
    fs_extents = XExtentsOfFontSet(data_ptr->fontset);

   /* max_logical_extent.y is number of pixels from origin
    * to top of rectangle (i.e. y is negative). */

    ascent = -fs_extents->max_logical_extent.y;
    descent = fs_extents->max_logical_extent.height +
      fs_extents->max_logical_extent.y;
  } else if (data_ptr->font){
    ascent = data_ptr->font->max_bounds.ascent;
    descent = data_ptr->font->max_bounds.descent;
  }
  data_ptr->ascent = ascent;
  data_ptr->descent = descent;
  data_ptr->line_height = ascent + descent;

 /* Arbitrarily pick an x,y location for the start of the
  * first line. */
  data_ptr->lines[0].location.x = 20;
  data_ptr->lines[0].location.y = 5 + data_ptr->line_height;
}


void InitializeIM(widget, data)
  Widget widget;
  DrawData *data;
{
  Arg args[6];  /* To set initial values to input method. */
  Cardinal num_args;
  XPoint xmim_point;
```

```
    XGCValues values;
    Pixmap bg_pixmap;
    int active_line = data->active_line;
    int data_pixel_length = 0;

/* Start the input method. */
    XmImRegister(widget, (unsigned int)NULL);

/* Determine background, foreground, and background pixmap
 * to be passed to the input method. */
    num_args = 0;
    XtSetArg (args[num_args], XtNforeground,
              &values.foreground); num_args++;
    XtSetArg (args[num_args], XtNbackground,
              &values.background); num_args++;
    XtSetArg (args[num_args], XtNbackgroundPixmap,
              &bg_pixmap); num_args++;
    XtGetValues (widget, args, num_args);

/* Provide the x,y location of where the next character will
 * be displayed so if the input method needs to pop up a
 * window (i.e. for over the spot input method), the
 * window will be where the user is looking. */

    if (data->fontset){
      if (MB_CUR_MAX == 1)
        data_pixel_length =
          XmbTextEscapement(data->fontset,
                            data->lines[active_line].text,
                            data->lines[active_line].num_chars);
      else
        data_pixel_length =
          XwcTextEscapement(data->fontset,
                            data->lines[active_line].wc_text,
                            data->lines[active_line].num_chars);
    } else if (data->font){
      data_pixel_length =
        XTextWidth(data->font, data->lines[active_line].text,
                   data->lines[active_line].num_chars);
    }

    xmim_point.x = data->lines[active_line].location.x +
      data_pixel_length;
    xmim_point.y = data->lines[active_line].location.y;
```

```
  num_args = 0;
  XtSetArg(args[num_args],
          XmNfontList, data->fontlist); num_args++;
  XtSetArg(args[num_args],
          XmNbackground, values.background); num_args++;
  XtSetArg(args[num_args],
          XmNforeground, values.foreground); num_args++;
  XtSetArg(args[num_args],
          XmNbackgroundPixmap, bg_pixmap);num_args++;
  XtSetArg(args[num_args],
          XmNspotLocation, &xmim_point); num_args++;
  XmImSetValues(widget, args, num_args);
}

void swap_colors(widget)
  Widget widget;
{
  Arg args[3];   /* To set initial values to input method. */
  Cardinal num_args;
  Pixel tmp;
  unsigned long valuemask = GCForeground | GCBackground;
  XGCValues values;

 /* Determine background, foreground, and background pixmap
  * to be passed to the input method. */
  num_args = 0;
  XtSetArg (args[num_args], XtNforeground,
          &values.foreground); num_args++;
  XtSetArg (args[num_args], XtNbackground,
          &values.background); num_args++;
  XtGetValues (widget, args, num_args);

  tmp = values.foreground;
  values.foreground = values.background;
  values.background = tmp;
  XChangeGC(XtDisplay(DrawArea), my_gc,
          valuemask, &values);

  num_args = 0;
  XtSetArg (args[num_args], XtNforeground,
          values.foreground); num_args++;
  XtSetArg (args[num_args], XtNbackground,
          values.background); num_args++;
```

```
    XtSetValues(widget, args, num_args);
    XmImSetValues(widget, args, num_args);
}

void IncrementActiveLine(widget, data, x, y)
  Widget widget;
  DrawData *data;
  int x;
  int y;
{
  int active_line;
  XPoint xmim_point;
  Arg args[1]; /* New spot location to the input method. */
  Cardinal num_args = 0;

 /* If this was a real application, we would need to do
  * some fancy calculation of line location, and allow the
  * user to easily change the active line.  However, for a
  * simple example of input methods in drawing areas,
  * we'll just increment the current active line and set
  * the x,y and num_chars for a new line.  If we hit
  * MAXLINES, leave it at the last line. */

  if (data->num_lines < (MAXLINES - 1)) {
    data->active_line++;
    swap_colors(widget);
    active_line = data->active_line;
    data->num_lines++;
    data->lines[active_line].location.x =
      data->lines[active_line - 1].location.x;
    data->lines[active_line].location.y =
      data->lines[active_line - 1].location.y +
        data->line_height;
    data->lines[active_line].num_chars = 0;
   /* Tell the input method the new x,y location of
    * the "spot". */
    xmim_point.x = data->lines[active_line].location.x;
    xmim_point.y = data->lines[active_line].location.y;
    XtSetArg(args[num_args], XmNspotLocation,
      &xmim_point); num_args++;
    XmImSetValues(widget, args, num_args);
  } else
    data->active_line = MAXLINES - 1;
}
```

```
/* The following routine is used to erase a line allowing
 * the updated line to be re-displayed.  It is necessary to
 * erase the entire line * to correctly display the result
 * of backspace.  If this was a real application, we would
 * try to be more clever and calculate the minimum amount
 * of real estate to be touched. */

void EraseLine(data, line_number)
  DrawData *data;
  int line_number;
{
  int num_args = 0;
  int x_seg_len = 0;
  XGCValues values;
  unsigned long valuemask;
  Arg args[2];

  /* Create the GC for drawing text in the drawing area. */
  valuemask = GCForeground | GCBackground;

  /* Swap the foreground/background colors in the GC to do
   * the erasure. */
  num_args = 0;
  XtSetArg (args[num_args], XtNforeground,
            &values.background); num_args++;
  XtSetArg (args[num_args], XtNbackground,
            &values.foreground); num_args++;
  XtGetValues (data->widget, args, num_args);

  XChangeGC(XtDisplay(data->widget), my_gc,
            valuemask, &values);

  if (data->fontset && MB_CUR_MAX == 1)
    x_seg_len = XmbTextEscapement(data->fontset,
                      data->lines[line_number].text,
                      data->lines[line_number].num_chars);
  else if (data->fontset)
    x_seg_len = XwcTextEscapement(data->fontset,
                      data->lines[line_number].wc_text,
                      data->lines[line_number].num_chars);
  else if (data->font)
   /* Can't reaonably handle MB_CUR_MAX >1 with font
    * structs, so don't try. */
```

```c
      x_seg_len =
        XTextWidth(data->font, data->lines[line_number].text,
                   data->lines[line_number].num_chars);

    if (x_seg_len)
      XFillRectangle(XtDisplay(data->widget),
                     XtWindow(data->widget),
                     my_gc,
                     data->lines[line_number].location.x,
                     data->lines[line_number].location.y -
                       data->ascent,
                     x_seg_len, data->line_height);

   /* Restore the GC. */
   num_args = 0;
   XtSetArg (args[num_args], XtNforeground,
             &values.foreground); num_args++;
   XtSetArg (args[num_args], XtNbackground,
             &values.background); num_args++;
   XtGetValues (data->widget, args, num_args);

   XChangeGC(XtDisplay(data->widget), my_gc,
             valuemask, &values);
}

void DA_Destroy (w, data, cb)
  Widget w;
  DrawData *data;
  XmDrawingAreaCallbackStruct *cb;
{
  XmImUnregister(data->widget);
}

void DA_Input (w, data, cb)
  Widget w;
  DrawData *data;
  XmDrawingAreaCallbackStruct *cb;
{
  int active_line = data->active_line;
  int position = 0;
  int num_chars = 0;
  int cur_end = 0;
  int tmp_num_chars;
  Status status_return;
```

```
int insert_length=0;
char insert_string[TEXT_MAX_INSERT_SIZE];
wchar_t wc_insert_string[TEXT_MAX_INSERT_SIZE];
XPoint xmim_point;
KeySym keysym;

insert_string[0] = NULL;

switch (cb->event->type) {
  case KeyPress:

    /* Get any characters entered from the keyboard; the
     * input method will set insert_length > 0 when there
     * is data. */

    insert_length =
      XmImMbLookupString(w, (XKeyEvent *)cb->event,
                         insert_string,
                         TEXT_MAX_INSERT_SIZE,
                         &keysym, &status_return);

    switch (status_return) {
      case XLookupNone:
        break;
      case XLookupKeySym:
      case XLookupBoth:
      /* process new_line */
        if (keysym == XK_Delete ||
            keysym == XK_BackSpace){
          if (data->lines[active_line].num_chars > 0){
            EraseLine(data, active_line);
            tmp_num_chars =
              data->lines[active_line].num_chars;
            position = --tmp_num_chars;
            data->lines[active_line].num_chars =
              tmp_num_chars;
            if (MB_CUR_MAX == 1)
              data->lines[active_line].text[position] =
                NULL;
            else
              data->lines[active_line].wc_text[position] =
                0L;
          } else {
            if (active_line > 0) { /* Backed up a line. */
```

```
                data->active_line = --active_line;
             /* Swap colors back to those used on
              * previous line. */
                swap_colors(w);
           }
         }
      } else if (keysym == XK_Return){
         IncrementActiveLine(w, data,
                  data->lines[active_line].location.x,
                  data->lines[active_line].location.y);
         active_line = data->active_line;
      }
      if (keysym == XK_Delete ||
          keysym == XK_BackSpace ||
          keysym == XK_Return) break;

      if (status_return == XLookupKeySym) break;

  case XLookupChars:
  /* If there's room, append it; otherwise,
   * replace it. */

    if (MB_CUR_MAX == 1) {
      if (insert_length +
          data->lines[active_line].num_chars
            <= MAXLINESIZE){
          strncat(data->lines[active_line].text,
                  insert_string, insert_length);
          data->lines[active_line].num_chars +=
            insert_length;
        } else {
          strncpy(data->lines[active_line].text,
                  insert_string, insert_length);
          data->lines[active_line].text[insert_length] =
            NULL;
          data->lines[active_line].num_chars =
            insert_length;
        }
      } else {
       /* Null terminate the string. */
        insert_string[insert_length] = '\0';
        num_chars = mbstowcs(wc_insert_string,
                             insert_string,
                             insert_length + 1);
```

```
        if (num_chars +
          data->lines[active_line].num_chars
            <= MAXLINESIZE){
          cur_end = data->lines[active_line].num_chars;
         memcpy(&data->lines[active_line].wc_text[cur_end],
              wc_insert_string,
              num_chars * sizeof(wchar_t));
          data->lines[active_line].num_chars +=
            num_chars;
        } else {
          memcpy(data->lines[active_line].wc_text,
              wc_insert_string,
              num_chars * sizeof(wchar_t));
          data->lines[active_line].num_chars =
            num_chars;
          data->lines[active_line].wc_text[num_chars] =
            0L;
        }
      }
      break;
    }


/* Force the modified string to be displayed. If this
 * was a real application, we would be much more
 * efficient about this. */

DA_Expose(w, data, cb);

/* Tell the IM the new location of the input location. */

xmim_point.y = data->lines[active_line].location.y;
if (data->fontset){
  if (MB_CUR_MAX == 1)
    xmim_point.x =
      data->lines[active_line].location.x +
        XmbTextEscapement(data->fontset,
                data->lines[active_line].text,
                data->lines[active_line].num_chars);
  else
    xmim_point.x =
      data->lines[active_line].location.x +
        XwcTextEscapement(data->fontset,
                data->lines[active_line].wc_text,
                data->lines[active_line].num_chars);
```

```
        } else if (data->font){
          xmim_point.x =
             data->lines[active_line].location.x +
               XTextWidth(data->font,
                           data->lines[active_line].text,
                           data->lines[active_line].num_chars);
        }
        XmImVaSetValues(w, XmNspotLocation,
                          &xmim_point, NULL);
        break;
  }
}

void CreateGC (data)
  DrawData *data;
{
  Arg args[5];
  int num_args;
  XGCValues values;
  unsigned long valuemask;

 /* Create the GC for drawing text in the drawing area. */
  valuemask = GCForeground | GCBackground;

  num_args = 0;
  XtSetArg (args[num_args], XtNforeground,
            &values.foreground); num_args++;
  XtSetArg (args[num_args], XtNbackground,
            &values.background); num_args++;
  XtGetValues (data->widget, args, num_args);

  if (!data->fontset) {
 /* If we don't have a fontset, need to add fontstruct to GC. */
    valuemask |= GCFont;
    values.font = data->font->fid;
  }

  my_gc = XCreateGC(XtDisplay(DrawArea),
                    XtWindow(DrawArea),
                    valuemask, &values);
}

void DA_Expose (w, data, cb)
  Widget w;
```

```
  DrawData *data;
  XmDrawingAreaCallbackStruct *cb;
{
  int line;
  MyLineRec cur_line;

  if (!XtIsRealized((Widget)DrawArea)) return;
  if (!my_gc) CreateGC(data);

  if (data->fontset) {
    for (line = data->num_lines - 1; line >= 0; line--) {
      cur_line = data->lines[line];
      if (MB_CUR_MAX == 1)
        XmbDrawString (XtDisplay(DrawArea),
                       XtWindow(DrawArea),
                       data->fontset, my_gc,
                       (int)cur_line.location.x,
                       (int)cur_line.location.y,
                       cur_line.text, cur_line.num_chars);
      else
        XwcDrawString (XtDisplay(DrawArea),
                       XtWindow(DrawArea),
                       data->fontset, my_gc,
                       (int)cur_line.location.x,
                       (int)cur_line.location.y,
                       cur_line.wc_text,
                       cur_line.num_chars);
    }
  } else {
    for (line = data->num_lines - 1; line >= 0; line--) {
      cur_line = data->lines[line];
      XDrawString (XtDisplay(DrawArea),
                   XtWindow(DrawArea), my_gc,
                   (int)cur_line.location.x,
                   (int)cur_line.location.y,
                   cur_line.text, cur_line.num_chars);
    }
  }
}


/* Tell the input method when we gain or lose focus.  This
 * allows it to alter its visuals to indicate its focus
 * status.  In addition, because in some models or
```

```
 * applications a focus change can accompany an input
 * location change (for example, text widget in explicit
 * focus mode), we tell the IM the location of the input
 * on focus change.  This isn't really needed in this
 * sample program, but in a real application (that allowed
 * the user to specify where data was to be drawn/input)
 * this *would** be necessary. */

void HandleFocusChange (w, data, event)
  Widget w;
  DrawData *data;
  XEvent *event;
{
  Arg args[2];
  int num_args = 0;
  XPoint xmim_point;
  int active_line = data->active_line;
  int data_pixel_length = 0;

  if (data->fontset){
    if (MB_CUR_MAX == 1)
      data_pixel_length =
        XmbTextEscapement(data->fontset,
                          data->lines[active_line].text,
                          data->lines[active_line].num_chars);
    else
      data_pixel_length =
        XwcTextEscapement(data->fontset,
                          data->lines[active_line].wc_text,
                          data->lines[active_line].num_chars);
  } else if (data->font){
    data_pixel_length =
      XTextWidth(data->font, data->lines[active_line].text,
                 data->lines[active_line].num_chars);
  }

  xmim_point.x = data->lines[active_line].location.x +
    data_pixel_length;
  xmim_point.y = data->lines[active_line].location.y;

  if (event->type = FocusIn){
    XtSetArg(args[num_args],
             XmNspotLocation, &xmim_point); num_args++;
    XmImSetFocusValues(data->widget, args, num_args);
```

```
    } else if (event->type = FocusOut)
      XmImUnsetFocus(w);
}

void main (argc, argv)
  int argc;
  char **argv;
{
  Widget BulletinBoard;
  Display *display;
  Arg args[20];
  int num_args;
  static char default_text[] = "This is the starting string";
  DrawData data;

  char *dummy;

  my_fd = catopen("drawIM", NL_CAT_LOCALE);

  dummy = catgets(my_fd, VALUE_SET, 1, default_text);
  strcpy(initial_string, dummy);

  (void)XtSetLanguageProc(NULL, NULL, NULL);

 /* Initialize the Xt toolkit. */
  XtToolkitInitialize();
  app_context = XtCreateApplicationContext();
  display = XtOpenDisplay(app_context, NULL, argv[0],
                          "XMclient", NULL, 0,
                          &argc, argv);
  if (!display) {
    printf(catgets(my_fd, ERROR_SET, 3,
          "Unable to open display\n"));
      exit(0);
  }

 /* Create message shell. */
  num_args = 0;
  XtSetArg (args[num_args],
            XmNallowShellResize, True); num_args++;
  Shell1 = XtAppCreateShell(argv[0], NULL,
                            applicationShellWidgetClass,
                            display, args, num_args);
```

```
    XtGetApplicationResources(Shell1, &data, resources,
                          XtNumber(resources), NULL, 0);

    num_args = 0;
    BulletinBoard = XmCreateBulletinBoard (Shell1,
                                        "BulletinBoard",
                                        args, num_args);
    XtManageChild (BulletinBoard);

    num_args = 0;
    XtSetArg (args[num_args], XmNresizePolicy,
            XmRESIZE_NONE); num_args++;
    XtSetArg (args[num_args], XmNheight, 500); num_args++;
    XtSetArg (args[num_args], XmNwidth, 800); num_args++;
    DrawArea = XmCreateDrawingArea (BulletinBoard, "DrawArea",
                                    args, num_args);
    XtAddCallback (DrawArea, XmNexposeCallback,
                (XtCallbackProc) DA_Expose,
                (XtPointer)&data);
    XtAddCallback (DrawArea, XmNinputCallback,
                (XtCallbackProc) DA_Input,
                (XtPointer)&data);
    XtAddCallback (DrawArea, XmNdestroyCallback,
                (XtCallbackProc) DA_Destroy,
                (XtPointer)&data);
    XtManageChild (DrawArea);
    XtAddEventHandler(BulletinBoard, FocusChangeMask, False,
                    (XtEventHandler)HandleFocusChange,
                    (XtPointer)&data);

    InitializeDrawStruct(DrawArea, &data);
    InitializeIM(DrawArea, &data);

    XtRealizeWidget(Shell1);
    XtAppMainLoop(app_context);
}
```

Quick Reference: Localizable Motif Resources

Many of the resources defined by the Motif widgets specify values that may need to be changed based on the locale of the user. Your software should avoid hard coding these values if possible. If the value is a procedure (such as the `Text` widget's `modifyVerifyCallback`), consider that different procedures may be needed based on the locale. Tables E.1 through E.6 identify these localizable resources and their associated widget; the resources are grouped by functional type.

Table E.1 Locale Sensitive Font List Resources

Widget Class	Resource Name
`VendorShell`	`XmNbuttonFontList`
	`XmNdefaultFontList`
	`XmNlabelFontList`
	`XmNtextFontList`
`XmBulletinBoard`	`XmNbuttonFontList`
	`XmNlabelFontList`
	`XmNtextFontList`
`XmLabel[Gadget]`	`XmNfontList`
`XmList`	`XmNfontList`
`XmMenuShell`	`XmNbuttonFontList`
	`XmNdefaultFontList`
	`XmNlabelFontList`
`XmText`	`XmNfontList`

Table E.1 Locale Sensitive Font List Resources (Continued)

Widget Class	Resource Name
XmTextField	XmNfontList

Table E.2 Locale Sensitive Resources: Labels and Buttons

Widget Class	Resource Name
Core	XmNbackground†
XmCommand	XmNcommand
	XmNpromptString
XmFileSelectionBox	XmNdirListLabelString
	XmNfileListLabelString
	XmNfilterLabelString
	XmNnoMatchString
XmLabel[Gadget]	XmNaccelerator
	XmNacceleratorText
	XmNlabelString
	XmNmnemonic
XmList	XmNstringDirection
XmManager	XmNstringDirection
XmMessageBox	XmNcancelLabelString
	XmNhelpLabelString
	XmNmessageString
	XmNokLabelString
XmPrimitive	XmNforeground†
XmRowColumn	XmNlabelString
	XmNmenuAccelerator
	XmNmnemonic
XmRowColumn (simple menu)	XmNbuttonAccelerators
	XmNbuttonAcceleratorsText
	XmNbuttonMnemonics
	XmNbuttons
	XmNoptionLabel
	XmNoptionMnemonic

Table E.2 Locale Sensitive Resources: Labels and Buttons (Continued)

Widget Class	Resource Name
XmSelectionBox	XmNapplyLabelString
	XmNcancelLabelString
	XmNhelpLabelString
	XmNlistLabelString
	XmNokLabelString
	XmNselectionLabelString
	XmNtextAccelerators

†. Foreground and background color names cannot be localized; X restricts the names of colors to the X Portable Character Set. However, the color may still need to vary for different locales.

Table E.3 Locale Sensitive Text and Keyboard Input Resources

Widget Class	Resource Name
VendorShell	XmNinputMethod
	XmNpreeditType
XmSelectionBox	XmNtextColumns
	XmNtextString
XmText	XmNcolumns†
	XmNmodifyVerifyCallback
	XmNmodifyVerifyCallbackWcs
	XmNvalue
	XmNvalueWcs
XmTextField	XmNcolumns†
	XmNmodifyVerifyCallback
	XmNmodifyVerifyCallbackWcs
	XmNvalue
	XmNvalueWcs

†. Note that the columns resource specifies the minimum number of characters that can be entered into a line of text.

Table E.4 Locale Sensitive List Resources

Widget Class	Resource Name
XmList	XmNitems
	XmNselectedItems
XmSelectionBox	XmNlistItems

Table E.5 Locale Sensitive Title Resources

Widget Class	Resource Name
TopLevelShell	XmNiconName
	XmNiconNameEncoding[†]
WmShell	XmNtitle
	XmNtitleEncoding†
XmBulletinBoard	XmNdialogTitle
XmScale	XmNtitleString

†. This resource should not be set. When using
XtSetLanguageProc(), this resource is set to a value that ensures that
the property encoding is passed automatically.

Table E.6 Locale Sensitive Pixmap Resources

Widget Class	Resource Name
Core	XmNbackgroundPixmap
WMShell	XmNiconPixmap
XmDragIcon	XmNpixmap
XmDropSite	XmNanimationMask
	XmNanimationPixmap
XmLabel[Gadget]	XmNlabelInsensitivePixmap
	XmNlabelPixmap
XmMessageBox	XmNsymbolPixmap
XmPushButton[Gadget]	XmNarmPixmap

Table E.6 Locale Sensitive Pixmap Resources (Continued)

Widget Class	Resource Name
`XmToggleButton[Gadget]`	`XmNselectInsensitivePixmap`
	`XmNselectPixmap`

Glossary

API

Application Programming Interface or Application Programmatic Interface — the routines provided by a library.

Base Font Name

A base font name is used in the creation of a font set to specify a collection of fonts with similar characteristics. A base font name may be a full or abbreviated XLFD; one or more of the XLFD fields may contain wild cards.

Basic Execution Character Set

The set of characters that the C programming standard says must exist in every code set of every supported locale on the system. In addition, the coded value of a character from the basic execution character set must be the same in every coded character set supported on a system

Bidirectional Text

In many languages used in world, some characters are written in multiple directions. Such languages are said to be bidirectional. For example, Hebrew is a bidirectional language. Some characters are written from left to right, while other characters are written from right to left.

C0

C0 characters are the control code characters defined in the graphics left portion of a coded character set. The eighth bit of the byte containing the coded control character is zero.

C1   C1 characters are the control code characters defined in
                                      the graphics right portion of a coded character set. The
                                      eighth bit of the byte containing the coded control
                                      character is set.

Caret Cursor   In the `PreeditDrawCallback` used with on-the-
                                      spot preedit style, the input method directs the client
                                      software to modify the preedit buffer contents, begin-
                                      ning at a specified location. This location is the called
                                      the caret cursor position.

Character   A character is any of the symbols (letters, numbers,
                                      punctuation, controls) used in the writing of a lan-
                                      guage. For example, the letter "A" is a character. A
                                      Japanese kanji or ideograph is a character.

Character Set   A character set is a collection of characters used to
                                      write one or more languages. For example, the letters a
                                      – z and A – Z, coupled with a set of punctuation marks
                                      and numbers, are a character set used to write the
                                      English language. The term repertoire is commonly
                                      used to mean character set.

Coded Character Set   A coded character set is a character set for which a
                                      unique numeric identifier or code has been assigned to
                                      each character. Computers can't easily deal with
                                      abstract graphical symbols the way you and I can.
                                      Instead, they assign a numeric value or code point to
                                      each character. This code point allows the character to
                                      be stored and manipulated in software. For example, in
                                      ASCII (American Standard for Character Information
                                      Interchange), the character "A" has a value of hexadec-
                                      imal 41 (0x41). In American EBCDIC (a coded charac-
                                      ter set sometimes used on IBM systems), the character
                                      "A" has a coded value 0xC1.

Code Set Independent   When software is written such that it does not depend
                                      on any particular code set, the software is said to be
                                      code set independent. Such software can usually sup-
                                      port new code sets without modifications.

Code Sets

A code set is either a coded character set or an encoding method implementation. Each locale requires that data be represented in either a coded character set or an encoding method implementation. For example, the code set of the U.S. English locale en_US.iso88591 is ISO 8859.1; the code set of Japanese Korean locale ko_KR.eucKR is the encoding method implementation eucKR — Korean EUC.

Compound Text

Compound Text is a way of representing text data such that the data contained is tagged, with the tag identifying the coded character set of the data. It is based on the ISO/IEC 2022 standard for data representation. Because text data is tagged, Compound Text allows data encoded in many different coded character sets to be mixed together.

Context Sensitive

In many written languages, the shape used to represent a character often depends on the characters the surround it.

Data Encoding

Data encoding is another term for the code set used to represent character data.

Encoding Method

An encoding method is a scheme or set of rules for combining several coded character sets in a data stream. Examples of encoding methods include ISO 2022, Compound Text, and EUC — Extended Unix Code. When an encoding method is applied to a specific collection of coded character sets, the result is an implementation of an encoding method. For example, EUC is an encoding method that combines up to four coded character sets in a data stream. When the rules of EUC are used to combine JISX0201, JISX0208, and JISX0212, the result is Japanese EUC — an encoding method implementation.

Font Set

A font set is a list of one or more fonts, providing glyphs for every printing character in the code set of the locale. It is created by calling XCreateFontSet().

G0

G0 characters are the graphical characters defined in the graphics left portion of a coded character set. The eighth bit of the byte containing the graphical character is zero.

G1	G1 characters are the graphical characters defined in the graphics right portion of a coded character set. The eighth bit of the byte containing the graphical character is set.
Glyph	A glyph is the visual representation of a character. It is not bound to any code point.
Graphics Left	Graphics left characters are the graphical characters defined in the graphics left portion of a coded character set. The eighth bit of the byte containing the graphical character is zero.
Graphics Right	Graphics right characters are the graphical characters defined in the graphics right portion of a coded character set. The eighth bit of the byte containing the graphical character is set.
Host Portable Character Encoding	The encoding of the X Portable Character Set on the system where an X application runs is called the Host Portable Character Encoding. The X specification does not define what encoding is used for the Host Portable Character Encoding. However, the coded character value of a character from the X Portable Character Set is guaranteed to be the same in all locales supported on a system.
Hot Key	With X11R6, when software wants to process a key itself (instead of allowing the input method to process the key), it declares the key to be a hot key. Hot keys are ignored by filters put in place by the input methods.
I18N	I18N (pronounced "eye eighteen en") is a shorthand notation for the word *internationalization* — the letter I, followed by 18 letters, followed by the letter N.
Input Context	An input context is an opaque object used for all communications between your software and the input method. You create an input context by calling `XCreateIC()`.
Input Method	An input method (IM) is a procedure, a macro, or sometimes a separate process that converts `KeyPress` events into a character encoded in the code set of the current locale. For each locale supported by X11R5 and X11R6 on your system, at least one input method is provided — though a vendor often provides several input methods for a locale.

Internationalization	Internationalization is a software design model in which a single source code version of software works according to the rules and customs of its user's written language, processing data encoded in the code set of the user's choice.
L10N	L10N (pronounced "el ten en") is an acronym for the term localization — the process of adapting software for use in a locale other than that for which it was originally designed. (See "Localization.")
Locale	The locale is a collective term for the language of the user, the location or territory of the user (which determines locale customs, such as currency formats), and the code set in which the user's data is represented. The locale is also a physical data file and/or collection of routines that are used to initialize an application's language sensitive environment. The definitions are often used interchangeably since the physical file is an implementation or instantiation of the language, territory, and code set.
Locale Modifier	Users control which input method is used with their application by specifying a locale modifier. Typically they do this by setting the `XMODIFIERS` environment variable, though your software may decide to implement a resource to supplement the ways in which a user can specify the modifier. For example, Motif's VendorShell widget defines the `XmNinputMethod` resource as an additional way to specify a locale modifier.
Localization	Localization, often abbreviated L10N, is a term that refers collectively to all work needed to make a product acceptable and work correctly for use in a different locale. This includes translating all text to be displayed to the user, translating documentation, modifying the behavior of language sensitive operations, and providing fonts and other special functionality when needed.
Localized	Software or data files that have been modified to make them acceptable for use in a locale other than that for which they were originally created. For example, a manual that has been translated is said to have been localized.

Localizer
A localizer is the person responsible for modifying software, data files, and documentation for use in a locale other than that for which they were originally created. The localizer of documentation and text files is also referred to as the translator.

Message Catalog
A message catalog is a file used to contain the localized strings (such as prompts and error messages) used by internationalized software.

MSE
The Multibyte Support Extensions (MSE) are a set of extensions to the ISO/IEC 9899 C Programming Language Standard. The MSE adds a number of I18N routines to the C library.

Multibyte
Multibyte is a term that means the data is stored as a sequence of bytes — one or more bytes per character; the data type for multibyte data is `char*`. The size of a single multibyte character can vary from character to character; this is a function of the locale.

Nibble
Nibble is one-half of an eight-bit byte, or four data bits.

Output Context
The X11R6 I18N rendering model is based on the concept of an output method (data type `XOM`) and an output context (data type `XOC`). An output context contains the I18N data (such as the font set) needed by an output method to draw the text.

Output Method
The X11R6 I18N rendering model is based on the concept of an output method (data type `XOM`) and an output context (data type `XOC`). An output method is locale specific software that knows how to draw text according to the locale. An output context contains the data (such as the font set) needed by an output method to draw the text.

Radix
The character used to separate the integer and fractional portions of floating point numbers. In the United States, the decimal point is the radix character — the character "." separates the integer value 10 from the fractional portion 25 in the string representation of the floating point value 10.25.

Repertoire
The collection of characters in a character set.

String Conversion

For complex input methods, a character is usually generated by typing a series of keys before the final character is generated. X11R6 introduced functionality that allows a character to be converted back into the sequence of elements from which it was composed. This process is called string conversion.

Tee Shirt Size Aliases

The Common Desktop Environment uses a collection of font aliases that avoid specific point sizes in their X Logical Font Descriptions. Instead, these aliases use strings typically used to size clothing (such as Tee-shirts) in the United States. For example, the aliases use the string "xs" to indicate "extra small" and the string "xxl" to indicate "extra, extra large."

Universal Coded Character Set

A Universal Coded Character Set (also known as a UCS) is a code set that contains all the characters possibly needed by any user. Examples of UCS include ISO/IEC 10646 and Unicode.

Wide Character

Wide character is a term meaning that data is stored in fixed width elements, one character per element. The data type for wide character data is wchar_t (one wide character) or wchar_t* (a wide character string). Type wchar_t is an integral data type whose content is opaque. The size of wchar_t is implementation defined.

XLFD

The X Logical Font Description (XLFD) defines a standard syntax for structured font names.

X Locale Database

The internationalization capabilities of X11R5 and X11R6 utilize data stored in a vendor-defined, locale-specific database called the X locale database. This database includes information such as which CHARSET_REGISTRY-CHARSET_ENCODING pairs are needed to represent characters encoded in the code set of the user's locale.

X Portable Character Set

The X Portable Character Set is a basic set of 97 characters that are present in the code set of every locale supported by the X library. The repertoire consists of the characters in the graphics left portion of ISO 8859.1, though the actual code values are not specified.

Index

Symbols

$set *see* Message Catalog

A

application manager 286
ASCII
    definition and table 23
Auxiliary Area 108

B

Base Name
    defined 75
    usage in creating an output context 98
    used in Motif font list 250
Basic Execution Character Set
    ANSI-C requirements 30
    defined 30
Bidirectional Languages
    defined 10
    determining directionality explicitly 90
    determining directionality implicitly 90
    extent of support for in X11R6 90
    Layout Services, pending tools 12
    Motif 1.2 support for 257
    querying for X library support of 93
    rendering support with X11R6 89
    software tools 12
Bounding Box 80
btowc() 37, 287

C

C0 25
C1 25
CallbackProc()
    syntax 166
Caret Cursor
    defined 168
    direction 171
    highlights 171
catclose()
    example usage 55
    Message Catalog
        closing with catclose() 53
catgets() 53
    example usage 55, 57, 85
catopen() 53
    example usage 55, 84
    example, handling errors 57
CDE
    controlling the input method started 285
    integrating localized software with application manager 286
    integrating localized software with workspace manager 286
    selecting the locale 284
    setting DTAPPSEARCHPATH 285
    setting DTDATABASESEARCHPATH 285
    style manager, controlling fonts in font set 282
    Xconfig, selecting the locale for all users 285
Character
    defined 21
Character Set
    defined 21
    repertoire of 21
CHARSET_ENCODING 74, 93
CHARSET_REGISTRY 74, 93
Code Set
    data interchange of 225
    data interchange of,
        see Data Interchange
    Japanese EUC defined 27
    number of bytes per character 26
    rendering, see Font Set
    standard tools for converting between 49
Code Set Independence
    defined 27
    guiding principles 30
    X/Open and X Consortium on design approach 31

Coded Character Set
    ASCII coded character set table 23
    control characters 25, 26
    definition 21
    graphics left characters 25, 26
    graphics right characters 26
    table showing location of control, graphics left, and graphics right characters 26
Complex Input Method 107
Compose Input Method 107
Compound String
    converting to compound text with XmCvtXmStringToCT() 252
    creating a segment with XmStringSegmentCreate() 252
    creating with XmStringCreate() 251, 252
    creating with XmStringCreateLocalized() 251, 252
    creating with XmStringCreateLtoR() 252
    default font tag, XmFONTLIST_DEFAULT_TAG 251
    defined 251
    using a font set with 251
    widgets using 251
Compound Text
    converting to compound string, XmCvtCTToXmString() 252
    defined 226
context sensitive 10
Context-Sensitive Languages
    explicit shaping 90
    extent of support for in X11R6 90
    implicit shaping 90
    lack of software tools 12
    Layout Services, pending tools 12
    Motif 1.2 support for 257
    querying for X library support of 93
    rendering support with X11R6 89
Cut and Paste
    see Data Interchange

D

Data Encoding
    defined 15
    see also Code Set
Data Interchange
    compound text 226
        converting to code set of locale, XmbTextPropertyToTextList() 229
        converting to wide character, XwcTextPropertyToTextList() 229
        generating 228
        generating from multibyte, XmbTextListToTextProperty() 227
        generating from wide character, XwcTextListToTextProperty() 227
    cut buffers, use of 226

example 231
example interaction 226
interoperability with pre-X11R5 applications, XStdICCTextStyle 228
Motif 1.2
    XmTextCopy() 254
    XmTextFieldCopy() 254
    XmTextFieldPaste() 254
    XmTextPaste() 254
owning the selection, XtOwnSelection() 231
performance tuning 230
primary selection 226
    Atom PRIMARY 226
    TARGETS 226
requesting the selection, XtGetSelectionValue() 235
sending window title to the window manager 225
setting icon names 254
setting the icon name 225
setting titles 254
with Motif 1.2 254
XA_STRING, predefined Atom 226
XICCEncodingStyle 228
    XCompoundTextStyle 228
    XStdICCTextStyle 228
    XStringStyle 228
    XTextStyle 228
XmbTextListToTextProperty() 227
XSetWMIconName() 225
XSetWMName() 225
XtConvertSelectionProc
    example procedure 232
XtSelectionCallbackProc
    example procedure 235
Data Interchnage
    code set of requestor same as code set of owner 230
Date Format
    examples of variations 63
    LC_TIME, controlling the locale 18
    LC_TIME, example usage 19
    localtime() 63, 64
    nl_langinfo() 64
    strftime() 63, 64
    strptime() 64
    variations described 62
    wcsftime() 63, 64
Dead-Key Input Method 107
Destroy Callback
    defined 203
DestroyCallback()

syntax 202
Drag and Drop
    see Data Interchange
Drawing Local Language Characters
    calculating size of, *see* Font Metrics
    encoded as multibyte 77
    encoded as wide character 77
    example 86
    output context, defined 89
    output context, using 102
    output method, defined 89
    R5 font set compared to R6 output context 91
    support for bidirectional languages 89
    support for context-sensitive languages 89
    X11R5 compared to X11R6 89
    XmbDrawImageString() 77
    XmbDrawString() 76, 77
    XmbDrawText() 77
    XwcDrawImageString() 77
    XwcDrawString() 77
    XwcDrawText() 77
DrawingArea Widget 323
    XmNdestroyCallback procedure 323
    XmNexposeCallback procedure 323
    XmNinputCallback procedure 323
dspcat 54
DTAPPSEARCHPATH 285
DTDATABASESEARCHPATH 285
dtstyle 281, 282
dumpmsg 54

E

Encoding Method
    example, Japanese EUC 27
    implementation of 22
Event
    data type, Xevent 105
    defined 105
    keyboard events, XKeyEvent 106
example usage 84
Explicit Shaping
    defined 90

F

Feedback Highlights
    see On-the-Spot Preedit Style, highlights for preedit data
fgetwc() 37, 38, 39, 287

`fgetws()` 37, 38, 287

Filtering Events
    performed by `XtDispatchEvent()`, `XtMainLoop()`, and `XtAppMainLoop()` 248

Filtering Events, see Input Method

Font
    bitmap fonts 71
    `ENCODING`, identification of glyph index 71
    `FILE_NAMES_ALIASES`, using file name as font name 73
    font name alias 73
    `fonts.alias` file 73
    glyph index 71
    glyph index compared to coded character value 72

Font List
    adding a font list entry, `XmFontListAppendEntry()` 271
    CDE
        location of resource file for `SystemFont` and `UserFont` 282
        Tee Shirt Size aliases 283
    CDE `SystemFont` font list resource 282
    CDE `UserFont` font list resource 282
    creation using a font list entry, `XmFontListAppendEntry()` 271
    data type `XmFontList` 250
    default font tag, `XmFONTLIST_DEFAULT_TAG` 251
    entry type
        data type `XmFontType` 272
        XmFONT_IS_FONT 272
        XmFONT_IS_FONTSET 272
    example resource specifications 251
    extracting a font or font set, example of 273
    font list entry
        creating a font set while creating an entry, `XmFontListEntryLoad()` 271
        creating from an existing font set, `XmFontListEntryCreate()` 271
        freeing associated memory, `XmFontListEntryFree()` 272
        programmatic creation, using an existing font set, `XmFontListEntryCreate()` 271
    programmatic creation, example 272
    programmatic creation of 271
    resource
        syntax 250
    resource converter and font sets 250
    use of font sets in 250

Font Metrics
    bounding box 80
    calculating ascent, descent, left bearing, and right bearing 80
    calculating ink metrics 79
    calculating logical metrics 79
    example 85
    example calculation 136
    `XExtentsOfFontSet()` 79
    `XmbTextEscapement()` 78

XmbTextExtents() 78
XmbTextPerCharExtents() 78
XTextWidth() 78
XwcTextEscapement() 78
XwcTextExtents() 78
XwcTextPerCharExtents() 78
Font Set 251
    base name, controlling the fonts in a font set 75
    calculating metrics with 78
    calculating metrics, example 80
    calculating metrics, *see* Font Metrics
    CDE
        controlling fonts with dtstyle 281, 282
        SystemFont resource 282
        UserFont resource 282
    CHARSET_ENCODING, identifying which fonts are needed in the font set 74
    CHARSET_REGISTRY, identifying which fonts are needed in the font set 74
    creating with XmFontListEntryLoad() 271
    creating with XCreateFontSet() 73
    default output context 98
    defined 73
    destroying a font set with XFreeFontSet() 76
    example, creating 85
    example, handling errors 85
    in Motif font list resource, syntax 250
    in Motif font lists 250
    locale of the font set 75
    obtaining font set info for an output context, XNFontInfo 101
    obtaining the list of base names for a font set, XBaseFontnameListOfFontSet() 76
    obtaining the list of font structures comprising a font set 76
    resource 247
    use in creating a font list entry, XmFontListEntryCreate() 271
    using resource converter, example 247
    using with compound string 251
    X locale database, usage in creating font set 75
    XCreateFontSet(), which fonts are selected for a font set 75
    XFontSet data type 73
    XLFD, wild cards in 75
    Xt resource converter, XtCvtStringToFontSet 247
    Xt resource for, XtRFontSet 247
fprintf() 37, 38, 65, 287
fputwc() 37, 38, 287
fputws() 37, 38, 287
fscanf() 37, 38, 65, 287
fwprintf() 37, 287
fwscanf() 37, 287

G

G0 25
G1 26
gencat 52, 53
    example usage 55
Geometry Callback
    defined 149
    syntax and usage 150
Geometry Management
    Motif 1.2 VendorShell, handled by 253
Geometry Negotiation 149
    example 150
    input method initiated 149
    when to negotiate 150
getwc() 37, 38, 39, 287
getwchar() 37, 38, 39, 287
Global Orientation
    changing 95
    defined 94
    querying for with XNQueryOrientation 93
Glyphs 29

H

Hiragana 110
Host Portable Character Encoding
    defined 242
Hot Keys 207
    example 207

I

I18N *see* Internationalization
ICCCM 225
iconv 50, 291
iconv() 50, 291
iconv_close() 50, 291
iconv_open() 50, 291
IM *see* Input Method
IMInstantiateCallback
    example usage 199
IMInstantiateCallback()
    syntax 198
implicit character shaping 93
Implicit Shaping
    defined 90
Ink Metrics
    defined 79

example
input 222
Input Context
    controlling preedit state when reset, `XNResetState` 206
    creating with `XCreateIC()` 122
    creating, example 123
    data type, `XIC` 121
    defined 121
    gaining keyboard focus 128
    losing keyboard focus 129
    notification of change to preedit state 206
    notification of failure, `DestroyCallback()` 202
    spot location, illustrated 146
    variable length argument list
        memory management 127
    `XGetICValues()`, syntax 127
    XIC data values 122, 295
        preedit attributes 122, 295
            nested variable length argument lists 123
            nested variable length argument lists, example usage 124
            `XNArea` 296, 299
            `XNAreaNeeded` 296, 299
            `XNBackground` 296, 299
            `XNBackgroundPixmap` 296, 299
            `XNColormap` 296, 299
            `XNCursor` 297, 299
            `XNFontSet` 297, 299
            `XNForeground` 296, 299
            `XNLineSpace` 297, 299
            `XNPreeditCaretCallback` 297
            `XNPreeditDoneCallback` 297
            `XNPreeditDrawCallback` 297
            `XNPreeditStartCallback` 297
            `XNSpotLocation` 296, 299
            `XNStdColormap` 296, 299
        setting and querying 127
        status attributes 122
            nested variable length argument lists 123
            nested variable length argument lists, example usage 124
            `XNArea` 297, 299
            `XNAreaNeeded` 297, 299
            `XNBackground` 298, 300
            `XNBackgroundPixmap` 298, 300
            `XNColormap` 298, 299
            `XNCursor` 298, 300
            `XNFontSet` 298, 300
            `XNForeground` 298, 300
            `XNLineSpace` 298, 300

`XNStatusDoneCallback` 298
`XNStatusDrawCallback` 298
`XNStatusStartCallback` 298
`XNStdColormap` 298, 299
variable length argument list 123
`XNClientWindow` 293
`XNDestroyCallback` 203, 213, 221
`XNFilterEvents` 294
`XNFocusWindow` 293
`XNGeometryCallback` 294
`XNHotKey` 207, 221
`XNHotKeyState` 221
    `XIMHotKeyStateOFF` 208
    `XIMHotKeyStateON` 208
`XNPreeditAttributes` 294, 295
`XNPreeditState` 222
    `XIMPreeditDisable` 205
    `XIMPreeditEnable` 205
    `XIMPreeditUnknown` 205
`XNPreeditStateNotifyCallback` 206, 223
`XNQueryICValuesList` 213
`XNQueryIMValuesList` 213
`XNR6PreeditCallbackBehavior` 214
`XNResetState` 206, 221
    `XIMInitialState` 206
    `XIMPreserveState` 206
`XNResourceClass` 294
`XNResourceName` 294
`XNStateConversionCallback` 222
`XNStatusAttributes` 294, 295
`XNStringConversion` 210, 222
`XNStringConversionCallback` 210
`XNVisiblePosition` 213
`XSetICValues()`, syntax 127
input context 122
Input Method
auxiliary area 108
choosing preedit and status styles 119
choosing preedit and status styles, example 119
complex input method 107
compose input method 107
connecting to 116, 117
connecting to using `XmImRegister()` 275
connecting with Motif 1.2 252
controlling preedit state 204
controlling which input method is used 116
dead-key input method 107
defined 106

determing supported preedit and status styles 117
determining which events the IM wants 124
disconnecting from using `XmImUnregister()` 275
filtering events 125, 248
    using `XtDispatchEvent()` 248
    using `XtMainLoop()` 248
handling keyboard focus 128
handling optional XIM values 204
hot keys 207
hot keys, example 207
IM values
    `XNDestroyCallback` 214, 215
    `XNQueryICValuesList` 214, 215
    `XNQueryIMValuesList` 214, 215
    `XNQueryInputStyle` 214
    `XNR6PreeditCallbackBehavior` 214, 218
    `XNResourceClass` 214, 215
    `XNResourceName` 214, 215
    `XNVisiblePosition` 214, 216
input context, *see* Input Context
instantiate callback, syntax 198
locale modifiers
    impact on input method selection 117
Motif 1.2
    controlling preedit style, `XmNpreeditType` 253
    controlling which input method is used, `XmNinputMethod` 253
notification of failure, `DestroyCallback()` 202
notification of IM start-up 197
notifying when focus is gained, using `XmImSetFocusValues()` 275
notifying when focus is gained, using `XmImVaSetFocusValues()` 275
notifying when focus is lost, using `XmImUnsetFocus()` 275
passing values to, using `XmImSetValues()` 275
passing values to, using `XmImVaSetValues()` 275
preedit area 108
preedit styles
    off-the-spot 111
    on-the-spot 111
    over-the-spot 111
    root 111
processing key press events, `XmImMbLookupString()` 275
processing `KeyPress` events 125
protocol between X library and input method 212
querying preedit state 205
reconnect callback, syntax 198
reconnecting to 197
selection with CDE, `XMODIFIERS` 285
setting preedit state 206
status area 108

trouble shooting 140
using input methods, synopsis 115
XIM data values
    memory management 197
    XNDestroyCallback 203
XIM values, setting 196
XIM values
    querying for preedit state, example 205
    querying for supported values, example 204
    setting preedit state 206
XIMStyle, using 119
XmbLookupString() 125
XMODIFIERS 116
XOpenIM(), syntax 117
XwcLookupString()
    syntax 125
input method 124, 219
insert cursor 166
Instantiate Callback
    syntax 198
Inter-Client Communications Conventions Manual
    see ICCCM
Internationalization
    architectural overview 6
    benefits of I18N design model 7
    code set dependent designs 28
    code set independence 27
    customer expectations 1
    locale defined 16
    locale-sensitive operations 15
    performance impact 12
    problems and associated costs 11
    relationship to localization ix
    schedule impact for use of I18N 12
    standards controlling I18N tools 13
    using a universal code set 28
ISO 8859.1
    data interchange of 228
    generating from the keyboard 106
    XA_STRING, predefined Atom for interchange of 226
ISO C
    comparison of I18N tools with XPG4 and MSE 287
iswalnum() 45, 289
iswalpha() 45, 289
iswcntrl() 45, 289
iswctype() 45, 46, 290
iswdigit() 45, 290
iswgraph() 45, 290

`iswlower()` 46, 290
`iswprint()` 46, 290
`iswpunct()` 46, 290
`iswspace()` 46, 290
`iswupper()` 46, 290
`iswxdigit()` 46, 290

J

Japanese EUC
    defined 27
JISX0201 27
JISX0208 27
JISX0212 27

K

Key Code
    defined 106
Keyboard Focus 128
Keyboard Input
    geometry management
        handled by Motif 1.2 `VendorShell` 253
    input method, defined 106
    Motif 1.2
        controlling preedit style, `XmNpreeditType` 253
        controlling which input method is used, `XmNinputMethod` 253
    Motif `Text` widget 252
    Motif `TextField` widget 252
    Motif `XmIm` routines 252
    processing `KeyPress` events 125
    see also Input Method
    selecting the input method 116
    using input methods, synopsis 115
    using `XmIm*` for input without `Text` or `TextField` widgets 275
    with an `DrawingArea` widget 271
`KeyCode` 106
Keymap
    defined 142
`KeyPress` 106
`KeyPress` Event
    modifiers 143
    processing 125
`KeySym` 142
Keysym
    data type, `KeySym` 142
    defined 142

L

L10N see Localization
LANG 19
Language-Specific Software see Local Version
Layout Services 12
LC_ALL
    defined 18
LC_COLLATE
    defined 18
LC_CTYPE
    defined 18
LC_MESSAGES
    defined 18
    example usage 19
LC_MONETARY
    defined 18
LC_NUMERIC
    defined 18
LC_TIME
    defined 18
    example usage 19
Local Language Software *see* Local Version
Local Version
    benefits described 3
    defined 2
    problems and associated costs 3, 4, 5
Locale
    categories defined 18
    code set 6
    defined 6, 16
    initializing using XtSetLanguageProc() 242
    LANG environment variable 19
    LC_ALL category defined 18
    LC_COLLATE category defined 18
    LC_CTYPE cateogry defined 18
    LC_MESSAGES category defined 18
    LC_MONETARY category defined 18
    LC_NUMERIC category defined 18
    LC_TIME category defined 18
    locale names 18
    performance tuning with category selection 19
    querying the locale with setlocale() 19
    selection, with CDE 284
    specifying with -xnlLanguage command line option 243
    specifying with -XnlLanguage resource 243
    territory, description of 6
    when to initialize 20

Locale Modifier
   defined 116
   impact on input method selection 117
`localeconv()` 65, 66, 67
Localization 8
   creating a message catalog with `gencat` 53
   defined 8
   `dumpmsg`, undoing `gencat` 54
   icons 59
   integrating localized software with CDE application manager 286
   integrating localized software with CDE workspace manager 286
   L10N, an acronym for 8
   message catalogs compared with resource files 255
   positional parameters, example usage 68
   positional parameter format specifier 68
   tools for creating message catalogs 53
   using message catalogs 52
   using resource files 52
Localized
   defined 2
Localized Software
   definition ix
Localizers 7
`localtime()` 63, 64
Logical Metrics
   defined 79
   example 80

M

`MB_CUR_MAX` 35, 36, 39, 289
   example usage 41
`MB_MAX_LEN` 39, 289
`mblen()` 39, 289
   error handling 44
   example usage 41
`mbrlen()` 40, 289
`mbrtowc()` 38, 40, 288, 289
`mbsrtowcs()` 38, 40, 288, 289
`mbstowcs()` 36, 39, 288, 289
   example usage 42
`mbtowc()` 36, 39, 288, 289
Message Catalog
   `$set` directive 57
   affect on geometry 61
   comments in source files 57
   common mistakes 60
   compared to resources 255

creating with gencat 53
default location when NLSPATH is not set 56
embedding tabs in source files 57
example 267
example creation and usage 55
example source file 58, 134
example, setting NLSPATH for testing 87
extracting message catalog source with dumpmsg 54
generating with gencat 52
LC_MESSAGES, controlling which locale's messages are used 18, 53
LC_MESSAGES, example usage 19
LC_MESSAGES, performance tuning with 56
long messages in source files 57
NL_CAT_LOCALE, controlling dependence on setlocale() 53
NL_MSGMAX, maximum message number in a catalog 53
NL_SETMAX, maximum set number in a catalog 53
NLSPATH, controlling the location of the message catalog 53
NLSPATH, example setting for testing 58
NLSPATH, wild cards in 53
opening with catopen() 53
position parameters with printf() and scanf() 67
positional parameters, an example 68
retrieving messages with catgets() 53
separating locale-dependent data from your application 52
source file for 57
tools for creating and using 53
use to translate format strings 58
Metrics *see* Font Metrics
MODE SWITCH Modifier 142
Monetary Format
currency symbol 65
LC_MONETARY, controlling the locale 18
localeconv() 66, 67
location of currency symbol 61
strfmon() 66
nl_langinfo() 66
Motif 1.2 257
connecting to an input method, XmImRegister() 275
developing internationalization software with 249
disconnecting from an input method, XmImUnregister() 275
input method selection, XmNinputMethod 253
keyboard input using XmIm* 252, 275
keyboard input with Text widget 252
keyboard input with TextField widget 252
notifying input method when focus is gained, XmImSetFocusValues() 275
notifying input method when focus is gained, XmImVaSetFocusValues() 275
notifying input method when focus is lost, XmImUnsetFocus() 275
passing values to an input method, XmImSetValues() 275

passing values to an input method, `XmImVaSetValues()` 275

preedit style control, `XmNpreeditType` 253

processing key press events, `XmImMbLookupString()` 275

supported preedit and status styles 119

MSE

comparison of I18N tools with ISO C and XPG4 287

conversion between multibyte and wide character 37

defined 36

I18N extensions to ISO C standard 36

Multibyte

ANSI C character handling routines 39

comparing strings for equality 49

conversion to wide character 36, 37

example parsing with 44

generating from the keyboard 125

influence of `LC_CTYPE` 36

`MB_CUR_MAX`, maximum size of character 36

MSE charcter handling routines 40

MSE routines for conversion

passed to on-the-spot `PreeditDrawCallback` 169

processing text as 39

size of character 32

sorting routines 48

standard tools for converting to/from wide character 287

usage compared to wide character 35

N

`NL_CAT_LOCALE` 54

defined 53

`nl_langinfo()` 64, 65, 66

NLSPATH

controlling the location of message catalogs 53

example default setting 56

example usage 55

setting for testing 87

Numeric Format

formatting floating point values 64

`fprintf()` 65

`fscanf()` 65

`LC_NUMERIC`, controlling the locale 18

`localeconv()` 65

`nl_langinfo()` 65

`printf()` 65

`scanf()` 65

`sprintf()` 65

`sscanf()` 65

`vfprintf()` 65

```
vprintf() 65
vsprintf() 65
wcstod() 65
```

O

Octet
    defined 28
OffTheSpot 254
Off-the-Spot Preedit Style
    adding support for 147
    feedback area, illustrated 153
    geometry negotiation 149
        geometry callback 149
        input method initiated 149
    handling changes to window size 147
    program example 148
Off-the-Spot Status Style
    adding support for 147
    feedback area, illustrated 153
    geometry negotiation 149
        example 150
        geometry callback 149
        input method initiated 149
    handling changes to window size 147
    program example 148
On-the-Spot Preedit Style
    adding support for 165
    application responsibilities 165
    caret cursor 168
    caret cursor direction 171
    caret cursor highlight 171
    example 175
    example, use of callbacks 191
    highlights for preedit data 170
    `PreeditCaretCallback`, defined 166
    `PreeditCaretCallback`, syntax 171
    `PreeditDoneCallback`, defined 166
    `PreeditDoneCallback`, syntax 167
    `PreeditDrawCallback`, defined 166
    `PreeditDrawCallback`, syntax 167
    `PreeditStartCallback`, defined 166
    `PreeditStartCallback`, syntax 166
    `XIMFeedback` 170
    `XIMText` data structure 168
On-the-Spot Status Style
    adding support for 165
    application responsibilities 165

caret cursor 168
caret cursor direction 171
caret cursor highlight 171
`StatusDoneCallback`, defined 166
`StatusDoneCallback`, syntax 174
`StatusDrawCallback`, defined 166
`StatusDrawCallback`, syntax 174
`StatusStartCallback`, syntax 173
`XIMText` data structure 168
Output Context
creating default output context 98
creating with `XCreateOC()` 97
data type, XOC 90
defined 89
destroying the default output context with `XFreeFontSet()` 98
destroying with `XDestroyOC()` 98
determining if created with `XCreateOC()` or `XCreateFontSet()` 98
freeing associated memory, `XFreeFontSet()` or `XDestroyOC()` 102
instead of font sets 91
output context values that can be queried 99
output context values that can be set with `XSetOCValues()` 99
output context values that must be set when creating 99
querying for output context values with `XGetOCValues()` 98
setting output context values with `XSetOCValues()` 98
using 102
when to use instead of font set 91
`XCreateOC()`, syntax 98
Output Context Values
querying for with `XGetOCValues()` 98
setting with `XSetOCValues()` 98
table of 99
`XNBaseFontName` 99
`XNBaseFontName`, defined 99
`XNDefaultString` 99
`XNDefaultString`, defined 100
`XNFontInfo` 99, 101
`XNMissingCharSet`, defined 99
`XNMissingCharSet` 99
`XNOMAutomatic` 99, 102
`XNOrientation` 99
`XNOrientation`, defined 100
`XNResourceClass` 99, 101
`XNResourceName` 99, 101
Output Method
closing with `XCloseOM()` 92
controlling the output method values with `XSetOMValues()` 92
data type, XOM 90
default output method, `XCreateFontSet()` 92

defined 89
example usage 95
obtaining the associated display with `XDisplayOfOM()` 92
obtaining the associated locale with `XLocaleOfOM()` 92
querying the output method with `XGetOMValues()` 92
table of output method routines 92
table of output method values 93
when to use instead of font set 91
Output Method Values
defined 93
example, querying for 95
`XNContextualDrawing` 93
`XNDirectionalDependentDrawing` 93
`XNQueryOrientation` 93
`XNRequiredCharSet` 93
Output Methods
opening a connection with `XOpenOM()` 92
OverTheSpot 254
Over-the-Spot Preedit Style
adding support for 145
calculating the spot location 146
program example 146
spot location, illustrated 146

P

Performance
data interchange 230
using locale categories in performance tuning 19
Pixmaps
loading appropriate pixmaps for the locale 255
Portability
I18N tools defined by ANSI C and ISO C 33
I18N tools defined by XPG4 33
Positional Parameters
example usage 68
positional format specifier
use with `scanf()` and `printf()` 67
Preedit Area 108
Preedit Attributes
defined 295
see also Input Context
Preedit Buffer 168, 171
Preedit Style
choosing 119
choosing, example 119
defined 111
determining which styles an IM supports 117

Motif support for in `Text` and `TextField` widgets 253
styles supported by `XmIm*` 274
`XIMPreeditArea` 118, 294
`XIMPreeditCallbacks` 118, 294
`XIMPreeditNone` 118, 294
`XIMPreeditNothing` 118, 294
`XIMPreeditPosition` 118, 294
   example usage 119
`PreeditCaretCallback`
   data type, `XIMPreeditCaretCallbackStruct` 171
   defined 166
   example 190
   syntax 171
`PreeditDoneCallback`
   defined 166
   example 182
   syntax 167
`PreeditDrawCallback` 168
   defined 166
   example 185
   syntax 167
`PreeditStartCallback`
   defined 166
   example 179
   return value 167
   syntax 166
`PRIMARY` 226
Primary Selection 231, 235
Prime Drawing Direction 100
`printf()` 37, 38, 65, 288
   example, using with message catalogs 55
   positional parameters 67
`putwc()` 37, 38, 288
`putwchar()` 37, 39, 288

R

Radix 64
Reconnect Callback
   syntax 198
Reconnection 197
Resource File
   localization affect on geometry 61
Resource Files
   separating locale-dependent data from your application 52
`RESOURCE_MANAGER` 282
Resources
   `app-defaults` file, `XtResolvePathname()` 247

CDE
>   `SystemFont` and `UserFont` font list resources 282
>   `SystemFont` resource 282
>   Tee Shirt Size aliases 283
>   `UserFont` resource 282
compared to message catalog 255
example `app-defaults` file 269
font sets 247
localized values 242
locating locale-specific resources, `XtResolvePathname()` 244
location of, `XAPPLRESDIR` 246
location of, `XFILESEARCHPATH` 247
location of, `XUSERFILESEARCHPATH` 246
resource names as XPCS 242
`RESOURCE_MANAGER` property 282
using font set resource converter, example 247
values encoded in host porbable character encoding 242
Root 254

S

`scanf()` 37, 38, 58, 65, 288
>   example usage 42
>   positional parameters 67
Selection Owner 240
`setlocale()` 35, 67, 84
>   categories defined 18
>   controlling locale of a category 18
>   controlling the locale of the message catalog 53
>   default language procedure for `XtSetLanguageProc()` 244
>   example usage 18
>   illustrated use in I18N architecture 17
>   initializing the locale 16
>   `LANG` environment variable 19
>   `LC_ALL` category defined 18
>   `LC_CTYPE` category defined 18
>   `LC_MESSAGES` category defined 18
>   `LC_MONETARY` category defined 18
>   `LC_NUMERIC` category defined 18
>   `LC_TIME` category defined 18
>   querying the locale 19
>   summary of usage 20
>   syntax 17
>   use of environment variables 19
>   when to call 20
Sorting
>   `LC_COLLATE`, controlling the locale 18
`sprintf()` 37, 38, 65, 288

`sscanf()` 37, 38, 65, 288

Status Area 108

Status Attributes
    defined 295

Status Attributes, *see* Input Context

Status Style
    choosing 119
    choosing, example 119
    defined 117
    determining which styles an IM supports 117
    Motif support for in Text and TextField widgets 253
    styles supported by `XmIm*` 274
    `XIMStatusArea` 118, 295
    `XIMStatusCallbacks` 118, 295
    `XIMStatusNone` 118, 294
    `XIMStatusNothing` 118, 295

`StatusDoneCallback`
    defined 166
    syntax 174

`StatusDrawCallback`
    data type, `XIMStatusDataType` 175
    data type, `XIMStatusDrawCallbackStruct` 174
    defined 166
    syntax 174

`StatusStartCallback` 166
    syntax 173

`strcat()` 30

`strcmp()` 48, 49

`strcoll()` 48, 291

`strcpy()` 30

`strfmon()`

`strftime()` 63

String Conversion 209

`StringConversionCallback`
    syntax 210

`strncmp()` 49

`strptime()` 64

`strtod()` 65

`StructureNotifyMask`
    use with off-the-spot style 147

`strxfrm()` 48, 291

Style Manager
    controlling fonts in font set 282

`swprintf()` 37, 288

`swscanf()` 37, 288

`SystemFont` 282

T

TARGETS 226
Tee Shirt Size Aliases 283
 example 284
 resolving, `XCreateFontSet()` 283
`Text` Widget
 supported preedit and status styles 253
`TextField` Widget
 supported preedit and status styles 253
Time Format
 examples of variations 63
 LC_TIME, controlling the locale 18
 LC_TIME, example usage 19
 `localtime()` 63, 64
 `nl_langinfo()` 64
 `strftime()` 63, 64
 `strptime()` 64
 tools for 63
 variations described 62
 `wcsftime()` 63, 64
`towctrans()` 47
`towlower()` 47, 290
`towupper()` 47, 290

U

UCS2
 defined 28
 languages encoded 28
UCS2 *see also* Universal Coded Character Set
UCS4 29
`ungetwc()` 37, 39, 288
Unicode
 defined 28
 internationalized software using 28
Universal Coded Character Set
 advantages of use
 non-spacing characters 29
UserFont 282

V

`VendorShell`
 geometry management 274
`vfprintf()` 37, 38, 65, 288
`vfwprintf()` 37, 288
`vprintf()` 37, 38, 65, 288
`vsprintf()` 37, 38, 65, 288

vswprintf() 37, 288
vwprintf() 37, 288

W

wchar_t
    defined 32
    typedef 34
wcrtomb() 38, 288
wcschr() 44, 289
wcscmp() 49
wcscoll() 49, 291
wcscspn() 44, 289
wcsftime() 63, 64
wcsncmp() 49
wcspbrk() 44, 289
wcsrchr() 44, 289
wcsrtombs() 38, 288
wcsspn() 44, 289
wcsstr() 45, 289
wcstod() 65
wcstok() 45, 289
wcstombs() 288
wcsxfrm() 49, 291
wctob() 38, 288
wctomb() 36, 288
wctrans() 47
wctype() 46, 290
Wide Character
    ANSI C character handling routines 39
    comparing strings for equality 49
    conversion to multibyte 36
    generating from the keyboard 125
    influence of LC_CTYPE 35, 36
    MSE character handling routines 40
    MSE scanning and parsing routines 44
    number of bytes per 33
    passed to on-the-spot PreeditDrawCallback 169
    sorting routines 48
    standard tools for converting to/from multibyte 287
    usage compared to multibyte 35
    wchar_t data type 32
    XPG4 and MSE case conversion routines 47
    XPG4 and MSE character classification routines 45
wmemchr() 45, 289
Workspace Manager 286
wprintf() 37, 288
wscanf() 37, 288

X

X Locale Database
    entries controlling font set creation 75
X locale database 74
X Logical Font Description 73
    see also XLFD
X Portable Character Set 230
X Resource Manager
    handling localized resources 241
    see also Resources
XA_STRING 226
XAPPLRESDIR 246
XBaseFontnameListOfFontSet() 76
XBMLANGPATH 256
XBufferOverFlow 126, 279
    handling, example 138
XCloseOM() 92, 93
XCompoundTextStyle
    defined 228
Xconfig 285
XCreateFontSet() 73, 85
    alternative to, XNBaseFontName 99
    alternative to, XNDefaultString 99
    altnative to, XNMissingCharSet 99
    behavior 75
    creating a default output method in X11R6 92
    default string return 76
    obtaining the list of base names for a font set, XBaseFontnameListOfFontSet() 76
    resolving Tee Shirt Size aliases, example 283
    syntax
    XFontSet, data type returned 75
XCreateIC()
    controlling preedit state 206
    example usage 123
    syntax 122
XCreateOC()
    output context values that must be set when calling 99
    syntax 98
XDestroyOC() 98
XDisplayOfOM() 92
XDrawImageString()
    use XmbDrawImageString() or XwcDrawImageString() instead 87
XDrawImageString16()
    use XmbDrawImageString() or XwcDrawImageString() instead 87
XDrawString() 76
    use XmbDrawString() or XwcDrawString() instead 87

XDrawString16()
    use XmbDrawString() or XwcDrawString() instead 87
XDrawText()
    use XmbDrawText() or XwcDrawText() instead 88
XDrawText16()
    use XmbDrawText() or XwcDrawText() instead 88
XExtentsOfFontSet() 79
    example usage 136
XFILESEARCHPATH 245, 247
XFilterEvent()
    called by XtDispatchEvent() 248
    example usage 138
    syntaxt 125
XFontSet 73
    compared with X11R6 output context 91
XFontsOfFontSet() 76, 99
    alternative to, XNFontInfo 99
XFreeFontSet() 76
    destroying the default output context 98
XFreeStringList() 75
    example usage 85
XGetICValues()
    syntax 127
XGetIMValues()
    memory management 197
    syntax 117
    XNQueryInputStyle 117
XGetOCValues() 98
    output context values that can be queried 99
XGetOMValues() 92
    values to be queried 93
XGetRGBColormaps() 298
XIC 121
XIC Data Values 207, 210, 294
    defined 122
    see also Input Context: XIC data values
    setting and querying 127
XICCEncodingStyle
    defined 228
XIM values 196
XIMAbsolutePosition 172, 173
XIMBackwardChar 172, 173
XIMBackwardWord 172, 173
XIMBitmapType 175
XIMCaretDirection 172
    defined 171, 172
XIMCaretDown 172, 173

`XIMCaretStyle`
    defined 171
`XIMCaretUp` 172, 173
`XIMDontChange` 172, 173
`XIMFeedback` 170, 216
`XIMForwardChar` 172, 173
`XIMForwardWord` 172, 173
`XIMHighlight` 170, 216
`XIMHotKeyState` 208, 221
`XIMHotKeyStateOFF` 208
`XIMHotKeyStateON` 208
XIMHotKeyTrigger 221
`XIMHotKeyTriggers` 207
`XIMInitialState` 206, 221
`XIMIsInvisible` 172
`XIMIsPrimary` 172
`XIMIsSecondary` 172
`XIMLineEnd` 172, 173
`XIMLineStart` 172, 173
`XIMNextLine` 172, 173
`XIMPreeditArea` 294
`XIMPreeditCallbacks` 118, 294
`XIMPreeditDisable` 205, 222
`XIMPreeditDrawCallbackStruct` 168
`XIMPreeditEnable` 205, 222
`XIMPreeditNone` 118, 294
    example usage 137
`XIMPreeditNothing` 118, 294
    example usage 137
`XIMPreeditPosition` 118, 294, 296
`XIMPreeditState` 222
    defined 205
`XIMPreeditStateNotifyCallbackStruct` 206
`XIMPreeditUnknown` 205, 222
`XIMPreserveState` 206, 221
`XIMPreviousLine` 172, 173
`XIMPrimary` 170, 216
`XIMResetState` 206, 221
`XIMReverse` 170, 216
`XIMSecondary` 170, 216
`XIMStatusArea` 118, 295
`XIMStatusCallbacks` 118, 295
`XIMStatusDataType` 175
`XIMStatusDrawCallbackStruct` 174
`XIMStatusNone` 118, 294
    example usage 137
`XIMStatusNothing` 118, 123, 295
    example usage 137

XIMStringConversionCallbackStruct 211
XIMStringConversionOperation 211
XIMStringConversionPosition 211
XIMStringConversionRetrieval 211
XIMStringConversionSubstitution 211
XIMStringConversionText 209, 212, 222
XIMStyles 118
XIMTertiary 170, 216
XIMText
    defined 168, 169
XIMTextType 175
XIMUnderline 170, 216
XIMValuesList
    defined 204
XIMVisibleToBackward 217
XIMVisibleToCenter 217
XIMVisibleToForward 217
XKeyEvent 106
    key code 106
    modifiers 106
XLFD 73
    alias 73
    example identifying XLFD fields 74
    Tee Shirt Size aliases 283
    wild cards in 75
XLoadFont()
    use XCreateFontSet() instead 87
    use XOpenOM() and XCreateOC() instead 103
XLoadQueryFont()
    use XCreateFontSet() instead 87
    use XOpenOM() and XCreateOC() instead 103
XLocaleOfFontSet() 76
XLocaleOfOM() 92
XLookupBoth 127, 279
    handling, example 139
XLookupChars 127, 279
    handling, example 139
XLookupKeySym 127, 279
    handling, example 139
XLookupNone 127, 279
    handling, example 138
XLookupString() 106
XmbDrawImageString() 77, 91
    use with output context 91
XmbDrawString()
    compared to XDrawString() 76
    defined 77
    example usage 86

XmbDrawText() 77
XmbLookupString() 191
    status return 126
    syntax 125
XmbResetIC()
    controlling preedit state when calling 206
XmbTextEscapement() 78
XmbTextExtents() 78
    example 80
    example usage 85
XmbTextListToTextProperty()
    syntax 227
XmbTextPerCharExtents() 78
XmbTextPropertyToTextList()
    syntax 229
XmCvtCTToXmString()
    syntax 252
XmCvtXmStringToCT()
    syntax 252
XmDrawingArea 249
    keyboard input with 271
XmFONT_IS_FONT 272
XmFONT_IS_FONTSET 272
XmFontList 276
XmFONTLIST_DEFAULT_TAG 250, 251
XmFontListAppendEntry() 271
XmFontListEntryCreate() 271
    usage 272
XmFontListEntryFree() 272
XmFontListEntryLoad() 271
    usage 272
XmFontType 272
XmGetPixmap()
    controlling search with XBMLANGPATH and XAPPLRESDIR 256
    syntax 255
XmIm*
    breaking the connecting to an input method, XmImUnregister() 275
    connecting to an input method, XmImRegister() 275
    geometry management, VendorShell 274
    input method selection 275
    input method values
        XmNbackground 276
        XmNbackgroundPixmap 276
        XmNfontList 276
        XmNforeground 277
        XmNlineSpace 277
        XmNspotLocation 277
   input method, font set selection from font list 277

notifying input method when focus is gained, `XmImSetFocusValues()` 275
notifying input method when focus is lost, `XmImUnsetFocus()` 275
notifying input method when focus is gained, `XmImVaSetFocusValues()` 275
passing values to an input method, `XmImSetValues()` 275
passing values to an input method, `XmImVaSetValues()` 275
preedit and status styles supported 274
processing key press events, `XmImMbLookupString()` 275
purpose and use 274
support of 274
usage 275
`XmImMbLookupString()` 275
   status return values
      `XBufferOverflow` 279
      `XLookupBoth` 279
      `XLookupChars` 279
      `XLookupKeySym` 279
      `XLookupNone` 279
   syntax 278
`XmImRegister()` 275
   syntax 275
`XmImSetFocusValues()` 275
   syntax 277
`XmImSetValues()` 275
   syntax 276
`XmImUnregister()` 275
   syntax 279
`XmImUnsetFocus()` 275
   syntax 278
`XmImVaSetFocusValues()`
   syntax 277
`XmImVaSetValues()` 275
   syntax 276
`XmNbackground` 276
`XmNbackgroundPixmap` 276
`XmNdialogTitle` 255
`XmNfontList` 276
`XmNforeground` 277
`XmNiconName` 255
`XmNiconNameEncoding` 255
`XmNinputMethod`
   defined 253
   interaction with `XMODIFIERS` 253
`XmNlineSpace` 277
`XmNpreeditType`
   defined 254
`XmNspotLocation` 277
`XmNtitle` 255
`XmNtitleEncoding` 255

XMODIFIERS 116, 351
    automatically set in CDE 285
    interaction with XmNinputMethod 253
XmStringCreate()
    syntax 252
XmStringCreateLocalized()
    syntax 252
XmStringCreateLtoR()
    syntax 252
XmStringSegmentCreate()
    syntax 252
XmTextCopy() 254
XmTextFieldCopy() 254
XmTextFieldGetStringWcs()
    example usage 253
XmTextFieldPaste() 254
XmTextFieldReplaceStringWcs()
    example usage 253
XmTextFieldSetString()
    example usage 253
XmTextPaste() 254
XNArea 296, 297, 299
    usage in geometry negotiation 150
XNAreaNeeded 296, 297, 299
    usage in geometry negotiation 150
XNBackground 296, 298, 299, 300
XNBackgroundPixmap 296, 298, 299, 300
XNBaseFontName 99
    defined 99
XNClientWindow 293
XNColormap 296, 298, 299
XNContextualDrawing 93
XNCursor 297, 298, 299, 300
XNDefaultString 99
    defined 100
XNDestroyCallback 213, 214, 215, 221
    defined 203
    preedit/status styles affected 220
XNDirectionalDependentDrawing 93
XNFilterEvents 124, 294
XNFocusWindow 293
XNFontInfo 99
    defined 101
XNFontSet 297, 298, 299, 300
XNForeground 296, 298, 299, 300
XNGeometryCallback 294
XNHotKey 207, 221
    preedit/status styles affected 220

XNHotKeyState 221
    preedit/status styles affected 220
XNLineSpace 297, 298, 299, 300
XnlLanguage 243
xnlLanguage 243
XNMissingCharSet 99
    defined 99
XNOMAutomatic 98, 99
    defined 102
XNOrientation 99
    defined 100
XNPreeditAttributes 122, 294, 295
XNPreeditCaretCallback 297
XNPreeditDoneCallback 297
XNPreeditDrawCallback 297
XNPreeditStartCallback 297
XNPreeditState 204, 205, 206, 222
    preedit/status styles affected 220
XNPreeditStateCallback 204
XNPreeditStateNotifyCallback 206, 223
    preedit/status styles affected 220
XNQueryICValuesList 204, 213, 214, 215
XNQueryIMValuesList 213, 214, 215
XNQueryInputStyle 117, 214
XNQueryOrientation 93
XNR6PreeditCallbackBehavior 214, 218
XNRequiredCharSet 93
XNResetState 206, 221
    preedit/status styles affected 220
XNResourceClass 99, 214, 215, 294
    defined 101
XNResourceName 99, 214, 215, 294
    defined 101
XNSpotLocation 296, 299
XNStateConversionCallback 222
XNStatusAttributes 122, 294, 295
XNStatusDoneCallback 298
XNStatusDrawCallback 298
XNStatusStartCallback 298
XNStdColormap 296, 298, 299
XNStringConversion 209, 210, 222
    preedit/status styles affected 220
XNStringConversionCallback 210, 212
    preedit/status styles affected 220
XNVisiblePosition 213, 214, 216
XOC 90
XOC Values 99
XOM 90

XOMCharSetList 93, 99
XOMFontInfo 99
    memory management of structure 102
XOMOrientation 93
XOMOrientation_Context 94
XOpenIM() 117
XOpenOM() 92
XOrientation 99, 100
XPCS
    resource names 242
    see X Portable Character Set
XPG4
    comparison of I18N tools with ISO C and MSE 287
XQueryTextExtents()
    use XmbTextExtents() or XwcTextExtents() instead 88
XQueryTextExtents16()
    use XmbTextExtents() or XwcTextExtents() instead 88
XRegisterIMInstantiateCallback()
    data type, IMInstantiateCallback 198
    syntax 197
XSetICFocus()
    example usage 140
    syntax 128
XSetICValues()
    controlling preedit state 206
    syntax 127
XSetIMValues()
    example 196
    syntax 196
XSetLocaleModifiers() 117
    called by XtSetLanguageProc() default language procedure 244
XSetOCValues() 98
    output context values that can be set 99
XSetOMValues() 92
    function without a purpose 93
XSetWMIconName() 225
XSetWMName() 225
XStdICCTextStyle
    defined 228
XStringStyle
    defined 228
XSupportsLocale()
    called by XtSetLanguageProc() default language procedure 244
XtAppMainLoop() 248
XtConvertSelectionProc
    example procedure 232
XtCvtStringToFontSet 247
XtDefaultFontSet 247

xtDefaultFontSet 247
XtDispatchEvent() 248
XTextExtents()
    use XmbTextExtents() or XwcTextExtents() instead 88
XTextExtents16()
    use XmbTextExtents() or XwcTextExtents() instead 88
XTextProperty 226, 229
    creation of 228
XTextStyle
    defined 228
XTextWidth() 78
    use XbmTextEscapement() or XwcTextEscapement() instead 88
XTextWidth16()
    use XbmTextEscapement() or XwcTextEscapement() instead 88
XtGetSelectionValue()
    example usage 235
XtMainLoop() 248
XtOwnSelection()
    usage 231
XtResolvePathname() 245
    locating locale-specific files 244
    syntax 245
    wild cards recognized by 246
    XAPPLRESDIR 246
    XFILESEARCHPATH 247
    XUSERFILESEARCHPATH 246
XtRFontSet 247
XtSelectionCallbackProc
    example procedure 235
XtSetLanguageProc() 16, 246
    default language procedure, setlocale() 244
    syntax 242
XUnregisterIMInstantiateCallback()
    syntax 198
XUnsetICFocus()
    example usage 140
    syntax 129
XUSERFILESEARCHPATH 246
XVaCreateNestedList() 123
    example usage 128
XwcDrawImageString() 77
XwcDrawString() 77
    example usage 140
XwcDrawText() 77
XwcLookupString() 191
    example usage 138
    status return 126

`XwcResetIC()`
    controlling preedit state when calling 206
`XwcTextEscapement()` 78
`XwcTextExtents()` 78
`XwcTextListToTextProperty()`
    syntax 227
`XwcTextPerCharExtents()` 78
`XwcTextPropertyToTextList()`
    syntax 229